Fundamentals for Practice with High-Risk Populations

Nancy Summers
Harrisburg Area Community College

THOMSON
BROOKS/COLE
Australia • Canada • Mexico • Singapore • Spain • United Kingdom • United States

To all the students who use this book
and go on to make a positive difference in the lives of others
and a useful contribution to their communities

Executive Editor: Lisa Gebo
Assistant Editor: Alma Dea Michelena
Editorial Assistant: Sheila Walsh
Marketing Manager: Caroline Concilla
Marketing Assistant: Mary Ho
Advertising Project Manager: Tami Strang
Production Project Manager: Stephanie Zunich
Print Buyer: Vena Dyer
Permissions Editor: Sue Ewing
Production Service: Sara Dovre Wudali, Buuji, Inc.
Copy Editor: Linda Ireland, Buuji, Inc.
Cover Designer: Lisa Berman
Cover Image: Getty Images
Compositor: Buuji, Inc.
Printer: Globus Printing Company

Printed in the United States of America
2 3 4 5 6 7 06 05 04

For more information about our products, contact us at:
Thomson Learning Academic Resource Center
1-800-423-0563
For permission to use material from this text, contact us by:
Phone: 1-800-730-2214 **Fax:** 1-800-730-2215
Web: http://www.thomsonrights.com

Library of Congress Control Number: 2002108817

ISBN 0-534-55866-6

Brooks/Cole–Thomson Learning
511 Forest Lodge Road
Pacific Grove, CA 93950
USA

Asia
Thomson Learning
5 Shenton Way #01-01
UIC Building
Singapore 068808

Australia
Nelson Thomson Learning
102 Dodds Street
South Melbourne, Victoria 3205
Australia

Canada
Nelson Thomson Learning
1120 Birchmount Road
Toronto, Ontario M1K 5G4
Canada

Europe/Middle East/Africa
Thomson Learning
High Holborn House
50/51 Bedford Row
London WC1R 4LR
United Kingdom

Latin America
Thomson Learning
Seneca, 53
Colonia Polanco
11560 Mexico D.F.
Mexico

Spain
Paraninfo Thomson Learning
Calle/Magallanes, 25
28015 Madrid, Spain

Contents

Preface

INTRODUCTION

In an agency serving older people, workers know how to recognize cognitive problems in older clients and refer them promptly to the people who can best address those problems. In an agency where single mothers come with their children after domestic violence in their homes, workers are able to develop a useful and individualized safety plan with each of the mothers. In a social service agency where most of the consumers are children, workers can tell the difference between normal development and development that is delayed and troublesome. How do these workers learn the specific considerations for each population of consumers?

When we enter the field of social work or human services, it is clear that we are seeking to be helpful to other people. We can easily see the people we want to help as being more or less a single group comprised of individuals who are experiencing difficulties. As we become professionals, we learn to be discerning, developing an understanding of the unique issues facing each population of clients.

PURPOSE

This textbook was written to give students a detailed picture of particular high-risk populations. Students who use this text will be introduced to the unique difficulties, considerations, and issues that confront individuals in a specific high-risk population and those that confront the workers who serve them. Giving the reader, who is interested in a specific high-risk population, the insight necessary to understand the consumer increases the likelihood that these consumers' cases will be handled competently. The circumstances and problems and the information about services and treatments that will best address these are given for each high-risk group. The hope is that readers of this textbook will feel confident that they can deftly address the needs of a specific population of consumers with increased professional skill.

ORGANIZATION OF TEXTBOOK

Chapter 1, At Risk, seeks to ground the reader in a definition of high risk and a theoretical means of looking at interventions. Chapter 2, Writing a Social History, gives readers a basic format for taking a sound social history when evaluation and assessment forms are not available from the agencies where they work. This chapter includes methods for asking difficult questions.

Chapters 3 through 8 are concerned with case management with six high-risk populations. The areas covered are: children, survivors of rape and domestic violence, chemical dependence, mental health, mental retardation, and aging. Each of these chapters follows a specific format. Every chapter contains special considerations for that particular population. Examples of such topics include men working in women's programs and various organizations that support the work of case management in a particular field.

In addition, the last six chapters contain considerable information on the assessment of clients in each of the fields discussed. Readers are introduced to the specific symptoms and life circumstances to look for when conducting intakes and monitoring client services. For example, the chapter on aging includes a detailed description of how to determine a cognitive impairment, particularly when receiving information from distressed family members; the chapter on children contains a detailed account of the problems children face and how they react at different ages when their parents separate or divorce; and the chapter on mental health provides clear suggestions for handling possible suicidality in clients with empathy and warmth.

Another feature of the chapters on different fields is that each contains information that the particular field is likely to use from the *Diagnostic and Statistical Manual of Mental Disorders* (4th ed., Text Rev.; *DSM-IV-TR*). Every chapter contains common treatments and medications and a list of typical services to which a case manager might make referrals, as well as information about least restrictive and least intrusive services for each population. Special services for each given population—such as day treatment for adolescents, day treatment for Alzheimer's patients, and crisis services for mental health consumers or for domestic violence and rape survivors—are described as well.

Finally, every chapter throughout the book ends with exercises to give the student practice in using the new information by applying it to case scenarios. In all the chapters on populations, the exercises are followed by intake forms and other forms from actual state and local agencies that are used to evaluate a consumer's situation and to determine services and treatment. Some of these forms are long and detailed, but they have been included with few modifications so that readers can see what they are like and what kinds of questions they ask.

TO THE STUDENTS

The challenge for educators in the social work or human services field is to prepare students for their first day on the job by giving them enough information and helping them develop enough skills that they will have entry-level competence. This is not easy when consumers of social service agencies are not present in the classroom or readily available for practice.

This book was written to give you the skills and information you will need to practice in a particular field. You may find yourself in a generic case management unit where all the social problems in a particular geographic region come into a single unit. More likely, however, you will find yourself working in an agency that serves the needs of a particular population of consumers.

Many textbooks present generic skills that prepare students to talk to consumers and collect information in an empathic and useful way, but what has been missing is information on how to do that with an understanding of the unique concerns that arise for each high-risk population. Students often express interest in a particular group of consumers and intend to work with that group in their social service career. If you are one of these students, this textbook will give you the basic information you need about these groups to get started in your chosen field of interest. You may also find, in reading the chapters, that you have an interest in other high-risk populations.

TO THE INSTRUCTOR: SUGGESTIONS FOR USING THIS TEXT

Today the social service field is scrambling for qualified workers. Many state agencies are accepting individuals with no credentials in the field in order to have someone present to direct consumers and patients. All of us who are educators in the social service field have been seeking ways to better prepare students for the demands they will actually encounter when their education is complete and they take positions in the field.

My previous textbook, *Fundamentals of Case Management Practice* (Summers, 2001) was written specifically to address basic skills. It laid a foundation for the attitudes, values, and skills needed to work successfully with other people. But who are these other people? How are they likely to present themselves to the case manager? How do we prepare students to make distinctions in collecting information and searching for clues with various high-risk populations? What are the initial concerns and issues that arise when doing intakes and working with individuals in various high-risk populations? To answer these questions, this text, *Fundamentals for Practice with High-Risk Populations,* was written as a supplement to *Fundamentals of Case Management Practice.*

Instructors cannot be expected to know all the distinctions among the various high-risk populations. What instructors will provide is the foundation in ethics and practice that helps students make good decisions. Using *Fundamentals for Practice with High-Risk Populations,* an instructor can teach the points that are most important to each high-risk group and monitor the student's ability to include the correct material and use insight in planning for each of these high-risk groups.

How to Use This Text

The text can be used as a survey of six high-risk populations. Another option is to have students, after they have read the first two chapters, choose two or three populations that interest them most and focus on those chapters in the text. Unless working with students who are about to become senior professionals but who have had little or no experience in the field, this book need not be read from cover to cover. Rather, it is a reference book, a source of information that is needed by those in the social service field to be more effective.

As mentioned, this textbook was written to supplement *Fundamentals of Case Management Practice* (Summers, 2001). Using the two together provides the tools for teaching entry-level skills. *Fundamentals of Case Management Practice* sets forth the basic foundations for generic best practice from ethics to documentation to monitoring of cases. *Fundamentals for Practice with High-Risk Populations* allows students to choose a particular type of consumer and move through the generic steps found in the first text, while using the unique and specific information that applies to a high-risk group.

As the instructor, you can function like an agency supervisor. Students can take initial inquiries from a variety of individual clients created by them or you, or they can take initial inquiries from the populations that interest them the most. As they move to the first interview and the intake evaluation or assessment, the realistic forms provided in the text for each population can be used and discussed with the class. Treatment planning conferences to plan services can be conducted in small groups while you lend ideas and confirm the more realistic plans.

Using one of the populations found in *Fundamentals for Practice with High-Risk Populations*, you will be able to walk a student through the case management process from intake to termination, as outlined in *Fundamentals of Case Management Practice*. Students can prepare for you a completed case in a manila file folder as a final examination mechanism.

Supplementary Teaching Material

Supplemental items are available for use in the classroom. For example, students can purchase the *DSM-IV-TR Handbook* and work on assigning likely diagnoses to clients they have created. Several concerns need to be addressed regarding the use of the *DSM*. Many instructors are reluctant to use it because entry-level workers do not determine diagnoses. Familiarity with the *DSM* does, however, allow students to be conversant with other professionals and to understand what other professionals are discussing. Some instructors believe that in working with the *DSM*, there should be only one correct answer or diagnosis. In fact, most diagnoses are open to lively debate, and this debate gives students a feel for the kinds of discussions that take place every day in social service agencies. It is useful, therefore, to focus on the exercises that work with the *DSM* as get-acquainted tools, and not to become overly concerned about whether the diagnosis is absolutely correct. The American Psychiatric Association also produces training tapes that give students a realistic look at consumers and allow them to use the *DSM* for practice purposes.

Finally, instructors do not have to be responsible for preparing lectures on all these different populations, but can supplement the textbook with additional information as they see fit. This can include videos on topics such as personality disorders and Alzheimer's. It might include guest speakers on particular high-risk populations or handouts on special topics. Class time also can be used to develop realistic service plans, discuss dynamics of clients being developed, and discuss possible problems that might arise for each of these clients, looking at how the case manager would go about preventing these.

BENEFITS AND ADVANTAGES

Using the material in this text in my own classroom has been enormously helpful in addressing the most common problems students encounter. Students using this material have described their "learning curve" in a new position as comparatively shorter than that of other entry-level colleagues. Having been given the opportunity to focus on the population with whom they will be working after they leave the classroom, they enter their new positions with confidence, possessing the skills and information necessary to begin serving consumers.

Three positive features of *Fundamentals for Practice with High-Risk Populations* make it particularly useful in preparing students for work in their chosen field:

1. The text gives the basic information needed to handle each high-risk population, as the case manager doing the intake, developing the service and treatment plans,

monitoring the progress, handling the crises and common difficulties likely to arise, and making a realistic termination if that time comes.

2. The exercises at the end of the chapters further acquaint the student with the skills for handling the issues, personal and family concerns, and unique problems of each high-risk group.
3. Every chapter on a high-risk population contains forms that are likely to be used for assessment and planning purposes for that population. Although students will encounter somewhat different forms when they actually begin to work in the field, the forms included here will acquaint them with what information it is important to collect for each group. Further, having worked with forms before, they will find it easier to do so in the field under pressure.

When the chapters and their features are put together, the classroom becomes much like a social service agency. This affords many opportunities for students to practice, discuss, consider the best plan of action, and make final decisions without the daily pressure of a social service agency. Few textbooks at present provide students with the specific information to collect or the warning signs that signal potential problems for each population.

ACKNOWLEDGMENTS

I would like to thank Sharon Grady, supervisor of the children's case management unit at the Dauphin County Case Management Unit, Harrisburg, Pennsylvania, for her help in preparing the chapter on children. In addition, I thank Charlie Brinich, family support worker, Diane McCurley, administrative case manager, and Marjorie Tomlinson, resource case manager of the Columbia, Montour, Snyder, Union (Counties) Base Service Unit for supplying me with considerable firsthand information about serving children and their families. Also helpful were Marsali Hansen, director of the Pennsylvania CASSP Training and Technical Assistance Institute, and Ann Litzleman, the Institute's Curriculum Development Specialist. Both of them offered assistance and information to enhance the chapter on children, for which I am grateful.

I received invaluable help from Leigh Malonee at the Pennsylvania Coalition Against Rape and from Jenny Murphy-Shifflet, director of the Sexual Assault Resource and Counseling Center of Lebanon County (Pennsylvania). I appreciate their assistance. I also appreciate the help I received from both the National Resource Center on Domestic Violence and the National Sexual Violence Resource Center. In addition, I am grateful to Brooke Hertzler, domestic violence/sexual assault children's counselor, and Shannon Kuhn, domestic violence/sexual assault counselor at the Harrisburg, Pennsylvania, YWCA, for their help in bringing together the important points in the chapter on sexual assault and domestic violence.

I want to thank Bill Milchak, clinical instructor of psychiatry at the Penn State University Milton S. Hershey College of Medicine, who supplied information and firsthand experiences to make the chapter on chemical dependency more relevant and interesting.

Dan Saussman, director of the mental retardation case managers at the Dauphin County Case Management Unit, and his staff were gracious enough to spend time working with me on the details of the chapter on mental retardation.

I very much appreciate the help given to me by the National Alliance for the Mentally Ill and the Pennsylvania chapter of the National Alliance for the Mentally Ill. I am especially grateful to Kelly Dunlap Preston, supervisor of adult administrative case management and intake, Dauphin County Case Management Unit, for once again taking the time to make certain the material contained in this book is realistic and helpful to case managers. I also want to thank Luciano A. Picchio, a psychiatrist in private practice and a consultant to the Dauphin County Case Management Unit, for reading over the chapter on mental health and giving me advice that enriched the chapter.

Thanks goes to Jill Burman, supervisor, Susan Pierce, and Lynn Shade of the Dauphin County Area Agency on Aging for their help in preparing the chapter on growing older. They gave time and examples that made the chapter more realistic.

I am indebted to Dahl Krow, who made his staff of the Dauphin County Mental Health and Mental Retardation Unit available to answer questions and give advice, and to Mary McGrath, executive director of the Adams Hanover Counseling Services, Inc., who supplied technical information on policies and laws.

I am deeply grateful to my husband, Martin Yespy, whose encouragement and enthusiasm for this project kept me going through some very difficult times.

I am also indebted to the reviewers who gave me helpful feedback:

Freddie Avant, Stephen F. Austin State University
Georgia Bland, Oregon Institute of Technology
Sabine Bolz, Solano Community College
Mary Ann Bromley, Rhode Island College
Lisa Deason, Tulsa Community College
Sue Ellen M. Dunn, New Hampshire Community Technical College

Finally, I want to thank my editors for their help in very difficult times. Lisa Gebo, executive editor, has always been available to give good advice and ideas. Alma Dea Michelena, assistant editor, was willing to discuss every problem or concern, sometimes daily. I am indebted to her for providing support when I needed it.

Nancy Summers

Chapter 1

At Risk

INTRODUCTION

You are in one of your first staff meetings at an agency that works with children whose parents are addicted to drugs. During the meeting the director talks about changes that will be made in the agency's services. "Our studies of the community show that the children who are at risk are not only those whose parents use crack and other street drugs, but also those whose parents are alcoholic," she tells the staff. "The County Drug and Alcohol Service Center is asking us to take a look at these at-risk children and provide the same service to them that we provide for children whose parents are addicted to street drugs."

You agree that children whose parents are alcoholic need attention, but the term *at risk,* which you have heard several times since you started working at the agency, is not entirely clear to you. What is meant by the term? At risk for what, exactly? And how does one decide who is at risk and who is not?

DEFINING *AT RISK*

The term *at risk* is used somewhat loosely in social services to characterize groups of people who are likely to experience problems that will affect their adjustment or ability to function successfully now and in the future. These groups are often referred to as populations. Each group of people or population will face different issues and challenges. The likelihood of the problem occurring and the reason the group is determined by researchers to be at risk is based on one or more circumstances in their lives that make this negative outcome probable.

At some time in our lives, all of us are at risk for something. The risk occurs because of certain circumstances in our lives that make it more likely that we will experience a problem. Furthermore, not all of these problems placing us at risk are social service problems. For example, insurance companies compile statistics to predict who is most at risk to have an accident while driving. One population they target is older drivers, drivers over the age of 55. That does not mean that all drivers over age 55 will experience an accident. It means that their statistics show that a driver over age 55 is more likely to have an accident than a driver who is under age 55. Many of these insurance companies have, therefore, developed programs to reduce the risk to older drivers, such as encouraging them to take a standard driver training course for older drivers.

To summarize, for the policy makers at the federal and state levels and those who determine social services for individual communities, the term *at risk* refers to populations of people who, because of certain circumstances, will be more likely to experience a problem related to adjustment and functioning. In other words, these people are more likely to experience problems that will interfere with their ability to reach their full potential.

WHO DECIDES

As noted, federal and state policy makers make some of the decisions about who is at risk. In 1963 the Congress of the United States passed legislation making services to those with mental illness more accessible and affordable. They chose, in this legislation, to address the needs of a broader population to include those contending with various psychological diagnoses. Funding for mental health services was made available to states only if they wrote legislation for their state to include the same broader populations of individuals eligible for mental health services. Individual communities within states then applied for money to start mental health centers. The staff in these centers determined who in their communities within this population was most at risk and developed programs specifically for them.

For instance, one community had a large number of older people, so the mental health center in that community would see more older adults than a center in another community. Compiling statistics on why older adults sought psychological help from the center uncovered a trend. One of the most frequent reasons older adults sought help was to cope with the death of a spouse. Therefore, in this community of older people, a large portion would be at risk for depression and withdrawal at the time a spouse died. In response, the center set up services specifically for those going through this normal life transition. The purpose was to help people make a better adjustment and remain as functional as possible following bereavement, which could help prevent the development of more serious psychological problems.

Certainly not all the older people in the community would be widowed and not all those who lost a spouse would experience incapacitating depression and withdrawal. In fact, as the center set up the programs, they called on some individuals who had gone through this life transition successfully to help them design more effective services. Because, however, they had recognized this problem as affecting more than a few people in their community, they were able to tailor their services to a specific group they found to be at risk.

A large regional state mental hospital was located in another community. As patients recovered and were discharged, many of them remained in that community rather than return to their homes in other parts of the state. Entering the community, these people were often at risk for relapse and the need for a return to the hospital. Here the mental health center devised programs specifically to help this population adjust to their life in the community, using several accessible partial hospitalization programs and good case management. These programs were meant to give information, support, and ongoing treatment as the clients met the challenges and made the adjustment to new surroundings.

Your community will have needs that are specific to it. At some point you will be involved in deciding who is at risk in your own community and what services would be most effective for them. You will look at populations who use services in your community most often. You will look at the kinds of problems that repeatedly bring people to social service agencies for service. This information will be the basis for new services and programs.

MAKING THE DECISION

A decision to develop services for a population at risk is not made on intuition, but should be made on statistics. Human services personnel often blanch at the very notion that they will have to use mathematics, but math is important in determining who is at risk, what variables make the risk more or less pronounced, and what interventions work better than others.

Your funding sources may do the studies that determine the needs in your community and direct your agency on how to access funds based on the services your agency provides. In other instances, you may need to do the research yourself to point out to funding sources and legislatures what is needed in your community or state.

Sometimes, in spite of the best practice, the decision is made for political, emotional, or anecdotal reasons. This, unfortunately, can result in ineffective use of funds and missed opportunities.

DETERMINING THE INTERVENTION

Interventions come in three categories: primary prevention, secondary prevention, and tertiary prevention. These can be defined as follows:

1. *Primary prevention:* Prevents at-risk populations from experiencing a problem that is likely to interfere with adjustment and functioning, or prepares the population to better handle a predictable problem that will occur. Primary prevention seeks to reduce the number of cases of a specific problem in the community before these cases develop.
2. *Secondary prevention:* Intervenes with small groups or individuals early, or just after the problem has started, with diagnosis, assessment, and treatment to address the problem before it becomes long-term. Secondary prevention is designed to shorten the duration of the problem and to assist individuals in the effective management of the problem so as to prevent further difficulties.
3. *Tertiary prevention:* Seeks to reduce the severity or disability caused by specific problems. The intervention here is treatment, which seeks to reduce the damage and rehabilitate people after the disorder or problem is fully developed.

Primary Prevention

There may be times when you will be asked to develop primary prevention programs for at-risk populations. Here the focus is on preventing a problem from occurring in the first place. There are four ways you can approach this:

1. *Strengthen the individual.* You might use education in order to strengthen individuals before the problem begins. Drug and alcohol prevention programs

provided before kids are pressured to use these substances and educational programs aimed at preventing teen pregnancy before young people are sexually active fall into this category. Other examples include parenting classes for expectant parents, communication classes for engaged couples, and groups at a local hospital for spouses of patients with terminal cancer to prepare them for the terminal stages of the disease and the death of their spouse.

2. *Remove the problem.* On the other hand, you might look at how you can remove the problem from affecting people at all. Working with city planners, you might suggest better transportation to neighborhoods of older adults as part of your plan to get older people out into the community and prevent their withdrawal. If there have been a considerable number of muggings in neighborhoods of older adults and these victims have been seen by your agency for help with the consequences, you might approach the local police to see if security can be strengthened in these neighborhoods to prevent or reduce the number of assaults.
3. *Remove the person from the stress.* Another approach might be to find ways to remove individuals from stressful situations before the situation creates a problem for them. For example, if you work in a small rural community where there is no middle school you might find that going directly to high school from 6th grade is stressful for young people. If your agency works with a number of 7th graders and finds that going from elementary school to 7th grade at a high school has been stressful for them, you might work with the school board to place these children in a middle school setting. In this way, you remove these children from a potentially stressful environment to one that will be far less stressful.
4. *Change the problem before it hits.* In the previous example, the school district might be small and unable to afford a separate middle school. In this event, you might work with school officials to change the arrangement of 7th grade classes and activities to better separate 7th graders from the confusing and more adult atmosphere of the high school. Here rather than working to strengthen the group of students, you would work toward changing the structure of the problem so that it would be less stressful for the students.

Secondary and Tertiary Prevention

Most of your professional efforts will take place in the area of secondary and tertiary prevention because funds for primary prevention are scarce. Secondary and tertiary interventions are usually associated with treatment and are carried out in small therapy groups, self-help groups, or individual case management and treatment. In other words, most of what we do is designed to shorten the duration of a problem that already exists and to make those individuals who are coping with the problem more effective at doing so. For example, there is no widely accepted way to prevent schizophrenia, but in a partial hospitalization program, people dealing with schizophrenia are taught ways to prevent psychotic episodes from occurring by making specific diet and behavior changes. This in turn allows people to prevent debilitating episodes and to work or function usefully in other ways.

Treatment and interventions in the secondary and tertiary categories are wide-ranging. For example, one person might be offered therapy to help him or her deal with the consequences of sexual abuse as a child, while another might attend a self-help group for individuals who were sexually abused as children and are now brought together to share ways to cope with the experience and regain emotional well-being. Other services might involve case management for adults who suffer from chronic episodes of depression and need support and medication. For other individuals suffering with depression, a group session once a week with a therapist may be extremely helpful because of the group support. Medication might be used to reduce the symptoms of anxiety for a person who has been laid off from his or her job, while another person may elect to join a support group made up of recently unemployed individuals.

In all these examples the person has already experienced the problem and the interventions are designed to shorten the duration, reduce the severity of the difficulty, and return the person as quickly and smoothly as possible to a sound level of functioning.

CASE MANAGEMENT WITH HIGH-RISK POPULATIONS

In the chapters that follow, we will look at six high-risk populations. For each population, general case management is the same. You will provide intake, planning, linking and monitoring. More information on these case management services can be found in *Fundamentals of Case Management Practice* (Summers, 2001). Each group or population, however, will have unique problems and issues.

For example, you will find that different populations of clients require different services. While services for older people might be focused on keeping people in their homes and addressing medical problems, services for a person who is in an abusive relationship would focus on getting the person to a safer location outside the abusive situation. In drug and alcohol services, you would be looking at ways to help the client remain sober, while in children's services much of your work might be with parents and teachers to help the child make the best adjustment.

In every case management situation, regardless of the referrals you have made, you will find that your clients will seek you out when they are in trouble. An older person who has been hospitalized will call. A man who has relapsed and is again using drugs will call. A mental health client who is out of medication will call. Not only will you arrange for the best services in those circumstances, but you also will be expected to listen. Listening is your best skill. Therapists may be booked; it may take time to get someone into a detoxification program; a psychiatric appointment may be several days or even weeks away. In the meantime, your clients will turn to you for help and reassurance. For this reason, you will need to have a thorough understanding of the unique problems and issues of your client population.

It is important to understand from the beginning that case management is always more than just arranging and monitoring services. That is only part of it. The client looks to you for support, crisis intervention, and direction. You would be wise to expect that your clients will see you in that way. Your preparation to handle the population you are seeing will make you an effective case manager.

Finally, in some agencies, intake and service are provided in the same place. In those agencies, the focus is on a particular high-risk group, and case management might be augmented by good listening skills on a continuing basis. In such an agency, you might have to be available to handle crises and run educational groups. In agencies of this type, you will be given considerable information beyond case management about how to handle the particular problems the clients bring to the agency.

IT IS NOT ALWAYS EASY

Jerome refused to work with Mr. Edwards. Of course, he could not take him off his caseload, but he refused to return Mr. Edwards's calls or to give him service. He confided to one of the other workers that he had tried to help Mr. Edwards, but the man was rude and demanding. Jerome told his coworker, "Why I even set up a job interview for him, and he didn't keep the appointment. Now he wants me to start over with him. I don't think so!"

Jerome entered the field ill-prepared for the realities of his work. He erroneously believes that all his clients should be reasonable and act in what he considers to be their own best interests. People do not always do that, and often when they do not, they end up needing our help. Many people entering this field do so with unrealistic expectations about the people who will be their clients.

Before we look in more detail at populations with which you are likely to work during your career, it would be wise for us to stop here and think about what it is we are attempting to do. Certainly we are not attempting to force change on anyone or make people do the things that would, in our opinion, be best for them. Rather, we are here to facilitate and support people as they move toward healthier and more positive lives. Some clients make great strides, and some clients who make great strides need very little support. Others need more. Some clients lurch toward positive goals, going forward and moving back again many times before they get to their goals. Sometimes the goals are very modest, and other times clients work on making considerable life changes. Some people never can reach their goals, often because the changes are too frightening or they do not have the capacity at the time to move toward their goals.

It is unfortunate that some students believe people in high-risk groups will all move in a healthy, constructive way toward what might be best. Your preparation is designed to help you understand and work with the setbacks that come with each population. The man who has been sober for months may show up at work intoxicated again. The woman who left her abusive husband could return home after you helped her get on welfare and find an apartment. The mother of an adult with mental retardation might refuse to allow her child to go to work. The child who seems to be settled and is doing better in school may run away. The parents who appeared to benefit from parenting classes might abuse their child again and get arrested. Rather than give in to exasperation, it is better to work on understanding what this behavior means and why the client made such choices at that particular time.

More important, we need to understand that the people with whom we work will not automatically agree with us or see the changes they need to make and then make them. They will not always be reasonable, pleasant, or logical. Some may be difficult, maddening, and unpredictable instead. It is pointless for you to take this personally or for you to enter this field believing that everyone will be cooperative and enlightened and delighted you are there to help. People need help because they have problems. Often these problems have to do with faulty perceptions, fear of change, a sense of being overwhelmed, and poor relationship skills.

So remember this as you start out: We cannot *make* people change. We will eventually wear ourselves out if we are not prepared for these two things:

1. Some individual clients will make poor decisions.
2. Some individual clients will not be particularly happy about our presence in their lives, *even when they have sought our help voluntarily.*

Do not take a client's anger, refusal to cooperate, or lack of progress personally. Instead, focus on what frightens and motivates your client.

CONCLUSION

In the following chapters, we will look at several broad population groups. The groups we will address are children, women, people with drug and alcohol problems, individuals with mental health problems, individuals with developmental problems, and people who are growing older. Not all the members of these populations will be at risk. For instance, not all women or all children or all older adults will be at risk for problems that require a social service intervention, but the material in these chapters will inform you about what to look for and how to help those who do require intervention.

In the chapters on specific population groups, we will look at some of the common issues and difficulties facing each population. The material in each chapter will familiarize you with what to look for in doing your intake and assessment, what services should commonly be available, and what specifically to monitor as you follow the client. You will learn what questions are important to ask and what information needs to be given to specific members of your treatment team. You will also learn to recognize coping strategies used by clients before they seek help that might be detrimental to them, such as self-medicating or confabulating to compensate for a failing memory. In addition, you will learn to spot certain symptoms that are indicative of problems that must be addressed.

It is important to note that each population faces different circumstances and challenges. Each population requires you to be vigilant about issues particularly relevant to that group. Each population requires different interventions on your part.

EXERCISES

Talk to a person who works in social services such as a social worker, psychologist, minister, counselor, or therapist. To make this assignment more interesting, select a person who works in a field that interests you. Ask this person the following questions:

1. What population within your caseload do you see as being particularly at risk in the course of your practice?

2. How was it determined that this group is at risk? Has any statistical research been done, or is this a hunch you have from looking at your caseload? Has a community needs assessment been done, and if so, may I see the assessment and the results?

3. What do you do to address these problems? What interventions do you use? Does the agency use any primary prevention techniques? Has anyone approached funding sources to express concern about this population? Has anyone tried to affect legislation for this population? Is the agency using any specific techniques designed just for this population?

Describe your findings in a paper with three sections, one for each of the three areas of questioning. Place a cover page on the front and submit it to your instructor.

In a small group of students, choose a high-risk population that is of interest to those in the group, and do the following exercise:

1. Describe the population, clearly defining what specifically places your population at risk and what the risk is.
2. Next, develop at least one primary prevention program for the population as a whole. Remember, this program will be for individuals who have not yet experienced the problem, but who appear to be at risk for it.
3. Finally, develop tertiary interventions for individuals within this population who are currently experiencing the problem in a way that is proving detrimental to their overall functioning and emotional health.

Present your plan to the class, using the following questions to lead a discussion with the class about these issues:

- Does the class agree that you have presented a suitable primary prevention program for this high-risk population?
- What would constitute secondary interventions?
- Do others in the class share your interest in this population?
- What practical problems (i.e., funding) might arise if you tried to implement your plan?

Chapter 2
Writing a Social History

INTRODUCTION

In each of the succeeding chapters we will study a particular high-risk population. Accompanying each of these chapters is a typical evaluation or assessment form. If you choose later in your career to work with one of these high-risk populations, you may find that the form used here is not the same as the form used in the agency where you work. Every agency has a different way of taking and recording relevant information during the initial intake process. Once you have used a typical form for a high-risk population, however, you will be able to move easily to other similar forms.

In some situations, you will be asked to take a social history, either as a supplement to the assessment forms used by your agency or in place of such forms. Just as the assessment forms may differ from agency to agency, so might the format for the social history. Nevertheless, having written social histories in the classroom, you will be able to adapt readily to whatever format is used in the agency where you work.

WHAT IS A SOCIAL HISTORY?

A social history provides the following information:

1. A description and history of the presenting problem (the problem that brought the client into the agency)
2. Background information on the person's life
3. The worker's impressions and recommendations

Taken together, these three sections of the social history give a picture in summary form of where clients were when they came to the agency seeking assistance. In this way, the social history functions as the baseline or foundation for decisions about services and for measuring clients' progress. It also gives some direction in regard to the problems that will need to be addressed. We will look at each of these sections individually, and at examples of each one, so you can see how the social history is developed.

LAYOUT OF THE SOCIAL HISTORY

Social histories always use subheadings set out to the left of the text. This is done to help people find relevant information quickly without having to read an entire text to find buried pieces of information. In most agencies, the outline of subheadings is the same for all clients, so workers become familiar with the outline and know exactly where to look for information. A typical outline might look like this:

> Presenting problem and reason for referral (including what the client is requesting and how the client sees the problem)
> Family of origin
> Birth and childhood
> Marriages and significant relationships
> Current living arrangements
> Education
> Military service
> Employment history
> Medical history
> Legal history
> Social and recreational interests
> Religious activities
> Client successes, strengths, and resources
> Impressions and recommendations

It must be stressed that this is one of any number of formats. You would use a different outline, for instance, if you worked in an agency with criminal offenders. Then the section on legal history might be called criminal justice background, and that section might be closer to the top of the outline. If you worked in an agency that served the needs of victims of domestic violence, the agency might place the section on marriages right after the presenting problem to augment the information on the presenting problem. If you were working with children, you might include a section on school adjustment in place of the section on education. In an organization devoted to helping people with their addictions, you would probably have several sections related to the course of the addiction and attempts to overcome the addiction in the past. Both criminal justice history and medical history would become more prominent in that outline.

The social history will have identifying information on each page so that it will not get separated from the chart or record in which it belongs. Sometimes it is printed on different colored paper so the social history will be easily identifiable in the chart or record.

In the following text, we will look at each of the usual sections in a social history closely. Examples will demonstrate how to write these summaries.

HOW TO ASK WHAT YOU NEED TO KNOW

If you follow the outline provided earlier, you will have assembled a considerable amount of personal information. Clients who are giving a social history probably are not very familiar with you or the agency, and talking openly about each of these aspects of their lives may be difficult. For that reason, you should use plenty of open questions. For more information on how to pose open questions to your clients, consult *Fundamentals of Case Management Practice* (Summers, 2001).

Certainly you will not use only open questions. Asking, for example, how many brothers and sisters a person has is a closed, but useful, question. You might, however, follow such a closed question with an open one: "Tell me a little bit about them." In another example you might ask these closed questions: "Were you ever in the military?" and "What were the dates of your military service?" Then you would follow up with an open question such as: "Can you describe your military service?"

Open questions soften the interview, making it seem to be less prying and making clients feel less like they are being grilled, since the clients choose which significant details to reveal. When questions are asked with respect and with a genuine interest in clients, the initial interviews can be helpful to the clients in sorting out, maybe for the first time, the factors in their lives that are relevant and significant.

Each section that follows provides open questions that you can use to solicit information needed for that section of the social history. These are only examples; with time and practice, you should become proficient in asking open questions on your own.

A History of the Problem

The first section is the history of the presenting problem. In a brief summary, the background to the presenting problem is documented. This is done in no more than two or three paragraphs; usually only one paragraph of summary is needed. Agencies differ in what they call this section: Background Information, Presenting Problem, History of Presenting Problem. Some agencies break the section into two parts: Presenting Problem and Background to Presenting Problem. For our purposes, we will call the first section Presenting Problem and Reason for Referral, and we will include both the problem and the background to that problem in this section.

Following are two examples of the presenting problem and reason for referral section in a social history. The first is about Kate, a 47-year-old woman who contacted the agency requesting help for a long-standing depression.

Presenting Problem and Reason for Referral

Kate is a 47-year-old woman who called requesting help for a depression that she states has lasted for almost two years. Kate describes the depression as beginning after a serious episode with the flu and the death of her mother approximately two years ago. At the time her mother was ill, Kate did not follow her doctor's recommendations that she take time off work and stay home. She was very involved in caring for her mother before her mother died. Kate states she was not aware of being depressed until after the funeral, but she grew depressed during the seven-month period in which she and her husband cleaned out her mother's house and settled her mother's affairs. She describes this work as "heart-wrenching" work that involved several legal difficulties. Currently Kate describes her depression as characterized by hypersomnia, an inability to go to work several days each month, and a loss of interest in social activities and friends. She states she is here in part because her husband insisted she get help.

The second presenting problem and reason for referral section is written about Carlos, who recently entered the country and is having problems adjusting to the new culture.

Presenting Problem and Reason for Referral

Carlos, a 38-year-old male Mexican citizen, contacted the agency at the suggestion of his boss, Ronaldo Rodriquez. Carlos states he came to the United States from Mexico because his only family is living here. His brother and parents came to this country in 1982, and his brother received a good education and went on to medical school. The brother currently practices medicine in Maryland. Carlos was left behind with an aunt when the family emigrated, "because I was hard to handle." Last year his aunt died and Carlos came to the United States to join his family, "who are all I have."

Carlos has been here for eight months and is not sure if he wants to stay or return to Mexico. He describes feeling "out of place" in American culture, particularly compared to his brother and his brother's lifestyle. He states he has no commitment to Mexico, but believes he would be more comfortable in familiar surroundings. In addition, he states his parents are "putting pressure on me" to remain in this country and get a better job. He describes them as critical of the few friends he has made and of his lax attendance at church.

In each of these examples, we see what information the worker assembled as being the most relevant to the immediate difficulty. We have a picture now of why each of these people called the agency and what might have precipitated the request for help.

Questions You Might Ask

- Can you tell me a little about what happened?
- Can you describe this problem for me?
- Could you give me some idea of what has been going on lately?
- Can you tell me a bit about what brought you here today?

Client's Appraisal and Requests

Always ask clients what it is they are seeking. A client new to the system may not know exactly what services are available or may have only a partial understanding of what a service actually is or can accomplish. Therefore, when you ask for the client's expectations, you may have to describe and explain what is available and how the service works, not only at your agency but also in other places in the community if these are relevant.

Ask clients for their assessment of the problem. Valuable information can be found in listening to how clients view what is going on in their lives.

Questions You Might Ask

- Tell me a little about what you see as the main problem.
- Could you tell me something about what you think is important here?
- Could you give me some thoughts on how you see the problem?
- Do you have any thoughts about the services you would like to receive from us?
- Give me some ideas you have for how you feel we could best help.

Background Information About the Person

As noted earlier, this part of the social history contains a number of sections on various aspects of the client's personal history. We will look at each of these areas.

Family of Origin

Here you document the relevant information about the family of origin, that is, the family into which the person was born. Information on parents and their occupations, siblings, and outstanding characteristics of or information about the family would be placed here.

Questions You Might Ask

- Can you tell me something about your brother?
- Could you describe your parents for me?
- Tell me a little about what your family was like.
- Can you describe what your home was like?

Birth and Childhood

In this section, note if the pregnancy and birth of the client were in any way complicated. Ask about important features of the person's childhood and what the person remembers. You want to determine the flavor of the client's perceptions of this period of his or her life. Was it happy or fraught with conflict? As a child, did the client feel appreciated or ignored? Was the client asked to shoulder adult burdens or allowed to remain a child?

Questions You Might Ask

- Can you tell me something about your childhood?
- Tell me a little about what growing up was like for you.

Marriages and Significant Relationships

In this section, you will document the marriages of the client. Be sure to include all significant relationships, whether or not the couple actually went through a marriage ceremony. If the client lived with someone for several months or years, note that here. Some clients have had more than one marriage or relationship. You should write a sentence or two on each, including information such as when the marriage or relationship took place, how long it lasted, and why it ended. Information about the current relationship of the client to an ex-spouse is also relevant.

Questions You Might Ask

- Tell me a little more about her (or him).
- Can you describe something about what that marriage (or relationship) was like for you?

Current Living Arrangements

In this section, give a brief description of the home, how the client feels about the home, and who lives there.

Questions You Might Ask

- Tell me a bit about your home.
- Can you describe what your life is like when you are at home?

Education

Document here the person's highest level of education. Also note any difficulties or successes the client experienced while in school.

Questions You Might Ask

- Can you tell me more about school?
- Can you explain a little about your problems in school?
- Tell me a bit about college.

Military Service

If the client served in the military, summarize the details of that service here. Always mention the type of discharge from the military and the client's status as a veteran. If the client was never in the military, simply state "No military service."

Questions You Might Ask

- Can you tell me about your military service?
- Could you describe a few of the things you did in the service?

Employment History

Here you will document the type of employment the client has held. Note any breaks in the client's employment history and the reasons for them. Also indicate how the client views the work he or she has done. If the person has never held a job, write "No employment history."

Questions You Might Ask

- Tell me a bit about what it is like to work there.
- Can you give me some examples of the work you did?

Medical History

Medical history will be extremely important to medical personnel who may be called upon to assess and give service to your client. A psychiatrist or a nurse may spot a possible underlying medical problem based on the information you assemble in this section. Ask about childhood illnesses and any other illnesses, allergies, or surgeries.

Questions You Might Ask

- Tell me a little about your health.
- Could you describe this surgery a bit more for me?
- Can you tell me a little about the polio?
- Can you describe those allergies?

Legal History

In many cases, clients will have no legal history. If that is the case, write "No legal history" in this section. If the client has a legal history, however, include the information here. Involvement in a lawsuit or a criminal case, as either the defendant or plaintiff, is usually a source of stress. Petty criminal activity that is current gives insight into how a client views authority and his or her place in society. Previous criminal activity may show how much the client has been able to turn his or her life around, or it may indicate an unfortunate pattern.

Questions You Might Ask

- Can you explain a little about the lawsuit?
- Can you tell me about those early encounters with the law?
- Could you tell me a bit about what brought you into contact with law enforcement?

Social and Recreational Interests

Because we are always interested in the strengths of our clients, we want to note what interests them and the kinds of social and recreational activities in which they participate. If a client has no activities to report, be sure to note this as well, since it gives important clues to the extent of a client's social involvement or withdrawal. Ask if this lack of social involvement has always been present or whether it is more recent in the client's life. Recent lack of interest in activities that used to be important can be a sign of depression. Note what interests the client most and what activities the client pursues.

Questions You Might Ask

- Tell me a little about what you do in your spare time.
- Fill me in on what you do for fun.
- Can you tell me a bit about what you like to do most?

Religious Activities

Some clients are very involved in their church, synagogue, or mosque. Others are not so involved but hold firm spiritual beliefs that they find sustaining. Still others have neither religious involvement nor any interest in spiritual matters. Ask clients about religious affiliation and activity or involvement. If a person does not have anything to report, explore with that person any spiritual beliefs that might have given him or her strength and comfort. This sort of strength and comfort is often enormously helpful to people as they recover or cope with illness and difficult problems. This is a sensitive area, however, so move on if you feel a client is reluctant to discuss his or her beliefs. For some clients, this line of questioning may be construed as an attempt on your part to push a specific religion. Be sure to make a note, in a matter-of-fact way, if a client shows discomfort with this topic.

Questions You Might Ask

- Could you tell me about your synagogue?
- Could you describe some of the beliefs you feel are most helpful to you?

Client Successes, Strengths, and Resources

This is a section you may not find on most social history outlines. As much as we want to see clients as whole people, agency policies and time pressures often prevent us from exploring anything other than problems with clients. This focus on the negative aspects of a person's life often causes workers to create a skewed picture of the person they want to help and to register barely disguised surprise over successes the client has had that come out during the social history. Asking clients what they are most proud of, or asking them what things they consider to be accomplishments, makes it clear that you expect each client to be a whole person, not a collection of problems. It is also good practice for you, as it helps you to develop the habit of asking about and documenting positive information along with information about the client's difficulties.

Questions You Might Ask

- Tell me a bit about the things that make you proud.
- Can you tell me a little about the things you consider successes for you?

In addition, note here the strengths and resources your client brings to the situation. Personal skills, financial assets, and social supports are all important to note in this section.

Impressions and Recommendations

This last section in the social history contains your own impressions and recommendations. Include information about the client's appearance during the interview, any problems with memory or reality, and any anxiety or depression that was present. Indicate how the client related to you. Your impressions give important clues to clients' present situations and how they are handling their problems emotionally and cognitively.

Much of the information included here about your client is referred to as a mental status examination. The method for taking a mental status examination is described fully in *Fundamentals of Case Management Practice* (Summers, 2001). This textbook also covers the points that are included as part of a mental status examination.

Finally, give your recommendations for services that might be considered when creating the treatment or service plan for the client. Be sure to note the client's input into these recommendations and that this input was or will be considered.

CAPTURING THE DETAILS

Sometimes people taking social histories for the first time are inclined to write the barest number of details. They might write something like this: "Alice worked at K-Mart for four years." In addition to knowing that, however, it would be useful to know when she worked at K-Mart, what she did there, and why she is no longer there. Here are some other examples:

1. "Madelaine's health is good. She states she had one surgery in 1998, but since then she has been fine." You would also want to include information about what type of surgery she had.
2. "Marie is the mother of four children." You would also want to include their ages and where they are now. Some place in the history you should note how these relationships are doing, whether there is frequent contact between children no longer in the home and their mother, and how she felt about their childhood and her role in it.
3. "Bill is currently active socially." You would want to note what activities are enjoyable for him.
4. "Carl describes his childhood home as happy, but today he does not know where two of his siblings are." You should also include what made the childhood home happy, what Carl remembers specifically about his childhood home, and how he lost touch with the two siblings.

While your history should be a concise summary of the main points of a person's life, too much brevity can leave a number of unanswered questions that, if answered, would shed considerable light on the client's life and problems now.

SAMPLE SOCIAL HISTORY

Figure 2.1 shows a completed social history for Kate, whose presenting problem was summarized earlier. By examining the figure, you will be able to see how a social history is constructed.

Social History

Name: Kathryn (Kate) Carter **Agency #:** 04587

Date: 7/10/2001

Prepared by: Winston Cramer

Presenting Problem

Kate is a 47-year-old woman who called requesting help for a depression that she states has lasted for almost two years. Kate describes the depression as beginning after a serious episode with the flu and the death of her mother approximately two years ago. At the time her mother was ill, Kate did not follow her doctor's recommendations that she take time off work and stay home. She was very involved in caring for her mother before her mother died. Kate states she was not aware of being depressed until after the funeral, but she grew depressed during the seven-month period in which she and her husband cleaned out her mother's house and settled her mother's affairs. She describes this work as "heart-wrenching" work that involved several legal difficulties. Currently Kate describes her depression as characterized by hypersomnia, an inability to go to work several days each month, and a loss of interest in social activities and friends. She states she is here in part because her husband insisted she get help.

Client believes she needs medication "to jolt me out of this." She blames herself for letting it go so long but says she felt it would lift on its own. She also states she did not want to disturb her husband with the problem. She is asking for a session with a "doctor" and a prescription. She seems uncertain that she needs therapy, stating, "I don't think there is anything wrong in my life, really."

Family of Origin

The client's father died when she was 6 years old, and Kate describes feeling responsible for her mother most of her life. She describes her childhood as a happy one. A number of aunts and uncles took an interest in her, and she grew up with a number of cousins close by. She describes happy family gatherings for holidays. She describes her mother as living off the social security that came after her father died and as being unable to sustain a consistent work history. The client states that her mother sought her advice often and that she feels she made many of the important decisions for the family. At present, only one aunt remains (in a nursing home), and client's cousins have moved out of the state. Client has some contact with them at Christmas.

Birth and Childhood

Pregnancy and birth were uneventful. In addition to what is noted above, the client and her mother never had enough money. "That's why I think my aunts and uncles took an interest in me." She spent weeks away from home in the summer at the homes of her cousins and often went to camp with them. Her mother would come for family picnics and was always warmly received.

Marriages and Significant Relationships

Kate has been married to her husband for 25 years. They have one daughter who is 20 years old and currently a student at the University of Minnesota. She is studying engineering. Kate remembers the pregnancy as easy, but she suffered severe and incapacitating depression immediately following the birth. She was unable to return to work at the end of her maternity leave, thus losing her job.

She describes her husband as "steady" and reports that he is an accountant with a local accounting firm. Kate wanted more children, but he discouraged her, fearing she would again suffer postpartum depression. As a couple they are fond of going to symphony concerts and plays. Her husband is a model railroader, and Kate helps with the activities of the club from time to time.

Her daughter is "quiet like her father." She did very well in school and got a scholarship to the university. Kate worries about her in that she has had few friends and no boyfriends. She is concerned that her daughter "may be prone to depression the way I am."

Current Living Arrangements

Kate and her husband live in a three-bedroom home on half an acre in Meadowview. There are no others living in the home. Kate has a cat that she is very fond of. She describes her home as "in need of work" and says that she would like to do more to fix it up but is not able to find the energy. The couple has lived in this house since they were married.

Education

Kate has an associate's degree in early childhood. She recalls that she did well in school and it was suggested she go to college and become a teacher, but her mother discouraged her due to the financial situation of the family. She has rarely used this education.

Military Service

There was no military service.

Employment History

Right after Kate got her degree, she worked for 3 years in a day care center, but was attracted to a job as an office manager in a small insurance firm. She has done office management for the last 27 years except for a time when she was off for a prolonged postpartum depression. This occurred at the time of the birth of her only child, a daughter. Following this episode she obtained an excellent position in a large law firm and has, until now, moved upward steadily with promotions and pay raises.

Medical History

Aside from the postpartum depression and the bad flu she suffered in 1999, Kate reports her health is good. She had few childhood illnesses and has a medical checkup about every three years. She denies using drugs, and states she never smoked. She states she will have a glass of wine once or twice a year when she and her husband go out to dinner. Recently, along with the depression she has noticed that she has more headaches. She has not seen a doctor about these.

Legal History

There is no legal history to report.

Social and Recreational Interests

Kate is very interested in sewing and has made all the curtains and draperies for her home. "I would make my own clothes, but I haven't the time with working." She is also an avid reader of mystery novels and does some "modest gardening" on the weekends. She has a cat that gives her a lot of pleasure. Since her depression she has noticed a gradual withdrawal from activities she used to enjoy.

Religious Activities

Kate states she is a Methodist and that she and her husband regularly attend the church just six blocks from their home. She used to sing in the choir but dropped out after her mother died and has not been able to "find the strength to add that to my list of things to do." She and her husband used to be active in Sunday school, but she does not want to go anymore, and he also has dropped out.

Client Successes, Strengths, and Resources

Client was unclear about what she could list as successes. She denies that raising her daughter was an accomplishment or that helping her mother to the extent she did was important. "I was just doing what anybody would have done." She smiled and shook her head, unable to think of anything she would list as a success. She did finally admit that she is proud of her recent promotions at work.

Client feels she can be open with her best friend, Sue, and describes her husband as a source of support. She reports no financial problems, and she attends college one night a week to improve her computer skills.

Impressions and Recommendations

This woman is a competent, but modest person who is coherent and oriented x 3. She came to the office today seeking help with a depression of two years' duration. Her appearance was very neat, and she sat with her hands folded in her lap and on the edge of the chair. Her affect was flat, but she seemed concerned that she give accurate and useful information to the worker.

She reports a loss of interest in activities that formerly gave her pleasure. This and her hypersomnia have increased recently, causing her to seek help. During the interview, client had difficulty discussing herself and her accomplishments. She tends to minimize her successes and focus on things she could have done better.

She is requesting medication and an appointment with a doctor. Recommend a psychiatric assessment prior to development of service plan.

Taken by *Winston Cramer*

Figure 2.1 A completed social history

SOCIAL HISTORIES IN OTHER SETTINGS

Limited Time for Intake

As a case manager having ongoing contact with your client, it may be possible to assemble an entire social history as outlined above. Certainly, compiling this complete picture of the client at the time of intake is best practice. Today, however, many agencies are unable to spend the time it takes to assemble such a history. Often the client is in and out of service in a matter of days, depending on the directions of the funding source. Many managed care organizations and insurance companies have severely limited the amount of service a client may receive. This is particularly true for adult services in agencies focusing on mental health and on drug and alcohol problems.

Brief Intakes

In some agencies, the emphasis is on the presenting problem, background to that problem, and your impressions and recommendations. In all cases, you are expected to discuss the services you provide with the client and seek the client's input, and to document this discussion. Unfortunately, you might not have the time to do this thoroughly or to note many of the other aspects of the client's life in the history.

Use of Forms

Because of the limited time in some agencies and the need to make sure that specific questions are covered in the initial interview, many agencies provide intake or assessment forms. These forms contain certain information the funding source requires and make that information easily accessible. Such a form may be similar, although a bit longer, to the telephone inquiry form you used if you learned how to do telephone inquiries from *Fundamentals of Case Management Practice* (Summers, 2001). These forms usually have names like Initial Assessment Form or Intake Evaluation Form. Other intake or assessment forms may be lengthy, with numerous questions to determine the client's needs and capabilities.

Remember, when you are using a form, it is important that you stop and ask open questions as you go through it. This increases rapport with the client and reduces the client's sense of being grilled by you.

WHO TOOK THE SOCIAL HISTORY

Generally agencies have the person who took the social history sign his or her name after a phrase such as "taken by," "submitted by," "prepared by," or "filed by." This signature appears at the end of the form. If the person signing the form has credentials such as BSW or MSW, these would follow the signature. In the example shown in Figure 2.1, the name of the worker who took the history is also typed at the top of the history so that anyone in the agency can look and quickly find out who did the history.

EXERCISES

1. On a single sheet of paper, write a note on how Kate appears to you from her social history shown in Figure 2.1. What are your impressions of her? What do you think she would be likely to do or not do? How likely is she to commit suicide following this visit? How readily can she stand up for herself? What strengths and supports does she have? What contradictions do you see in looking at her life?

In the following two exercises, do not place your name anywhere but in the designated places, since you will be practicing taking social histories the way they are actually taken in agencies. Do not hand in social histories or forms with your name anywhere but in the designated places for your name and signature.

2. Write a social history of Carlos using the presenting problem paragraph provided earlier in this chapter. Invent other information as needed. This will give you practice in organizing information.
3. Take a social history from a friend or classmate. Be sure to let this person know that he or she *does not* have to answer any question that makes him or her uncomfortable; he or she can make up information to fill in the gaps. The important thing is for you to practice taking a social history and then organizing the information in the useful format provided in this chapter.

Chapter 3

Case Management with Children and Their Families

INTRODUCTION

Isaiah was 7 years old the night his mother and father and little sister had roasted hamburgers on the back porch on the charcoal grill. Having learned about fires in school, Isaiah suggested to his dad that they pour water over the hot charcoal after the hamburgers were cooked. His father explained that putting water in the grill would rust it and they could close the lid and shut the vents and the fire would go out. He and Isaiah did that and the family gathered for dinner around the kitchen table.

Sometime later in the night a stiff wind blew up and the grill tipped over. The back of the house caught fire, and the smoke alarms went off throughout the house. The family managed to escape, but with very few possessions. Neighbors awakened by the fire took the family into their homes. Isaiah was found sitting on the curb, holding his ears, his eyes tightly closed, and rocking. Over and over he kept saying, "Make it stop, make it stop." A neighbor took him gently into her house and reunited him with his family.

In the weeks following the fire, the family moved into a similar house in the neighborhood that was for sale, the owner having agreed to take it off the market for six months while the family got settled. Getting settled, however, was difficult. The insurance agency did not want to give the family the amount it would take to rebuild the portion of the house that was burned and repair the smoke- and water-damaged areas. Clothes, books, and toys were lost. Six months later, rebuilding still had not begun, and the family was facing a decision about what to do for living arrangements should the house be sold.

At first Isaiah seemed to take it all in stride, as did his much younger sister, but as the weeks passed he became less communicative and more silent. Several times he lashed out at his parents in uncharacteristic anger, and on occasion he made it clear that he had told his father how to put the fire out and his father had ignored him.

Isaiah's parents were deeply concerned, particularly when he began to announce that he had not been born into this family at all, but came from another planet and was an alien, living among people alien to him. To the parents this seemed like psychotic behavior. They quickly made an appointment with case management to bring their child into the children's mental health system where he could be seen by a psychiatrist.

In taking the social history, the case manager learned that Isaiah was continuing to do well in school, but without the same enthusiasm. He was also continuing to handle getting ready for school and other responsibilities. It seemed highly unlikely that Isaiah was psychotic, but it did seem likely that he was having trouble handling the fact that he might have known more than his father, who was supposed to be protecting him, and that he had lost so much in the fire. The case manager shared this impression with the parents, who were greatly relieved, and arranged for a psychiatric evaluation. The psychiatrist's assessment supported the case manager's conclusions, and the family began attending family sessions together to talk about the fire.

The sessions with a therapist went well, and throughout the time the family was in therapy and attempting to rebuild their life at the same time, the case manager was a source of support, visiting in the home and playing with and talking to Isaiah. Later the mother said she was convinced the therapy had "turned things around," but she credited the case manager for his perceptions and support in helping them to look at the situation "through our son's eyes."

SPECIAL CONSIDERATIONS

The Ecological Model

When working with children and their families, the ecological model is an important tool. Interaction within families will differ. So will the expectations for the children in the family and the attitudes toward children. Every family is different. The ecological model is described and explained more fully in *Fundamentals of Case Management Practice* (Summers, 2001). From studying that model we can see that the interaction between the child and the parents helps to define the problem, if there is one.

A child who is born into a family with little patience and few parenting skills might have problems. A child who is placid and cooperative might handle these parents with compliance, while a tense and anxious child might become depressed or defiant. Further, families differ in what they can tolerate. Parents who expect absolute obedience and who are themselves tense and anxious may be more demanding and less satisfied with their child than parents who are relaxed and have a sense of humor. For example, some parents can tolerate difficult children and explain their children's behavior as stemming from independence or determination. Another set of parents, looking at their children with the same behavior, might call that behavior defiance. The first set of parents tolerates the behavior because they see it as a good thing, while the second set of parents is angered or overwhelmed by their children's behavior and seeks help.

Although it is tempting for families seeking help for their children to describe it as a problem that rests entirely with the child, that is rarely the case. Thus, when we work with children, we are really working with the entire family, including the family's interactions with and expectations for one another, and the degree of tolerance and understanding family members have for each other.

The Child's Point of View

As a case manager, part of your work with children is to understand the family from the child's point of view. This is not the same thing as taking the child's side against the parents. Young workers are often inclined to see the problem from a child's perspective and to blame the parents exclusively, while older workers are often inclined to have a more balanced view of the contributions all family members have made to the difficulties.

Understanding how the child views his or her family and the interactions within the family helps us to understand the problems the child is having more clearly. The ability to be empathic, put yourself in the child's shoes, is invaluable. Children often cannot express their feelings and opinions about their families. Many times they are only vaguely aware of family dynamics. It takes an observant and empathic case manager to shed light on how the child perceives the family and the problems occurring there.

Respect

In all the work done to learn how to be a respectful professional, little is said usually about respect for children. Many case managers tend to see children as unimportant in determining the problem and finding resolutions. These case managers talk to the children in a condescending or patronizing manner. They talk when they should be listening and give advice when they should be asking the child for his or her ideas.

Another way in which case managers show disrespect for children is to become intimidating or call children names. They mistakenly believe that they are being tough with children, showing them who is ultimately in charge, with the purpose of forcing the child into submission. Talking to children respectfully is seen as being "soft." Being firm, but respectful, is entirely different from intimidation and name-calling. Case managers working with children must know the difference or they will turn away the very children they are supposed to help.

Respect is important when working with any client. It is mentioned here because so many case managers fail to show children the same respect they would show adult clients.

Prevention

Prevention efforts are given more emphasis with children than with most populations. The reason is that catching the problems of children early in their lives really can prevent problems in later life. Also, programs that strengthen children, whether or not they exhibit problems, can prevent later problems. A successful prevention program we all know about is Project Head Start, and there are other preschool prevention programs. Typically these have a multitude of dimensions ranging from helping children develop school readiness skills to medical interventions. For example, Head Start has four major components: (1) education to prepare a child to enter school and to make up for a deficit of early life experiences; (2) education for parents; (3) parent involvement in planning, decision making, and even teaching; and (4) community involvement to strengthen the parents' ability to negotiate the community and to involve the community in the education and the experiences of Head Start children.

Some studies have shown these programs to be successful, while others claim the effects do not last beyond the elementary grades. Findings in follow-up studies generally have indicated that children do benefit cognitively, emotionally, and in interpersonal skills from these very early programs. Higher intelligence scores, a greater achievement orientation, and a more positive attitude toward school on the part of the family have been some of the positive results of these programs according to the findings.

With school-age children, prevention programs have generally focused on interpersonal skills, impulse control, and empathy for others. Some of the programs help children consider the consequences of their actions or teach problem-solving skills.

For parents, training and education can make them more effective and competent. Parent training and support for very young parents, single parents, or first-time parents can be an important prevention technique. Parents who receive such support can parent more effectively and have support or information when things become overwhelming or bewildering.

Prevention programs should be an important part of programming that addresses the needs of children in a community. Some of the training needs can be addressed by obtaining training packages from established universities or institutes. These usually come with learning booklets, exercises for participants, advice for the instructor, and information the instructor can share with participants. If these are too expensive, many good programs for parents and children have been developed by communities, looking at a number of different models and developing a program to meet the needs of their own community.

Vulnerablility

Children are one of our most vulnerable populations, and for that reason careful attention must be paid to their protection. They cannot protect themselves from exploitation by adults or even agencies. They cannot protect themselves from abuse and neglect. They are unable to protect their own confidentiality and must trust that when we reveal the details of their situation, we will do so only to responsible people who will not use the information as a basis for gossip. Make certain that every action you take on the part of children will not harm them and that you are protective of children in the course of your work with them.

CHILD AND ADOLESCENT SERVICE SYSTEM PROGRAM OR SYSTEMS OF CARE

For many years professional groups have registered their concern for children with mental health problems. The numbers of children, the lack of comprehensive and coordinated services in most communities, and the general lack of interest in serving this population have worried many in the social service field. For example, because children can be involved in more than one system, such as the school system, medical system, and child welfare system, parents have often received contradictory information about their children and had to deal with differing requirements for the family. In addition, parents have been left very much alone to handle difficult and bewildering behavior on their own. When their efforts have failed, largely due to a lack of support, the children have been routinely removed from their care and placed in institutions. Finally, the services a family most needs often have not been available, and the services that have been available have not always met their needs or have been inadequate.

In 1982 Jane Knitzer, writing for the Children's Defense Fund, documented the large number of children with emotional problems receiving inadequate services or no services at all. Knitzer estimated that there were 3 million children suffering from mental health problems, most of whom were receiving no attention. Her study was titled *Unclaimed Children* to emphasize the fact that children have been essentially overlooked or barely taken into account in service planning in most communities.

In 1984, largely spurred by Knitzer's work, the National Institute of Mental Health started a program called Child and Adolescent Service System Program (CASSP). Today the U.S. Department of Health and Human Services has responsibility for this program, lending technical support and dispersing a budget of $10 million throughout all 50 states in order to develop services for children with emotional disorders. A major focus has been on a concept called systems of care. In fact, in some states, CASSP is actually called Systems of Care. The goal of this concept, which is the foundation for efforts to serve children, is to provide children with a variety of useful services in their own community and, further, to have all agencies and programs that serve children coordinate and collaborate on the delivery of these services to children and their families.

Cross-Systems Collaboration

Cross-systems collaboration is a term you will hear often in children's services. It refers to the goal to marshal services that address the needs of each particular child from all of the systems in the community. Ideally, this collaboration is to be done without barriers (e.g., income or gender) to treatment and service. According to Stroul and Friedman (1986), "(A)n important aspect of the concept of systems of care is the notion that all components of the system are interrelated and that effectiveness of any one component is related to the availability and effectiveness of all other components."

Children typically are involved in a number of different systems, beginning with family and school and sometimes extending to a social service agency. In addition, other agencies may be involved (e.g., medical facility, juvenile justice, substance abuse services, child welfare, recreational systems, or vocational services). The CASSP or systems-of-care concept mandates an interagency approach to serving children. Old turf concerns over whose prerogative or area of concern should address the child's problems have largely been diffused by this approach.

In some communities, interagency teams address the needs of a single child, creating an individualized plan for that child that spans the services of many different agencies, each acting as a resource in the child's life. Older children are encouraged to participate in this planning wherever possible, and parents are always part of the planning team.

Case managers are often extremely inventive in creating service plans that use indigenous community resources, rather than spending for new services. Existing recreational programs and incentives such as pairing children with interested adults who can give guidance on particular career choices involve the child in the community and cost very little. Children's case managers look at what the child and family need and try to find ways to meet the need. This is very different from the more traditional approach where children and their families are informed that their child will need to fit into existing services, regardless of whether these services actually meet the needs of the child. Under that approach, services are developed by professionals who assume they know what the community needs, but with the new approach, the focus is on individual children and their families. Both professionals, including case managers, and the family participate in finding out what will work best for the particular child.

Lindsey was 14 when her home burned down in a serious fire after a row of homes in the city was set afire by a teenage arsonist. Until the fire, she had been a good student and enjoyed school. After the fire, she began to lose interest in her schoolwork and her grades plummeted. Lindsey's mother brought her into the case management unit complaining that Lindsey was depressed and needed attention. Before the fire Lindsey had talked often of going to college, and her mother worried that Lindsey's goals would soon be lost if she continued to do poorly in school. The case manager listened to the mother and then talked at length with Lindsey. Lindsey explained that during the fire all her schoolbooks were lost, including notebooks with notes in them and her dictionary. School officials at the inner-city school had been reluctant to issue a new set of books because they rigidly adhered to a regulation that students got only one set a year and were "responsible for the replacement of any damaged books."

The case manager, working with the school business office, managed to secure a new set of books for Lindsey. She and Lindsey went shopping for notebooks, pens, and a dictionary, using agency contingency funds. Then the case manager linked Lindsey with a teacher at the school who helped Lindsey secure notes and other material she needed from other teachers. In addition, the case manager approached the school about letting Lindsey make up exams she had been unable to take successfully without her textbooks. Lindsey showed relief in the first interview, as the case manager suggested the plan they might follow together. At the end of a month Lindsey was once again engaged in her schoolwork and was doing well as she had done before.

In this case, a child who might have been diagnosed as seriously depressed, placed on medications, and seen for weeks in a mental health center received care from a case manager who was willing to come up with solutions outside the usual therapeutic avenues, using natural supports in Lindsey's own environment.

For Communities

For communities, the systems-of-care concept has motivated social service systems to look at exactly what services are offered to children and their families. The ideal is to have options that range from less restrictive in-home services to more restrictive institutional care. In addition, communities have taken a look at the number of available slots for services they have in their service delivery system for children. A community may offer an array of valuable services, but have few slots in each of them, leaving many children without service because they cannot get into these programs. In situations where service slots are few, agencies begin to erect barriers that will help them to determine who gets the service and who does not. The ideal is to have enough slots that all the children who need service will be able to attain it.

There are other barriers to good care in communities, and in the course of your career you are likely to run into several, if not all, of them. Gordon R. Hodas (1996) provided a list of barriers that need to be addressed in communities to ensure that children get the best care. In his discussion of barriers, Hodas pointed out that regulations can interfere with collaboration with families and that regulations can be contradictory. Funding can be sparse, or agencies may refuse to see children whose families cannot pay enormous sums for service. Sometimes professionals become caught up in their own rigid ideas about what constitutes treatment and cannot participate in the more flexible planning that is better for children. Further, some professionals are not committed to collaboration with parents or lack the training and education to follow CASSP principles.

Hodas (1996) also stated that communities can have too few services for children. Sometimes conflicts erupt within communities about which discipline should perform which task or which system should serve what child. Your sensitivity to these possible barriers to good service will enable you to address them during your career.

CASSP Is Becoming the Norm

During the course of your work with children, you will run into CASSP or systems-of-care principles and ideas. The work on children's mental health has progressed in recent years, and more and more states and communities are subscribing to this concept in providing services for children and their families.

CASSP Core Values

Child-Centered and Family-Focused

The needs of children and their families are the determining factor in what services will be given. These services need to be appropriate to the child's developmental level and should take into consideration where the child lives and what strengths and supports the child and family have.

Case managers acknowledge the primary role of the family and make the family a full partner in planning, monitoring, and evaluating services and the child's progress. Not all families work well with case managers and other professionals. The chapter on disarming anger in *Fundamentals of Case Management Practice* (Summers, 2001) discusses a number of reasons why people are difficult and a number of ways to diffuse situations in which people become angry or uncooperative. Case managers committed to the best interests of the child will use all these skills to make certain that even a difficult family participates in their child's service planning.

Community-Based

Case managers need to be able to draw on community resources first, looking for both formal services and informal resources that will integrate the child into his or her community in a healthy and successful way. Looking beyond formal social service agencies and being able to use natural supports is one of the case manager's greatest skills. Cultural, religious, extended family, and social supports should all be taken into account by those planning for a child's needs.

Culturally Competent

The CASSP concept has emphasized from the beginning that anyone who works with children must be culturally competent. A brief discussion about ways to approach different cultures and ethnic groups can be found in *Fundamentals of Case Management Practice* (Summers, 2001). Every case manager who works with a particular ethnic, cultural, or racial group has an ethical obligation to learn about that population. Service given by case managers should always demonstrate an understanding of and be responsive to the particular needs and points of view of the populations with whom they work.

The Pennsylvania State CASSP Advisory Committee to the Office of Mental Health and Substance Abuse (1995) lists the following cultural considerations: "behavior, ideas, attitudes, values, beliefs, customs, language, rituals, ceremonies, and practices characteristic of a particular group of people." A case manager is expected to be respectful of all of these even when they differ sharply from the case manager's own culture.

Assignment

In most communities where you practice, these principles will be followed in children's case management. Find out whether CASSP or Systems of Care is recognized on the state level in your state. Next, learn whether CASSP or systems-of-care principles and values are actively followed in your community, particularly in children's mental health.

CULTURAL COMPETENCE

Cultural competence is important in working with any population, but it is particularly important in working with children. Traditional services for children often overlook cultural differences and find children deficient when they do not live up to the norms of the dominant culture. This insistence on judging children in terms of a culture other than their own places an unnecessary burden on the child at the very time the child is struggling with other issues.

Thus, good case management implies that the case manager will be able to establish rapport and collaborate with many different cultures. In addition, case managers should be familiar enough with the cultures of their clients to know what healthy informal supports exist and to encourage the family to access them. Finally, the case manager needs to be able to relate well to young people of all cultures.

Different Cultural Expectations

Different cultures have different expectations for their children and the role of the family in the child's life. Those differences can involve the rate at which a child is expected to develop, the role the caregiver should have in the child's life, the extent the extended family should be involved, and appropriate responses to and discipline for a child's behavior. Different cultures respond differently to the distress of an infant. Cultures differ in what they expect the role of the father and of the grandparents to be. Cultures also have norms about what gender differences should be as children mature.

For older children, cultural differences can exist in how the child's peer group will function in the child's life, how parents should respond to the new independence and responsibilities of growing up, and the degree of independence that should be given. Parenting expectations for each gender can differ. For example, in some cultures girls are strictly regulated while boys are given considerable freedom and independence.

Assisting Families to Negotiate the Dominant Culture

A good children's case manager should be able to help families when their cultural practices go against state or federal laws. For example, you might run into a situation where a family uses forms of corporal punishment that are defined as child abuse in your state. Case managers would help parents in such situations, giving assistance and support to them as they make changes and handle the legal requirements of the dominant culture.

Many of the referrals that case managers make for families may be to agencies that are not familiar with any culture other than the dominant one. Case managers should be available to help the agency understand the culture of the family and the impact that the culture has on the way the family organizes itself and addresses problems. On the other hand, the case manager should give support and be available to help the family work with the agency as well. This will ensure that the child actually gets services and that an adversarial relationship does not develop between the family and the agency in question.

Finding Strengths in the Culture

The case manager needs to be able to recognize the strengths of a particular culture. The way the family members relate, discipline, care for one another, and involve one another in each other's lives can all be healthy and lend strength to the child and support to the family. A good children's case manager will recognize where these strengths are, even when they differ considerably from those found in the case manager's culture.

Religion and the spirituality of a family are important sources of strength and can differ from culture to culture. Case managers should be able to see the strengths in particular religious practices and spiritual beliefs. The idea that religion is unmentionable or that these topics are off-limits can eliminate from the planning process important sources of support and comfort for children and their families.

Stereotyping and Racism

Families and older teens from different cultures experience both racism and stereotyping in our society. A culturally competent case manager will be able to help young people address these troubling issues as they encounter them. Being able to talk openly about what the young person has experienced and how he or she feels about that is important. Children in your caseload have enough problems without facing these negative attitudes alone. If your relationship is such that you can talk openly with the children you serve, they will be able to discuss these unsettling experiences with you.

CHILD DEVELOPMENT

Child development is an important course of study for anyone working with children and their families. The subject of child development is much too detailed and lengthy to be covered in this chapter, but anyone wishing to work with children should have an understanding of how children develop and what constitutes normal development. This section discusses four primary areas of child development and provides some suggestions for case managers. The suggestions are based on the work of the Pennsylvania CASSP Training and Technical Assistance Institute, which put together detailed material on what constitutes competence for those working with children in *Child, Family and Community Competencies* (Hanson et al., 1999). The four primary areas of child development are:

1. Social development
2. Cognitive and language development
3. Emotional development
4. Physical development

Social Development

Children develop social skills as they grow. They learn to interact with adults and peers, and they acquire language to facilitate that interaction. Children are normally self-centered in the early years, but as they begin to interact with peers, normal competition and appropriate generosity are developed. Case managers need to be able to distinguish between normal ways of interacting and inappropriate ways of relating.

By the preteen years, children are very involved with same-sex friends and are beginning to learn something about their own sexuality. Young teenagers are very involved in their peer groups and harbor mostly ambivalent feelings toward the opposite sex. Certainly, in these early teen years the line between taking responsibility and needing supervision fluctuates.

Older teens have learned their sexual preference, and their involvement in social activities and relationships with peers remains very important to them. These years, as well as the early teen years, can be misleading to observers. Normal teenagers struggle with social issues and try out different ways of adapting and relating; some see that struggle as unhealthy, while others view it as normal.

Case managers should know how to document and understand the impact of problems that exist between parents and children. In addition, case managers should know enough about child development to recognize serious developmental delays, inappropriate lack of self-control, and high-risk behaviors. A good children's case manager can identify extremes in social behavior, particularly risky behaviors.

Because case managers relate to both adults and children, it is important that children's case managers know how to interact with young children and to connect with children of every age group. This can occur only when the case manager shows genuine respect for young people. At every stage, case managers need to be able to communicate and relate to children. A case manager working with infants and toddlers would recognize normal attachment and bonding that takes place at this stage and the predictable response to strangers. Certainly a case manager needs to be able to hold and interact with infants and be able to help caregivers find the most appropriate means of interaction with their very young children. With young children, case managers are obligated to know how to engage in playful activities that interest this age group. With older children, case managers should be able to show a real interest in the things that interest this age group, as well as discussing normal parental concerns and talking about risky behaviors with their young clients.

Carson was a sullen 12-year-old when he was brought into the case management unit by his mother. The problem stemmed from the mother's ex-boyfriend who had sexually molested the boy for over three years before it was discovered by the mother who put a stop to the molestation by moving out. The move had been hard on the family financially, as Carson's mother was a waitress and did not bring home much in the way of weekly earnings.

Carson had lost interest in school and other activities long ago, possibly when the abuse first began. He was monosyllabic with the case manager, saying little and rarely smiling. The case manager could see that sitting in the office with Carson would not be helpful to him, so the case manager, a man with quite a bit of experience with children, bought Carson a football. He would pick Carson up after school, and they would throw the ball around, often in silence. Gradually, however, Carson came to appreciate being picked up by a male person who was genuinely interested in him. Over time Carson began to talk about his situation and his own goals for himself and even for his mother. These goals were translated by the case manager into services that could help Carson meet his goals. It was the case manager's ability to connect to an angry, frightened child and the case manager's considerable patience in waiting for Carson to be able to relate to and trust the case manager that made the difference in Carson's life. Today Carson is finishing his first year at a community college and still keeps in touch with his old case manager on occasion.

Cognitive and Language Development

Children's case managers are required to know something about how language is acquired and show parents how to support the cognitive development of their child and the child's attempts to communicate. Again, case managers should be able to recognize developmental delays or deviations. Some children live in environments that do not stimulate their cognitive development, while other children live in environments that are overly stimulating. Case managers need to recognize and know how to evaluate the type of environment in which a child is living.

Augustine brought her son Alfonso into the case management unit after Alfonso was seen in the emergency room for strep throat. The doctor in the emergency room suggested to Augustine that she have Alfie evaluated because, as he put it, "I think this child could be doing more for his age than he is right now." Alfie did seem immature to the case manager and behind where a normal 4-year-old would be. His mother was still dressing him and feeding him, and she complained that she did not know how to get Alfie to do these things for himself. She had a job cleaning homes for a cleaning service and had to be out the door and on her way by 7:30 every morning. Alfie was dressed and fed by her before she left, and then she dropped him off at her mother's. "My mom really loves him," Augustine told the case manager. "He don't want for nothing if my mom can give it to him." In the evening Augustine was in a hurry to get Alfie to bed so she could have some time to herself. Again she did everything for him to hurry the dinner and bedtime process along. The problem was that Alfie was not learning age-appropriate skills to become more independent, and he had no experience with other children his own age. Working with both the grandmother and the mother, the case manager devised a service plan that involved parent training to help them both begin to move Alfie toward more age-appropriate behavior. In addition, the case manager arranged for Alfie to attend kindergarten where he learned how to do many of the tasks himself and began to interact socially with other children.

A good children's case manager is obligated to identify the early warning signs of learning disabilities. As children make their way though school, academic problems and conduct problems may surface. Case managers are urged to look for root causes in their assessment of the child and his or her family for these problems. In addition, children's case managers often advocate for children and their families with the schools or give support to parents who are advocating for their children. Thus case managers need to be able to collaborate with schools in order to best serve the child.

By the early teen years, children are moving toward more abstract thinking. A case manager should be able to tell the difference between concrete and abstract thinking. Further, with older teens, when cognitive abilities appear to be impaired, it is important to be able to ascertain if the impairment stems from developmental problems or from substance abuse.

Emotional Development

Certainly all children's case managers are required to know the range of emotions children can show at any given age. As children grow, they need more and more independence and mobility. They also learn healthy ways to express emotion and control emotions. Case managers need to recognize separation anxiety in young children as well as real concerns about the level of activity or the ability of the child to relate to others. In addition, it is important to be able to spot the beginnings of disruptive behavior, depression, sadness, or anger in young children. All children have emotional needs for unconditional love and security. Case managers must recognize when these needs are not being met and be able to discuss the emotional needs of the child with the parents.

Preteens seek more autonomy and self-reliance. A case manager should be able to discuss with children their feelings and concerns. By the early teen years, children usually experience a wide range of moods and emotions. This is certainly a trying time for adults, who often become engaged in adversarial relationships with their children at this age. Case managers should know how to remain calm in provocative situations and be able to discuss emotionally charged issues with children.

Older teens continue to move rapidly toward autonomy and look for self-respect and a sense of belonging. The case manager should be able to connect with this age group and be able to balance the needs of the parents and the child. It is at this stage that case managers often have the hardest time, since many identify to an unhelpful extent with either the parents or the teen. Keeping a balance while listening to both the parents and the teenager is an important skill for working with this age group.

Physical Development

Children develop at different rates. Some children develop more quickly than others; some children adopt a slower pace. There is a range for normal development, and as long as a child develops within that range, the development is considered within normal limits. Some children may be early in the range and others later in the range, but their development is still considered normal. Case managers should be able to spot problems that delay a child's development. For example, a child may not develop at a normal rate because the expectations in the home are such that the child is not expected to reach that milestone until much later or the child is not provided with the appropriate guidance within the home. In addition, abuse and neglect can impact development negatively.

Physical development involves capabilities from crawling and learning to feed oneself to being able to run and jump and balance. A child whose physical development is appropriate will do better at age-appropriate tasks, have greater emotional well-being, and be more successful socially with peers and adults.

Case managers need to be able to work with parents of all age groups to find the best referrals to assist a child with physical delays and be able to collaborate with medical personnel and others working to assist the child and his or her family. Parents can find these referrals alarming or upsetting. Case managers are urged to find ways to discuss the need for a referral in a manner that does not unnecessarily alarm parents. Another skill particularly useful to case managers is the ability to collaborate with the parents on choosing the best place to which to refer the child and family. This involves discussion with the family about the various options available to them.

Abuse and neglect are topics a case manager wants to address tactfully with parents. With teens, uncertainty about their sexuality, concerns about their physical development, and worries about physical abilities are topics a case manager should be able to talk about frankly. Older teens face other problems that affect them physically. Substance abuse, AIDS, and sexual activity are topics that are likely to arise, and a case manager needs to be able to discuss these topics in an open and helpful manner.

MANDATED REPORTER

All states have laws requiring social service workers to report child abuse and neglect. State laws differ, however, in what constitutes abuse or in when the abuse should be reported. In some states, workers are required to witness the abuse. In other states, a worker learning of abuse secondhand is required to report it to authorities. In working with children, it is safe to assume that you are a mandated reporter of child abuse and neglect in your state. You need to know the circumstances under which the abuse must be reported and how and where to report that abuse.

New workers often go first to their supervisors to discuss the abuse and to indicate that the abuse needs to be reported to the proper authorities. Some supervisors discourage reporting or will not make the report themselves. There are several reasons why supervisors may not report abuse, even though such an action is illegal. Many are not informed of the law and do not take reporting of abuse seriously. Many consider reporting abuse something that could interfere with the rapport the agency has established with the family. Others find the reporting of abuse and the subsequent consequences too time-consuming or troublesome.

Carla was a case manager for a large public child-care system. She was assigned to a child-care center and worked on service plans for children in the center. A woman brought in her 3-year-old one morning; she was discouraged and angry. The 3-year-old boy had "talked back" according to the mother, and she had rubbed hot red peppers on his tongue, gums, lips, and around his mouth. The child's mouth was red, and there were abscesses on his gums and inner lips. Carla made a report to child welfare. The following morning the mother backtracked. She claimed that an older child had actually rubbed the hot red pepper on the 3-year-old's mouth when the mother was out of the kitchen getting ready for work. She made light of it, as though it was a funny story.

The report was filed, and child welfare workers investigated the family, beginning with a visit in the family home. The family called the director of the child-care center the next morning. They were indignant and indicated they were suing the center for falsely accusing them of child abuse. The director, uninformed about the laws in her state, immediately reprimanded Carla and suggested a meeting of the family with both the director and Carla in which Carla was to apologize. The case management supervisor was able to intervene.

Laws in all states prohibit suits against the reporters of child abuse unless malicious intent can be proved on the part of the person doing the reporting. The onus of proving malicious intent rests with the person bringing the suit. Further, failure to report the abuse could result in the agency losing their license to provide child care for any children. Carla had no choice about whether to report the abuse. The role of the child welfare authorities would be to sort out whether this was abuse or an inadvertent accident. That was not the role of either the case manager or the director of the agency. The case manager supervisor was tactful but firm, and the meeting between the parents and the child-care personnel did not take place. The parents took their child out of the center, but the investigation continued and they were found guilty of having engaged in child abuse in more than that one instance.

There is no choice about reporting child abuse. If you are aware of the abuse and have discussed it with your supervisor, document that discussion in the record. Your supervisor is as responsible as you are for reporting abuse in most states, and if your supervisor holds a license to practice, that license can be pulled by the state for failure to report abuse. In some instances, you may need to tactfully point that out to superiors.

Assignment

Look at the laws in your state governing the reporting of child abuse and neglect. Find out who is mandated to report the abuse, how abuse is to be reported, and where such reports are made. Learn whether or not your state has a hot line to report child abuse.

OTHER LEGAL AND ETHICAL CONSIDERATIONS

There are other legal issues that come up when working with children. How they are handled differs from state to state and from county to county. Depending on where you work, you may be involved in these legal issues to a greater or lesser degree. Here are some of the legal issues you are likely to encounter:

- The civil and legal rights of children with disabilities
- Custody proceedings and adoption proceedings
- Paternity suits
- Age of consent issues, particularly consent for treatment and family planning
- Rights of parents and grandparents
- Duty to warn others when your client presents a danger to others

In addition, there are ethical considerations. Many of these are the same for all cases you handle. The subject of ethical considerations is covered in detail in *Fundamentals of Case Management Practice* (Summers, 2001). Here we will look at those you are most likely to encounter as you work with children.

Confidentiality is the foundation of a good professional relationship. There are always exceptions to confidentiality, such as when your client presents a danger to others or is a danger to him- or herself.

Avoiding dual relationships is also important. You would not, for instance, want to work with a child who was your student in Sunday school or whom you coached on a little league team. This would be considered a dual relationship. In some rural areas, dual relationships are harder to avoid. If it is impossible to avoid a dual relationship, the case manager has an even greater obligation to adhere to confidentiality and be vigilant about not letting one relationship interfere adversely with the other.

Maintaining professional boundaries is another ethical principle. You do not want to cross professional boundaries by establishing a friendship with the family. In some cases, accompanying the family to social events to support them and the child is accepted practice, but it is done as a professional obligation. Becoming part of the family's social circle, confiding your own problems to the family, or dropping in to chat would be unprofessional.

INVOLVING THE FAMILY

Every chapter in this textbook emphasizes the importance of working successfully with families. With children, the ability to relate well and collaborate with parents is essential, since the family is a child's primary support system. If the family is not included in planning for the child and in monitoring and evaluating the services, an important part of the child's life is left out and even alienated. Therefore, families should sit at the table with all the other professionals when planning is taking place. They should be encouraged by the case manager to participate fully. In this way, team decisions are owned by the family as part of a team who has planned for their child.

Barriers to Good Planning for Children

Attitude

Parents have identified the attitude of professionals as one of the chief barriers to their seeking and receiving good services for their children. For example, parents, and particularly mothers, have complained that they are often blamed for their child's problems when there are other possible explanations, such as neurological or genetic ones. Parents have complained that there is a tendency to blame mothers for failing to develop a proper attachment with the child or for failing to let go sufficiently and allow the child proper independence.

Marlene, a 19-year-old, was the mother of 4-year-old Bellita. Bellita was referred to the case management unit by her kindergarten teacher. This teacher had numerous interviews with the mother and complained to the case manager when she made the referral that Marlene was incompetent and unwilling to be involved in her child's life. In fact, the mother was studying to be a math teacher at the community college and came at once to the center for help when that was suggested.

Bellita was eating paper, cigarette butts, and dirt. She was restless, whiney, and aggressive toward other children and adults. She did not focus in school and seemed angry, blurting out obscenities and frequently hitting and kicking other children. The case manager suspected lead poisoning among other possible reasons for the child's behavior. The first part of the service plan was to get a complete physical examination. This revealed serious lead poisoning, so severe that Bellita was placed in the hospital on intravenous medications to counteract the high lead levels in her blood.

While the kindergarten teacher was willing to see Bellita's problems as entirely the mother's fault and a matter of poor parenting, the case manager was able to consider poor parenting along with a number of other possible reasons for the unusual behavior in this 4-year-old child. The case manager could have simply accepted the kindergarten teacher's explanation, assuming the teacher had more contact and experience with Marlene. In being willing to consider a number of reasons for Bellita's behavior, however, the case manager uncovered a serious medical condition, and it was treated. In the months following Bellita's hospitalization, the child calmed down immensely. She began to focus and to learn. While she remained slightly behind other children in her kindergarten class, she made considerable headway by the end of the year, and her aggressive behavior and need to eat things other than food subsided. The case manager also worked on a lead remediation project in the apartment building where Bellita and her mother lived and arranged for temporary housing during that project.

Too many professionals focus entirely on the weaknesses and the pathology within families and tend to overlook or dismiss the strengths and resources that families provide to their members.

Big Words

Families have objected to the use of academic words by psychologists, psychiatrists, and social workers. Such terms are understood by professionals but are unfamiliar to the family. When professionals give information about the child or discuss treatment options using words parents do not understand, they distance themselves from families. A patronizing demeanor toward families widens the gap and makes collaboration difficult.

No Real Collaboration

Finally, families have criticized professionals for talking about working with families "in the best interests of the child" when, in reality, the agency's and family's understanding of that concept are very different. Families expect and need collaboration, but some agencies define partnership as the family's unconditional willingness to accept whatever treatment plan the professionals develop, to receive services and education on becoming a better parent rather than giving input, and to be present to receive information when requested. Families who want a more extensive role in planning and feedback have often been considered uncooperative.

Case managers and other professionals hold a certain amount of power. The power stems from the case manager's education, expertise, and access to needed resources. It can be disconcerting to define the very people seeking your help as having expertise of their own to bring to the situation, but families know their children best. They are the ones who see their children every day and who know the children's needs, habits, anxieties, and behaviors. Unless families are made full partners in planning, monitoring, and evaluating the services their children receive, the children will not get adequate service. Collaboration with families is crucial to developing the very best service to children.

What Case Managers Can Do

Respect Families

Involving families begins with mutual respect for one another. Case managers need to demonstrate, beginning with the initial interview, their respect for what the family has to bring to the situation and the case manager's intention to work collaboratively with the family.

Respect for families includes respecting the way in which families choose to live and their culture, lifestyle, and values. This does not mean that you will tolerate abuse or neglect because that is how a family has chosen to discipline their children or conduct their family life. What it does mean is that you must understand that families are different, that not all families are like your own, and that families will make their own choices about values and culture and lifestyle.

Sometimes you will disagree with parents, or you may want to add ideas of your own. Consult the chapter on expressing concerns in *Fundamentals of Case Management Practice* (Summers, 2001) for the most respectful way to do that so that the family can hear and make use of what you have to say. After you have expressed your concerns and encouraged the family to respond, listen carefully. This can be tricky because your concerns, however valid they may be, can be expressed in ways that make the family feel defensive. Then, of course, they can no longer hear you or collaborate with you successfully.

Paquita brought her son, Hector, to the case management unit one day, complaining that he had ADHD (attention deficit/hyperactivity disorder). Hector was only 2 years old, and while Paquita described normal behavior for a 2-year-old, Hector sat quietly in the playroom with another worker, drawing with crayons and playing with toy trucks. Paquita found Hector's insistence on trying to do things himself and his propensity for saying "no" an indication of a real behavior problem. She was seeking play therapy and medication for Hector, because that is what the case manager had done for Paquita's nephew. But Paquita's nephew was 10 and had definite and clear signs of ADHD.

The case manager suggested numerous plans for the mother, but she was insistent that this was not her problem and that she wanted Hector to get the help she felt he needed. The case manager listened to the mother with respect and empathy, and then arranged for Hector to come to the center several times during the next two weeks. Because she was able to develop good rapport with the mother, the case manager was then able to suggest that the mother take parenting classes. Paquita was simply very unfamiliar with the developmental stages of young children. Once she accepted the case manager's idea and began attending the classes, she discovered that Hector was really a normal 2-year-old. Paquita was deeply relieved, stopped seeing Hector as a problem child, and began to use some of the techniques she learned in the parenting classes to work better with Hector.

The case manager made regular home visits to Paquita's home and lent support, particularly when Paquita was not sure how to apply the new parenting skills or when she applied them and they did not seem to work. Paquita and her case manager had many talks about applying specific skills to specific situations. In this way, the case manager was able to help Paquita become an effective parent.

Be Available and Communicate

While children are receiving services, case managers need to communicate often with the families. This communication serves to keep the families informed about what is taking place and gives case managers important information about how children are progressing and what other needs have arisen.

Ask and Listen

Always ask families what goals they hold for their children. Ask them where they would like to be in several months or a year. Listen to their evaluation of the problem, their ideas about what needs to change, and their thoughts on what would be most helpful. Listen to the information you receive. Treat what families tell you as expert information, useful to you in planning and understanding the children better. Indicate your willingness to be available to hear the concerns families raise about their children as treatment progresses. Demonstrate that you value the perspectives families bring to you.

Communicate Clearly

Communication between case managers and families needs to be clear and understandable to the family. Professional jargon serves to erect barriers between you and families. Give families explanations and information they can use. Be willing to explain things more than once or in more than one way so that all members of the family can make use of the information.

CHILDREN'S MENTAL HEALTH

Children bring a variety of problems and issues to case management as those closest to them seek answers for unsettling behaviors or moods. In this section we will look at some of the common problems, along with the *DSM-IV-TR* criteria for diagnosing them.

Attention Deficit/Hyperactivity Disorder (ADHD)

Attention deficit/hyperactivity disorder is generally referred to as ADHD in the literature and written that way when the diagnosis is discussed. At present ADHD is viewed as a problem more influenced by neurology and genetics than by the social environment of the child. The environment can play a part in making the problem worse, however. Studies indicate that ADHD tends to run in families.

In general ADHD is characterized by an inability to self-control one's behavior, often accompanied by inattention. Therefore, the diagnosis is made by looking at two distinct sets of symptoms: those that relate to hyperactivity and impulsivity and those that relate to inattention. When making the diagnosis, the clinician is asked to designate one of three separate subtypes. Is the diagnosis, for instance, attention deficit/hyperactivity disorder, combined type? Or does the child have only one of the sets of symptoms? In this case, the diagnosis would be either attention deficit/hyperactivity disorder, predominantly inattentive type, or attention deficit/hyperactivity disorder, predominantly hyperactive-impulsive type.

It is possible for a child to be inattentive without being hyperactive or to appear hyperactive while paying attention. For the most part, the two occur together and are generally noticed when a child must perform in the regulated environment of school. The *DSM-IV-TR* spells out the criteria for inattention and requires that the child have at least six of the symptoms listed. The same is true of the symptoms for hyperactivity-impulsivity, for which the child must have at least six. (See Table 3.1.)

Parents and teachers of children with ADHD may complain to you about behaviors such as not listening when instructions are given; being distracted by other children, television, music, or other things going on around them; leaving homework unfinished; making careless mistakes in chores and on homework; being disorganized and often losing important instructions, assignments, and books; and appearing to be day dreaming. All children will exhibit these symptoms from time to time. What sets the child with ADHD apart is that the child exhibits these symptoms in several different settings and the symptoms interfere with the child's ability to function successfully and make friends. Some teens will lose their hyperactivity and impulsivity later in life. Some make a satisfactory adjustment and are successful in adulthood. Others do less well in their careers and adjustment. Many drop out of school or suffer from anxiety or depression.

There has been considerable controversy over whether children should be placed on stimulant medications, such as methylphenidate (Ritalin). Stimulants increase the neurotransmitter dopamine in the brain, leading many to conclude that ADHD may be a result of too little dopamine in the central nervous system. Dopamine is central to supporting purposeful activity, making one alert and motivated. These are all desirable characteristics of successful school-age children.

In addition to medication, parents and teachers are often taught how to employ behavioral techniques with mechanisms such as time-out for brief periods to deescalate impulsive or uncontrolled behavior and positive reinforcement by adults of appropriate behavior on the part of the child. Clinicians will work with the child and the child's parents, designing specific interventions for the parents to use with their child. Children can learn problem-solving skills and social skills that will assist them in making friends and solving problems thoughtfully.

After doing a through assessment with the parents of an ADHD child, you will make referrals to agencies where the best treatment plans can be developed for the child and the family.

Table 3.1 Diagnostic Criteria for Attention Deficit/Hyperactivity Disorder

A. Either (1) or (2)

(1) six (or more) of the following symptoms of **inattention** have persisted for at least 6 months to a degree that is maladaptive and inconsistent with development level:

(a) often fails to give close attention to details or makes careless mistakes in schoolwork, work, or other activities
(b) often has difficulty sustaining attention in tasks or play activities
(c) often does not seem to listen when spoken to directly
(d) often does not follow through on instruction and fails to finish schoolwork, chores, or duties in the workplace (not due to oppositional behavior or failure to understand directions)
(e) often has difficulty organizing tasks and activities
(f) often avoids, dislikes, or is reluctant to engage in tasks that require sustained mental effort (such as schoolwork or homework)
(g) often loses things necessary for tasks or activities (e.g., toys, school assignments, pencils, books, or tools)
(h) is often easily distracted by extraneous stimuli
(i) is often forgetful in daily activities

(2) six (or more) of the following symptoms of **hyperactivity-impulsivity** have persisted for at least 6 months to a degree that is maladaptive and inconsistent with developmental level:

Hyperactivity

(a) often fidgets with hands or feet or squirms in seat
(b) often leaves seat in classroom or in other situations in which remaining seated is expected
(c) often runs about or climbs excessively in situations in which it is inappropriate (in adolescents or adults, may be limited to subjective feelings of restlessness)
(d) often has difficulty playing or engaging in leisure activities quietly
(e) is often "on the go" or often acts as if "driven by a motor"
(f) often talks excessively

Impulsivity

(g) often blurts out answers before questions have been completed
(h) often has difficulty awaiting turn
(i) often interrupts or intrudes on others (e.g., butts into conversations or games)

B. Some hyperactive-impulsive or inattentive symptoms that caused impairment were present before age 7

C. Some impairment from the symptoms is present in two or more settings (e.g., at school [or work] and at home)

D. There must be clear evidence of clinically significant impairment in social, academic, or occupational functioning

E. The symptoms do not occur exclusively during the course of a pervasive developmental disorder, schizophrenia, or other psychotic disorder and are not better accounted for by another mental disorder (e.g., mood disorder, anxiety disorder, dissociative disorder, or personality disorder)

Source: Reprinted with permission from the *Diagnostic and Statistical Manual of Mental Disorders*, Fourth Edition, Text Revision. Copyright 2000 American Psychiatric Association.

Oppositional Defiant Disorder (ODD)

This diagnosis is given to a child who appears to consistently defy authority figures with disobedience and hostility. These children are alarming to parents and are difficult to relate to. They characteristically fight and argue, refuse to carry out simple requests, and are sensitive and touchy. In addition, often they annoy adults on purpose, and sometimes they are even spiteful. They appear to be resentful and angry most of the time and tend to blame everyone else for the way they feel and the way they behave. Many children with ODD are inclined to test the limits and stubbornly refuse to go along with routines, even when they are obviously in the child's best interests. Some clinicians have suggested that ODD may be the result of environmental conditions where fighting and arguing have been necessary to survive or where the child has been subjected to extreme marital discord involving domestic violence.

Many of the risks that seem to make ODD more likely occur early in life; thus, early interventions are a key element in helping the child. Clinicians can screen the child for both early events or traumas and aggressive behavior to give a more accurate picture of the problem. Treatments that involve the family and that teach parents how to handle the behavior and how to reward appropriate behavior have been shown to be effective. Parents working with difficult children in their homes may follow techniques learned in training sessions, but they will need case management support when things do not go as well as expected. Parents cannot be expected to learn a technique and use that technique to solve all the problems. The goal is to keep children in their homes, and to meet that goal, case managers need to stand by to support parents' efforts.

Medication is useful for some children and not for others. As more is understood about the brain, medication may prove useful in more instances in reducing aggressive behavior. It is believed that in some cases the medications prescribed for ADHD may be helpful for a child with the symptoms of ODD.

Conduct Disorder

Often ODD turns into conduct disorder. The behavior becomes much more aggressive and dangerous to both the child and others. Fighting with others, bullying and intimidating vulnerable people, physically or sexually assaulting others, or coercing others into having sex can be ways a child exhibits conduct disorder. Vandalism and destroying the property of others, such as by setting fires or breaking windows, and theft are common. So also is truancy, running away from home, promiscuity or prostitution (particularly in girls), and early substance abuse. Certainly this behavior interferes with school success, and many are expelled from school or run into problems with the law and end up in the juvenile justice system.

Again, there are measuring devices used by clinicians to make an early diagnosis and thus allow for early interventions, which are key to a good prognosis.

Separation Anxiety Disorder

Most infants and toddlers become anxious when their parents leave them in the care of someone else. In older children, particularly adolescents, this becomes inappropriate. According to the *DSM-IV-TR*, the diagnosis becomes separation anxiety disorder when the anxiety related to leaving "home or from those to whom the individual is attached"* is

---

* The quotes here and throughout are reprinted with permission from the *Diagnostic and Statistical Manual of Mental Disorders*, Fourth Edition, Text Revision. Copyright 2000 American Psychiatric Association.

"developmentally inappropriate and excessive." Children with separation anxiety disorder can worry excessively "about losing, or possible harm befalling, major attachment figures" or that an "untoward event will lead to separation from major attachment figures," such as a kidnapping or accident.

Children with this condition may refuse to go to school or find it difficult to do so. Others may be unable to be alone without significant adults nearby. Some children refuse to go to sleep without reassurance that attachment figures are nearby. For these children, sleepovers with friends would be impossibly frightening. If these children experience nightmares, the common theme is separation from attachment figures. Parents may first seek a physician's assistance because children with this disorder may complain of headaches or stomachaches when attachment figures may be about to leave.

For the diagnosis to be given, the disorder must have lasted at least four weeks, started before age 18, and significantly impair the child's social, academic, or occupational functioning. This means that many children with this disorder will be unable to go to scout meetings, go to camp, or participate in choir or after-school sports or lessons.

Depression

According to the National Alliance for the Mentally Ill (NAMI), many children, particularly teenagers, will experience difficult times that lead them to feel sad. Cliques at school, a rebuff by a friend, a romance that has ended, the pressure to do well in school, hormonal fluctuations, and even family problems can all be the cause of feeling down or blue.

Adolescents, like adults, can suffer from major depression, and NAMI (n.d.) estimates that 5% of those under 19 will experience major depression. This diagnosis should be considered when the teen is showing the same symptoms adults show when they are depressed: trouble falling asleep or wanting to sleep all the time, withdrawing from friends, neglecting hygiene and personal appearance, losing appetite or eating excessively, and having trouble doing well at school or at work.

However, the *DSM-IV-TR* gives the following caution when looking at children and teens: Whereas adults may be depressed most of the time, children and adolescents may be irritable most of the time. Further, while adults may experience significant weight loss, children may fail to gain weight when they should be doing so. Clinicians who have treated very young children note that they often mask depression with somatic complaints, separation anxieties, and becoming whiney along with other, more common symptoms of depression.

In other words, depression in adolescents can look similar to depression in older adults, but there can be a difference. Some depressed teens will "act out" and become angry. Some depressed teens may become aggressive or delinquent, abuse drugs or alcohol, do poorly in school, or run away (NAMI, n.d., p. 7). Thus, it is not unusual for a child to be diagnosed with both depression and conduct disorder or an anxiety disorder as well.

Children and adolescents who are depressed are more likely to commit suicide. According to the National Institute of Mental Health (NIMH), the suicide rate among adolescents and young adults has doubled. In 1996, the most recent year for which statistics are available, suicide was the third leading cause of death in 15- to 24-year-olds and the fourth leading cause of death among 10- to 14-year-olds (NIMH, 1999). NAMI estimates that suicide among adolescents has increased 300% (NAMI, n.d., p. 7).

Bipolar Disorder

Children who are or have been depressed may also, at some point, exhibit manic symptoms. In that case, the diagnosis is a bipolar disorder. Children who experience manic symptoms are likely to feel irritable, have considerable physical energy, demonstrate boundless self-confidence to the point of sounding grandiose, and may engage in activities that have a high potential risk.

NAMI (n.d.) describes a child with bipolar disorder as one who might refuse to sleep and who might energetically pursue activities late at night and talk incessantly, often grandiosely. Such a child may refuse to pay attention and may disobey authority and behave impulsively. The *DSM-IV-TR* states that mixed episodes of depression and mania are more likely in young people. This means that the mania and the depression can occur at the same time or with rapid cycling back and forth.

NAMI (n.d.) also states that "recent research finds that one in four children with ADHD are suspected to develop bipolar disorder." This disorder is, according to NAMI, "over-represented in children and adolescents with ADHD."

Generalized Anxiety Disorder

Children can become anxious and worried to an extreme extent. Children who have a generalized anxiety disorder are likely to worry about their own school and athletic performance and anticipate unfortunate events that are unlikely to happen. Many of these children do well and have not experienced any catastrophe. The *DSM-IV-TR* states, "the anxieties and worries often concern the quality of their performance or competence at school or in sporting events, even when their performance is not being evaluated by others. There may be excessive concerns about punctuality."

These children tend to be perfectionists, to attend to the smallest details, and to conform to the expectations of adults. If work they have done is not as good as they think it should be, they commonly throw it out and start over, insisting that it be completed perfectly. Adults find that these children need their approval and reassurance much of the time. As the *DSM-IV-TR* puts it, "They are typically overzealous in seeking approval and require excessive reassurance about their performance and their other worries."

The *DSM-IV-TR* gives this diagnosis to children when they exhibit only one of the following symptoms, along with the other criteria for generalized anxiety disorder. The symptoms are:

- Restlessness or feeling keyed up or on edge
- Being easily fatigued
- Difficulty concentrating or mind going blank
- Irritability
- Muscle tension
- Sleep disturbance

Social Phobia

Children with social phobia or social anxiety disorder are likely to have a persistent fear of being embarrassed in public and in social situations or when asked to perform in some way before others. These symptoms are similar in adults; however, adults and adolescents are generally aware that these fears are unreasonable. Young children usually have no such awareness, although they sometimes do understand that others might think they are "babies" for acting the way they do.

Adults appear anxious and may even have a panic attack, while children show this anxiety in other ways. Tantrums, freezing up in social situations, clinging to parents, and shrinking away from unfamiliar people or social events are ways a child demonstrates this problem. To others the child appears inappropriately timid, shy, and unusually fearful of leaving parents for his or her age. However, the *DSM-IV-TR* cautions that the developmental stage of the child must be considered. If a child is capable of age-appropriate relationships with familiar people, then there is reason for concern. Further, the symptoms must appear with peers as well as with adults.

Posttraumatic Stress Disorder

Children, like adults, can suffer from stress following a traumatic event. For children, those traumatic events are often related to physical and sexual abuse. The pattern of recurrent and intrusive memories of the event, dreams of the event, and psychological stress when exposed to reminders of the event are all common in children. For a more detailed description of posttraumatic stress disorder (PTSD), consult Chapter 6 of this text. Children do show the signs of PTSD a little differently than adults. For example, young children may engage in "repetitive play . . . in which themes or aspects of the trauma are expressed." A child may have nightmares, but the content of the nightmares may not be familiar or recognizable. The child is anxious and experiencing that anxiety through frightening dreams.

When PTSD is not addressed in children who have gone through a traumatic event or series of events, more is often expected of them than is possible, given their emotional state. Individuals working with children often expect the child to change his or her attitude and behavior without ever addressing the PTSD and the events that caused this condition. When you take the social history, look for events that could cause PTSD for your client and discover whether these events were ever addressed.

Divorce Reactions

Many parents bring their children to social service agencies because they are worried about their children's reaction to a divorce. Children tend to react with either anger or sadness. Almost all children are upset by divorce and feel they are going through extremely difficult times. This feeling is made worse when parents tend to focus on themselves and forget to communicate with the children. Table 3.2 gives common reactions children have to divorce.

Many of the reasons children have difficulty when their parents divorce is because parents do insensitive things to children at the time of the divorce. For example, divorce should not be a divorce between parents and their children. When one of the parents disappears from a child's life, it is extremely hard on that child. Some parents try to get children to side with one parent over the other. These maneuvers place unnecessary strain on children at a time when they need their energy to do well in school and with peers.

Younger children are often left out of the planning and what will take place. They can easily sense the atmosphere at home but are often left to guess what will happen next. Such children often come up with unrealistic ideas about what is going on and very often believe a happy reunion of their parents is possible when it is not.

You may see children who have lost a parent because that parent refuses to participate in the child's life anymore. Very young children may have no idea where the other parent is or if this parent is all right. For very young children, having to leave home with no place to go is frightening, but some parents never give the reassurance children need.

Table 3.2 Children's Reactions to Divorce

	Preschool Ages (3-5 years)	Middle Childhood (6-12 years)	Adolescents (13-18 years)
Both Boys and Girls	Anger or sadness Sad and more tearful and demanding Regression to earlier behaviors (thumb sucking, pacifier, security blanket) More anxious and insecure (nightmares, bed-wetting, fear of leaving parent)	Mostly sad and tearful May think departing parent is rejecting them Self-esteem becomes poor Depression May take sides and assign blame May be hard to discipline	Concern is with the future. One of three reactions likely: 1. Adjust well because more independent. Distance themselves and pursue own plans. Mature as a result. 2. Feel betrayed and disengage from family. May act out. 3. Become depressed and withdrawn. Lose ambitions and give up plans.
Boys	Noisier, restless, and angry Trouble with friends Withdrawal from friends Disruptive, uncooperative in group activities	Miss their fathers intensely May be more likely to disobey or defy mothers (This is worse if the father does not take an active role in the boy's life.) When father is custodial parent, may do better with same-sex parent	
Girls	Occasionally angry May become perfect little adults May be neat and clean May lecture and scold others as an adult would	May function well with mothers as custodial parent	

Some children you see may be encouraged by their custodial parent to distance themselves from the other parent. Parents with visitation may aggravate a child's anxieties by failing to come on time or at all for scheduled visits.

Other children you see may be caught in the middle. They are asked to spy for one parent against the other, asked to help facilitate a reunification of the family, or offered rewards for taking one parent's point of view over the other's. Some children watch their parents gloat over one another's misfortunes or shortcomings, and some parents encourage their children when the children show normal childhood dissatisfaction with the other parent.

Sixteen-year-old Joyce's mother brought her to the case management unit because she claimed Joyce had become "sassy." Following the divorce, Joyce had continued to have contact with her father, and because she could drive and was active at school, Joyce and her father had a rather relaxed and flexible visitation schedule. Joyce's mother was deeply resentful. The issue that brought the matter to a head was Joyce going to her father when her car broke down. While Joyce was in school, her father took the car to his local garage and got it fixed. That evening Joyce's mother became furious. She accused Joyce of siding with her father because she went to him with this problem. She told Joyce that she had deliberately given the father the keys to her car with the house key on the key chain. To the mother, this was colluding with the father, who she suspected had a key made to their home. In the first session with the case manager, Joyce blurted out, "Well, what am I supposed to do? He is my frigging father after all." The mother used this as an example of how sassy Joyce had become and how little she cared about the mother's feelings in the divorce.

In this situation, the case manager had to work carefully to help the mother see that she might be contributing to the problem. The case manager did this with considerable tact and a good bit of empathic listening. Soon, Joyce and her mother were seen together for relationship therapy, arranged by the case manager. Eventually, the therapist was able to get the mother to begin to work on her own issues about the divorce, and Joyce no longer attended all the sessions with her mother.

What is unfortunate about children is that they are very likely to blame themselves for the divorce. That is because children tend to think egocentrically. The world revolves around them. For this reason, children can easily assume they caused the parting of their parents to happen. If parents do not explain the part they played in the divorce or deny all responsibility for the breakup, a child is all the more likely to take the blame. Some parents blame the child's behavior for the separation. Children allowed to take responsibility for the divorce of their parents generally end up with very low self-esteem.

Substance Abuse

Adolescents are the most likely to be using alcohol or drugs on a regular basis. For young people who are experiencing the symptoms of depression or early schizophrenia, the availability of drugs and alcohol appears to them as a useful way to self-medicate in an attempt to address these uncomfortable or incapacitating symptoms. In addition, many young people find the pressure to do well in school, excel in extracurricular activities, and get into good colleges overwhelming. Substances like drugs and alcohol are often a means of relieving the pressure and stress.

Young people who use drugs and alcohol regularly can become addicted and be unable to break off that use, which eventually begins to interfere with their performance and exacerbate symptoms of emotional disorders. When taking a social history from a young person, always inquire about substance use, and look for some of the reasons mentioned previously for why the use started and what the young person needs to address through the use of substances.

Eating Disorders

Most of the clients you will see with eating disorders will be female and adolescent. These disorders can be extremely life-threatening, as the young person fails to get adequate nutrition, sometimes over a period of years. Today, the following three types of eating disorders are recognized.

1. *Anorexia nervosa.* According to the *DSM-IV-TR,* the person "refuses to maintain a minimally normal body weight, is intensely afraid of gaining weight, and exhibits a significant disturbance in the perception of the shape or size of his or her body." There is an unrealistic sense of one's body size and weight, along with intense fear of becoming overweight.
2. *Bulimia nervosa.* The *DSM-IV-TR* describes the essential features of this disorder as "binge eating and inappropriate compensatory methods to prevent weight gain." Again, there is considerable focus on body weight and shape. The compensatory methods to prevent weight gain include such things as induced vomiting following a binge-eating episode, inducing diarrhea through the use of laxatives, and using enemas.
3. *Binge-eating disorder.* Recently clinicians have looked at this disorder, not included in the *DSM-IV-TR,* as binge eating without the use of compensatory methods to avoid weight gain.

It is not clear why young people develop these eating disorders. Many young people with these disorders are also experiencing depression or anxiety and may be using substances to allay these symptoms. Look in your social history for attitudes toward food and body image and note, of course, unusually low body weight.

ASSESSMENT

Your intake assessment paves the way for the development of a sound treatment plan. Documentation of the details regarding the problems and the reasons the child is being seen in a social service agency is significant in this planning. What you learn and document at intake will be brought to the interdisciplinary team that develops the individualized plan for the child. For that reason, careful intake is important.

Strengths-Based Assessments

In children's case management, initial assessments carefully note both the child's capabilities and problems. The case manager is responsible for developing a picture of a whole person, not a collection of problems.

Gordon R. Hodas (1996), writing for the Pennsylvania CASSP Training and Technical Assistance Institute, pointed out the importance of focusing on a child's strengths. He wrote, "One goal of strengths-based treatment is to enable the child to experience him- or herself as a unique and interesting individual in the eyes of others" (p. 5). This should be the goal of case management as well, in both the initial assessment and in the ongoing relationship you have with the child.

In order to achieve this goal, a case manager must be willing to genuinely want to know about a child's dreams for the future and the goals the child has thought about for him- or herself. Rather than asking rote questions such as "What are your three favorite things?" or "If you had three wishes what would those be?," ask real questions that indicate your genuine interest in this child.

Hodas (1996) pointed out another reason to focus on strengths both during the assessment and afterward. "Parents experience pride when their child is treated as a competent person by the professional or the mental health worker. Similarly, children experience pride, even if they do not verbalize it, when their parents' capabilities emerge" (p. 5). Opening the assessment with a focus on strengths is one good way to establish rapport early. Hodas (1996) wrote, "The information gathering process is sequenced, with strengths explored first, so that relationships can begin to develop and the recitation of problems does not demoralize or alienate the participants" (p. 5).

Communication

A good assessment of children and their families depends in large measure on the case manager's ability to relate to children of all age groups, as well as the adult members of the family. This means being able to use appropriate means of communication with children who are very young and those who are older and more articulate. Communication entails the ability to talk about difficult and sensitive topics with parents and older children.

Recognition of Problems

Case managers also should be able to recognize severe psychiatric problems and document the parents' concerns and descriptions of behaviors that are the focus of attention. Children often are seen because of certain impairments in their cognitive or physical abilities. The case manager will need to document all of these concerns in the assessment.

The Mental Status Examination

Part of the assessment must focus on a mental status examination, looking at such things as how the child interacted with the case manager and with the parents during the interview, how the child appeared, and what emotions the child seemed to express. For a more detailed explanation of the mental status examination, refer to *Fundamentals of Case Management Practice* (Summers, 2001).

In developing the assessment, the case manager should also note:

- Signs of abuse or neglect
- Signs the child might present a danger to him- or herself or others
- Signs of strength in the parent-child relationship
- Strengths and supports within the family and community
- Risky behaviors such as substance abuse, dropping out of school, sexual activity, and pregnancy
- Factors in the child's environment that contribute to negative behaviors

A good mental status examination is culturally competent. That is, the case manager is able to distinguish the norms of the culture from true problems. For instance, various cultures welcome infants in different ways. A case manager should be able to assess how this is done in families where an infant is the focus of concern.

Summary

To summarize, your assessment should record both strengths and needs, competencies and deficits. The assessment should discuss a whole person and relate to the context of the child's family, community, and culture. The assessment should note who was present and should be able to demonstrate that interested family members other than the child were present and were encouraged to give input. This assessment then serves as the basis of planning for the child.

When you, as a case manager, attend a planning session with an interdisciplinary team, you should be prepared with ideas that will, whenever possible, keep the child in his or her family, and you should rely on the natural supports that are present in the child's life and community.

MEDICATIONS AND TREATMENTS

There are medications and treatments available that are routinely used to help children and their families cope with the problems and issues children are having. This section discusses some common therapies and medications used for children.

Medications

There is little enthusiasm for giving children medications. Aside from the recent trend to medicate children with ADHD, most clinicians are somewhat reluctant to medicate children. This is because few long-term studies have been done to help us better understand what the medication may do to a person who is physically and mentally developing. Many of the medications used for adults have not yet been approved for use with children. Further, children can appear to have the symptoms of a mental disorder and actually be going through a phase that passes quickly on its own. Labeling and medicating normal children handling difficult, but normal, transitions is seen by some as injurious.

Nevertheless, medications are given to children. Many of these are the same medications listed for mental disorders (see Chapter 6). Some medications are used more extensively than others. It is helpful for you to know the names of these.

ADHD

The medications given to children diagnosed with ADHD are given to help the child focus and concentrate. Thus the doses generally coincide with the child's school schedule, giving the child the advantage of focusing and concentrating while in school. Most children placed on stimulants experience few side effects, as the medication appears to be metabolized and to leave the body within 1 to 4 hours. When the child appears to have side effects from the stimulants or is not responding to them, other medications are tried either in combination with stimulants or alone. While these other mediations may be effective, they are rarely as effective as stimulants. Here are common medications given to children with ADHD as their diagnosis:

Stimulants

Adderall (amphetamine: dextroamphetamine)
Cylert (pemoline)
Dexedrine (dextroamphetamine)
Ritalin (methylphenidate)

Antidepressants

Norpramin (desipramine)
Wellbutrin (bupropion)

Treatment of ADHD has better results when medication is combined with parent education and sessions with the child if the child is old enough to monitor and correct his or her own behavior. In addition, other interventions in a variety of settings where the child functions are most effective when combined with medication. Such a treatment plan is generally referred to as multimodal.

In helping parents understand and support a child with ADHD, the focus is generally on behavior modification techniques in which parents are encouraged to reward and attend to positive behaviors and ignore negative behaviors that are not life-threatening. Many parents with ADHD children have become so exasperated with the hyperactivity and impulsivity of their child that they rarely are able to note and praise positive behavior. This is true in the school setting as well, and some treatment focuses in part on the proper school placement or on helping the child's teacher use good behavior modification techniques.

Depression

Most of the medications given to adults for depression have been given to children. Chapter 6 lists the most commonly used types of antidepressant medications. These include MAO inhibitors, tricyclic medications, selective serotonin reuptake inhibitors (SSRIs), and other mediations used to treat depression. You would do well to look at that section of Chapter 6 and become familiar with what medications are often used. Prozac (fluoxetine) has received the most research on use with children, and this medication or another of the SSRIs is generally preferred for children because it appears to have fewer side effects or long-term complications. Further, it is nearly impossible to overdose on the SSRIs. These medications are relatively new, however, and the complete understanding of how they might affect people, particularly when taken in childhood and over the long term, is not fully understood.

In addition to medication, cognitive therapy has been useful for many young people, in which they are taught to recognize and correct their own negative thinking. The focus is on helping the child rethink some of the distortions in thinking that are seen to contribute to the depression and to find ways of behaving that will relieve some of the feelings of helplessness and passivity.

Other Disorders

Oppositional defiant disorder and conduct disorder do not appear to respond as positively to medication. In some cases, antidepressants do seem to reduce aggressive behavior, but in others there is no effect at all. What does appear to be helpful are programs that offer parents support and new ways of relating to their child that focus on the child's positive behaviors and attributes and do not focus on negative behaviors exclusively. In some places, this treatment is intensive, and workers go to the home to assist parents in correcting and revising relationships within the home.

Support Groups

Support groups in which teens with similar problems talk about their issues and concerns can be especially helpful. Sometimes a school or mental health facility will sponsor such a support group.

Parents also can benefit from support groups, or from support groups combined with parent education. These groups function to allow people to know they are not alone with the problems facing them. In addition, group participants often learn from one another or from the group facilitator good ways to resolve their problems. The groups often foster the development of friendships outside the group, breaking the sense of isolation.

SERVICES

People who work with children refer to systems of care. That is because children are likely to be known to or be receiving services from a variety of social service systems. The more systems there are available to support the child and the child's family, the more likely the child is to receive the help he or she needs. There is, however, a caution. With the wide variety of services comes the need to ensure that these services are coordinated for each individual child and family. This takes considerable case management skill.

Stroul and Friedman (1986) list the components of the systems of care for children (see Table 3.3).

Case Management

Case managers are often called upon to facilitate meetings of professionals interested in developing the best plan for a specific child. As a facilitator of such a meeting, you will want to make sure the meeting does not deteriorate into listing the many deficits of the child and the child's family. Try to start by presenting what is strong and what will be good support within the family. Allow the family to describe their concerns and the goals they have for their children.

The central question the case manager needs to keep as the focus during intake and during planning meetings is what this child would be if he or she was well-functioning and exhibited emotional well-being. Asking parents to visualize what they would like their child to become is important. Asking a group of professionals considering a particular child how a typical child from a similar community and culture would appear is also important. Once this is established, the group can move on to consider what needs to take place to bring this about and what barriers need to be overcome to make this happen.

If a child and the family engage in real strengths-based planning and assessment with the case manager, the collaboration is more likely to continue as the case manager monitors the services and the child's progress. One important goal for you as the child's case manager is to invite and facilitate the family's active participation both in the initial assessment and in evaluating services and future planning.

Table 3.3 Components of Systems of Care for Children

I. MENTAL HEALTH SERVICES

Nonresidential services
- Prevention services
- Early identification and intervention
- Assessment
- Outpatient treatment
- Home-based services
- Day treatment
- Emergency services (crisis intervention)

Residential Services
- Therapeutic foster care
- Therapeutic group care
- Therapeutic camp services
- Independent living services
- Residential treatment
- Crisis residential services
- Inpatient hospitalization

II. SOCIAL SERVICES
- Protective services
- Financial assistance
- Home-aid services
- Respite care
- Shelter services
- Foster care
- Adoption

III. EDUCATIONAL SERVICES
- Assessment services
- Resource rooms
- Self-contained special education
- Special schools
- Home-bound instruction
- Residential schools
- Alternative programs

IV. HEALTH SERVICES
- Health education and prevention services
- Screening assessment services
- Primary care
- Acute care
- Long-term care

V. SUBSTANCE ABUSE SERVICES

Nonresidential services
- Prevention
- Early intervention
- Assessment
- Outpatient services
- Day treatment
- Ambulatory detoxification
- Relapse prevention

Residential Services
- Residential detoxification
- Community residential treatment and recovery services
- Inpatient hospitalization

VI. VOCATIONAL SERVICES
- Career education
- Vocational assessment
- Job survival skills training
- Vocational skills training
- Work experiences
- Job finding, placement, and retention services
- Supported employment

VII. RECREATIONAL SERVICES
- Relationships with significant others
- After-school programs
- Summer camps
- Special recreational projects

VIII. OPERATIONAL SERVICES
- Case management services
- Juvenile justice services
- Family support and self-help groups
- Advocacy
- Transportation
- Legal services
- Volunteer programs

Source: From *Systems of Care for Children and Youth with Severe Emotional Disturbances*, by Stroul and Friedman, 1986, p. 126. Copyright 1986. Georgetown Child Development Center. Reprinted with permission.

Wrap-Around Services

The term *wrap-around* refers to surrounding the child with the necessary services to support the child in his or her community. Using whatever resources or innovations are available, interdisciplinary teams, including case managers, work to develop service plans for children that truly support them.

A variety of individuals connected to the child are asked to sit on the team. Generally the list may include:

1. The parents, guardians, or surrogate parents, who are invited to describe exactly what is needed to support the child at home
2. The appropriate representative of the state, such as a social worker or probation officer, if the child is in custody
3. An important teacher or guidance counselor
4. The appropriate counselor or therapist, if the child is in mental health treatment or should be
5. A case manager or service manager, who will ensure that services are implemented and coordinated
6. An advocate of the child and/or parent
7. Any other person who is important to the child or the parents who can contribute meaningfully to the construction of an effective service plan. Neighbors, ministers, friends and relations, and physicians are all examples of others who may play an important role
8. The child, unless there are serious reservations about the proceedings having a detrimental effect on that child. Input from children is often invaluable in shedding light on some of the real issues that need to be addressed

Planning should take into consideration a number of factors that will strengthen the plan and make it more effective. Following are the common factors that are considered during planning.

The Community

The plan that is developed is usually designed to keep a child in his or her community. Therefore, the team looks at every resource and any innovative measure they can create to maintain the child at home or at least in the same community where his or her family lives. Placing children in institutions is done ideally only for very brief intervals, and these placements are seen merely as a means of bringing stability to the situation. A child's community and the child's place in that community is seen as important. Separating children from their communities is viewed as disruptive to the child's progress.

Unconditional Services

The services are, in most communities, given to all children regardless of the severity of their disability. At one time providers denied services to children who suffered extreme problems. They simply said they were "not equipped" to deal with the problem, or they stated that they only treated a specific type of client, excluding those who had severe problems that were difficult and time-consuming. Today an individual provider can still say that, but with interdisciplinary teams making the decisions, agencies willing to engage in wrap-around planning and services are the ones that are most likely to stay in business.

Unconditional also means that when the child changes or when the child's family changes, services will be adapted to meet these changes. The ideal is that children and their families are not rejected from service because they fail to fit some criteria. In addition, a child would not be excluded from service as punishment for failing to progress or for behaviors that are due to the emotional disturbance being treated. As illogical as it sounds, some programs do admit children whose behavior is a direct result of their emotional disturbance and then focus on changing the behavior, without addressing the underlying emotional disturbance; and if their attempts are unsuccessful, these programs often expel the child rather than examine their own techniques.

Strengths-Based Planning

The team looks at the positive supports and resources available to the child and the family, and the team considers the strengths the family and child can bring to the situation. The child's interests and abilities are considered, and the family's religious, cultural, and community supports are included in the assessment. Look also at the child's extended family, neighborhood, family friends, and religious leaders, all of whom may be a resource in supporting the child. All of this is considered when forming the treatment plan. There are always positive aspects of the family, the child, and the child's community, all of which should play a part in determining what is the best plan for the individual child.

Interpreting Your Observations You will see many children and their families for the first time when they are distressed with one another. Parents may shout at or hit their children in your presence. They may call their children names and tell you there is nothing good to say about the child. Children may be surly to you and to their families. They may sit in your office in sullen silence and tell you the questions you are asking are none of your business. It is fairly easy, after such an encounter, to assume that the parents are unable to parent or that the child is hopelessly incorrigible.

Instead, remember that although your observations are important, you also need to look at the participants' points of view. Do the parents need help with parenting skills? Are the parents afraid because things seem to be out of their control? Are the children feeling betrayed by others in their lives? Do they feel hopeless about circumstances they face?

You will note your observations, and many assessment forms will provide space for your impressions. Be very careful to indicate the pieces of the story that are missing: the fact that your observations represent only a fraction of the actual interaction between parents and their children, and that you need additional exposure to the family to truly understand the problems they all face. In this way, you will not assume a lack of strengths and resources before you have the whole picture and develop plans that are ineffective based on a single observation or two.

Individualized Plans

Children and their families are not all alike. Each plan addresses the specific needs of the child and the child's family, based on the idea that no child is untreatable. Individualized services may include many elements that are not considered traditional treatment. For instance, staff may spend time in the family home, or the child might be enrolled in a special recreational or art program. The idea is that every individual child counts. The hope is that communities will plan more for individual children and less for children to be served as groups.

There are intervention models available that stipulate the best intervention for particular diagnoses. These are commonly used by therapists but are used in conjunction with other approaches when designing plans for children. Traditional therapies can be part of the plan, but it is expected that these therapies will be designed specifically to meet the child's needs. Such therapies should be highly individualized.

Natural Supports Case managers are creative and flexible in determining with families how best to address the child's needs. They think outside of the traditional services in communities and look at a number of creative solutions as well. Formal social services can have positive value and should not be excluded if they can be helpful, but children function in a variety of places, relate to many role models, and have numerous interests. Using these as a basis for planning creatively will make the plan more individualized.

Informal supports built into the service plan are often referred to as natural supports because they come from the child's natural environment. A child who has community activities and attachments already may need fewer hours in a treatment program or less of the case manager's time.

When you take the social history, identify any natural supports you find there. Look for them in the reports of others such as psychologists and psychiatrists who may also see the child for evaluation or treatment. When writing your social history, make sure you include the use of natural supports in your recommendations, and when you are planning for the child with a team, be prepared to point these out so the team can incorporate them into the child's plan.

Basic Human Needs

Wrap-around services often refer to life domain areas. Here the reference is to the basic human needs that everyone experiences. At one time or another these can be:

1. A place to live (residential)
2. A family or surrogate family
3. Friends and social contacts
4. Education and/or vocational training
5. Medical care
6. Psychological and emotional care
7. Legal support
8. Safety and the need to feel safe
9. Other needs such as cultural, ethnic, and special community needs

Planning for children looks at the basic human needs of the child and evaluates the need for such things as safety or a home. Many times helping the family to achieve basic human needs will address the child's problems as well.

To summarize good wrap-around services, we would say that the intervention developed for each child would be approved by an interdisciplinary team, provided to the children in their own community, and provided with as few barriers to service as possible. In addition, interventions would be centered on the strengths of the child and the family, carefully coordinated, and highly individualized.

Planning and Case Management

Articulate What Is Ideal

At some point during the planning process, everyone should put on the table how the ideal plan should look. Many hesitate to do this because they are convinced that neither the community nor the child's context can provide all the supports the team might identify. If the opportunity to brainstorm about what an ideal plan for this child would be is missed, however, the team is likely to move to traditional services, and all the care plans will begin to look alike. Sometimes unusual ideas can actually be implemented using the collective information of the entire team.

Be Ready to Change the Plan

Children who have emotional and psychiatric problems typically have many different problems occurring over the course of their childhood. These problems are each addressed in the most effective way, which often means that over the course of a childhood, the child will come in contact with a number of different agencies. One service program generally is not enough. Case management offers the ideal solution because case managers are trained to coordinate services and address the needs of the whole person. It is the case manager who prevents the child's service plan from deteriorating into fragmented pieces.

Do Not Try to Address Everything at Once

It is tempting to give the child every service the child needs if the services are available, but such an approach can be overwhelming to the child and to the family. It is important to separate what must be addressed at once from what can wait, and to prioritize the problems after that. Certainly basic human needs would be addressed first, since a child must have a safe, secure foundation on which to build changes.

Build Success into Your Plan

Fundamentals of Case Management Practice (Summers, 2001) contains an entire chapter on formulating goals and objectives for clients. One of the cautions in that chapter is to be very careful about not creating goals and objectives that are unrealistic or complicated. Instead, break your objectives into small achievable steps to ensure completion and thus success. When the family or the older young person complete even the tiniest step, be jubilant with them, pointing out that they are that much closer to achieving what all of you have agreed is important.

Case Management and Advocacy

Advocacy begins with the ability to articulate and document the ideal case plan for the client. The case manager then faces the need to implement the plan. At this point, the case manager may find that not everyone involved is enthused about implementing the plan. This is particularly true when others are being requested to change their way of doing business.

Advocating for clients is an art. It involves all your best communication skills. Every situation is different, and every approach on behalf of the child should be tailored to meet the particular situation. For example, you might want to ask your supervisor to talk to a director or supervisor at the agency serving your client. You might decide to discuss the needs of the child directly with a teacher at the school or a worker in the agency. In rare cases, a funding source may need to be involved. Following are some common errors:

1. *The case manager does not really know the agency.* The case manager has made the referral, but is not completely informed about the agency's policies, state and federal regulations that limit them, and eligibility requirements. The agency may wish to carry out the referral exactly as it is proposed, but be unable to do so because of agency or legal policies and regulations.
2. *The case manager does not stop to think about what the goal is.* A case manager may confront a particular agency without thinking about what outcome he or she is seeking. Without thinking about this carefully, the case manager can alienate the agency and jeopardize the service to the client, and perhaps to future clients as well.

3. *The case manager becomes too involved with the client.* In such situations, the case manager begins to feel protective of the client and superior to those who are seeking to understand the client. This can lead to dissatisfaction on the part of the case manager with any attempts on the part of another agency to give service to the client.
4. *The case manager sets up an adversarial relationship.* Unwittingly case managers can profess their deep concern for the client in such a way as to indicate that no other agency cares as much. This stance may be interpreted by the family and the client as the case manager's disapproval of the agencies giving service. This sets up a situation in which the family or an older child can play the agency off against the case manager, circumventing any real change.

Case Management with Older Children

Older children are better prepared to be full participants in the intake, assessment, and planning. Case managers who work with teenagers need to genuinely like and respect them. Following are some ideas for working with older children. The Brandeis University's Center for Human Resources (1989) put together a number of excellent ideas about case management with older children. The following list is based in part on their ideas.

1. *Be willing to share responsibility.* You will be more successful with young adults if you are willing to explicitly share the responsibility for reaching the goals with the young person. As the teen matures, that responsibility should increase.
2. *Help the teenager move toward independence.* All young people eventually become adults. Case managers have a unique role in facilitating this transition and making it successful. Part of the success is in getting to the point where the young person no longer needs a case manager. This self-reliance can be achieved only if the case manager is willing to gradually give the young person more and more responsibility. In delegating more responsibility, the case manager needs to know how much the teen can actually handle at any given time. Some teens need skills training to handle certain situations, while others need a lot of positive verbal support.

Peter had known Jim, his case manager, for years. Peter lived in a chaotic family where the family, involved in constant fighting and drug abuse, paid little attention to Peter or his needs. Jim had worked with Peter, setting up services, accompanying him to visits with his pediatrician, helping him get enrolled in Boy Scouts, and being available for after-school talks. Sometimes, Jim would take Peter out for ice cream and they would talk about things going on at school and in Peter's home.

Jim never minimized the hardships Peter was facing, but he always pointed out areas where he felt Peter had acted wisely or competently. Jim openly acknowledged the hardships Peter faced in growing up well in such a chaotic situation and made it clear that as unfortunate as it might be, Peter was going to have to learn some skills for taking care of himself if he were to survive successfully. As Peter grew older, Jim began to give him more and more responsibility. He discussed with Peter after-school jobs and let Peter seek and obtain one on his own. He talked to Peter about Peter's relationship with his girlfriend and the need to either abstain from sex or practice safe sex. He gave Peter the responsibility of making sure he followed through on that advice, and he discussed frankly with him the consequences of not doing so. By the time Peter was in his senior year in high school, he was applying to a local college on his own and determining what course of study to pursue. He still made regular contact with Jim, but it was much less frequent, and Jim was helping Peter prepare to move off the caseload when he reached 18 and became self-reliant.

3. *Help the teenager gain control.* Teens often feel as if life just happens to them. They may express to you the sense that they are simply hapless victims in an unjust life. Case managers can be helpful in showing how certain behaviors result in particular outcomes. What teenagers really need is predictability, and when a case manager helps the teen to set goals and systematically work toward them, the case manager is teaching the teen how to control circumstances to achieve desirable outcomes.

   Some teens will point out correctly that they did not cause their problems. It is important to acknowledge this and to point out respectfully that it is the teen's responsibility to work with you to create solutions and change things. However unfair that might seem, the teen is responsible for making his or her life better.
4. *Be flexible.* Do not become flustered and upset when the teenager's life changes or unplanned circumstances arise. Expect that the plans will need revision. The primary goal may remain the same, but you and the teen may need to find new ways of reaching that goal.
5. *Get to know your teenage client first.* Teenagers have issues with adults to begin with. If you take the time to really get to know your client, you will establish important rapport. Many case managers want to leap immediately to the problems posed by the young person without ever really knowing him or her. Later, after spending time learning who your client really is, you can turn to the problems and issues that need to be addressed. That may be later in the interview or it may be at the next session.
6. *Communicate clearly.* Do not be ambiguous about your expectations. Let the teen know clearly what you expect and how well-equipped the teen is to rise to that challenge, however hard it may be. When you are first assessing the teen's situation, tell him or her definitively the purpose of the assessment.

   Your service plan should clearly present the long-term goals and short-term objectives and what will be needed to achieve those goals, including any new skills the teen must learn to better implement the plan. Your plan should spell out all the responsibilities of each person involved in the plan: yours as well as those of the teen, the parents, and anyone else who is participating. Finally, your plan should have time lines for when certain objectives are to be accomplished. These elements in your plan make it crystal clear what the plan is and who is responsible for each part of it.
7. *Be firm.* You need to be firm when that is necessary. If the teen makes certain promises or commitments and does not follow through, insist that these be met. Point out that you are a team and that you are not the only one responsible for meeting the goals the two of you have chosen. Everyone on the team, including the teenager, must take responsibility.
8. *Have integrity.* This is an ethical obligation, and certainly one that makes trust and rapport more likely. Do not say things you do not mean, promise things you are

not sure you can make happen, or create unrealistic expectations. Instead, make every effort to follow through on what you have promised, and certainly let the teenager know when you have made a mistake. Owning our mistakes is a way to model for teens that they are not expected to be perfect people, but they are expected to be responsible.

9. *Share test results and other assessment information with the teenager.* Some case managers are tempted to assume that the data they receive from other evaluators are absolutely correct and give an accurate picture of the teenager. It is better to share the assessments with the teen to determine where the young person agrees and where he or she disagrees. Listen carefully to why the teen is disagreeing. In this way, your picture of the teen becomes more accurate. From this accurate base you can move forward in planning or revising plans.
10. *Prepare the teen for referrals to other services.* If you have established good rapport with your teenage clients, they may feel abandoned when they are suddenly referred to another agency where service will be given. Teens need to know in advance that a referral is going to be made and why the referral is important in meeting the goals that the teens and the case manager have agreed upon. Case managers need to go a step further and make it clear that they will remain available and be the teens' case manager for the duration. Help young people to see a referral as bringing in additional resources, not as a transfer to someone else.
11. *Let the young person make choices.* Wherever possible, let the young person choose the service or direction that would be best. Offer a variety of options and describe them fully. Giving young people the right to set the direction of the plan and to choose the best way to reach their goals is a step toward important self-reliance.
12. *Help them learn to access services for themselves.* This never means handing a young person a telephone number and a brief description of what an agency does and telling him or her to go call the agency. It does mean that as you work with your client, you will gradually give the teen more responsibility for making contact with those who are providing services. The goal is to help the teen move toward self-reliance and rely less on the case manager.
13. *Write a contract with the young person.* A contract is a written agreement in which responsibilities and time lines are clearly spelled out. The hope is that if everything is carefully spelled out, there will be less reason for the young person and the case manager to misunderstand one another. It is hard to put together a contract that the teen really feels is his or hers. Many adolescents who are confronted with an adult, particularly one they like, will feel a need to go along with the case manager's wishes. If young people do that, they will never really feel the plan belongs to them. For that reason, develop the contract very carefully, consulting the teen about the exact contents and even the exact wording before completing it.
14. *Be prepared for resistance.* Young people can be sullen, unenthusiastic, and disconnected from adults. Many of them distrust adults. They come to the agency with cynical attitudes. Perhaps they have been in services somewhere before and those services provided little in the way of facilitating real change.

    As case management progresses, teens may complain that the case manager is expecting too much of them, that the goals are unrealistic. Long-term goals with little short-term gratification can be boring. Others may voice objections and attempt to drop out of services when the assessment and planning involve an honest appraisal of themselves and their situation. This is sometimes threatening (they might have to change some things) or unnerving (they did not know things were that bad).

Rapport is the only answer to getting past the resistance. That is why it is so important to take the time to really get to know your client, to consider the young person's ideas and interests, and to respect their opinions. In addition, case managers need to show that case management can actually address some of the issues with which the young person is grappling, and can address them in ways that are not necessarily traditional in their approach.

We turn now to the services you might be likely to include in your service planning for children, services to which you would make a referral for a child to receive the necessary treatment.

Outpatient Treatment

Outpatient treatment is used by children and their families and usually provided in a private office or a public clinic. Children and their families can have a number of sessions, often determined by the insurance coverage. These sessions are usually weekly, but recently more intense therapies have evolved that provide for treatment in the child's home or make case managers more available to families to support the therapeutic interventions of clinicians.

Community-Based Interventions

One of the goals for children's mental health is to keep children in their own communities, rather than isolating them in institutional settings. Case managers and therapists have looked at various ways to accomplish this. Following are some of the interventions you might use in your practice.

Intensive Case Management

This form of case management requires the worker to have fewer cases and be more available. Often the caseload is shared with others so that the family and the child have someone to call, 24 hours a day, in a crisis. Others on the team may be clinicians who are familiar with the family and their problems. In intensive case management, workers become involved with the family in order to give support and to prevent hospitalizations or removal from the home, which are expensive options. More importantly, case managers give the much-needed support to help families cope and grow, not only planning with the family members and linking them to relevant services, but also advocating for the child and assessing the needs of the family as the case unfolds.

Home-Based Services

Here intensive forms of therapy are provided within the child's home. It is the goal of home-based services to give the family enough support and options for change that the child will not need to be removed from the home. In addition, the services are designed to keep the family connected to social service agencies that can help them and keep the family together. These services are known by different names in different communities or depending on who provides the service. For instance, juvenile justice, mental health, and child welfare all develop and deliver home-based services; these services might be called in-home services, family preservation services, family-based services, or intensive family services.

Intensive programs are effective in part because the family is seen as a colleague by the professional staff and given the opportunity to help in defining the problem and choosing services. Most of these programs have someone available to the family 24 hours a day. Case management is generally very involved in coordinating services and in helping the family meet basic needs for food and shelter.

Therapeutic Foster Care

This would be the least restrictive placement for a child outside his or her own home. The foster parents have received considerable training in how to handle difficult children and children with multiple problems. Children are placed in a home setting with a real family, but the setting is therapeutic because the parents have had special training. Many of these programs have support available the entire time the child is in care so that foster families are able to seek support for situations that threaten to destabilize the family setting.

Partial Hospitalization/Day Treatment

Here children spend a part of the day in a structured setting, generally returning home to their families in the evening. Obviously this service is not as restrictive as inpatient treatment, but it does provide daily opportunities for the child to discover him- or herself and to make changes. Generally families are involved, as they would be in an outpatient setting, to learn ways to support positive behavior and to receive support themselves. This is also a place where children can attend group sessions and begin to work with other children who have similar problems.

At present, there is evidence that this form of treatment is more successful than outpatient treatment, but insurance companies and other third-party payers have been reluctant to pay for this treatment due in part to the length of time a child might spend in such a program.

The goal is to get children back in school and functioning normally again, and it appears that partial hospitalization programs help to facilitate that. For this reason, some schools have transition programs that ease the child back into school. Many feel that these programs prevent hospitalization or removal from the home and should receive closer attention from policy makers and third-party payers.

Residential Treatment Centers (RTCs)

A small percentage of children with mental disabilities will need to be referred to residential care, but such care is expensive. Children live in settings where they are given medication, education, and many different forms of established therapy in order to help them form a better self-image, relate better to others, and find ways to be useful and productive citizens. Many children who come to such centers cannot go home because they have been severely abused. For that reason, center staff must be familiar with the symptoms of posttraumatic stress disorder and be able to work with children who have extremely complicated problems.

For case managers, the hardest task is integrating a child successfully back into his or her community when the child is released from an RTC. Without proper coordination of services and preplanning before the release, the child is likely to encounter problems upon returning home.

Many RTCs use the Outward Bound program for young people in residential programs. Camping, self-sufficiency in the wilderness, and an appreciation of natural surroundings are often seen as positive in helping children to see themselves and the world in a new light.

Inpatient Treatment

This is, of course, the most restrictive type of care for any population. There is some controversy about the use of hospitals to treat children. For instance, many feel the services can be provided in less restrictive settings and in a supportive community environment. At present, most feel hospitals are important for children with severe emotional disturbances that require the child to receive intense treatment away from the family and community. Typically these inpatient stays are brief, and to be successful they should include involvement of the family. Case managers need to assist with the transitions to the hospital and back to the community.

Crisis Services

These services are generally available 24 hours a day, 7 days a week. The services for children and their families may be part of a larger regional crisis team or a crisis service specifically for children and their families. The crisis team may go to homes, emergency rooms, and other locations where the child is having trouble, or they may direct others, through a hot line, to take the child to a specific place. For example, some teams are connected with hospital emergency rooms and direct those calling about children who are in need of immediate attention to bring the child to the emergency room so that the crisis worker can assist the family there.

The best teams are those whose members are specifically trained to deal with children and their families and are willing to go out to locations where the disturbed child needs immediate attention. Such teams are good at helping the family to stabilize the situation, at making the correct referrals, and at giving supportive follow-up.

Crisis services serve to deescalate family problems and help in the transition to therapeutic services. Crisis workers assess the problem immediately and give the family some treatment to stabilize the situation. In addition, these workers link the family to the needed services so that the family can obtain the support they need to stay together and avert future crises. Such services prevent visits to the emergency room and often prevent the need for hospitalization or some other form of removal of the child from the home. Some crisis centers for children have short-term residential services where children can go until the situation is stabilized. These may be referred to as respite care. In other crisis programs, intensive in-home services are given until the family can be referred to other services.

It is the case manager who helps to make the transition from crisis services to other long-term services and who coordinates what has been done by the crisis team with what remains to be done in order to strengthen the family and assist the child.

OTHER SERVICES USING CHILDREN'S CASE MANAGERS

Child Welfare

In 1974 a piece of federal legislation was passed titled the Child Abuse Prevention and Treatment Act (CAPTA). States wishing to receive monies provided in this bill were required to write state legislation that included immunity from prosecution for those who report child abuse and clearly stipulating who is mandated to report child abuse. The problem, however, is that experts do not always agree on the definitions of abuse and neglect. Extreme cases are rare; the cases that are most often seen by children's workers fall into a gray area that some consider obvious abuse and others do not. CAPTA contained a definition: "the physical and mental injury, sexual abuse, neglected treatment and maltreatment of a child under 18 by a person who is responsible for the child's welfare under circumstances which indicate the child's health and welfare is harmed and threatened thereby." When other adults harm children, it is considered an assault and referred to the criminal justice system.

Downs et al. (2000) discusses family structure as one of the predisposing factors to child abuse and neglect: "Abuse and neglect are more likely to occur in single-parent households, with father-only families at somewhat higher risk than mother-only families." The problem appears to be related to a single parent trying to fulfill the roles of both parents and experiencing considerable stress as a result. Other factors often found in abusive or neglectful families are domestic violence, social isolation, psychological disorders, and a poor understanding of children, including how to discipline them and what to expect of them as they mature. Downs et al. (2000) writes that these parents interact with their children in "limit(ed), negative, controlling" ways and may lack the capacity to give "emotional nurturance."

The consequences of abuse and neglect to the child are enormous. Abuse and neglect can interrupt normal physical, psychological, cognitive, and social development, leading to impairments in all those areas. When abuse is severe or occurs early, it can leave the child with permanent disabilities, mental retardation, and perhaps sexually transmitted diseases. Some children suffer language difficulties as a result of the abuse or neglect they encounter. Abused and neglected children grow up to have problems with their peers because of their inability to trust other people or to empathize with them. Downs et al. (2000) points out that neglected children "are more likely to be passive and withdrawn and to exhibit helplessness under stress."

Agencies that work to protect children, investigate complaints of child abuse or neglect, and seek to help families stay together in healthier, safer ways employ case managers to develop plans for families and for their children. This is an area in which you might work if protective services and family preservation are of interest to you. In your work, you would, ideally, join a team in cross-systems collaboration on behalf of the children and families you would be serving.

Juvenile Justice Systems

Some children come in contact with the juvenile justice system because of the abuse or neglect they have suffered or because they are suffering from a mental disorder. Some of these children have been or will be diagnosed as having conduct disorder. In coming to the attention of the juvenile justice system, these children may have become involved in the use and sale of illegal drugs, carried weapons, engaged in shoplifting, set fires, broken into schools or homes, vandalized property, or injured other people.

Most colleges offer a course in juvenile delinquency that will give you a good foundation in what delinquency is and an understanding of the role case managers play in the juvenile justice system. A young person who has entered the juvenile justice system will need evaluation and services if the behavior is to be prevented from becoming more pronounced in adulthood. There are a number of services available that a case manager can use in planning for a young person who is in the criminal justice system for the first time or who is being discharged from a detention center for youth. The problem is that case managers, often referred to as juvenile probation officers, must help young people within the limits of the laws governing juvenile delinquency in their jurisdiction. Therefore, they may have less latitude in choosing services and in developing an individualized plan than they do in working with other services for children.

The services that case managers in the juvenile justice system might use include: residential treatment facilities, which remove children from their environment and give them structure within which they are expected to be successful; restorative justice programs, in which the young person, often under a court mandate, gives something to the community as a volunteer or works to repay the victims of his or her crime; intense treatment programs, where therapists have contact almost daily with the family and the child for several months; and psychotherapy and family therapy. Some of the therapy programs seek to change the way the child thinks about him- or herself using cognitive therapy techniques, while other therapy programs involve all the important people in the child's life and include all the areas (such as family and school) in which the child is involved in order to modify and affect the child's environment in positive ways.

DOING YOUR ASSESSMENT AND FOLLOWING YOUR CLIENT

The information in this chapter gives you a realistic picture of the types of problems children encounter as they mature and how they are likely to come in contact with a social service agency. In addition, the chapter spells out the role of the case manager in assisting the child and the family to correct negative situations and resolve problem behaviors. This information will help you to develop believable children's cases and prepare you with ideas about how to handle these cases and what referrals to make. As you follow your children and families, you will be able to anticipate the kinds of problems and concerns that are likely to arise. Use the information in this chapter to develop a hypothetical child and his or her family, and then imagine yourself as the case manager dealing with the problems the child is experiencing.

EXERCISES

Developing Service Plans

Instructions: Develop a service plan for each child and his or her family. For each component in your plan, explain what that component is supposed to address.

1. Kevin is 8 years old. His mother, Mrs. Moore, brought him into the center, saying he is hyperactive and often unmanageable at home. She told you she is looking for a prescription for Ritalin "so he will stop bouncing off the walls." During the first interview with Mrs. Moore, she described a child at home who will not sit and watch TV or do his homework. "He hums, jumps from chair to chair, fiddles with his food at the table, shouts when I talk, and is driving me crazy." Much of the rest of the interview was spent discussing in graphic detail the abuse she experienced at the hands of Kevin's father from before Kevin was born until she divorced him when Kevin was 4 years old. During this initial interview, Kevin played in the playroom with another worker who indicated that Kevin played

normally and did not appear to be hyperactive, but focused on the projects he was working on with the toys. In the waiting room, Kevin was observed sitting quietly with his mother while waiting for the appointment.

With Mrs. Moore's permission, you interview Kevin's 3rd-grade teacher. She tells you that Kevin could do a little better in school, but that overall he is an average student and presents no disciplinary problem in the classroom. Based on this and your observations at the case management unit, you make two home visits. During both of these visits, Mrs. Moore again discusses, in graphic detail, the abuse she experienced at the hands of Mr. Moore and the problems she had with the divorce. During her description, Kevin turns up the TV, sings loudly, runs through the room yelling, jumps on the sofa, and interrupts. "See what I have to put up with at home?" Mrs. Moore asks. "I am going crazy with this, and no one else seems to agree with me. I'm glad you were here when this happened. He is bouncing off the walls!"

Your Service Plan

2. Manejeh's family moved to the United States from Afghanistan. They escaped Afghanistan after the Soviets invaded and targeted her extended family as important Afghanis who needed to be eliminated. Manejeh was an infant when the entire family made their escape through Pakistan. Manejeh's paternal uncles also came, as well as all her aunts and cousins, but Manejeh is the only girl among the cousins. The family lives now in a small town where her father, who was once a government official, is now working in a warehouse. He is extremely strict with Manejeh and has sought help from you because she does not obey, and he understands this is a place where he can bring children who do not obey their parents.

Manejeh's father reports that Manejeh disappears from home or comes in late, wears indecent clothes, and is not observant of Islam. Manejeh is 17. The day you interview her, she appears to be a lively, normal, 17-year-old high school student. Her grades are very good, she is planning to go to college, which her family supports, but Manejeh tells you she is not happy. She talks about an extremely restrictive setting in which she is constantly being compared to her male cousins who faithfully observe Islam and who are scandalized by her clothes, dating, and missing Friday services on occasion to be with her friends. She tells you that the times she has missed Friday prayers were times she went to play rehearsals at school.

Manejeh is often out late or leaves home without asking permission because she knows she will not be given permission to meet her friends or do things with them if she asks. She tells you about another family from Afghanistan that is "completely Americanized." She says that she spends a lot of time with the daughter in that family and that her friend's mother is very supportive of Manejeh and what she wants to do. Recently Manejeh began to date an American boy. He is not Muslim. Manejeh's father has forbidden him to enter the house and forbidden Manejeh to go out with this boy.

Your Service Plan

3. Two-year-old Ardella is brought to the center by her mother, who is asking that she be put on medication. Ardella's mother is 19 years old. She seems burdened by the care of Ardella, whom she had at 17. "When I had her, I had already dropped out of school. I couldn't stand school. All that stuff they make you do." The family is on welfare. The mother insists that Ardella is "not right." She describes Ardella as getting into drawers and cupboards, picking up things and putting them in her mouth, and "not listening." The mother says, "I mean, I told her not to touch the things on the coffee table and not to look at my magazines, but she tears them up anyway. She puts stuff in her mouth. She's bad!" The mother tells you she does not know how to make Ardella listen: "I smacked her, I yelled at her. It don't do no good. She just won't listen, no way!"

Your Service Plan

4. Margurita and her boyfriend are separating. They have been together since their son, Emanuel, was born. Emanuel is now 6. Margurita tells you she knows the separation is hard on Emanuel. "His daddy was using drugs before he left. He was out of it all the time, and bringing these no goods around night and day. Then he started to get in trouble with the law for stealing and stuff like that. I didn't want Emanuel to grow up like that." Her concern is that Emanuel is now "acting like a baby." She goes on to describe his behavior. "I mean, he whines before school, fusses, you know, about he can't tie his shoes or button his shirt. He wants help brushing his teeth, and hangs around me all the time." Margurita has not allowed Emanuel to see his dad since he left. "He can't take care of Manny. He can't barely take care of himself. How's he going to look after Manny?" She refuses to talk about the father and changes the subject when Emanuel brings it up. "I don't want him to get upset. He needs to forget about him. Anyway, they weren't close or anything. He didn't do anything with Manny or nothing." Margurita says Emanuel started school this year and is doing well. She would like to work, "But I got no skills, you know." She and Emanuel are on welfare. "I was supposed to find a job, but so far they haven't pushed that and I'm glad. I was waiting for Manny to start school. I didn't want to leave him with no strangers, like the welfare said I had to."

Your Service Plan

5. Jenkins is brought in by his mother and father. They tell you that the school psychologist suggested it. Jenkins was tested by the school psychologist because he was so far behind in class work. Jenkins is 11 and appears to you to be withdrawn and sad. He says little during the interview, often shrugging when asked for his input or mumbling, "I don't know." His parents tell you he has always been that way. "Even when he was little," his father tells you, "he would rather sit in his room than be out playing. I used to try to do things with him, but he would rarely want to do anything with me." Jenkins has one friend, "if you could call it that. I think they walk to school together and maybe talk at school, but they never do anything after school or on the weekends." The friend, Barry, is a Boy Scout and swims at the YMCA after school. The parents describe a normal birth and childhood, but say they have always been a little worried because Jenkins always seemed so sad. "He can cry at the drop of a hat. He always seems down or blue. A lot of the time when he is in his room he is just sleeping." Pediatric records show that a recent complete physical revealed no medical problems. The pediatrician did note the child had a "flat affect" and, in another note, commented, "This is not an animated child."

Your Service Plan

Intake Form for Children and Adolescents
Wildwood Case Management Unit

Date ______________________ CMU# ______________________

GENERAL INFORMATION

Name(s) of significant other (SO) ______________________

Relationship of SO to child ______________________

SO's address ______________________

____

Home phone ______________________ Work phone ______________________

May we leave a message? __________

Child's name ______________________ DOB ______________ Age ________

Child's address if different from the SO's ______________________

____

Child's school ______________________ Grade ________

FAMILY BACKGROUND

Household members

Names	**Relationship to child**	**Age**

Are there people to whom the child feels especially close? ______________________

____

Describe the relationship ______________________

____

____

____

Are there people with whom the child has particularly difficult relationships?

____

Describe the relationship ______________________

____

____

Does the SO believe the child feels safe at home? ______________

Other family issues or events

______ Divorce ______ Custody dispute ______ Financial concerns

______ Separation ______ Domestic violence ______ Death of a relative

Other ______________

____

Interviewer comments:

SCHOOL AND SOCIAL INFORMATION

Does the child attend school regularly? ______________

Describe peer relationships ______________

Are there behavior problems in school? ______________

Describe ______________

____

____

____

____

____

Does child complete homework? ______________

Describe child's relationship to teachers ______________

____

____

Subjects liked best ______________

____

____

____

Subjects liked least ______________

____

____

____

Describe the type of student the child is:

☐ Far below average ☐ Somewhat below average ☐ At grade level
☐ Somewhat above grade level ☐ Far above grade level

Does child belong to clubs or organizations? ______________

Describe ______________

____

____

Does child attend any religious activities? ____________________

Describe ____________________

____

____

What is child most likely to do when alone? ____________________

____

What does child do most often with friends? ____________________

____

What does child like to do best? ____________________

____

Interviewer comments:

HEALTH AND MEDICAL INFORMATION

Describe and date each:

Medical problems ____________________

____

____

____

____

Last physical examination ____________________

Problems addressed as a result (other than emotional) ____________________

____

____

____

____

Physician who conducted examination ____________________

Family physician ____________________

Last eye examination ____________________

Surgeries ____________________

____

____

____

____

Last dental checkup ______________________________

Immunization status ______________________________

Pregnancies ______________________________

Drug use ______________________________

Alcohol use ______________________________

Smokes? ☐ Yes ☐ No How much? ______________________________

Current medications ______________________________

____

____

____

____

____

Interviewer comments:

MENTAL AND EMOTIONAL HEALTH INFORMATION

Symptom Checklist

☐ *Depression*

_____ Looks sad

_____ Cries a lot

_____ Irritable

_____ Withdrawn

_____ Sleep problems (insomnia or hypersomnia)

_____ Decreased appetite

_____ Appears listless

_____ Loss of interest in things formerly interested in

☐ *Anxiety*

_____ Panic attacks

_____ School avoidance

_____ Persistent worry

_____ Afraid to leave parent/caregiver

_____ Somatic complaints

_____ Unusual fears

_____ Nightmares

_____ Obsessive/compulsive behavior

☐ *Mania*

_____ Euphoric

_____ Agitated

_____ Grandiose ideas

_____ Pressure of speech

☐ *Suicidal*

_____ Vague death wish

_____ Thoughts without plan

_____ Thoughts with plan

_____ Verbal threats

_____ Gestures

_____ Attempts

_____ Self-injurious

_____ Means available

☐ *Homicidal*

_____ Thoughts without plan

_____ Thoughts with plan

_____ Gestures

_____ Attempts

_____ Toward a specific person or persons

_____ Weapons available

☐ *Poor Attitude*

_____ Toward school

_____ Toward parents

_____ Toward siblings

_____ Toward authority figures

_____ Toward community

_____ Cynical

_____ Angry

_____ Sullen

_____ Defiant

☐ *Psychosis*

_____ Hallucinations

_____ Auditory

_____ Name-calling

_____ Command

_____ Vague

_____ Visual

_____ Other ______________________

____

____

_____ Delusions

- _____ Erotomanic
- _____ Grandiose
- _____ Jealous
- _____ Persecutory
- _____ Somatic
- _____ Mixed
- _____ Unspecified

(consult *DSM-IV-TR* pp. 324–325)

Interviewer comments:

BEHAVIORS

	Home	School	Work
☐ *Acting Out*			
____ Temper tantrums	☐	☐	☐
____ Verbally aggressive	☐	☐	☐
____ Physically aggressive	☐	☐	☐
____ Stealing	☐	☐	☐
____ Lying	☐	☐	☐
____ Does not follow rules	☐	☐	☐
☐ *Hyperactive*	☐	☐	☐
____ Disruptive	☐	☐	☐
____ Impulsive	☐	☐	☐
____ Fidgets	☐	☐	☐
____ Inattentive	☐	☐	☐
____ Cannot focus	☐	☐	☐

☐ *Other Behaviors*

____ Poor hygiene
____ Fire setting
____ Running away
____ Encopresis
____ Enuresis
____ Irresponsible
____ Easily hurt
____ Suspicious
____ Overly anxious to please
____ Plays with genitals
____ Obscene language
____ Daydreams a lot
____ Peer problems
____ Tics
____ Compulsive behaviors
____ Sexual behaviors
____ Secretive
____ Demanding
____ Threatens others
____ Stubborn
____ Thumb sucking
____ Shows off/clowns
____ Vandalism
____ Behaves like opposite sex

Interviewer comments:

PAST MENTAL HEALTH TREATMENT

Diagnosis: ______

Hospitalizations: ______

Medications: ______

Therapy: ______

Suicide attempts: ______

PRESENT MENTAL HEALTH TREATMENT

Diagnosis: ______

Hospitalizations: ______

Medications: ______

Therapy: ______

Suicide attempts: ______

Interviewer comments:

Developmental problems ______

______

______

Exposure to medications, drugs, alcohol, cigarettes during pregnancy ______

______

______

Problems with pregnancy or delivery ______

______

______

Interviewer comments:

OTHER AGENCIES INVOLVED

1. ______

Treatment ______

Primary therapist or worker ______

How long? ______

2. ____

Treatment ____

Primary therapist or worker ____

How long? ____

3. ____

Treatment ____

Primary therapist or worker ____

How long? ____

4. ____

Treatment ____

Primary therapist or worker ____

How long? ____

Interviewer comments:

CHILD ABUSE ISSUES

☐ *Physical Abuse*

When ____________________ By whom ____________________ Reported ________

Comments ____

☐ *Emotional Abuse*

When ____________________ By whom ____________________ Reported ________

Comments ____

☐ *Sexual Abuse*

When ____________________ By whom ____________________ Reported ________

Comments ____

☐ *Neglect*

When ____________________ By whom ____________________ Reported ________

Comments ____

☐ *Witness to Violence*

When ____________________ By whom ____________________ Reported ________

☐ Nightmares ☐ Flashbacks

Comments ____

MENTAL STATUS IMPRESSIONS

Appearance

_____ Appropriate

_____ Disheveled

_____ Unconventional

_____ Other ________________________

____

Thought Processes

_____ Clear and coherent

_____ Difficult to follow

_____ Flight of ideas

_____ Loose associations

_____ Other ________________________

____

Mood

_____ Depressed

_____ Euphoric

_____ Normal

_____ Expansive

_____ Irritable

_____ Anxious

Intelligence

_____ Above average

_____ Average

_____ Below average

Affect

_____ Appropriate

_____ Restricted

_____ Flat

_____ Inappropriate

_____ Labile

Motivation for Treatment

_____ Good

_____ Fair

_____ Poor

Client Response to Interview

_____ Good

_____ Bad

_____ Indifferent

_____ Hostile

_____ Avoidant

_____ Guarded

_____ Cooperative

_____ Uncooperative

Speech

_____ Normal

_____ Overtalkative

_____ Undertalkative

_____ Pressured

_____ Other ________________________

____

Thought Content

_____ Appropriate

_____ Delusions

_____ Hallucinations

_____ Preoccupations

Memory

_____ Adequate

_____ Impaired

Insight

_____ Good

_____ Fair

_____ Poor

Orientation

_____ Time

_____ Place

_____ Person

Impact of Problems

____ Health

____ Relationships

____ School/Work

Family Response to Interview

____ Good

____ Bad

____ Indifferent

____ Hostile

____ Avoidant

____ Guarded

____ Cooperative

____ Uncooperative

GAF Score ________________

IMPRESSIONS AND RECOMMENDATIONS

____

CASE MANAGER COMPLETING ASSESSMENT

Chapter 4

Case Management for Survivors of Rape and Domestic Violence

INTRODUCTION

It was a June day, and Megan was working in her garden. She did so furtively because her husband, Chris, might appear at any moment. He was supposed to be at work, but lately he had taken to coming home at odd times, supposedly for lunch or because he forgot something. Each time he had been critical of what Megan was doing.

It had started as verbal complaints. "You're wasting your time on that project. Find something more constructive to do!" At first Megan had not taken these complaints seriously. She worked in a social service agency during the week, and her husband, who had an excellent job at the glass factory, often worked on weekends to pick up overtime and put himself in line for a promotion. They had been married only a year and had no children. In the evenings and on weekends, Megan liked doing things around the little house they rented. She made curtains for the kitchen windows, made a dust ruffle for the bed, took care of a collection of potted plants, and started a small flower garden in the backyard. She also liked to read.

In May she noticed that things seemed to be getting worse. Just as some irises were ready to bloom, Chris pulled them out, saying he thought she should plant dahlias instead. She doubted he really knew what dahlias were. In addition, she had begun to notice that some of her books were missing. Often she discovered them hidden behind the refrigerator or in other places she would never have left them. She knew that Chris was critical of what she read, and of her reading at all. "All you do is read that shit and keep your nose in a book. Find something useful to do."

These encounters had been painful to Megan. She wanted a husband who supported what she wanted to do. She had many interests when she and Chris married, but she could feel herself gradually giving them up or not starting something new because she feared Chris's criticism. She felt angry and betrayed, but she really wanted to make this marriage work. After all, the wedding had been a wonderful affair with all their friends and family. Everyone had predicted a terrific marriage to follow. If she caused trouble, she would be the one ruining what everyone else saw as a good relationship. So she did not discuss her hurt feelings with anyone.

After she finished her work in the yard, she went into the kitchen to make some lemonade. It was a hot day, and she thought that would be a refreshing treat for Chris when he came home from work. Instead, Chris arrived while she was making the lemonade. When he saw what she was doing, he shouted at her that she should know he never drank lemonade, and said to just look at all the lemons she had wasted, for God's sake. He demanded that she clean up the kitchen and dispose of the lemonade at once, and then he went into the back yard. In a few minutes, he came back. "You've been working in that damn garden again, haven't you? I thought I made it perfectly clear that you were to give that up." Chris slapped Megan. "If this doesn't teach you what you can and can't do around here, then nothing will." He slammed out of the house.

Megan cried most of the rest of the afternoon. Her feelings were hurt. She did not want to live like this, but she could vividly remember the happier times she and Chris had shared before they were married. Couldn't they somehow get back to that?

At dinnertime Chris arrived home with flowers. He was apologetic and loving. He asked Megan to forgive his "outburst" and promised never to do such a thing again. Of course she could do the things she liked to do. He was sorry. Megan forgave Chris that night and on many subsequent nights as the abuse grew more intense and Megan became less and less confident about herself and her ability to make decisions. Coworkers had expressed concern about Megan's bruises and talked to her about seeking help, but Megan remained afraid to be the one to break up a relationship that most of her friends and all of her family still believed was a happy one. "A match made in heaven," her mother had told her just before the wedding. She did not want to disappoint everyone. Besides, on each abusive occasion, Chris had managed to convince her that he would seek help and never "lay a hand on you again." He also convinced her that he needed help and that she alone could help him "through this." Each time she thought about leaving, he begged her to stay, and since she really had not thought about where to go, she did stay. The idea of leaving and deciding what to take with her was exhausting to her, so she did nothing.

The following June Megan had to go to her parents' home because her father was sick. He had suffered a heart attack. The family went together to the hospital, but Chris did not go because he was working. When he returned from work and got Megan's note about the emergency, he flew into a rage. He felt she should have put him first and made sure she returned from the hospital in time to take care of his dinner. He even considered himself as being "reasonable" for not objecting to her going to the hospital in the first place.

As the evening dragged on, Chris fumed and became angrier. At 7:00 Megan called. Her father had taken a turn for the worse. The family was all with him. She would be home when she could. Chris became enraged on the phone and threatened her. He told her to "get your ass back here in the next 15 minutes or I'm coming for you, and you won't like the scene at the hospital." Megan complied. She made an excuse to her mother and said she would be right back. She was terrified of any scene that might make things worse for her family at this critical time.

At home Chris raged and yelled. He threw furniture, broke dishes, and punched Megan several times. Bruises and welts began to appear. Retiring that night, Megan felt utterly overwhelmed. She had never returned to the hospital. Her mother had called about 11:00 to say her father was stable. Chris had already gone into his contrite mode, asking forgiveness and promising never to treat her like that again. He applied ice packs to her bruises and wanted to help clean up her cuts and abrasions. But Megan had heard all this before. Furthermore, her father needed her, and so did her family. She knew that what was going on was unhealthy and that she must do something.

The next morning, Megan feigned that everything was fine and left for work as usual, but she went straight to a women's shelter where she stayed for the next three weeks until she found a place of her own. Chris called the shelter several times seeking forgiveness and promising to change. He even went to a therapist. But somehow Megan was able to admit to herself and to her family that this was not a relationship made in heaven, but rather a nightmare for her that, for the sake of her own emotional health and physical safety, she needed to leave.

The case manager in the shelter immediately understood Megan's ambivalence about leaving her marriage. After listening and taking information, the case manager made some suggestions and helped Megan choose services that might work best for her. Together Megan and the case manager developed a safety plan that would allow Megan to return to work. Megan then attended a group, recommended by her case manager, with other women who had recently left abusive relationships. She suffered from nightmares and flashbacks of the incidents of abuse that were most intense. Her case manager arranged for Megan to have a good feminist therapist and medication.

Megan's situation is typical of what many women face when they are battered by someone they originally loved and trusted. In this chapter, we will look at abuse and rape and the consequences of these actions. We will also examine your role as a case manager in this field. This chapter was prepared with the help of both the National Resource Center on Domestic Violence and the National Sexual Assault Resource Center.

SPECIAL CONSIDERATIONS FOR WORKING WITH VICTIMS OF RAPE AND DOMESTIC VIOLENCE

If You Are Male

Men rarely work in the field of domestic violence and rape. Agencies set up specifically to address these issues are generally run and staffed by women. This is because the majority of victims of rape and domestic violence are women or female children. Nevertheless, as part of a generic crisis team, or in the event that there are few well-qualified individuals to work in these agencies, you might be in a position to help women who are victims.

It is important to keep in mind that, as unfortunate as this is, the majority of perpetrators are men. For this reason, most of your clients will have strong feeling about men, and they may initially be very afraid of you as a male person. Your understanding and acceptance of this can go a long way toward making your client's transition to safety and emotional health a smooth one.

In a domestic violence situation, your client has probably come from a very coercive relationship. In spite of your good intentions, such a female client could very easily mistake your suggestions for imperatives. Practice collaboration consciously. (For more information on how to collaborate during problem solving, consult Summers, *Fundamentals of Case Management Practice,* 2001.) Make certain that the woman with whom you are working understands that you want to share information with her, but you do not want to make decisions for her or pressure her to make certain choices. If you are concerned for her safety and about the choices she is making, express this very tentatively by using "I messages" as outlined in *Fundamentals of Case Management Practice* (Summers, 2001).

In some situations, you may want to acknowledge how hard it must be for the woman to have to deal with a male person after such a trauma. Assure her that you want to be helpful and not frightening, and ask her (if appropriate) how you can help.

Interchangeable Terms

A number of terms are used to describe domestic violence in the literature on the subject. One term is *domestic violence,* which is used in many instances to cover any violence inside the home. *Abuse* and *battering* are other terms that often mean the same thing, but are generally used to refer to abuse by a partner.

Other Forms of Domestic Violence

As you will see in other chapters, domestic violence is not limited to adult partners. Children are abused by parents of either sex in some homes. Elderly people are sometimes abused by their children of either sex. There can be violence against pets as a form of controlling a victim. Live-in partners sometimes abuse children living in the home, and relatives who have access to children can abuse them. For our purposes, we will address abuse between adult partners and rape or sexual abuse between adults, although we will look briefly at sexual abuse where children are the victims and same-sex abuse.

The Victim as "She"

For the most part, this chapter will refer to the victim as a female person. Certainly abuse can and does happen to male people, and it is not our intention to make light of that. We are using the female designation in most instances within the chapter because an overwhelming number of victims are women or female children.

Organizations That Serve Women

This chapter was prepared with the help of the National Sexual Assault Resource Center and the National Resource Center on Domestic Violence. Both organizations make information and technical support available to women's programs throughout the United States. They can be a resource to you as you serve clients in this field.

BACKGROUND

Programs for women arose during the women's movement, a period in U.S. history when women were speaking out about the condition of women and raising awareness of the crimes committed against them. During the 1960s, women participated in the civil rights movement and other movements that involved the civil rights of others. By the 1970s, women had begun to look more closely at the discrimination and bias they often experienced. Feminism, as the movement came to be known, was a call for political and economic rights for women equal to those of men.

In the course of their work together, women realized that violence against women was one of the ways in which their inferior position was maintained. Historically, violence in the home between intimate partners was dismissed as being between two adults. As long as the violence was between individuals who lived together and knew each other intimately, it was considered a private matter, and intervention was considered an intrusion. Rape was similarly dismissed as generally being a crime women brought on themselves, usually through the way they dressed, their poor choice of partners, or the places they went.

As the women's movement took shape and women began to talk among themselves, the tendency to blame themselves diminished, and women began to view these violent acts as crimes involving an abuse of power. In addition, individual women who had tended to go along with society's assessment and blame themselves now began to view violence against women in political terms. Society, including women themselves, had colluded to make these crimes seem somehow less important than other crimes. Women could now see these crimes as a part of the way society was structured, allowing men to abuse power and exert extreme control using violence, often with impunity, while holding women responsible in some measure for their own victimization.

In 1971–1972, the first hot line for victims of rape was opened in Washington, DC, and a group was formed in Berkelely, California, to address the needs of rape victims. During the 1970s, state coalitions to combat rape were also established. These groups encountered, among other problems, a lack of legal and emotional support for victims, a lack of good documentation of the crimes, and insensitive practices on the part of the police and hospital emergency rooms.

Working together, women began to make effective changes in their communities and states. Rape shield laws were enacted that prohibited a rape victim from being questioned about previous sexual behavior. Laws were repealed in which a victim had to have a corroborating witness before charges could be filed. Techniques were developed to improve evidence gathering, and methods were devised to help police become more sensitive in handling these cases.

In 1980 a mistrial was declared in a rape case because Ann Pride, director of Pittsburgh Action Against Rape, refused to give a client's records to the defense attorney. For this she was held in contempt of court. The case went to the Pennsylvania Supreme Court where judicial recognition was given to the confidentiality of the counselor-client communication. Soon thereafter the Pennsylvania legislature passed a law guaranteeing total confidentiality for any communications between a rape victim and her rape crisis counselor.

Assignment

Find out what laws exist in your state to protect the confidentiality of clients and their counselors in women's programs. Do these laws extend to support groups?

WORKING IN WOMEN'S PROGRAMS

Because of the way in which violence against women is viewed, work in a women's program is quite different from work in other programs. The views of those who staff women's programs are consistent with the political view of crimes against women described earlier. Women are seen not so much as victims, but more as survivors. They have strength and common sense. The abuse or assault has served to throw them temporarily off balance, but they are not sick or helpless.

For this reason, the worker and the client form supportive and collaborative relationships, relationships between equals. Since the women clients have been the victims of abuse of power and control, these agencies and the workers within them seek to put the woman in control, to value her desires and perspective, and to give her control over the process of her therapy and her legal decisions.

You may find, for instance, that the agency is staffed by individuals, many of them volunteers, who have had similar experiences. You may see staff being more open with clients about these personal experiences than you would in another kind of agency. Support groups are encouraged, giving women an opportunity to share their experiences and the effects these experiences have had on their lives.

Your Role

First, you must help your client negotiate the system. The system can include hospitals; the criminal justice system, including courts and probation and parole; legal systems for divorce, separation, and support; and child protective agencies. Helping the victim to navigate these systems is one of the most important responsibilities you have.

After an assault, most people are in emotional turmoil. Making decisions at such a time may be very difficult. Often, however, decisions about safety, reporting to the criminal justice system, and regarding children's welfare must be made immediately. You will not make these decisions for a victim, but you will need to be available to discuss her concerns and needs and to support the choices she believes would be best. Some of your clients may not speak or read English and may have no idea what their rights are. In such cases, you are responsible for going over everything verbally and seeking a translator if possible.

All your contacts with the victim should be documented, and you must maintain up-to-date records. You are also responsible for seeking the help you need when you encounter a situation that is particularly difficult to sort out.

Confidentiality

Maintaining confidentiality is an absolute ethical standard in any program. Women are often reluctant to seek help if they do not understand your ethical commitment to maintain confidentiality. Any communication between you and your client, either written or verbal, will be kept confidential. In addition, your observations of the client and any information you receive about the case are also confidential. Women need reassurance of this from the beginning of their relationship with you. (For a more complete discussion of confidentiality, see Summers, *Fundamentals of Case Management Practice*, 2001, pp. 8–16.)

There are times when you can and must break confidentiality. They are:

1. When the client has been determined to be legally incompetent and has a court-appointed guardian, the guardian has the right to consent to disclosure.
2. During a medical emergency where the client is unable to authorize a release of information, you may release information relevant to the medical emergency only.
3. If during the course of your work, you believe that a child is being abused or neglected, you must report that to the proper authorities according to the guidelines in your state.
4. If your client informs you of her intention to commit a violent act against another person, you should disclose that information to the proper legal authority and warn the victim directly if your state requires that.
5. If your client informs you that she is contemplating suicide, you may inform mental health crisis teams or act as a petitioner for a mental health commitment to protect the woman from harming herself and to obtain the mental health services she needs.

STATISTICS AND PREVALENCE

Rape

According to the U.S. Department of Justice, rape is committed primarily against young people. Their findings showed that 54% of all rape victims were under age 18 when raped for the first time, and an additional 45.6% of the victims were between 18 and 26 years of age when raped for the first time (Tjaden & Thoennes, 1999). The National Crime Victimization Survey (1996) estimated that teens are 3.5 times more likely to be raped or to experience attempted rape than the general population.

The National Victim Center found, based on their surveys, that 1.3 women over age 18 are likely to be raped in the United States every minute, meaning 1,871 rapes occur in this country every day (Kilpatrick, Edmunds, & Seymour, 1992). Although the focus is usually on rape by a stranger, nearly three out of four rape victims knew the perpetrator, and 76% of women who were raped or assaulted after age 18 "were assaulted by a current or former husband, cohabiting partner, or date" (Tjaden & Thoennes, 1999).

Generally women do not report rape. A 1994 survey found that only about 32% of rapes were reported, and nearly 80.4% of attempted rapes went unreported (National Crime Victimization Survey, 1996). The reasons for not reporting were determined in a survey conducted at the National Victim Center. Forty-three percent of rape victims believed nothing could be done about the rape, and 27% thought the incident should remain a personal matter. Some (12%) were afraid of how the police would respond, and others (another 12%) did not think it was important enough to report to authorities (Kilpatrick, Edmunds, & Seymour, 1992). In 1992, the average sentence for those convicted of rape was 117 months, but the average release occurred after only 65 months (Greenfield, 1995).

Surveys have shown that rape causes mental health problems, with 31% of victims developing posttraumatic stress disorder during their lives (Kilpatrick, Edmunds, & Seymour, 1992).

Domestic Violence

Johns Hopkins did a survey of 2,000 women in 1995 and found that one in three women experienced domestic violence as a child or adult, one in five women experienced domestic violence in adult life, and one in twenty women experienced domestic violence the previous year (McCauley et al., 1995). The Department of Justice reported in 1996 that women are more likely than men to be victimized by an intimate partner; this includes a spouse, boyfriend, girlfriend, ex-girlfriend, or ex-boyfriend (Craven, 1996). Female homicide victims are more likely to have been killed by husbands or boyfriends than male victims are to have been killed by wives or girlfriends. In incidents of homicide between intimate partners, boyfriends killed 26% of female murder victims, while girlfriends killed 3% of male victims (Craven, 1996).

Domestic violence is repetitive, with one in five women victimized by a husband or spouse reporting that she had been the victim of at least three assaults over the previous three months. Twenty-seven percent of the women injured by intimate partners required medical attention, while 15% of the men did. Women experience over 10 times as many incidents of violence from intimate partners as do men (U.S. Department of Justice, 1994).

In 1994 a nationwide study of emergency rooms indicated that 27% of all women who sought treatment for injuries resulting from violence had been hurt by a current or former intimate partner (Craven, 1996). This actually increases the number of cases of domestic violence over the Bureau of Justice crime statistics.

BATTERERS AND RAPISTS

Men who batter their intimate partners generally tend to minimize the abuse or deny it altogether. Rarely do they accept responsibility for the abuse. They often blame the victim for causing the violence. Most batterers are complacent in believing they will not suffer any legal or economic consequences as a result of their abusive behavior.

Carl was sure that the "little bit of fighting" he and his partner, Karen, did was "normal." "Every couple has their ups and downs," he told the worker. He did not see any reason for him to get help and denied that the physical abuse he applied to Karen to get his own way gave him an unfair advantage. "Hell, women hit men, too. She could hit back." When confronted by the fact that Karen had needed treatment for severe lacerations, Carl told the worker, "Look, she tends to make a big deal about these things. She knows I love her, and sometimes she forgets that. It makes her feel better to see someone and get a lot of attention." As for accepting help himself, Carl was dubious. "Help for what? Because I fight with my girl friend. C'mon. You have to be joking!"

For the most part, batterers do not act violently outside their home. Experiences and influences have made their violent behavior likely, but these are extremely varied, and there are no clear patterns to use in predicting whether a person will be abusive.

In general, batterers are seeking power over and control of the victim. Contrary to what many believe, men are not suddenly out of control. Battering is a choice made for a specific purpose. According to the Pennsylvania Coalition Against Domestic Violence (1997), the choice includes:

- Who will be battered
- When the person will be abused
- How the abuse will be dealt
- How severe and how often the abuse will be
- The methods of abuse, such as physical or emotional abuse or a combination
- Who will witness the abuse and from whom it will be hidden

Rapists are generally known to the victim. Although rape does occur between strangers, most rapes occur between the victim and someone she knows. Strangers were more likely to use a firearm and to inflict more injury than were individuals whom the woman already knew. Less than 10% of all rapes are committed by more than one person (Tjaden & Thoennes, 1999). Often the rape is committed while the rapist is using drugs and, more often, alcohol. Rape is considered a crime of assault and is carried out as a means of control and domination.

VICTIMS

For too long people assumed that women bring abuse or rape on themselves. We now know that being a victim is due to the behaviors of the abuser or rapist, not the behaviors of the woman. Traditionally rape was considered to be the woman's fault because of her dress or demeanor or the places she went. In domestic violence, men often assert that their partners' behavior is responsible for the violence and that if their partners would just do as they were told, the violence would stop. Women in abusive relationships do not fit a particular personality profile; they come from every ethnic and socioeconomic group.

Attempts to develop sound theories for the notion that women of a certain personality or from a certain economic class are more likely to be abused or raped have been notably mixed. For instance, according to the Department of Justice, white and black women had equivalent rates of violence committed by intimates or other relatives (Tjaden & Thoennes, 1999). Hispanic and non-Hispanic women tended to experience the same rates of violence committed by intimates. This study did show that an income under $10,000 places women in a higher risk category, and that those with incomes over $30,000 are less likely to experience violence by an intimate. Differences were also apparent in regard to education, with college graduates less likely to have experienced this kind of violence than women who had not graduated from high school. Nevertheless, incidents of rape and abuse do occur in every age, economic, and education bracket.

Reluctance to Seek Help

One of the issues you will help many women overcome is the reluctance to seek help at all, regardless of the abuse or assault they have experienced. You may find, for instance, that in some cultures the woman is blamed for the rape or is considered damaged as a result. You might find that victims of domestic violence feel responsible for the abuse and that this is being reinforced by religious leaders and others in their immediate culture.

> Helena was terrified that her rape and the help she had sought would be discovered by her family. In her culture, the rape would have been seen as something she brought upon herself, and she would forever be considered damaged and unsuitable for marriage with a "nice boy." For these reasons, she would not file charges, even though she knew who her assailant was. She declined to come to a self-help group because she might be seen entering the building. The case manager, who met Helena in the emergency room, could do little more than give support at the time of the rape and offer to be available should Helena ever need further support or services. The fact that Helena could call her case manager if she felt she needed to seemed to give her some reassurance at the time, but her case manager never heard from her again.

Another reason a woman might not go for help is that she fears involvement with the criminal justice system. There are mixed results when we look at how the criminal justice system has treated women who were victims of domestic abuse and rape. Although most police departments are working to become more sensitive and aware, many women still feel that they will not be heard and that the male rapist or abuser will be given preference. If the woman is a person of color or an ethnic minority, this may compound her fear of the police. Sometimes women are confused about a private victim service and believe it is part of the criminal justice system. Individuals who have come from countries where police corruption and brutality are common will assume that the situation is the same in this country.

If a woman does not speak the language, if the agency has no bilingual workers to assist, and if the woman fears being deported, she may not come into the agency and seek help for the assault.

WHAT IS DOMESTIC VIOLENCE?

Domestic violence takes many forms, all of it coercive in nature. The definition covers a wide variety of behaviors that include physical, sexual, psychological, and economic abuse. The term *domestic violence* is most often associated with physical assault that can, and often does, result in physical injury. It also can take the form of sexual assault or rape within an intimate relationship.

Types of Abuse

There are four ways to consider domestic violence. These are as follows.

1. *Physical abuse* is what is most often thought of when people mention domestic violence. Dawn Berry (2000) lists "slapping, hitting, kicking, burning, punching, choking, shoving, beating, throwing things, locking out, restraining, and other acts designed to injure, hurt, endanger, or cause physical pain." Indeed, batterers use a variety of household objects such as baseball bats and cigarette lighters, and they also, of course, use knives and guns. Women who have suffered physical abuse can end up with numerous types of injuries from bruises and scratches to actual broken bones and life-threatening injuries. Further, forcible rape between intimate partners is also considered to be domestic violence (Berry, 2000).
2. *Psychological abuse* throws the victim off balance and is designed to make the victim feel less confident and independent. Psychological abuse can take the form of demeaning insults, particularly in front of others. Long-term and denigrating criticism or threats can have psychological ramifications as well. Name-calling is one of the common ways a batterer demeans the victim. Psychological abuse also occurs when the victim is forcibly isolated from family and friends, and held to unreasonable rules in conducting her life both inside and outside the home. Ann Jones (2000) points out that forcing a victim to do something she does not want to do, or preventing her from doing something she wants to do, can be part of psychological abuse. Further, she points out that sometimes yelling, threatening, swearing, and sulking are written off by others as the batterer just getting things off his chest.
3. *Emotional abuse* is closely related to psychological abuse. The abuser may destroy valued property or pets, abuse children and pets, and withhold food and clothing, all of which creates fear in and takes a considerable emotional toll on the victim. Jones (2000) writes, "But it is the unspoken agenda of the batterer that makes it so difficult for a woman to think of what to do, or even to grasp what's going on. (Battered women commonly report great confusion and the fear that they must be going crazy.)"

Miyako is from Japan. She met her husband, Paul, when he was stationed there in the military. Paul has never hit Miyako, and in public he is a most considerate and loving husband. At home, however, he has strict rules about what Miyako can do. Paul has determined who she can talk to on the phone, when she can go out, what she can wear, and what makeup she can use. He accompanies her on all shopping trips, stating he needs to keep track of how the money is spent, as he earns that money. Miyako is prevented from attending any outside activities. She is disciplined (usually no supper, or no TV) if Paul feels the home is not as clean as it should be or the dinner is not prepared to his specifications. Miyako is unhappy and homesick, but because she recently came to this country, she is unaware of the help she could receive.

4. *Economic abuse* takes the form of cutting the victim off from any independent financial source such as a job or money to meet her own needs. Andrea Lissette (2000) writes that economic abuse "can include abusing mutual assets by placing ownership of vehicles, registrations, property, leases, stocks, bonds, or credit cards in one partner's name in exclusion of the other's rights and use." A batterer may attempt to keep a woman from being successful in her work by keeping her up late at night, failing to provide transportation or child care so she can work, hiding her clothes or the tools she may need to take to work, and causing visible injuries the woman is too embarrassed for others to see.

In 1995 the National Safe Workplace Institute did a survey in which they found that 94% of the corporate safety directors in the survey ranked domestic violence as a high security problem. Research from the National Workplace Resource Center (1995) showed that 26% to 50% of abused women have lost their jobs because of abuse-related performance problems. Seventy-five percent of victims of domestic violence are harassed at work, and 90% of these victims lose at least one day of work a month due to injuries sustained from domestic abuse.

According to Ann Jones (2000), laws regarding domestic violence have been changed partly because of the cost to businesses. She writes, "Advocates pointed out to businessmen the economic costs of battery: federal officials estimate that 'domestic violence' costs U.S. firms $4 billion a year in lower productivity, staff turnover, absenteeism, and excessive medical benefits." Jones also notes that victims of abuse are more likely to miss work, be late for work, and use "company time and company phones to call friends, counselors, physicians and lawyers they didn't dare call from home."

Other Aspects of Domestic Violence

Aside from the considerations raised by the four major areas of domestic violence, other aspects of such abuse that also demand attention include the following.

1. *Abuse of former partners.* Stalking, assault, and harassment of former and current intimate partners are all part of the picture of domestic violence. It may be violence against the person the perpetrator is dating, married to, or living with—or it may occur after separation and even after divorce. This type of violence can happen in both heterosexual and homosexual relationships. It is always a pattern of purposeful behavior that seeks to control the victim and gain complete compliance.

2. *Relationship link.* Domestic violence occurs within a relationship. Often this leads society to take this kind of violence less seriously. The "family" nature of the relationship gives perpetrators social, if not legal, permission to use tactics to control their victims. Many feel they are entitled to use these tactics. Unlike stranger-to-stranger violence, perpetrators have continual access to their victims and know their daily routines and their vulnerabilities. Being intimate partners, however, means that after a violent episode, perpetrators continue to be able to exercise physical and emotional control over their victims' daily lives. Perpetrators have intimate knowledge of their partners' problems and concerns and use these as leverage to assure compliance (e.g., withholding medication when the victim has a medical condition, or threatening the children or a beloved pet).

When Kitty took her cat to a no-kill shelter because her husband continually hit the cat and threw things at it, she was severely beaten for "not asking permission" to remove the cat from the home. Besides, her husband told her, he loved that cat, and the cat had preferred his company to hers.

3. *Patterns of abuse.* Abuse does not occur as a single isolated event, but is instead a pattern of various tactics used by perpetrators against their victims over the course of the relationship. An episode of abuse can consist of one tactic, such as punching, repeated over and over. Another episode may involve a combination of tactics, such as punching and name-calling, threats, or harm to personal property. Later episodes may again consist of a single tactic, such as a slap or a certain threatening look. In some cases, physical assault is used less often, while name-calling, threats, and intimidating gestures are used daily. One of the ways of maintaining control over the victim is to remind her of what happened the last time with threats to repeat the abuse if she does not comply.

   Some abuse, such as physical assault, sexual assault, menacing, arson, kidnapping, and harassment, is obviously illegal in all states. Some forms of abuse are legal, although they are not considered healthy or productive. These include abusive tactics such as name-calling, interrogating one's children, and denying one access to money or the family automobile.
4. *The escalation pattern of abuse.* Early in a relationship, abuse is often hard to spot. As the abuser takes more and more independence away from the victim, he typically does so under the notion that he is doing it out of love and concern for her. He may, for example, isolate her and take charge of all finances. In time there may be an acute episode that involves a display of physical force and makes it perfectly clear the abuser has control over his partner. It may involve physical force against the victim or begin with physical damage to pets and personal property.

   There generally follows a de-escalation process in which the batterer apologizes profusely, offers to get help or stop drinking, insists that she is the only one who understands him and that he cannot go on without her, and promises the behavior will never be repeated. In this phase he successfully avoids the consequences of his battering, denies the seriousness of it, and enlists the woman in going on as if it never happened.

   After this period of remorse, tension begins once again to build in the relationship until another acute episode occurs. These episodes generally increase in violence and severity the longer the relationship lasts.

5. *Psychological damage.* The victims of domestic violence respond to the entire pattern of their perpetrators' abuse, not to a single episode. As a case manager, you may be dealing with a single episode that resulted in injury, but your client is dealing with this episode in the context of all the other episodes, ranging from overt and obvious abuse to the subtle threats she has endured on a daily basis.
6. *Problems when leaving.* While the rest of society may think the victim is in part responsible because she stays with the perpetrator, most victims are well aware that leaving poses severe risk. In fact, the statistics bear this out. Separated and divorced women were 14 times more likely to report violence by a spouse or ex-spouse. In fact, 75% of all reported spousal abuse comes from separated and divorced women, who comprise only 10% of the population. When a woman finally leaves or indicates she is leaving for good, she is at heightened risk for homicide. It has been estimated that about half the homicides of female partners or spouses occurred after the women left the batterer. Women who are partners of batterers often sense this clearly and do not risk their lives by leaving (Harlow, 1991).

LEAVING AN ABUSIVE RELATIONSHIP

Understanding why your client might be reluctant to leave can be one of the most frustrating problems you will encounter in working with victims of domestic abuse. You know abuse is going on and you believe your client is in danger, but she is either reluctant to leave, or she leaves and then returns to her abuser. You need to understand this from her perspective.

The Leaving Process

"Leaving is a process" (Hart, 1990b). Very few women leave one day and never go back. For most women, it takes time to fully break with the relationship emotionally and begin to envision an independent life without the abuser. The first time a woman seeks your help and actually leaves may be a test. She is hoping that by leaving him, he will change or get help—that he will see how important she is to him and take real steps to end the abuse. The second time a woman leaves it may be to gather information about what supports and resources are out there for her. The third time she leaves she may be leaving for good. Nevertheless, a woman may leave more than once to try to force her abuser to get help or stop the abusive behavior. If each time he promises to reform his behavior, she may be lured back into the relationship.

Most women in abusive relationships do leave in time. They find that easier to do when the community in which they live makes leaving easier. This means that friends, family, social service agencies, police, clergy, shelters, courts, medical personnel, educators, and therapists must be ready to make considerable effort to assist the woman who is leaving. As you look at your community, see if you can find hindrances to a woman's being able to leave an abusive relationship.

Barriers to Leaving

There are seven barriers that often keep women from leaving an abusive relationship. Understanding the possible barriers your client faces as she contemplates leaving will make your work with victims of domestic violence more effective. These barriers, which are discussed in the following text, come from a paper written by Barbara J. Hart, Esquire (1990b), who has devoted much of her life to the problem of domestic violence.*

Hope for Change

In general, abusive mates become remorseful after they have inflicted violence. The batterer may allow the woman to feel she has the upper hand for a while, promising never to hit again if only she will promise to stay. Women often strike that bargain with their batterers. They, in turn, will threaten that if another episode of abuse occurs, they will leave for good, but this tactic rarely works. Nevertheless, the abusive mate may promise never to hit again, agree to seek counseling, and demonstrate his love for her in ways that are meaningful to her. He may point out how hard he works and the terrible stress he is currently under. He may acknowledge how wrong he has been, and he may apologize to the entire family and ask their help in stopping this behavior. A woman in a committed relationship, one that she expected to last a lifetime, hopes that the abuser's tears of contrition and promises to seek help and reform will actually bring about positive changes.

Isolation

Many women have no support for leaving. Many batterers make a systematic effort from the beginning of the relationship to isolate the woman from those who would give her support. Ways this can be done are to prohibit her from using the phone, censor her mail and other contacts, humiliate her in front of her friends and family, and drive her everywhere she goes, including work. The behavior illustrates a sense of entitlement and ownership in which the man feels a right to expect absolute obedience and all of her attention. This possessive and jealous attitude may belie a sense of insecurity about the woman's allegiance, and many women wage a futile struggle to assure their men of their loyalty. In addition, men often know that those who care about the women would urge them to leave if they knew the truth.

Societal Denial

Many batterers are otherwise socially well liked and successful. Their abusive behavior is only practiced within the family where others cannot observe it. In considering leaving, women may fear that no one will believe their description of the abuse. Agencies may make light of a woman's situation without understanding her feelings of being imprisoned or her fears of being seriously injured or killed if she stays. She may encounter physicians who think she is hysterical and prescribe Valium for her, ministers who tell her to pray for her husband, or therapists who see the problem as one of poor communication. If no one takes her seriously, she is likely to believe they would not support her breaking up the family.

Barricades to Leaving

Women who decide to leave may find their way blocked as their partners threaten to obtain custody of the children, withhold support, interfere with their employment, advise prospective landlords that they are not credit-worthy, or attempt to turn the children and other family members against them. Some men threaten to commit suicide if the woman leaves. You will often encounter women who are afraid to go because of a threat like this. Helping the woman to recognize whose decision it actually is to commit the suicide can be helpful. Escalating violence as the woman appears to be ready to leave or is leaving is also common.

Source: From *Seeking Justuce*, by Barbara J. Hart, Section 6, pp. 1–3.

Belief in Batterer Treatment Programs

Some men enter treatment specifically to keep the woman from leaving. A woman may be convinced that the program will help her partner to make the necessary changes to stop the battering. She may feel that if she leaves, she will be responsible for her partner dropping out of treatment or for breaking up a relationship prematurely. It is helpful to give the woman accurate information about these programs, including how many men revert to their original abusive behavior following treatment. In addition, helping a woman to recognize that a man must get help for himself, rather than simply to keep her in a relationship, is a worthy goal. He needs to make decisions for himself, and she needs to make decisions in her best interests.

Dangers in Leaving

Many women know that leaving will cause a considerable increase in the violence. As noted, many women die at the hands of their batterers at the time of leaving or after leaving the relationship. The planning, particularly when children and pets are involved, can be overwhelming. Legal safeguards have to be considered as well. If you have a shelter or agency that assists women in leaving, you have ready answers to these issues.

Make certain that there are ways to accommodate the children and their needs to continue school and be safe. In addition, if pets cannot be accommodated at the shelter, work with a no-kill animal shelter to see if arrangements can be made for them. A woman may return to the home to rescue a pet and end up being hurt further if this detail is not addressed.

Economic Autonomy

According to Barbara Hart (1990b), the "most likely predictor" of whether a woman will return to her abuser is her economic situation following her departure. Economic supports such as welfare, employment, job training opportunities, and even legal support decrees are all important if the woman is to develop a life independent of her batterer. The economic situation is one of the first things you should explore with your client.

STALKING

Stalking is most often associated with domestic violence. Anyone being stalked must invest considerable energy into hiding or making herself safe from her stalker 24 hours a day. Fear, anxiety, and a disrupted daily life are all results of being stalked.

Stalking by former boyfriends and husbands is often done by the stalker as a way of exacting revenge on the woman for leaving or as an attempt to force the woman to return to the relationship. One study estimates that 90% of the women killed by current or former partners were stalked first. The Pennsylvania Coalition Against Domestic Violence (1997) provides the following definition of stalking:

1. Repeatedly following the other person on foot or by vehicle
2. Repeatedly harassing the other person by such methods as numerous phone calls or hang-up calls; sending unwanted gifts, cards, or letters; and threatening by phone or mail
3. Repeatedly intimidating the other person by watching him or her outside the home or workplace; appearing at the same places he or she goes, such as restaurants or movies; and joining the same organizations or showing up at the same activities

In 1991 California passed the nation's first antistalking statute in response to the often deadly consequences of stalking. Since that time, all states have passed a similar law. Most states view stalking as an intentional action designed to make the victim feel afraid for her safety and to cause her substantial emotional stress.

Assignment

Find out what laws exist in your state against stalking. Is stalking a misdemeanor? At what point does it become a felony? What are the maximum sentences? What happens if the stalker has been convicted of stalking before?

SAFETY PLANNING

Safety should be a top priority in your work with clients of domestic violence services. In many cases, it will take precedence over any other intake procedure. You will work with your client to plan for her safety. There are a number of things to consider that she may not have thought about in the anxiety of the current situation. Here are some things to discuss with your client as the two of you work out a safety plan for her.

1. *For her daily schedule,* she can park close to the entrance of her home or wherever she is going, vary her daily routines and routes, and vary her places for shopping and other activities. She should also consider accompanying her children to the school bus stops.
2. *To protect herself in the use of her mail,* she should consider removing her address and telephone number from her checks, destroying any mail she discards, and receiving mail at a private company such as Mail Boxes Etc., which will ensure her more privacy than a post office box. She can use this as her official mailing address.
3. *To secure the telephone,* she can make sure her telephone number is unlisted and unpublished. She can also use a tracing device to trace unwelcome and harassing phone calls. The trace must be done immediately after the call. Check with the local telephone company to find out how a person does that. In addition, the woman can use caller ID and "blocking" of her own phone lines so her name and number cannot be revealed when she places a call, and she can screen calls with an answering machine.
4. *At work,* the woman might have coworkers screen her calls, visitors, and incoming mail. She can supply them as well as company security with a photograph of her stalker and a description of his vehicle. She can make sure she never leaves the workplace alone, particularly at night.
5. *In the car,* she should park in well-lit places, keep her car doors locked, change the car locks if she and her stalker shared the car at one time, get locking hood and gas cap devices, and know where the nearest police and fire stations are where she can get help if needed while she is out.
6. *At home,* the woman should keep her doors and windows locked, change any locks for which he might have a key and install deadbolts, keep lights and a radio or television on at all times, and maintain a smoke detector and an operating fire extinguisher. In addition, she may want to inform trusted neighbors or her apartment manager about the stalker, giving them a description or a picture of him and his vehicle. Finally she should identify visitors before she opens the door

and arrange a signal (e.g., lowering a certain window shade or turning a porch light on and off) for neighbors to call the police.

Documentation

When you plan with the client about her concerns for her own safety, help her to understand the importance of documenting any contacts she has with her stalker. Get her to note the date and time as well as the location the incident took place, and have her fully describe the incident. She may not see the importance of this initially, but if stalking becomes a dangerous problem, she will have the documentation required to demonstrate her need for more vigorous protection.

Reasons Not to Require a Safety Plan

It is never a good idea to require women to pursue specific safety options as a condition for receiving services. In some states, centers and shelters for victims of domestic violence are required to make women seeking assistance take specific steps on their own to ensure their safety. Women may be asked to keep their batterers from interfering with their work activities, but this may not be something they are able to do. Women cannot be held responsible for their batterers' behavior. Another example is insisting that women take out protection-from-abuse orders. As we will see later, this can actually increase the risk to a woman's safety. At other places, women are required to pursue safety options that are not really available to them or do not exist in their own community. For example, a woman might be required to enter a shelter when there are none in her area, or to attend a support group when the nearest group is two hours away. She might agree with the welfare office to do certain safety activities only to discover later that they are not available to her.

Individualize the Safety Plan

All safety plans, like all service plans, should be individualized. Some women create safety plans that seek to eliminate all of the abuse that is occurring, including psychological and emotional abuse. These plans are not limited to just the physical abuse. Some women create plans that allow them to stay in the home, while others have plans for leaving the home. Some women may work with you to develop a long-range plan for safety and leaving, but others may plan only for the short term.

There are two reasons why safety plans should be individualized. First, it is important that the woman be safe; and second, her opinions and needs should be the basis of any plan. She alone has lived with the situation, and she has definite ideas about when she might be in danger and when she might not be. For instance, some women want to inform their employer of the abuse and the need for safety at work, while others fear losing their job if the company feels threatened by the presence of an employee who is likely to attract an abuser to company property.

Plans change as circumstances change. One circumstance that affects the plan is the abuser's reaction to the woman's strategies and whether or not the strategies are successful. If she finds that something she tried did not work well, she will want to make some revisions. Accept that you and she will work on the plan, adjusting it to meet the current situation. Do not act as if the plan is written in stone and cannot be changed.

Safety at the Hospital

If you are called to the hospital to interview a person who is a victim of domestic violence or rape, make sure that you conduct the interview with the woman in private. The abuser may insist on being present and that the physical injuries be termed an accident. The situation can be confusing to a new worker, so it is important that you understand before you get to the emergency room how to handle this.

In most hospitals, close family members are allowed to accompany their relatives back to examining and treatment rooms. Some of these hospitals do not draw a distinction between domestic violence or rape injuries and other accidents, allowing the abuser or rapist to accompany the woman to the room for treatment.

Insist that you conduct all your interviews in private. *Do not ever turn to the victim and ask her if she wants the family member or significant other present in the interview room.* Make it look as if it is your policy and the policy of your agency. Be warm and put the person you are asking to leave at ease, saying that you want to speak to him after you complete your interview. Do not even glance at the victim to see what she might want. An abuser or rapist who needs to control his victim will blame her for the decision to exclude him from the interview, and this may result in serious abuse after they leave the hospital. If the person will not leave, you may have to get security personnel at the hospital to assist you.

New workers often feel intimidated by an abuser or rapist who is loud and demanding. Once you allow the abuser or rapist into the interview, however, the woman cannot freely discuss what has happened, and you have lost the opportunity to be helpful to her.

If the victim insists that the abuser or rapist remain in the room in spite of your attempt to conduct the interview privately, continue the interview, but be aware it is compromised. In closing the interview, make sure she has information about how to reach you. Be matter of fact in handing her your card.

Assessing Lethality

In an article entitled "Assessing Whether Batterers Will Kill," Hart (1990a) discusses how to assess lethality. Some elements appear to make it more likely that a batterer will actually kill his victim or even take his own life. Most victims of domestic violence are not killed, but every case needs individual assessment. Following are some points to consider in the assessment:*

1. Have there been threats to kill others or himself?
2. Has the batterer a plan or a fantasy that includes killing himself or his victim?
3. Does the batterer have access to weapons?
4. Does the batterer insist that the woman belongs to him and that no one else can ever have her? Does he indicate she is not entitled to any life apart from him?
5. Is the batterer virtually isolated except for his partner whom he depends on to organize and sustain his life?
6. Does separation or the hint of separation cause great rage?
7. Is the batterer depressed, with little hope of improving the situation?
8. Does the batterer have easy access to the victim?
9. Has there been a history of violence with calls to law enforcement?
10. Has there been a sudden change in risk taking in which the batterer appears to have no concern for the consequences of his behavior or for himself?

**Source*: From *Seeking Justuce*, by Barbara J. Hart, Section 6, pp. 8–9. Copyright Pennsylvania Coalition Against Domestic Violence. Used with permission.

If any of these elements are present in the history you take, you may conclude that the batterer is likely to kill his victim or himself. In such a case, you need to take extraordinary precautions in working out the safety plan with your client. If you are assessing and treating the batterer, and you conclude that he is likely to inflict harm on the victim, many states require that you inform both the police and the intended victim of your suspicions. You may need a mental health commitment, if this seems reasonable. Always talk frankly to the victim about what these indicators could mean.

There should be considerable concern when a batterer takes a hostage. It is estimated that between 75% and 90% of all hostage taking in the United States is related to domestic violence.

Batterer Programs

As mentioned, women often mistakenly feel safer when their abusers are enrolled in a batterer's program. Programs can range from educational groups to self-help to a counseling format. Some are court-mandated and can be used in some communities to avoid prosecution, for plea bargaining purposes, or as a condition of probation or parole. Programs may be sponsored by a domestic violence program, a mental health program, or a family services agency.

In most programs, men are confronted with the consequences of their behavior and held responsible for this behavior. Rationalizations and excuses are confronted, much as excuses for drug and alcohol abuse are confronted in recovery programs. Alternative behaviors are explored.

Such programs, however, have had mixed results. In many of them, batterers are likely to drop out or not show up at all. There is no clarity at this point about how to structure programs for batterers that are successful. Some believe counseling is the best approach, while others use the educational approach; some are long-term, while others are less than three months; and some address mental health issues while others do not.

PLANNING TO LEAVE

Another issue that requires careful and individualized planning is how the woman leaves. She may call you saying she wants to leave her abusive relationship, but she probably has not thought the process through entirely. Your help in thinking about everything that needs to be considered may make the difference between her leaving safely and endangering herself.

First, consider emergencies in which the woman's life is in danger. She needs a plan for how to leave the house safely in a crisis. Go over with her what windows, doors, stairwells, or fire escapes she might use to leave the presence of her abuser. Help her to think of a safe place to keep her purse and car keys so that she can get to them quickly. She might leave money, keys, important documents, and extra clothes with a close friend or someone else she trusts, so that she is not trying to gather things at the last moment or in a crisis.

Talk to her about where she will go when she leaves. Many women do not leave because they fear placing others in danger if they go to another's home. Discuss the possibility of going to a shelter if there is one available. Ask the woman if she knows of other safe places she might go in an emergency.

Be sure she has committed the phone number of the hot line or shelter to memory. Discuss a code word that she can use to indicate to her children that they are leaving or to family and friends that they are coming.

Long-term planning to leave might include opening her own bank account, obtaining her own credit cards, and redirecting mail from those accounts to a mailbox at a private firm such as Mail Boxes Etc. To prepare financially, a woman might take job training or start school if she is able to do that without escalating the violence.

CHILDREN AND DOMESTIC VIOLENCE

According to Dawn Berry (2000), "Adults frequently underestimate the level of suffering and damage inflicted on children who witness domestic violence" (p. 131). Most experts agree that homes in which domestic violence is present are homes where children are very likely to be abused as well.

Two areas of a child's health and development can be affected when there is domestic violence in the home.

1. *Physical injuries* can result from being hit by objects thrown by the abuser. Young children caught in this type of crossfire sustain more serious injuries than older children because of their small body size. Older children can be hurt physically when they attempt to protect the victim. Boys often try to protect their mothers, while girls often try to protect younger siblings.
2. *Emotional abuse* occurs when children witness or hear abuse and experience ongoing tension in their homes. Child development experts and children's counselors warn that children exposed to violence can become violent themselves, and many have witnessed this violence toward others in children as young as 3 or 4 years of age.

In both physical and emotional abuse situations, children often come to blame themselves and continually look for ways to keep their parents from fighting again. According to Berry (2000), children from abusive homes "exhibit poor health, low self-esteem, poor impulse control, difficulty sleeping, and feelings of powerlessness. Problems at school often include difficulty getting along with others, fewer interests and social activities and misconduct."

The abused parent can rarely give support to the child because she is often focused on her own survival, and she might be depressed. This makes her unavailable to give her children the type of support that might mitigate, to a small degree, the damage caused by witnessing abuse in their home.

In other words, children exposed to violence in their homes have less chance of growing into healthy, productive adults. That is why changing the cycle is so important, but as Berry (2000) points out, "Society has accepted the fact that direct abuse should be considered a serious and unacceptable social issue, but few see these secondary victims in the home where only the mother is battered." As a society, we are not adequately addressing or taking seriously enough the damage that occurs to children who live for prolonged periods in abusive homes.

Leaving, Visitation, and Support

For many women, leaving is complicated by the need to consider their children. One of the most important ways children can be helped is by removing them from the violent situation. This cannot be done easily, and the victim of abuse has many things to consider before deciding to leave. Berry (2000) points out that children who are removed to the homes of friends or relatives can end up in a cycle of moves from place to place, including return to their homes where abuse is taking place. Some mothers fear that leaving will cut off support needed to feed and clothe their children. Another concern is losing custody. It is common for abusers to threaten to gain custody if the woman decides to leave. "In fact, children are better off in a peaceful, loving, one-parent home than a violent, threatening, two-parent home" (Berry, 2000).

A battered woman may be blamed for the trauma her children experience from witnessing the abuse, but most experts agree that women go to considerable lengths to protect their children and carefully weigh the options and dangers in the choices they have available. Such a decision is entirely the woman's to make, and what may appear to others as vacillation or indifference is often a woman trying various solutions and weighing her choices.

Visitation and support are issues taken up by the court and are areas in which women face increased risk. Visitation rights for the abuser may open an avenue by which he can stalk and harass the mother. The abuser may be given the right to come to the home to pick up the child, may threaten or injure the child for leaving with the mother, or may threaten the child if the child returns. Some children are forced to see parents they do not want to see at present. Some courts, looking at these likely outcomes to visitation privileges, arrange for supervised visitation where the child and abusing parent meet in a location away from the home. If children have been abused by the abuser in the past, it is important to question the wisdom of letting them visit their abusive parent alone or unsupervised. If you are supporting a woman through this phase of her leaving, you might suggest she ask for supervised visitation arrangements.

Collecting support is another area that leaves women vulnerable. They may find that in seeking enforcement of support orders, they are further harassed or threatened. Rules for collecting welfare can jeopardize women from abusive relationships. They can be forced to seek support in order to receive welfare, but in doing so, they may open themselves to further abuse. In some states, welfare offices are making exceptions for women seeking welfare in order to remain independent of an abusive relationship.

Children are a major consideration when addressing domestic violence. If the cycle of abuse from one generation to the next is to be broken, and if children are to grow up to be healthy, productive people with better methods for resolving conflict, we must focus on the toll domestic violence takes on the children who are involved in it.

Assignment

Look at the state regulations regarding applications for welfare. Does your state or local office make any provisions for women who are leaving an abusive relationship? Are there staff who are specifically trained to work with these women? Does the welfare agency have specialized services or referrals for victims of domestic violence when they apply for welfare?

PROTECTION FROM ABUSE ORDERS (PFAs)

These orders, which are generally issued by a judge, are basically "no contact" orders. Most programs to assist the victims of domestic violence assist victims of stalking and harassment in obtaining such an order. Discuss this carefully with your client. While the order will ensure specific consequences for violations against the woman, it often inflames the situation, making the man more determined to get to the woman to show her "who's the boss," often with deadly consequences.

Assignment

Find out whether PFAs are available in your community and how a victim of stalking or harassment would go about getting one. Find out where they are filed and whether all local police units have access to the order even when regular business hours are over.

Protection orders may not work for the following reasons:

1. The batterer may refuse to obey the court order regardless of the consequences to him.
2. The batterer may increase the violence when he is served with the order.
3. The protection order may not include the children. If the children are with her and he still has access to the children, he may still have access to her.
4. The batterer may lose his job as a result of the order. This can reduce the support a woman is expected to receive.
5. She may lose her own job when she misses work to go to court to obtain the order.
6. The protection order may include his having to leave the home, and she may not be able to afford to stay there on her own.
7. The batterer may end up finding the woman who is in hiding because during the legal process to obtain the court order, he is able to obtain information about where she is, and he has contact with her in court.

When a woman has chosen to use a PFA, it is important to go over some strategies she might follow. First, she needs to keep the order on her or nearby at all times. She should copy the order and give copies of it to police departments in communities where she lives, works, and visits. Her employer should also have a copy. It might be useful to give a copy to a close friend and to leave a copy at her children's school and day-care center. Advise her that if her PFA is destroyed or lost, she can get another from the court that issued the original, and that if her abuser violates the order, she can notify the police.

HOUSING

Housing becomes a priority for women who must leave their homes. Often women begin by moving into an emergency shelter. Generally these are 30-day or 6-week programs, giving the woman enough time to begin to plan for herself and her children. Many shelters today are overcrowded, forcing programs to place women in less secure arrangements such as motels, hotels, or converted private residences. These are often expensive alternatives and do not meet the needs of children.

After her stay at the shelter has ended, the woman may move into short-term housing programs. These are often a year in length and may be as long as two years. For example, in one community, women left the shelter for apartments run by an agency for women and children. The program, which lasted two years, provided case managers to assist the women in developing a plan for job training, employment, and the needs of their children. A children's case manager then worked on plans for each individual child, seeking ways to overcome the trauma of the violence they witnessed or experienced and looking at each child's special talents, interests, and academic needs.

Long-term housing is next, housing in which the woman lives on her own and hopefully is self-supporting or working toward financial independence. In many communities, there is a lack of this sort of housing. Children and a limited income often make it hard to obtain long-term housing. Many do not want to rent to women with children or to women who may have a potentially violent ex-partner on the premises. If a woman needs to conceal her living arrangements from her former partner, she may need to move to an entirely new community, a difficult adjustment at best.

Public housing often has long waiting lists, and some women have no place to stay while they wait to get in. In some communities, however, battered women can identify themselves as such and be selected from the waiting list ahead of others because of the potential for harm to them and their children.

When working with your clients to develop a plan, housing may prove to be one of the more difficult issues to address.

ADDRESSING THE NEEDS OF DIVERSE POPULATIONS

We have been looking at domestic violence as an issue as it occurs in the majority of situations. There are other circumstances that must be considered if the goal is to reduce violence between domestic partners.

Rural Communities

Practicing in rural communities is difficult for several reasons. Your own center may be in a more urban area, making it difficult to get out to rural areas. In those places people are often reluctant to ask for help because they know everyone in their small community. Even judges and court staff may know them to some extent. Another barrier to getting help in rural areas is isolation. Women who live out on back-country roads are often unaware that there is help, or they have no protection even if they get a PFA. Another difficult issue is the view in rural areas that men have a right to control women and that asking for help outside the home is bringing shame on the family. These traditional attitudes can extend to the courts where judges may feel a man has more right to the family home than the woman, leaving her to find shelter for herself and her children while her partner remains in the home with all its amenities.

Poverty in rural areas can make taking out a PFA too expensive, and in many rural communities no provisions are made to allow the woman to waive this fee. Surveys of rural court personnel have shown a lack of understanding of abuse and a reluctance to help the abused woman.

Domestic violence programs that serve rural areas face a challenge in advocating for women and in educating law enforcement and the courts. This work may become part of your responsibility if you serve rural areas.

Gay and Lesbian Communities

Domestic or partner abuse can occur among gay and lesbian couples, just as it can among straight couples. Asking for help can put the gay or lesbian victim at double risk. Not only are the usual concerns about asking for help apparent, but gay men and lesbians must also reveal their sexual orientation in the process. Violence between same-sex couples is not a mutual activity, nor is it part of sadomasochistic sexual behavior; these are myths that are used to dismiss the real violence a partner in a same-sex relationship may experience.

Anyone who asks for help because he or she has been abused, controlled, and manipulated is in charge of the definition of abuse. That person can identify when abuse has occurred and seek help for that abuse. Regardless of the sexual orientation of the person seeking your help, you owe him or her the same respect and thorough advocacy that you would give to any client of your agency. Anything less diminishes you as a professional.

Domestic Violence in Later Life

Older women may seek services because they are currently enduring domestic abuse, but often they are reluctant to do so. Our society tends to devalue age, and an older woman in an abusive situation may feel that at her age she is not worthy of the attention and assistance of your agency. When working with older women, you are likely to find one of four scenarios:

1. Some women report that the abuse began in their childbearing years and has continued throughout the relationship. Some of these women have had contact with domestic violence services or law enforcement in the past.
2. Some older women may indicate that they were married for some years before the abuse began. These women are often concerned that there is something wrong with their spouse, a mental health or physical problem that has caused the abuse to begin. Generally these women report having made a good life together with their spouse, including children, family traditions, and friends, before the abuse began.
3. Another group of older women seeking help are women who began their relationships later in life. Some of them find themselves in their first abusive relationship. Some are widows or divorced, and some have their own jobs and financial resources. For them the abuse may be frightening and confusing, or they may take steps to protect themselves as soon as they identify the abusive behavior.
4. A final group of women have entered the relationship later in life, and some time after that the abuse began. Each partner may have older children, and each may have lost friends and family. Leaving the relationship may feel like yet another loss, one too difficult to sustain.

Agnes and Harry were married for 40 years before his retirement. After Harry retired, he became irritable and angry. Agnes felt he was at loose ends without his job and tried to interest him in other activities. Instead Harry followed Agnes around the house, commenting on what she was doing and often offering suggestions and being extremely critical. Agnes made light of this, assuming that Harry was having trouble adjusting to retirement.

As time went on, however, Harry became more and more abusive. One evening as Agnes was sweeping the kitchen, Harry grabbed the broom and hit Agnes with it because she was not sweeping the kitchen as he thought it should be swept. Agnes tried to leave the kitchen, but Harry grabbed her arm and twisted it. He ended up breaking her arm. At the hospital, Harry joked to the case manager that "we were just fooling around."

Eventually it was the couple's daughter who convinced Agnes that this could not go on. The daughter took Agnes into her own home and took her father to a doctor. In the ensuing examinations, it was determined that Harry had suffered a stroke and had high blood pressure. The doctor and the case manager were able to work out a plan for the couple that placed Harry on medication and got him involved in activities outside the home. The doctor was hopeful that with proper medication, Harry would be less irritable and more likely to develop interests on his own. The case manager would remain in touch with Agnes, but it would be some time before it would be clear whether these interventions were successful.

Reluctance to leave or to get help on the part of these women often stems from erroneous beliefs and attitudes. For instance, they may have decided that they are somehow responsible for the abuse because they have not yet figured out how to behave "correctly" to avoid it. You may find that they make excuses for the abuser's behavior, citing his age, deteriorating health, retirement, and so forth. Some will tell you that it is not as bad as it used to be when the couple was younger.

Older women may feel exceptionally vulnerable. Leaving raises fears of retaliation, particularly if they have been threatened by their abusive partner. The abusive partner may have threatened to kill the woman, her friends, her children, or her pets. As we have seen, leaving can be extremely dangerous for women.

You may find that adult children have mixed feelings about their parents separating. Some may have been abused as children or may be in abusive relationships themselves. An older woman may tell you that she is unwilling to upset her children by leaving.

The health of your client may make leaving particularly difficult in later years. If she hears and sees less well than she did previously, or if she is having trouble walking, she may be less likely to leave. Such a situation may require extra help from you. If the woman actually has dementia, you would need to report the situation to protective services as a case of elder abuse. Some older women are in good health, but are reluctant to leave because the abusive spouse is in ill health and they feel a need to stay and care for him.

Economics play a part in the decision to leave. A woman may fear losing financial security and feel her choice is between continued violence or poverty. Many report having no employment history or education. They may not be eligible for Social Security or Medicare benefits.

In our society, we tend to focus on younger people or people in our own age bracket. Older women who seek help from your center may need particular sensitivity from you regarding the issues they face.

Violence Against Latinas

You must consider racial and cultural differences when working with Latina victims of domestic violence. Some try to excuse the violence of Latino males toward Latinas, using culture as the excuse. Abuse is a crime, regardless of culture, and culture should never be used as a reason for not enforcing the law. Understanding the culture, however, will make you better able to help Latina woman in a domestic abuse situation. Getting help is often difficult because of language differences and the lack of bilingual and bicultural services.

Latina women are often the foundation of their families. They are expected to be dutiful mothers, daughters, and wives, putting their needs last. Women are expected to take partners for life, and usually they defer to their husbands, although in family matters they often have an equal say. Patriarchal families are not uncommon. Many Latina women believe that if their partner is abusive, it is God's will.

As we have seen, in many cultures males believe they have the right to control and abuse their partners. In Latino families, the woman, unlike her counterpart in other cultures, is more likely to accept and revere the authority of men and see the abuse as the will of God. In many Latino communities, the woman is expected to follow Catholic dogma and to be traditional and conservative in her religious beliefs.

Seeking help may be "seen as a public act of disrespect and as an act against God," according to David Abalos (quoted in Barrientos, 1995), a professor of Latino culture at Seton Hall University. "That certainly puts women in quite a bind. If you are defying God's will, you don't have a leg to stand on. The importance of the family in Latino culture should be understood. A woman may say she would rather take the abuse than leave the abuser."

What you may find is that Latina women may be "ignored by men because they are women, ignored by white culture because they are women of color, and often ignored by the English-speaking because they speak Spanish" (Castillo, n.d.).

Teen Dating and Violence

Violence against teenage girls occurs for the same reasons as violence against women: power and control. Teenagers, however, have fewer resources to which to turn in this situation. Often they are unaware of programs for battered women, and they may believe violence is the price they have to pay for having a boyfriend. Friends often dismiss the violence by telling the girl she is lucky to have boyfriend, and peer pressure can prevent her from leaving the relationship. In addition, the possessive nature of the abuse and the jealous reactions of her boyfriend, coupled with his dominance, are often interpreted by a teenage girl as positive signs that her boyfriend has made a loving commitment to her.

Lily did not like what was happening between Rob and herself. He had taken to holding her down until she agreed to do what he wanted. His demands were about little things, really, she told herself, like not going to the movies with her friends that night, or not wearing her hair a certain way because he liked it better another way. At first it was exciting to Lily to have a boyfriend, and to have one so intensely interested in what she was doing. Rob was attractive, and Lily's friends made playful remarks about how lucky Lily was to have Rob as a boyfriend.

When the slaps and pinching escalated to hair pulling and punches and Lily sustained bruises, Lily's mother became involved. She had not liked Rob's constant need to know where Lily was and what she was doing even when she was with her family. She and Lily went together to see a therapist; Lily's mother expressed her concerns, and Lily was able to talk about the relationship. In time Lily broke away from Rob and began to resume her interest in her schoolwork. She was accepted at a good college, and began to feel better about herself.

Abuse of adolescent girls lowers their self-esteem and isolates them, making a full and productive life all but impossible. This occurs at just the time the girls would be experimenting with their interests and talents and looking forward to living out their potential.

Instead, girls who are being abused often withdraw from their peers and from their studies. They sometimes dress differently, drop old friends, and behave in ways that are unlike how they behaved previously. Someone else is controlling them. Battering often occurs when these young women insist that their partners wear a condom or abstain from sexual activity. "[T]wenty-six percent of pregnant teens reported they were involved with a man who physically hurt them, and 40% to 60% said that the battering had begun or escalated" when their boyfriend discovered they were pregnant (Worcester, 1993).

Many believe the "messages" that violence against women is tolerated and that dominance, aggression, and abuse of power and control are appropriate masculine behaviors (Worcester, 1993). Many of the young men who abuse girls come from homes in which their male role models abuse females.

The center where you work may address teen abuse through programming in the schools. There are a number of curricula that are designed for teenagers regarding dating violence and violence-free relationships.

WHAT IS RAPE?

According to the *National Women's Study* (1992), rape is defined as "an event that occurred without the woman's consent, involved the use of force or threat of force, and involved sexual penetration of the victim's vagina, mouth, or rectum." In addition to actual penetration, sexual assault comes in other forms as well. Victims may be violated sexually in forcible and unwanted ways, such as being forced to disrobe, touched inappropriately, or forced into sexual acts that do not involve penetration. In the following text, we will look at various areas of sexual assault of concern to sexual assault workers.

CHILD SEXUAL ABUSE

All states have mandated reporter laws regarding child sexual abuse. You need to look at the laws in your own state to determine under what circumstances suspected abuse should be reported to the authorities and how this is to be done. (See the exercise in Summers, *Fundamentals of Case Management Practice,* 2001, p. 16.)

According to the American Academy of Pediatrics (1994), 61% of all rape victims are under age 18. The U.S. Department of Health and Human Services reports that in 1998, child protective service agencies received 2,806,000 referrals of possible abuse (Shalala, 2000). Upon investigation, it was determined that 66%, or 903,000 children, were experiencing abuse, and 12% of those children were experiencing sexual abuse. Most of those abused are girls. Only a small percentage is boys, although this may be due to underreporting of sexual abuse of males. It is difficult for men to report an incident in which they were powerless and controlled by another when it so obviously conflicts with the image of masculinity in which men are self-reliant and strong. Because most sexual abusers are male, the fear of being seen as homosexual is another reason men and boys tend not to report the abuse.

Risk Factors

Although sexual abuse of males may be underreported, it is still believed that girls are at higher risk. Social class does not appear to make one more or less likely to experience sexual abuse. European American and African American children experience about the same risk.

A number of risk factors may play a role in how likely a young girl is to be raped:

1. Living away from one's mother or father tended to make a child more at risk.
2. Frequent parental illness appeared to be a risk factor in some studies.
3. In situations where there was a lack of parental support, particularly from the mother, the risk increased.
4. Conflict between the parents increased the risk.
5. The presence of a stepfather seems to be another risk factor. (Pennsylvania Coalition Against Rape, 2000)

Signs of Child Sexual Abuse

There are certain signs that a child may be sexually abused. It is important, however, not to assume that every child who exhibits some of these signs is experiencing or has experienced sexual abuse. These signs are red flags that indicate something is wrong in the child's life; what is wrong may bear further investigation.

Refer to Table 4.1 for the usual developmental responses to sexual assault and the best way to handle the immediate situation.

Characteristics of Child Sexual Assault

The following are common characteristics of child sexual assault according to the Pennsylvania Coalition Against Rape:

1. *Engagement.* The perpetrator finds that he has access to the child. Once the relationship is established, the perpetrator will create opportunities to be alone with the child. Generally, no force is used. Instead the child is enticed to play games or cooperate for favors.
2. *Sexual interaction.* Here the line is crossed from signs of affection to sexual activity. Exposing oneself to the child or getting the child to expose herself may be the beginning of a progression into more sexual activity. This activity can escalate over months or years, with the perpetrator determining the time sequence.
3. *Secrecy.* This phase begins during the sexual interaction phase. Using subtle methods, such as making it a game or a little secret just between the two of them, the perpetrator influences the child to keep the relationship secret. Children comply with the perpetrator because they enjoy the attention, receive material rewards, feel loyalty to the parent, have been threatened with physical harm or injury to others close to the child if she tells, or have received threats to break up the family.
4. *Disclosure.* Disclosure may be accidental, as when someone discovers the activity, or because the child has developed a sexually transmitted disease. Purposeful disclosure is sometimes made by the child to obtain help in escaping an intolerable situation. When the child discloses the abuse, a crisis ensues. The entire family is affected in some way by the disclosure. The perpetrator will be at odds with other family members, a crime has been committed, and family members will have to make difficult decisions about what to do next. During this phase, the perpetrator is likely to be hostile, deny the events, blame the victim, and use whatever power he has to regain control of the situation.

   If the perpetrator is one of the parents, the other parent will initially be shocked and protective of the child. Eventually these reactions can give way to

Table 4.1 Developmental Responses to Sexual Assault and Management of Immediate Situation*

Age	Physical and Behavioral Indicators	Management of Emergency Situations
Infancy and Early Childhood (up to 3 years)	Crying, fussiness Underweight Fear of strangers Abnormally withdrawn Abnormally quiet Abnormally noisy Very lethargic or very active Sexually transmitted disease Physical trauma Clinging, whining to nonabusive parent	**Introduction** Introduce yourself and explain why you are there. Explain confidentiality. **Working with Children—Key Issues** A child will reflect the feelings of the parents. Issues can be obscured by parental feelings and attitudes. Parents are also in crisis and react as other victims. Parents feel responsible and ashamed that they could not protect the child. The child needs to be believed.
Preschool (4–6 years)	Distracted with short attention span (less than is usual for a preschooler) Anxious about discussing the incident(s) Confused with inconsistencies when discussing the incident(s) Baby talk, thumb sucking, clinging, fretful Strong manifestation of fears (of all men, all strangers, strange places, going home) Exhibits aggressive behavior Sexually transmitted disease Physical trauma Frightened parents Clinging, whining to nonabusive parent	Penetration is less likely to have occurred (usually fondling and masturbation are typical abuse of children). More physical injury occurs to infants. Toddlers' perceptions of the abuse will seem very concrete; they do not understand the dynamics of the situation. Children (6–12) can relate to what happened and feel embarrassed. Many male children are victims. With intervention, children up to 6 years can "bounce back" easily because they do not internalize feelings like adults. **Working with Children After Sexual Assault** Be calm! Your affect will help shape the child's reaction. Ascertain how the child perceives the assault.
Elementary School (6–9 years)	Complaints of headaches, stomachaches Reluctant to discuss or even admit to incidents Temper tantrums Will not obey rules or observe limits Extremely docile Poor school performance	Speak on the child's level. You may have to use several approaches before you can really communicate with the child. For instance, you may need to play with the child and use imagination.

(continued)

Source: From "Warning Signs of Child Sexual Abuse," in *The Trainer's Toolbox*, pp. 241–242. Copyright Pennsylvania Coalition Against Rape. Used with permission.

Table 4.1 *continued*

Age	Physical and Behavioral Indicators	Management of Emergency Situations
Elementary School (6–9 years) *continued*	School phobia Sexually acting out with peers far beyond average knowledge for elementary school Knowledge of sexual behaviors Sexually transmitted disease Physical trauma Running away Wary of adult contacts	Explain to the child why he or she is at the hospital (to make sure he or she is not hurt, or if there are injuries, so the doctor and nurse can help). Explain the pelvic exam by using words that identify body parts a child uses or understands. Ask the child if he or she wants you to be in the examining room. Although children are not little adults, it is as important to give children control over events as it is for other victims. Reassure the child that he or she is not to blame. The offender is responsible; it is okay to be upset. The child may have ties to the offender, so do not blame the offender. Use as many of the communication skills you have learned to allow for comfort. The extent to which you can use skills depends on maturity, age, and ability to articulate. **Counseling Parents** Help parents understand that the child's reactions result from their attitudes, feelings, and behavior. Explain medical exam and legal proceedings. Help parents focus on the child's pain and refocus their anger on the offender. Help parents understand that their support will facilitate the child's recovery and that lack of support will hamper recovery. Stress to parents that the child should not be forced to talk about the assault, nor should the child be shut off from talking. However the child chooses to react should be supported by everyone.
Preadolescence (9–12 years)	Socially withdrawn: no friends, no school activities, to the point of complete avoidance of peers School truancy Physical trauma Running away Pregnancy Wary of adult contacts Frightened of parents Suicides, delinquency Violent behavior Sexually assaults or victimizes younger or weaker individuals Promiscuous sexual behavior, prostitution	
Adolescence (13–18 years)	Self-destructive behaviors: drugs, alcohol, attempting suicide Truancy Pregnancy Wary of adult contacts Frightened of parents	

Management of Emergency Situations

Counseling Parents *(continued)*

Encourage parents to bring the child for counseling. This is particularly important for children who feel guilty or protective of parents. Explain that it is understandable that they might not know how to deal with the assault of their child. A trained counselor can help.

Explain to parents that if the perpetrator is in a caretaker role (babysitter, foster parent or stepparent, blood relative), the assault must be reported to the agency handling child abuse.

Working with Adolescents—Key Issues

Adolescence is frequently a crisis period in the life of a young person.

The sexual assault may aggravate the larger developmental crisis. This could include severe problems with drugs and alcohol, disrupted home life, and pregnancy.

Feelings of guilt, shame, and extreme vulnerability are apparent in the victim's struggle to maintain independent identity from parents and other adults.

Counselor must affirm confidentiality policy. Primary concern is for the victim, not the parents.

Victim will often express attitudes of peer group.

Assess the victim's reaction to the assault. A teenager's peer group may view rape as a rite of passage.

Victim's age will determine: physical and emotional trauma, acting out behaviors, and counseling needs and the reactions of significant others and professionals.

(continued)

Table 4.1 *continued*

Management of Emergency Situations

Working with Adolescents—Key Issues

Victim's age will determine reaction to protection from the offender. Does the child see removal from the home as punishment?

Prosecution of male breadwinner can lead to financial problems. Nonoffending parent tends to deny incident as loss of spouse, loss of money, and social stigma become apparent.

Working with Adolescents After Sexual Assault

Let the victim know you are there to advocate and to help.

Explain medical and legal proceedings.

Be sensitive and calm. Your reactions can shape the victim's reactions.

Assure the victim you believe him or her.

Betrayal of trust may need to be addressed.

Deal with the anger adolescents may express. Most adolescents have been tricked or promised rewards.

Always assure the victim that the assault was not his or her fault.

Explain why others (parents, siblings) will react as they do.

When appropriate, help victim make decisions about what he or she wants to do.

pressure by the perpetrator and a situation in which the mother feels she must choose between the child and the offender. Often the mother and other family members withdraw from participation to protect themselves. The child is left isolated and comes to feel that she will not be believed, helped, or protected.

Thirteen-year-old Marie had been sexually abused by an uncle who lived next door since she was 9. As the years went by and her parents seemed not to notice the attention he paid to her, Marie became more and more uncomfortable with the situation. She went out of her way to avoid ever being home alone, and she avoided her uncle as much as she could. One night after she had managed to avoid him for some months, he appeared in her room after she had gone to bed. He raped her. Marie pleaded with him to stop, but she did so quietly, hoping that no one would hear and that her uncle would just go away. Marie's mother heard the noise, however, and entered the room to find the two together.

From there the situation became very complicated. Marie's mother went screaming to Marie's father. While the father threw his brother out of the house, the mother called the police. Charges were filed, and Marie's mother accepted the offer of the case manager at the hospital to have Marie attend a group for teenage victims of sexual abuse.

As time went by, the uncle's wife began to blame Marie for the trouble. She indicated that "blood is thicker than water" and that the family should drop the charges. The uncle, too, began to insinuate that Marie had "asked for it." Marie's parents became less interested in pressing charges as other family members continued to pressure them to "think of the family." In the end, Marie's long-term support came from her case manager and the group she attended.

5. *Suppression.* Intense pressure is brought to bear on the child to make her suppress what has occurred. Threats about what will happen to the family if others find out are one way to make her remain silent. The family may work together to suppress publicity and details of the abuse and to resist interventions by the case manager or law enforcement. The child can be convinced by others in the family to minimize what happened.

What Children Need to Be Told

If a child does not receive support from her family and others close to her, the case manager may be the only person giving the child the support she needs. Following are some ways you can make it easier for the child to trust you.

Children need to be told over and over that they are not to blame. Children may feel that they are in part responsible and must be told that they are not at fault. Be sure that when you work with the victim of child sexual abuse, you make this point many times.

Children will not be sure that you believe them, even if they do not come out and say so. The adult may be denying the allegations or telling an entirely different version of events, and adults have more power. Make it clear to the children with whom you work that you believe them.

Children, particularly older children, may be horrified by what happened to them and afraid that you will feel the same way. Children need to know that this has happened to other kids and that you have talked to other kids about it. Let the children know that you are not going to be made uncomfortable by what they have to tell you.

Let children know that you will do all you can to keep them safe. You cannot promise realistically that the child will never go through this again, but you can promise to work hard to protect her.

Finally, let the child know what will happen next. If she will have to tell her story to others after she talks to you, tell her that. Do not trick the child into telling you the story by promising her that you are the only one who will hear it. These children have been tricked already and should not be tricked by you.

Trauma of Child Sexual Abuse

Children have many fears about disclosing what has happened to them. Fear is one of the main reasons children are reluctant to tell what happened. Common worries children have are:

- Getting in trouble for their part in the abuse
- Causing trouble for other people
- Being punished as a result of telling others or telling the secret that was not supposed to be told
- Losing important adults in their life
- Being removed from their home

Children will also often feel anger toward a variety of people. They may feel anger at the perpetrators who used power to abuse them or anger at others in the family who did not protect them. Sometimes children are angry at themselves, particularly when they see that their disclosure has caused so much trouble. If someone else disclosed the abuse, children may feel anger toward that person.

Guilt and shame are common reactions that are related to the children's belief that they engaged in something bad, or caused the abuse to take place. They may feel they deserve to be punished. Children may believe unrealistically that they could have and should have stopped the abuse themselves.

In an article written by Finkelhor and Browne (1988) entitled "Assessing the Long-Term Impact of Child Sexual Abuse," the authors used four categories that they referred to as traumagenic dynamics: traumatic sexualization, stigmatization, betrayal, and powerlessness. "A traumagenic dynamic is an experience that alters a child's cognitive or emotional orientation to the world and causes trauma by distorting the child's self-concept, worldview, or affective capacities." The following text examines these four categories in more detail.

1. *Traumatic sexualization.* Here the child's view of sex and her own sexuality are influenced in ways that are not appropriate for the child's age. The child may come to associate painful memories of sexual abuse with sex in general, or a child who was rewarded for sexual favors may come to use sex as a way of manipulating others. The child may begin to believe that her sexuality is her only important asset.
2. *Stigmatization.* The child is stigmatized by others who communicate shame, guilt, and immorality to the child. Secrecy demanded by the perpetrator can add to the shame, and the reactions of others to the disclosure can increase feelings of guilt. The authors believe that stigmatization is the primary reason victims of child sexual abuse are often self-destructive, isolate themselves, or engage in criminal behavior.

3. *Betrayal.* Trust is destroyed by the trauma of child sexual abuse. Children are likely to feel abandoned by others, and this feeling is made worse when they realize that they were harmed by the very people who should have protected them. During the course of the abuse, children can be manipulated and lied to, and their needs can be cruelly disregarded. If others who could protect the child or believe the child's description of what took place fail to do so, there is further betrayal. Betrayal may make it hard in the future for victims to have healthy intimate relationships; such people may be vulnerable to further victimization.
4. *Powerlessness.* The child generally lacks the power to stop the abuse and often lacks the power to make others around her believe that the abuse is taking place. Powerlessness is thought to contribute to general fearfulness, nightmares, running away, and even delinquency.

Child Sexual Abuse Accommodation Syndrome

According to *The Trainer's Toolbox* (Pennsylvania Coalition Against Rape, 2000), the accommodation syndrome is a pattern of behavior that is generally present as children attempt to cope with sexual abuse. First, the children must contend with keeping the secret because keeping the secret has been held out as a guarantee that everything will be all right as long as they do not tell. Children know, on the other hand, that the secret is being kept because there is something wrong and even dangerous about the abuse they are experiencing.

Children submit to the abuse with feelings of helplessness and without resistance because they do not have the power to stop the abuse. Gradually the children develop survival skills in order to handle the ongoing abuse. They may deny the events are taking place, blame themselves unrealistically, or dissociate. To ease the pain, some children use drugs or alcohol.

If and when disclosure does occur, it is likely to be delayed. Often it occurs only after the victims feel the disclosure can no longer inflict damage on others or during a time when separation from parents is important. The disclosure may not be convincing. If children appear to be well adjusted after disclosure, adults may believe that something as terrible as sexual abuse never happened. If children are rebellious, adults are likely to interpret the disclosure as punishment of the adult who has set limits and given discipline. In either of these cases, the children's stories are not believed.

Finally, the child may very well retract the disclosure. If the perpetrator has told his victim that she is responsible for holding the family together, for protecting her other siblings from abuse, for protecting her mother from falling apart, and for protecting her father from temptation, he has acted irresponsibly and made the child feel responsible for things the adult should be handling. These responsibilities often cause a child to retract the disclosure.

Working with Nonoffending Parents

When the offender is a parent, often the nonoffending parent (usually the mother) finds that the disclosure threatens her marriage. The parents' reaction may create additional pressure on the child to retract the disclosure. In addition, parents may become hysterical, and the hysterical reaction may be more upsetting to the child than the crime. Sometimes when the parents become overprotective, the child experiences that as punishment.

You need to give time to parents whose children have been sexually assaulted and refer them for more counseling when that seems indicated. Discuss with the parents in detail how their reactions will affect the child. Make sure that you stress to parents the need to refrain from blaming the child for what has happened. Prepare the parents to help their child handle internal blame.

Some parents become entirely caught up in their own needs. For example, they may feel that talking to you threatens them in some way. They may want to keep the abuse a secret from others. You should be aware of parents' needs and help parents to look at the fact that what they need may not be what their child needs at the moment.

To work with parents, listen. Recognize the parents' needs and concerns through active listening (see Summers, *Fundamentals of Case Management Practice,* 2001, pp. 134–152). Give parents the time they need to adjust to what has happened.

SEXUAL ASSAULT: THE ISSUES

When you work with individuals who have been sexually assaulted, a number of issues need to be addressed in the healing process. The issues listed in this section may sound like issues for therapy that should be addressed in a therapist's office to which you have made a referral. Actually, many of your clients will need or request a therapist. Many, however, will enter support groups that are run by workers in shelters or rape crisis centers. In these groups, the women talk about the abuse with each other, attempting to clarify what happened and to put the events in some clearer perspective. Following are the issues noted in *The Trainer's Toolbox* (Pennsylvania Coalition Against Rape, 2000) with which you may hear women grappling in support groups.

Rebalancing Power

Women who have been in a situation in which they were not in control and were powerless need to reassert their own power in their lives. You can facilitate this by allowing your client to make her own decisions and to take control over the way her life will proceed from here.

Clarifying Blame, Guilt, and Responsibility

Victims of sexual assault do not always believe that they are not to blame for what happened. What seems obvious to you, for example, that an older child or adult is the perpetrator of the crime, may be unclear to the victim. Children often blame themselves. For instance, they may feel they did something wrong that brought on the abuse or that they should have found a way to stop the abuse.

Some victims have a hard time excusing themselves. You may find, for example, that your client cannot really accept that she is not to blame because to do so would leave her with feelings of powerlessness and rage that are very uncomfortable and troubling. As long as she can believe she had some part in the assault, those feelings are less painful.

Establishing Self-Identity and Bodily Integrity

Women often need to address the fact that they are not deserving of the abuse they have experienced and that their body is entirely their own. Many women find that sexual abuse makes them feel damaged or dirty, or leaves them feeling that they are powerless individuals at the mercy of others who are stronger and more powerful. Children often experience sexual abuse as a literal body experience; as a result, they may develop distinct somatic complaints. Adults may experience the pain of the abuse in a more mental and emotional way and seek to handle that pain through drugs, alcohol, suicide attempts, eating disorders, or self-mutilation.

Defining One's Own Sexuality

Sexual abuse is not sexually motivated. It is motivated by a need to control and take power. Nevertheless, a victim may have conflicting views of what is appropriate sexual behavior. Guilt, anger, or fear may accompany normal sexual feelings, making it difficult for the woman to enjoy close, intimate relationships.

Tolerating Diverse Feelings

An example of how a victim must tolerate diverse feelings is found in the situation of the daughter who is abused by her father. The daughter must tolerate feeling rage at her father and love for her father all at once. A woman may not see that there is room for all her feelings. She may believe she is unbalanced in not being able to choose mutually exclusive feelings, when in reality mixed feelings are perfectly normal.

Reparenting from the Age of Assault

Most clients could not have survived emotionally without freezing certain parts of themselves and their feelings. It is not uncommon to find individuals who have gone on after sexual abuse as if the abuse never occurred, sometimes for years. Sometimes developmental needs are frozen in the process. A victim may need to back up and look at those issues and get the support to grow and heal.

GENERAL INFORMATION ABOUT CRISIS INTERVENTION

A crisis in a person's life refers to an event or situation that has rendered that person unable to cope, particularly using methods that have worked for him or her during ordinary difficulties. Crises throw people off balance to the extent that they cannot direct their own lives and feel that the circumstances have overwhelmed them. Rape and domestic violence are only two of the crises you may be involved in with your work. Elderly individuals have crises in their lives, as do individuals with mental disabilities. Women's centers generally have a crisis intervention process in place because of the unpredictable nature of rape and domestic violence and the shattering consequences they have on people's lives. What is written here about crisis intervention will be useful to you in handling many different crises in your work.

All individuals have a normal way of functioning that has more or less worked well for them prior to the crisis. When the usual ways of handling stressful circumstances fail, the person's behavior becomes less and less effective. If these ineffective and random attempts to handle the crisis are uninterrupted, the person is likely to experience psychological disintegration, and the disorganized behavior may become more permanent. A person may deal with the crisis in many different ways: contemplating suicide, drinking or taking drugs, overdosing on medication, crying, exploding with hostility, withdrawing from family and friends, or showing depression or panic.

Crisis intervention seeks to interrupt the downward spiral immediately, before the person has time to engage in many ineffective and maladaptive actions in trying to solve his or her problem. The crisis worker intervenes, acting as a person on whom the client can rely and from whom the client can receive direction when that is needed.

A crisis in a person's life appears to run an almost predictable course. *The Trainer's Toolbox* (Pennsylvania Coalition Against Rape, 2000) lists seven stages from the point of crisis to the rebalancing and moving on. These stages are:*

1. *Shock and disorientation.* This is where you will come in and hopefully offer support and stability.
2. *Expression of feelings.* Your presence and good communication skills should facilitate this.
3. *Denial.* At some point, the enormity of the situation may lead the client to minimize the event or situation and assure you that he or she is doing all right.
4. *Sadness.* Recognition that the events were not in the client's control and the resulting guilt, self-blame, and loss of esteem and personal security lead to profound sadness.
5. *Letting go.* After receiving services, processing, having a good listener, and integrating the experience, perhaps through support groups or therapy, the person is able to let go of the event and begin to focus on the future with more hope.
6. *Acceptance.* Once the person has accepted what happened and the changes it has created in his or her life, the future can be approached more positively.
7. *Reflecting.* For many years afterward, the person may reflect on what happened, often searching for the good that came of it or the spiritual reason this event took place. Reflection is done with the separation from the event that is provided by the passage of time.

Your agency will have a carefully outlined procedure for dealing with a person experiencing a crisis. This procedure will seek to manage the crisis, not solve the person's problems. Once your clients have returned to their normal level of functioning, they may need further assistance in resolving the issues that brought on the crisis. In that case, you would make a referral where counseling and psychotherapy would take place. Do not confuse crisis intervention with therapy. Instead, view it as a process to manage a life crisis so that the person experiencing the crisis can return to his or her normal way of functioning and find rational solutions to resolve the problems.

According to James L. Greenstone and Sharon C. Leviton, in their book *Elements of Crisis Intervention* (2002), there are six steps to a successful intervention. These are discussed in the text that follows, along with an additional step that is useful in crisis situations.

1. *Act immediately.* This is done to interrupt the somewhat chaotic responses in which the individual is engaging. The minute you come in contact with the client, on the phone, at the hospital, or at the crime scene, you are beginning the process of crisis intervention.
2. *Take control.* Many students comment on how difficult it is to see themselves as the person in control when they are just out of school. At the time of a crisis, the

---

**Source*: From "Crisis Theory," in *The Trainer's Toolbox*, p. 186. Copyright Pennsylvania Coalition Against Domestic Violence. Used with permission.

client does not know and does not care that you are just beginning to practice. What the client sees is a person who has come to help and upon whom the client can rely. Do not make things more complicated by hanging back and acting tentative. Even when you are unsure, act as if you know what needs to be done. You can call others for direction if you are unsure, but make the phone call look as if it is a part of your routine procedure. It is your job to appear supportive and to lend support and structure to the crisis.

Make Accurate Observations

It is not easy to take control if you have not observed the client and situation carefully. Enter the crisis with caution, and be alert to everything you see and hear (including nonverbal cues) and to what you sense or feel about the situation. Careful observation is your basis for establishing a good foundation for resolving the issues.

Remove the Client If Useful

Part of taking control is to remove the victim from the crisis scene. In your work with rape victims, you may remove them to the hospital and find a place for them to stay afterward that is removed from where the rape took place. In domestic violence situations, you generally have the option of offering shelter to the client to remove her from the abusive situation.

The Client Interview

Victims of rape and domestic violence need information that you can readily supply. Tell the client what the likely course of reactions will be. Let your client know that he or she may react in a unique way and that these reactions are common and to be expected. One way to help victims heal is to talk to them about pairing their panic reactions to the cues in their environment. Helping victims to recognize what triggers these panicky feelings will help your clients know what to work on and diminish the feelings of "going crazy." Tell your clients that flashbacks are common; and in follow-up discussions, you may want to ask victims if they have experienced these.

3. *Listen.* Allow the client to talk about the crisis. This is particularly important when the person has been the victim of a violent crime, such as rape or domestic violence. Talking about what happened can desensitize the person to the events. As the client tells the story several times, he or she begins to hear the events and to integrate them into his or her total life experience. A small degree of acceptance of what happened begins with the listening you do during the crisis intervention. Not allowing enough time to listen can circumvent a good recovery. It is your responsibility to give the client time to talk thoroughly about the event.

   You may find that the victim with whom you are speaking wants to protect family and close friends. Many centers give support to family members, and victims need to know that. Assess whether the client is likely to neglect his or her own needs for those of the people closest to him or her. Look at the support networks clients have available to them.

   This is the time clients may discuss with you the concerns they have about the incident. For instance, concern about HIV/AIDS may come up now for rape victims. Domestic violence victims may raise concerns about prosecution. A client contemplating suicide may be concerned about what living holds in store for them. Let clients tell you about their concerns, and discuss possible ways to address these.

Some clients are not ready to talk at the time of the crisis. Let the client know that the center will be there to listen when the client feels more comfortable. Explain that most people want to talk about it eventually, and if there is no one close to the client to listen, there will be people to give support at your center.

4. *Assess the situation.* This is part of your keen observations. Look at what the immediate concerns are at the time. Document what caused the crisis at this time and not at some other time. Ask yourself what exactly is troubling the client right now. Do your assessment at once. Unlike therapy, where the therapist has time to make an assessment over several sessions, the crisis worker must assess immediately, and that assessment begins as soon as he or she comes in contact with the client. Do not concern yourself with extensive background. Instead, look at the last 48 hours to determine what precipitated this crisis. All the listening and interviewing skills you will need to handle a crisis are covered in the chapters on communication skills in *Fundamentals of Case Management Practice* (Summers, 2001, chapters 8–11).

   While you interview your client and listen to him or her, remain calm and supportive. Do not judge your client's reaction. Allow the person to feel what he or she feels and to express what he or she needs to express. Be willing to listen to whatever the client wishes to talk about. Clients do much better if they have been able to ventilate their feelings to a person who is empathic and supportive.
5. *Decide how to handle the situation.* Your presence and your supportive demeanor make it easier for the client to sit with you and explore possible options and creative solutions. Alone the client has felt that nothing can help and the situation is out of control and beyond resolution. With your help, possibilities can emerge. Help the client look at personal resources and ways to effectively bring those into play.
6. *Make a referral if needed.* If your agency does not have the specialized services your client needs, refer the client to an agency that does. In domestic violence programs and rape crisis centers, specialized services for victims of those crimes are usually available, but some clients need more. Sometimes the client has an issue or problem that the agency cannot address. At other times a client may have problems that fall outside the scope of your agency's focus. Another agency may better address those difficulties. For more information on how to make a referral, consult *Fundamentals of Case Management Practice* (Summers, 2001, pp. 270–273).
7. *Follow up.* Following up is enormously important in giving your client a sense of stability. As the person moves away from the crisis and into services, your follow-up adds continuity. In small agencies, you may be the person who follows the client through services and follows up to ensure that the client makes contact successfully with the service provider and that the client is able to use the services. Again, rape crisis centers and domestic violence programs usually offer most of the services needed, which makes follow-up simpler to accomplish.

HOT LINE SKILLS

You can find most of the communication skills you need to work on a hot line in the companion textbook, *Fundamentals of Case Management Practice* (Summers, 2001). You need careful preparation in communication skills to handle hot line calls and other crises. Some of these calls will be from victims of abuse or rape immediately following the incident. Others may call months or years after the event, feeling that they cannot make sense out of it or integrate what happened to them. Some victims call because they are contemplating suicide.

Rape victims, it has been determined, are four times more likely than noncrime victims to have thoughts about suicide and thirteen times more likely than noncrime victims to have attempted or completed suicide. Individuals who call you because they are suicidal want to end the pain they are feeling because that pain has become unbearable. Their call to you is a last-ditch attempt to find another way to cope.

You need to be able to talk openly about suicide with the caller while providing support and hope. Do not make false promises, but discuss openly the other options to suicide that are available to the person (hospitalization, medication, therapy). Talk with the client about what a good situation would look like, and ask the client what specifically needs to change in the present situation.

Use good listening skills. Empathize, ask open questions, reflect feelings, and ascertain why the client called you now, and not at some other time. Do not put the client on hold. If the suicide seems imminent or the person has already taken an overdose of some sort, have a coworker get the call traced so that medical help can be on the way. Find a way to have clients come to a place where help is available.

Crank Calls

All hot lines experience crank calls from time to time. They may be from adolescents who are playing what they consider a practical joke, or they may be from others who are disturbed and need to obtain some form of gratification. Your agency should have a procedure for handling crank calls. If such a procedure is not available, initiate the task of writing one for the future. Following are the kinds of crank calls you are likely to get and ways to handle these.

1. *Hang-ups.* Stay perfectly matter-of-fact. If hang-ups persist, take the phone off the hook for a few minutes. You can also tell the caller that the line is tapped and the phone company is recording all phone numbers of calls coming into the hot line.
2. *Heavy breathers.* First ask if you can help them. It is wise to begin by assuming these calls are sincere, since it is possible a person could be having extreme difficulty talking about his or her victimization. Tell the caller that whenever he or she is ready to talk, you are there to listen, and acknowledge how difficult talking about assault can be. If the caller has not spoken after a sufficient length of time has passed, hang up.
3. *Obscene calls.* Remain matter-of-fact. Do not allow the callers to think they have upset you. Remain disinterested and hang up.
4. *Pseudo calls.* These calls may sound genuine at first, but often the caller's purpose is to carry on an obscene conversation with you. Watch for requests to use intimate words or expressions. If the caller is a repeat caller, listen for changing facts and exaggerated circumstances. Certainly provide information and referrals if requested. Hang up if you are absolutely certain the call is not from a real victim.
5. *Resistant or chronic callers.* As with all other calls, assess the needs and work toward resolution. Chronic callers should be limited to one or two designated helpers, and the calls should be scheduled. If the caller is resistant to the help, suggest small accomplishments. Focus the call on needs and problem solving, not on social exchanges, in order to prevent people from using the hot line as a means of socializing. If the caller continues to call repeatedly, remind him or her of the agreed-upon schedule and hang up with firm kindness.

Never end any hot line call disrespectfully or angrily. You can vent your frustration and anger to a coworker after you hang up, but do not vent those feelings to clients, who are vulnerable in spite of their frustrating habits.

RESPONDING TO A RAPE OR DOMESTIC VIOLENCE CRISIS

These guidelines are reprinted with permission from *The Trainer's Toolbox* (Pennsylvania Coalition Against Rape, 2000).

At the Scene

You may be asked to go to the scene of the crime while the police are still there. When you arrive, introduce yourself as a worker or advocate from the rape crisis center to the officer in charge, and ask him or her where you can sit and talk with the victim. If the victim is already in an interview with the police, do not interrupt. Instead, listen carefully to what the victim is telling the police.

Be very careful not to contaminate the crime scene in any way. Do not handle things, rearrange things, or walk through areas that the police have designated as part of the scene. In some cases, the scene may be taped off to prevent others from entering.

When you talk to the victim, let her know what is going on. Point out that there will be collection of evidence, that the police will want to identify and interview any witnesses, and that there may be a pursuit and apprehension of her assailant. You will know from your work at the center how your local hospital handles rape victims and collects evidence. Use this time to prepare the victim for what will happen at the hospital.

At the Hospital

If you are meeting the victim for the first time at the hospital, introduce yourself to hospital staff and ask to meet with the victim. Seek privacy; ask for a private interviewing room where possible. Begin by explaining to the victim who you are and why you are there. Before you continue, ask the victim if there is someone she would like you to call.

If a rape has taken place, a particular procedure will take place at the hospital. The doctor or nurse will gather evidence from the victim's body using what is called a "rape kit." This process carefully collects evidence and documents it. The victim may assume that she will be having a typical gynecology examination, so she needs to know beforehand that it will involve other procedures. Hair samples may be pulled, body orifices may be swabbed for evidence, and nails may be scraped and blood samples taken. In addition, the victim's clothes will be taken as evidence. All of the evidence will be sent to a laboratory for analysis. Let the victim know that similar evidence will be taken from the assailant if he is found. The evidence will be used in court to support the victim's testimony about what happened.

Stay with the victim during the wait to be seen by medical personnel. This is a difficult time, during which the victim may be in the first stages of recognizing and accepting what has happened to her. Your listening skills are very important here (see Summers, *Fundamentals of Case Management Practice*, 2001, pp. 121–177).

Following the examination and any medical care, talk to the victim about what she will do now. The objective is to make sure your client is safe. If she has been involved in a domestic violence situation, you may be able to offer her shelter. With a rape victim, talk about places (e.g., with friends or family) she can go for the night. Explain what will happen if charges are to be pressed. Explain that there will be an ongoing police investigation, during which the victim may be questioned further. Tell the victim that if that is the case, you or someone from your agency can accompany her to these meetings with law enforcement. Point out how difficult these interviews can be, often leaving the victim feeling as if she is on trial. Prepare your client for the questioning, and give her the reasons for the questions that will no doubt be asked.

Before you leave, be sure that you inform the victim of several items in a way she can hear and remember. First, be sure the client knows that your center will be available for ongoing support. Make sure the information the victim needs to contact your agency is given. Give your card, and if the agency has a brochure explaining services, give that to the client as well. Ask the client if you can call the next day to see how she is doing. This is called a follow-up call. In most crisis situations, it is important to follow up the next day, and even several days or a week after that. The victim will be coming to terms with the event during this time, and a good listener is crucial to long-term adjustment.

Your client has several rights of which she should be made aware. First, the client has the right to decide whether she will report the crime to the police. This decision belongs to her, not to you or others assisting her. If police or emergency room staff are not interested in protecting her rights or are not aware of her rights, they may ask questions that are not relevant to the incident, but instead pry into her private life. Your client does not have to answer questions that are not related to the investigation, court proceedings, or medical treatment. Finally, she may encounter officials who doubt that a rape took place or who trivialize the incident, particularly if she is in an intimate relationship with her assailant. If your client encounters negative attitudes and begins to doubt herself, you will need to remind her that any unwanted sex act forced upon a person is considered sexual assault.

There are some special considerations you should know about individuals who may become your clients from various populations. For children at the hospital or in an emergency, refer to Table 4.1.

Female Victims

Female victims will generally need to ventilate, and you will need to use good listening skills and not cut off this phase of the interview too soon. During the initial interview with the victim, you may find that embarrassment may be the main factor in whether or not she tells her family and friends. The decision not to tell them can cut her off from valuable support she might need in order to recover, but the decision is hers.

As you talk with the victim, remain calm. Let her know why you are there and assure her that everything she tells you will remain confidential. Ask her if she would like you to be present while she is examined, and explain the medical examination to her. She may question the need for the examination, in which case you will need to explain why it is necessary. First, the medical examination provides evidence for the police, and second, it allows medical personnel to treat the victim for injuries from the assault, prevent pregnancy, and treat her for any sexually transmitted diseases. You will also want to make sure she knows what services are available and what legal options she has available. She may feel ambivalent about prosecuting the offender. During your time with her, this is an area you can help her clarify and resolve.

If you do not have a good opportunity to really inform the victim of the services and procedures or to really listen to her, ask if you can call her soon to see how she is doing. If she agrees, follow up within a day or so.

Male Victims

Men, like women, have many feelings about the rape and a sense of loss of control. Particularly acute may be a sense of a loss of manhood. Adult men will have a more difficult time verbalizing how they feel. For them, remaining unaffected and in control may be far more important than ventilating how they are feeling. Men are particularly likely to feel embarrassment and an intense fear of having others know about what happened. Homophobia, the fear of homosexuality, may be apparent in what a male victim says to you, and you will need to address this with him. Reassurance that an assault does not make him homosexual is extremely important. This is a crime committed against his will, and not something he brought on himself. Help him to focus on the responsibility of the offender, and reassure him that he, or something about him, did not provoke the attack.

When you enter the room, introduce yourself and tell him why you are there. Use all your listening skills to help him ventilate to the extent that he feels comfortable. Do not pry or ask multiple questions. Assure him that his masculinity is intact. Assault is an act of power and violence. It is expressed through sex, in this case. Help him to see that the myths he has learned about rape are probably not true. Go over the physical examination. Explain that he will be examined both orally and anally for forensic evidence and that a rape kit will be given to the police.

Parents of boys who have been raped need to receive support. One thing they need to know is that the rape will not affect the boys' future sexual functioning. Parents need to know that their reactions can shape their sons' reactions. It is best for them to remain calm and matter-of-fact, while at the same time supporting their children's feelings and actions. Make it clear that their support is key to whether their sons will recover well.

Elderly Rape Victims

It is important to know that an older person will suffer more physical pain than a younger person. Bones are more easily broken, and there is a higher incidence of tissue damage. Preexisting medical problems such as heart disease or high blood pressure may be aggravated by the assault. The age of the victim will determine the extent of the physical and emotional trauma, the degree to which the victim acts out, and the counseling the person needs. The reactions of professionals and others to the rape of an older person also will be different.

The most common psychological reaction in an older person is to feel vulnerable and less physically resilient than before. Some focus on their old age and feel that death is imminent. If the victim was sexually inactive for years, the sexual assault, especially sodomy, can be particularly traumatic. Most sexual assaults of older women occur in their own homes, often in association with a burglary. For this reason, your client may indicate a fear of going home.

One of the first things you will want to do is to assess the support the older person has available. Without support there can be long-term symptoms of the crisis. In addition, you may need to assess the person's cognitive ability (see Chapter 8). A decreased cognitive ability may make it harder for the older person to remember details or to cope with the event. The older person may resort to more childlike behavior. A stressful crisis such as rape can make it that much harder to cope.

Begin by addressing your client as Mr., Mrs., or Miss, and do not use the person's first name unless you are specifically asked to do so. Do not treat the older person in a patronizing manner because your goal is to help the person regain dignity and respect. While you are talking to the client about what happened, assess the attitudes and feelings she holds about rapes and sexual assault. These attitudes and feelings will give you a clue about how she will cope with this event. Your client may have a hard time describing what happened for a number of reasons. Seeing and hearing impairments, as well as dementia, all contribute to reduced awareness. If your client appears to be so cognitively impaired that she cannot understand what is happening or why you are there, she will still respond to a caring attitude on your part. Be sure to look at whether she needs emergency funds if she was robbed, and whether she needs shelter if she cannot or is afraid to return to her own home.

The suspicion was that Mrs. Parnes had been raped by an attendant at the home where she was staying. Mrs. Parnes had cognitive impairment and was partially deaf, making the interview difficult. A nurse giving Mrs. Parnes a bath became suspicious when she saw the patient flinch during bathing. On closer examination, it was obvious that Mrs. Parnes had suffered abuse, and from the evidence the nurse felt it was sexual in nature. The nurse had Mrs. Parnes taken to the emergency room, and a case manager from the rape crisis center was called to meet Mrs. Parnes when she arrived.

The evidence collected in the emergency room strongly indicated that a rape had taken place. In addition, Mrs. Parnes had suffered a small fracture to her wrist. The case manager found her client to be frightened and afraid to return to the home. Most of the work the case manager did in the next few days was to give comfort and support to Mrs. Parnes as the family made arrangements for her to be placed elsewhere. The case manager also supported the family and the home when charges were filed against the perpetrator.

Victims Who Use Drugs and Alcohol

Use of an intoxicating substance can make a person more vulnerable to sexual assault, in part because of the impaired judgment that occurs as a result. The presence of such a substance does not necessarily mean that the victim is addicted to the substance that was used. If the victim is intoxicated, giving her coffee will not make her sober, and may make her more agitated. Furthermore, the person may have been forced to use drugs or alcohol or may have been drugged without her knowledge.

When you approach the victim, be calm and nonjudgmental. If there is considerable impairment, you will have to explain the procedures more slowly, and you may need to take on some of the tasks the victim might ordinarily handle, such as calling family or friends.

Victims with Mental Disabilities

You will have particular considerations in dealing with victims with mental illness or mental retardation. You may find that the disability has made the victim more vulnerable to sexual assault. You may find that your attempts to talk to the victim are difficult because of the victim's ways of thinking, which might include tangential thinking, flight of ideas, or delusions. (For a complete list, see chapter 17 in Summers, *Fundamentals of*

Case Management Practice, 2001.) Behavior may be inconsistent, reactions may appear inappropriate, and hallucinations may be present in which the person responds to voices. The victim may be extremely fearful of you and of hospital staff and have a difficult time remembering basic information about herself. As you listen, you may find that the person speaks slowly and moves deliberately. A person who is mentally retarded may have a concrete understanding of what happened in the same way that a child would understand the situation.

Give support in any way possible that you find has a positive effect upon the person. If the person is having trouble sticking to the subject, do not try to use active listening. You might want to begin with some reality-testing questions such as "Where are you?" or "Do you know why you are here?" Find out from the victim if there are social service personnel, family, or friends who can be called to give support. Other agencies that are serving the client with mental or developmental disorders will not be as familiar with the needs of sexual assault victims as you are, and you will find yourself acting as an advocate for the client to help other agencies give the support that is needed.

You will want to try to explain the medical and legal procedures. This may be difficult if the person is having trouble understanding what you are saying. Try to keep the information from being too technical, and use words the client is likely to use. If you have established rapport with the victim, accompany her to the physical examination and lend support. For some clients with mental disabilities, the examination may seem like another assault, and your reassurance during the process may be imperative.

COMMON CONCERNS

As you talk with the victims of violent crimes, you may come across predictable concerns. Following are some of those concerns and ways to address them.

Embarrassment

The victim is often embarrassed about having to talk to the police about the incident. Victims of domestic violence often perceive that others will blame them for not leaving, and victims of rape may find it embarrassing to go through the physical examination and to describe what happened. Be matter-of-fact and explain that these feelings are perfectly normal. For some people, describing the event may cause enormous embarrassment because they find it necessary to use words they have never used in public. Your role is to be patient and to make the client feel comfortable while talking about what happened.

Who Will Have to Know?

Male family members may have a difficult time accepting what happened, and the victim of rape may be well aware of this. If the rape or assault occurred during underage drinking, that may be another reason why the victim may think that family and friends will blame her, rather than the offender. If the family is at the hospital, try to have a counselor available for them, and let them know that a counselor at the center is available to discuss their concerns.

Other victims fear the incident will appear in the paper. Although most papers do not give the victim's name in a rape situation, they are likely to do so in domestic violence situations. Even without the name, details often make it quite easy to identify the victim. If the media appears to want to print the story, help the victim to understand that the media usually portrays rape victims as either virgins or vamps, and prepare the victim for the likely media response.

The victim may fear the neighbors knowing what happened. In small rural areas, where the victim is likely to be known and perhaps seen as responsible in some way, this can be a real problem. Support the victim in recognizing that she is not at fault and that many people are simply very insensitive.

When Denise was raped, she was in her second year of college. Her parents had asked her if she would baby-sit for a friend of a friend, and Denise had agreed to do it. The children were quite young and in bed when Denise arrived at the home. The parents encouraged her to use the time to study, and then left for the evening. A few hours later the husband returned alone, saying he had forgotten some tickets. He went to the bedroom to look for them and asked Denise to help by looking in other drawers in the bedroom. After a few minutes he came up behind Denise and raped her. He threatened her by saying, "This is a nice neighborhood, and you are a nice girl. I wouldn't tell anyone about this, or I assure you I can ruin your reputation and your family, too." With that he left. Denise's first impulse was to go on as if nothing had happened. No one was there with the very young children, and she felt she should stay with them until the couple returned. When they did, Denise and the couple all acted as if nothing had happened; in fact, Denise assumed the wife did not know what had taken place.

Eventually, Denise found her way to a rape crisis center and was able to talk to a counselor. Her failure to report the rape immediately, to seek medical care, and to tell anyone, even her parents, stemmed from her fear of who would find out and what would happen as a result. It was only after she learned about the confidentiality laws covering crisis centers that she was able to talk to a counselor there.

How to Pay for Medical Care

Your client may refuse treatment because she is concerned about how that treatment will be paid for. Most states have laws to cover the medical treatment of rape victims. Know the laws in your state. Where no laws exist, learn what resources are available for women to receive the care they need.

Whether to Prosecute

Prosecution is strictly up to the victim in a rape case. In a domestic violence case, there may be laws that make it mandatory for police to prosecute whether the woman wants to or not. Some states have passed such laws, taking the responsibility for prosecution away from the woman to protect her from further abuse. Prosecution is difficult psychologically and often embarrassing to the woman. Often she fears having to disclose her prior sexual history. There is always the potential for a second victimization by the criminal justice system. In any case, prepare your client for the realities of prosecution and support her and her decision as she goes through the prosecution process.

In some places, a polygraph test is administered in sexual assault cases. If this is the case, your client could be extremely nervous about the test. You will need to explain this practice to your client and try to alleviate her fears with the facts. If the victim wants you to accompany her to the test and you are allowed to be present, consider doing so. Also explain to her that she has a right to refuse the test.

Shock and Bitter Hatred

The victim may be extremely shocked by the extreme violence and degradation of the act, and may never have experienced hatred with so much intensity before. The strong emotions might seem to be out of the victim's control and therefore frightening. Help the victim to direct the anger where it belongs, toward the offender. She is entitled to those feelings; remind her of that.

Hester had a very difficult time in the group for survivors of rape. She told the group that she was often overwhelmed with a desire to kill the perpetrator, even though he was currently serving time for her rape and the rape of two other women. She was deeply confused by these feelings. "I hate the feelings as much as I hate him! I never hated anyone like this before. I see him as the sole cause of everything that went wrong after he raped me. But I don't want to feel like this. I want to move on to be happy again and full of energy like I was before, not all bogged down with this fury."

It took numerous sessions in group before Hester admitted that her anger was acceptable under these circumstances. In time she came to see that the perpetrator had brought about these perfectly normal feelings. When she accepted them as a normal reaction, she began to move beyond them, and the intensity of her feeling diminished.

Issues Regarding HIV for Victims of Rape

After a rape, fear of contracting HIV is a very real concern for victims. For this reason, women may go first to a medical clinic for testing before they contact the police or seek help from your agency. Some women, for the reasons cited earlier, are reluctant to seek any help, and this may cut them off from valuable sources of information about HIV. In addition, you may find that women have a difficult time describing every detail of the rape. For example, a woman might be ashamed or feel guilt over the fact that the rape was anal. Anal rape, however, places her at greater risk for HIV.

While the victim waits for her test results, she may feel as if all the rest of her life is temporarily on hold. The threat of HIV/AIDS complicates the victim's adjustment to the rape. For instance, she may be very reluctant to tell a partner about the rape for fear of the added potential exposure to the virus. If she does tell her partner, he may become distant because he fears exposure to the virus. In fact, some partners leave. If the victim had been planning to have a child in the immediate future, pregnancy must be delayed. She needs to wait for up to a year to determine whether she has the disease.

Your role in this difficulty is to listen and to help the victim sort out these concerns. Help the victim identify a support system. If she cannot construct one from close family members, help her to look to other sources, such as her clubs or church, for support. Make note of the partner's reaction to the rape. Is he being supportive or trying to distance himself from the victim? Long-term support is crucial during the one-year period in which the victim must await the test results. You might consider forming a support group of individuals awaiting their test results.

Once the test results are known, it is up to the victim to decide with whom she will share them. It is best if you do not go with your client for testing, to allow her to keep the results confidential and to keep the focus of the two agencies separate. For this reason, you should not be the person who gives your client the results of her test. If her test results are positive and she chooses to share this information with you, she will need your support in redefining herself in light of this new status in her life.

Some states require that perpetrators, once convicted, undergo testing for HIV/AIDs. This does not, however, substitute for HIV/AIDs testing and education for the victim. Some perpetrators may never be caught, and some who are caught do not come to trial for many months. In states where the victim must request that the perpetrator be tested, she may be reluctant to do so because she may correctly assume that individuals within the criminal justice system will assume she has HIV/AIDs as well.

The test performed to determine the presence of the virus is a blood sample. It is taken from the victim or the offender and analyzed for the presence of antibodies to the HIV virus. The analysis is not for the purpose of looking for the virus itself.

ONGOING CRIMINAL INVESTIGATIONS

After the initial crisis, a criminal investigation is likely to take place. Encourage the victim to share everything she remembers about the incident with the investigating officer. When rape is involved, there are a number of circumstances she could be reluctant to share. If she was drinking at the time, if she and the perpetrator had consensual sex in the past, or if the assault occurred as a result of her presence in a bar, the victim may feel that sharing these circumstances will impugn her rather than her assailant.

As stated earlier, in many states, the victim of domestic violence does not have to press charges. The police are authorized to press assault charges without her. Laws have been passed to give the police this authority because so many victims of domestic violence feel intimidated by their abusers and may suffer further abuse for pressing charges themselves. In situations involving rape, the victim generally has a choice about whether charges will be filed. If your client has decided to press charges, she will need your support and encouragement as she provides all the information to the investigator.

During the investigation, maintain contact with the victim. If she is in a shelter, contact her frequently there. You will be able to help her understand what is going on with her case and the investigation procedures. Check with the investigating officer and the district attorney to see if the victim needs to meet with them, and offer to accompany her to such meetings.

Be available to accompany your client to court appearances. You will know, from your work and training at your agency, what to expect in the local courts, police department, and district attorney offices. Share this information with your client to prepare her for these meetings. Explain the purpose of the preliminary hearing and that, during that hearing, she will be asked to testify before a judge. Prepare her for the possibility that she may be asked to look at a lineup of suspects at the police department.

Occasionally you may encounter insensitive and rude court personnel or police officers. Your agency should have protocol in place to handle these grievances. Do not take it upon yourself to chastise these officials on the spot. Give support to your client at the time, and report the incident or the attitude to your supervisor. Most agencies that serve women have ongoing contacts with law enforcement and have developed effective methods for handling individuals who display unprofessional behavior and attitudes.

Even after the case is settled, your client may need to continue receiving support. Feelings and emotions could still be surfacing, and the client may still feel the need to talk, to join a support group, and to have someone to turn to when emotions are too painful. All of these things are extremely important in the healing process.

DSM-IV-TR STRESS DISORDERS

The *DSM-IV-TR* lists two separate stress responses to a traumatic event. The difference between them is the timing. The first stress response is acute stress disorder. This is a reaction to the event that "lasts for a minimum of 2 days and a maximum of 4 weeks and occurs within 4 weeks of the traumatic event." The second response is posttraumatic stress disorder (PTSD), in which "the duration of the disorder is more than 1 month." This second diagnosis requires a specifier: The PTSD is considered acute if the person has experienced symptoms for less than 3 months, and chronic if the duration is 3 months or longer. The clinician also must specify if the condition is PTSD with delayed onset. Delayed onset means the person began to experience the symptoms at least 6 months after the traumatic event.

Each of these diagnoses defines a traumatic event in the same way: "The person has been exposed to a traumatic event in which both of the following were present:

1. The person has experienced, witnessed, or was confronted with an event or events that involved actual or threatened death or serious injury, or a threat to the physical integrity of self or others
2. The person's response involved intense fear, helplessness, or horror" (*DSM-IV-TR*, pp. 463–472).

The *DSM* goes on to note that, for children, "this may be expressed instead by disorganized or agitated behavior."

Both of the diagnoses, acute stress disorder and PTSD, have the symptom of "persistently re-experiencing" the event in any one of a number of ways. Some individuals have recurrent nightmares. Others have intrusive thoughts or memories of the event that they cannot stop (often referred to as flashbacks). Victims may indicate that they are having these memories by responding physically to the event, for example, by cringing, putting up their hands, or ducking. For some victims, the environment contains cues that cause them to feel extreme distress. Such cues can include things like a car that is similar to the one driven by the assailant, a particular location, or a piece of music that was playing before, during, or after the assault.

In the acute phase, victims are likely to go out of their way to avoid cues in their environment, to have an exaggerated startle response, and to be hypervigilant. The symptoms are likely, at this stage, to cause significant interference with the victims' normal work and social routines. This will often block victims from getting the help they need or the support that will help them get through this.

In PTSD, the victim also experiences increased arousal indicated by the exaggerated startle response, being hypervigilant, having difficulty falling asleep or concentrating, and outbursts of anger. In addition, there is a "persistent avoidance of stimuli associated with the trauma and a numbing of general responsiveness." Victims will tell you that they feel detached or estranged from others, numb to their own emotions, and unable to express emotions or engage other people. They will discontinue activities that were once important to them. They may indicate in their talks with you a view of their life as ending prematurely. Commonly you will find that clients are unable to recall important details of the assault and go out of their way to avoid thoughts, feelings, conversations, activities, or people that bring back memories of the assault.

In discussing acute stress disorder and PTSD here in relation to assault, it should be noted that these responses are common in any person, adult or child, who has been through something traumatic. Both men and women have experienced these conditions following car accidents, tornados, traumatic medical procedures, and other events that fit the first criteria. (For more information on how to use the *DSM-IV-TR*, see Summers, *Fundamentals of Case Management Practice*, 2001, chapter 16.)

Differences in Domestic Violence

In her book *Trauma and Recovery*, Judith Herman (1992) argues that victims of domestic violence often suffer the same trauma as individuals who were held in captivity (prisoners of war, concentration camp victims, kidnapped individuals, and hostages). The abuse takes place over a long period of time during which the victim is in fairly constant contact with the perpetrator. It is not a single event. As a result, the victim must submit to coercion or risk her life.

During the period of captivity, violence is often unpredictable, which has the effect of making victims fear for their lives while being grateful they are still allowed to live. Over time it destroys the victims' sense of autonomy. Destruction of victims' other relationships results in their becoming entirely dependent on the abusers.

Many of these victims complain of numerous somatic difficulties and tension. They are unable to recall what it felt like when they were calm and comfortable. A solitary inner life develops that is helpful while in captivity but is a hindrance later in the person's healing process. Herman (1992) believes "this constriction in the capacities for active engagement with the world, which is common even after a single trauma, becomes most pronounced in chronically traumatized people, who are often described as passive or helpless" (p. 90). In addition, victims complain of the feeling that the perpetrator is still present because during the captivity they had to focus entirely on the abuser and what he might do next.

Many victims of captivity, including women leaving abusive relationships, will experience, in addition to PTSD, a persistent depression. Without former close relationships, isolation can aggravate the depression. Herman (1992) speaks as well of the "loss of faith." "They suffer not only from a classic post-traumatic syndrome but also from profound alterations in their relations with God . . ." (p. 95).

Many victims are convinced that their abusers will hunt for them. Often they complain that they feel confusion and a sense of worthlessness without the relationship. It is enormously difficult for a woman who has been held captive in an abusive relationship to suddenly see the options she has available in creating a new life. Redirecting her life will take considerable time. Workers need to be prepared to help the client visualize another way of living while remaining patient with the time it takes to replace one all-consuming relationship with a life that is directed by the client. All your listening skills are important in helping the victim to regain her autonomy, and a new view of herself and her life.

COMMON EFFECTS OF RAPE AND ABUSE

Disorganization Phase

People who have studied the responses of rape victims report symptoms that fit the criteria for posttraumatic stress disorder found in the *DSM-IV-TR*. Responses begin in what is termed the "disorganization phase." This set of common responses to rape is called the rape trauma syndrome. Immediately following the event, you may see two different responses. Some people respond with composure, keeping their emotions under control and maintaining a calm external appearance. Others are more expressive; they may cry, become belligerent and angry, be obviously tense, or smile nervously.

What victims of both rape and physical assault are experiencing is fear. This is a response to the perception that their life or their physical body was in extreme danger. During the assault, both domestic violence and rape, the woman had reason to fear possible mutilation, permanent physical injury, or death. There are other emotions that account for the fact that many victims appear to have mood swings. An assault victim can be angry and embarrassed, feel helpless, and blame herself.

Physical reactions nearly always include sleep disturbances, nausea, and a decrease in appetite. Some women experience urinary tract problems or genital problems following rape, and they may experience pain in their stomachs. The victim may report feeling sore all over and stiff.

Emotionally the victim almost always attempts to keep the memory of the event out of her mind. As we have seen in looking at the criteria for diagnosing the two stress disorders, one of the common features is avoidance of reminders of the event.

Victims of rape also experience sexual disturbances. Some find that sex is no longer gratifying, and others find it abhorrent.

Reorganization Phase

In reorganization, the victim begins to heal. Talking about the abuse or assault, often to a counselor at the agency or in a self-help group, is the first step. Talking about the event helps victims to remember what happened. It is an acknowledgment of the truth that may occur only gradually. Victims who are remembering a traumatic event may need to talk about it many times and describe it over and over. Your listening skills have considerable therapeutic importance in helping the person to hear the event and come to terms with it. It is always up to the clients to decide the extent to which they will reveal what happened and to whom. Never force clients to talk to you by telling them that talking to you will help them to heal. Talking to you may be useful, but clients have the right to decide when and how much to tell, and to whom they will tell it.

In reorganization, clients may move, rearrange their homes, or take on a new job or a new activity. They may choose to become closer to certain friends and family members. Many clients read and write about abuse or sexual assault. Eventually many victims want to help others, often through volunteering at a center to take hot line calls or running self-help and support groups.

DOING YOUR ASSESSMENT AND FOLLOWING YOUR CLIENT

The information in this chapter gives you a realistic picture of the types of problems and issues that arise for victims of both rape and domestic violence. The chapter also gives you ideas about how these victims handle their problems and become survivors. In addition, the role of the case manager in helping survivors reorganize their lives and handle the consequences of abuse is laid out in this chapter. This information will help you to develop a believable case of a survivor and give you ideas about how to handle the case and what referrals to make. As you follow your client, you will be able to anticipate the kinds of problems and concerns that are likely to arise for him or her. Use the information in this chapter to develop a case of someone who has been sexually or physically abused and is seeking help from you as the case manager.

EXERCISES

Assessing Lethality

Instructions: In the following vignettes, see if you can come up with a reasonably accurate assessment of the lethality of the perpetrator. Remember that behavior is not entirely predictable. You are making an appraisal based on your knowledge, however, which is always more sophisticated than just guessing.

1. Annette, who has spent years in a domestic violence situation, wants to return home for her clothes. In spite of what she has been through, she feels it is reasonably safe to go back. Her live-in boyfriend has told her that he has accepted the fact that she has left for good, and he has also told her that he has a new girlfriend and is thinking of moving in with this other woman. Therefore, he has encouraged Annette to come over and take her things out of the house before he moves out and leaves the house vacant.

   Annette tells you that she has stayed away from the house until now even though most of her clothes and some sentimental items remain there because she was afraid of what her boyfriend might do to her if she were to go back. She feels more relieved now, knowing he has a girlfriend and that he seems to have accepted the breakup of the relationship. She tells you that in the past when she threatened to leave, her boyfriend threatened to kill both of them. "Those were bad times," Annette tells you. The boyfriend had a gun and kept her confined to the house for two days until she retracted her threats to leave. She tells you that her boyfriend still has the gun "as far as I know." "Anytime I ever said I was leaving or even hinted I was leaving he would get very angry, break up things, and hit me. I don't know how I got out of that situation at all." Right after Annette went to the shelter, her boyfriend sent her a letter that Annette turned over to the police in which the boyfriend threatened to kill her if he ever saw her with another man.

   When you ask Annette how sure she is that her boyfriend has another girlfriend and has accepted the breakup of their relationship, she tells you that she is basing her information on two phone conversations she has had with her ex-boyfriend in the last week. "I don't know. His mood just changed." Would you encourage Annette to return for her clothes? If so, under what circumstances? Jot down some notes in the space that follows about how you reached your decision.

2. Carla is wondering if she should come into the shelter. She has called from a pay phone at the supermarket where she was "allowed" to go for milk for the baby. The only reason her husband did not accompany her was that he was watching a football game on television and did not feel like going out. Otherwise, she tells you, she is rarely alone. Even when he goes to work, she feels he has someone watching, or he comes back at odd times to check on what she is doing.

    Carla tells you that she must get permission to go out, and usually she is accompanied by her husband. If he does not accompany her, he often becomes enraged, imagining that she was with another man. He has told her that she belongs to him and that the day she attempts to take up with someone else is "the day you die!" There has been a history of violence, and the police have been called to the home several times. Her husband was in a batterer's program, but he dropped out, and his probation officer never pushed the matter. During that time, things "were better," but recently they have begun to escalate again. She tells you her husband has no friends except her, and that has been one of the reasons she has stayed. "He really needs me. He doesn't get along well with people or with his family, and I am really all he has. I don't know what he would do if I weren't there for him."

    When asked, Carla says her husband has a small handgun he keeps in the table drawer beside the bed. Carla just wants information about your services, quickly, so she can get home before her husband suspects anything. You give her the information, and in your mind you begin to think about the danger Carla might be in if she attempted to leave or use your services and was discovered. Make some notes in the following space about the degree of lethality there is in Carla's situation.

Barriers to Leaving

Instructions: In the following vignettes, see how many barriers you can find to the woman's leaving her abuser.

1. Tameka tells you she is interested in coming into the shelter as the two of you had planned, but her husband has come home very apologetic about the most recent outburst of violence. He brought roses and took her out to dinner and has promised to seek help. Tameka is reluctant to jeopardize his career if this could really work. Her husband is a well-liked city official, and most people would have

trouble believing he could be a batterer. "They would believe him before they believed me, anyway, because he knows everyone and I'm here at home. No one really knows me." What barriers are there for Tameka?

2. Kimberly is in the shelter and wants to return home. When she came in, she was determined not to return; but now, after several conversations with her husband, she is wavering. She says they only recently moved here and she does not really know anyone but the people at the shelter. Her family is in another state. They begged her to stay when her husband moved here. Kimberly says, "He has a really good job, and he's threatening to take the kids if I go through with this. Besides it could jeopardize his new job. That's going really well for him right now." What barriers are there for Kimberly?

3. Meg comes to you, saying she needs to leave her home but just cannot see her way clear to do that. "My boyfriend is really jealous," she tells you. "I left just once before and he got me to come back by promising to change if I did and promising to see that I lost my job if I didn't. I went back and lost my job anyway because he kept coming there and making scenes or he'd keep me from going to work or from calling in for days at a time." She describes constant humiliation in front of friends and family so that she stopped seeing other people. Meg tells you, "I tried to get help from our doctor, but he gave me Prozac and said I was just depressed." What barriers are there for Meg?

4. Ivette wants to leave an abusive relationship with her boyfriend of one year, but she tells you she is afraid of what her boyfriend will do. Twice when she has threatened to leave, he has threatened to commit suicide. She feels that if he did commit suicide, it would be her fault. She also tells you she thinks he will become even more violent if she leaves. He has a gun and has threatened her with it on more than one occasion. In addition, her cat is there, and she feels strongly that if she leaves, the cat will be in extreme danger. Lately any attempts on her part to continue former friendships, see her family, or participate in office gatherings have resulted in increased violence. "I just go to work and come home. He drops me off, and he is there well before I get out to pick me up." What barriers are there for Ivette?

Using the *DSM-IV-TR*

Instructions: Look at the following situations and discuss what diagnosis would be appropriate in each of these cases. For more information on how case managers use the *DSM-IV-TR,* see chapter 16 in *Fundamentals of Case Management Practice* (Summers, 2001). Use the chapter in your *DSM-IV-TR* on anxiety disorders.

1. Ever since Angelina was raped by an older man at a party, she has not left her house. The man at the party was a distant acquaintance, and he lured her into his car with the promise of a ride home. Instead he took her to a nearby field and raped her more than once. Then he beat her and left her for dead. The next day people walking their dog found her and called an ambulance. Angelina was hospitalized for a week and has not recovered her vision in her left eye. From the day she returned from the hospital a year ago, she has not left her home. In the following space, provide your tentative diagnosis and the reasons for your diagnosis.

2. Linda was raped by two teen boys after a soccer game. She knew the boys well, as they were classmates of hers. Not only was she raped twice, once by each boy, but she also was threatened for hours with death because the boys thought she would tell. Linda recalls being absolutely terrified. For a number of months Linda was able to function normally, but about seven months after the rape, she began to have recurrent and vivid memories of the rape. She tried in vain to turn these off, but they continued and interfered with her ability to fall asleep. She felt especially fearful and anxious when she passed the soccer practices on her way home. She has now started walking home by another route. She tells you it is hard for her to remember all the details of the rape. Her grades have dropped significantly, and she cannot find the energy to go on with the school activities that she used to enjoy. She is talking to you because she finds she cannot concentrate on anything. "I sit down to watch TV and get right up. I start my homework and just give up." In addition, her parents want her to get help because the trial of the two boys is coming up. It is now a year since the rape. Linda's parents have noticed that Linda has been more irritable lately, and they fear that the trial will trigger more severe symptoms. In the following space, provide your tentative diagnosis and the reasons for your diagnosis.

3. Melissa and her roommate were raped by a stranger who broke into their house one night. The rape by a person she could not see was quick and over in minutes. She heard her attacker leave and called the police. He was not caught. Melinda tells you she felt very helpless at the time and extremely frightened. "I would say the very next morning I couldn't really remember all that had happened. It was as if it really happened to someone else. I became detached from everything, as if I was another person watching myself matter-of-factly living my life. I kept thinking I should be upset, angry, afraid, but I felt nothing really. I had nightmares about it at first, but these have gone away. At night I had a lot of trouble falling asleep. I was very alert to the possibility that he might come back. I would jerk awake all of a sudden every time I dozed off. All that seems to have subsided now. It is about eight weeks since this happened to me, and I feel as if I have my life back on track. It helps that I moved, but I really think I was able to handle this and move beyond it now." In the following space, provide your tentative diagnosis and the reasons for your diagnosis.

INTAKE FORM
DOMESTIC VIOLENCE AND RAPE CRISIS
WILDWOOD CASE MANAGEMENT UNIT

Date ______________________ [ ] Adult

Update ______________________ [ ] Child

Former client (when?) ______________________ [ ] Significant other

Former hot line client ______________________ [ ] Telephone or
[ ] In person

Intake case manager ______________________

Time spent on intake ______________________

PERSONAL

Client's name ______________________

Address ______________________

Phone number: Home ______________________ Work ______________________

Age __________ Date of birth ______________________ Gender [ ] Female [ ] Male

Place of employment ______________________

Client's children

Name	F/M	Age

Contact person client designated for safety reasons ______________________

Address ______________________

Phone number: Home ______________________ Work ______________________

Safe to call? [ ] Yes [ ] No Best time to call ______________________

LEGAL

Perpetrator's name ______________________

Address ______________________

Phone number: Home ______________________ Work ______________________

Place of employment ______________________

Police called [ ] Yes [ ] No [ ] Unknown

Jurisdiction [ ] Local [ ] State police

Officer's name ______________________

Case number ______________________

Specific charges filed ______________________________

____

____

Criminal court dates ______________________________

Civil court dates ______________________________

Victim offender relationship

[ ] Stranger

[ ] Friends

[ ] Lover/boyfriend

[ ] Parent

[ ] Siblings

[ ] Clergy

[ ] Other ______________

[ ] Acquaintances

[ ] Authority figures

[ ] Spouse/Ex-spouse

[ ] Stepparent

[ ] Other relatives

[ ] Other professional

[ ] Unknown

Location of assault ______________________________

Took place in

[ ] Automobile

[ ] Perpetrator's residence

[ ] Perpetrator and victim's shared residence

[ ] Street

[ ] Other ______________

[ ] College campus

[ ] Victim's residence

[ ] Public environment

[ ] Workplace

Weapons used? [ ] Yes [ ] No If so, what kind? ______________

Include guns, knives, household objects, and fists or hands

MEDICAL

Was medical care obtained? [ ] Yes [ ] No [ ] Unknown [ ] Not applicable

Hospital/facility ______________________________

Response team: Physician ______________________________

Staff person from agency ______________________________

Rape kit collected [ ] Yes [ ] No

Description of injuries ______________________________

____

____

____

____

Primary care physician ______________________________

Address ______________________ Phone ______________

Disability:

[ ] Mental/emotional

[ ] Physical

[ ] Other ______________________________

[ ] None

[ ] Unknown

Substance abuse? [ ] Yes [ ] No

Substance(s) ______________________________

Medical coverage/insurance carrier ______________________________

Policy number ______________________________

REFERRALS AND SERVICES

Referrals received from:

[ ] Criminal justice

[ ] Self

[ ] Mental health

[ ] Medical facility ______________________________

[ ] Physician ______________________________

[ ] Clergy ______________________________

[ ] Other professionals ______________________________

[ ] Friends/relatives/others ______________________________

[ ] Other social service agency ______________________________

[ ] Children and youth

[ ] Unknown

Referrals made to:

[ ] Criminal justice

[ ] Self

[ ] Mental health

[ ] Medical facility ______________________________

[ ] Physician ______________________________

[ ] Clergy ______________________________

[ ] Other professionals ______________________________

[ ] Friends/relatives/others ______________________________

[ ] Other social service agency ______________________________

[ ] Children and youth

[ ] No referrals

Client requesting (select all that apply):

[ ] Hot line information and referral

[ ] Legal advocacy and accompaniment

[ ] Case management

[ ] Medical advocacy and accompaniment

[ ] Group counseling

[ ] Supportive counseling

[ ] Follow-up contact

[ ] Hot line counseling

[ ] Crisis counseling services

[ ] Victim compensation assistance

[ ] Assessment

[ ] Criminal justice information

[ ] Safety planning

[ ] Other ____________________

Does client have stated goals? ____

____

____

____

Does client have transportation? [ ] Yes [ ] No

Additional information important to the case ____________________________________

____

____

____

____

IMPRESSIONS AND RECOMMENDATIONS

____

____

____

____

____

____

____

____

____

____

____

____

____

____

____

____

____

CASE ASSIGNMENT

Signature of intake worker ____

Date completed ______________________

Primary staff person assigned ____

PERSONAL SAFETY PLAN

For ____

Instructions: Check all the things you will do, and fill in the blanks of those items where required.

SAFETY AT HOME

___ If I need shelter, the domestic violence hot line is ______________________

___ I will tell ______________________ about the violence and ask them to call the police if they hear signs of violence coming from my house

___ I will teach my children how to contact the police and fire department

___ I will be sure my children know our address and can give it to the police and fire department

___ I will get a programmable phone, or if I have one, I will program emergency numbers into it

___ I will teach my children to auto dial

___ I will avoid making long-distance calls from the home phone because my partner can learn whom I called by looking at the phone bill

___ I will make long-distance calls, if I need to, from ______________________

___ When I expect my partner and I are going to have an argument, I will try to move to a place where I am less at risk, such as ______________________ (avoid the garage, bathroom, kitchen, rooms where there are weapons, rooms with no outside exit)

___ I will use my judgment and intuition to determine if the situation is serious. I will, where possible, give my partner what he wants until the situation is under control and I/we are out of danger

___ I will teach these protections to some/all of my children, where appropriate

PLANNING AHEAD FOR LEAVING

___ If it's not safe to talk openly, I will use ______________________ as the code word/signal to my children that we are going to go or to family and friends that we are coming or leaving home

___ My safety route out of my home will be ______________________

___ I will rehearse my escape plan and, if appropriate, practice it with my children

___ My purse and car keys are kept ______________________

___ I will leave money and an extra set of keys with ______________________

___ I will leave extra clothes with ______________________

___ I will keep important documents and copies of important documents at

____

___ If I have to leave, I will go to ______________________

___ If I can't go there, I will go to ______________________

INDEPENDENT MEASURES BEFORE I LEAVE

____ I will ask for help in planning from the domestic violence program

____ I will keep change and important numbers with me at all times

____ I will open my own bank account in my name

____ I will seek credit in my own name

____ I will take classes or get job skills

____ I will get a mailbox at a private mailbox company and receive my personal mail there

____ I will increase my independence in other ways ______________________________

____

____

____

AFTER LEAVING

____ I will install deadbolts where I live

____ I will change the locks where I live

____ I will check all my windows for access from the outside and take steps to bar entry into my home through the windows

____ I will replace all wooden doors with steel/metal doors

____ I will install a security system in my home

____ I will install rope or chain ladders to be used for escape from upper stories

____ I will purchase fire extinguishers

____ I will install smoke detectors on every floor

____ I will teach my children how to reach me collect if they are concerned for their own safety

____ I will inform the school or others who take care of my children about who has permission to pick up my children and I will make sure the school personnel can recognize these people

____ I will give those who take care of my children copies of custody and protective orders and emergency numbers

____ I will tell ____________________________ and ____________________________ that I am no longer with my partner and ask them to call the police if they believe I or my children are in danger

AT WORK AND IN PUBLIC PLACES

____ I will inform these people at my job

- ____ My boss
- ____ The security supervisor
- ____ The employee assistance program

The employee assistance number is ______________________________

___ I will ask ______________________________ to screen my calls at work

___ I will protect myself when arriving at work by ______________________________

____

____

___ I will protect myself when leaving work by ______________________________

____

____

___ When traveling to and from work, if there is trouble, I will ______________________________

____

____

___ I will carry a cell phone with me at all times

___ I will vary my routines

___ I will vary my route to and from usual destinations

___ I will avoid places my partner is likely to find me (Laundromat, banks, stores, doctors' offices I used before leaving)

MY PROTECTION FROM ABUSE ORDER (PFA)

___ I will keep my PFA on or near me

___ If my partner destroys my PFA or if I lose my PFA, I will get another copy from the court that issued it

___ I will give a copy of my PFA to the police where I live

___ I will give copies of my PFA to the police in communities I frequently visit

___ I will give a copy of my PFA to my employer or my employer's security department

___ I will give a copy of my PFA to my religious advisor

___ I will give a copy of my PFA to my closest friend

___ I will give a copy of my PFA to my children's school

___ I will give a copy of my PFA to my children's day care center

___ I will report violations of my PFA to the police

___ I can call my advocate, my attorney, or my case manager if my partner violates the PFA

My attorney's number is ______________________________

My advocate's number is ______________________________

My case manager's number is ______________________________

___ I will call a domestic violence program if I have questions about how to enforce my PFA order

___ I will call a domestic violence program if I have trouble getting my PFA enforced

RECOVERING MY EMOTIONAL HEALTH

___ I will call ______________________________ if I feel lonely, blue, or confused about what to do next

___ I will get a checkup at a doctor's

___ If I have left my partner and I am considering returning, I will call ____________________ or spend time with ____________________ before I make the decision

___ I will remind myself daily of my strengths

They are ____

____

____

___ I will remind myself daily of my good qualities

They are ____

____

____

___ I will attend a support group to help build a support system

___ I will go to workshops and take classes on domestic violence and recovering from domestic violence to get the information I need to grow beyond this experience

___ I will take precautions not to drink or take drugs in a way that jeopardizes my safety

___ If I drink or take drugs at all, I will do it with people who are committed to my safety

___ I will read one or more books written for battered women recommended by my domestic violence program

___ I will take other steps to feel stronger and more independent

These steps are ____

____

____

WHAT TO TAKE WITH ME WHEN I LEAVE

Check these off as you get them together in a safe place

___ Personal identification

___ My birth certificate

___ Social Security card

___ Public assistance ID/Medicaid cards

___ Keys to house

___ Keys to car

___ Keys to office

___ Money

___ Checkbook

___ ATM cards

___ Credit cards

___ Insurance papers

___ Divorce and separation papers

___ Lease, rental agreement, house deed

___ Car payment book

___ Mortgage payment book

___ Driver's license

___ Car registration

___ Passports, green cards, work permits

___ Medication

___ Children's toys

___ Children's security blankets

___ Children's Social Security cards

___ Sentimental items

___ Personal safety plan

___ Other ______________________

____

____

____

____

Chapter 5

Case Management in the Field of Drug and Alcohol Dependence

INTRODUCTION

Clarisse told the case manager that the morning Brad came in, took a shower, and went back out again, after being out all night, she knew things were out of control. She recalled rolling over in bed and feeling an overwhelming sense of helplessness. Clarisse had good reason to feel this way. Brad was her 14-year-old son. Her husband had died 10 years before, after a losing battle with alcoholism. There had been periods of sobriety and wonderful family times, and then gradually the drinking would begin again, followed by arrests for drunk driving, loss of license, months on work release in county jail, and a return home with the promise never to drink again.

The accident that took the life of Clarisse's husband happened one foggy night and was assumed to have happened while her husband was in a blackout. He drove headlong into a barricade on the highway, but there were obvious signs that he had tried to avert the crash at the last minute. Now Clarisse was watching her son starting down the same road. There had been signs of marijuana smoking in the garage with friends. Then the drinking had started. She had confronted the behavior, but there were angry outbursts, followed by sullen silence for days. Lately there had been a few nights where Brad did not even bother to come home. When he did come home, he often refused to stay, showering and changing clothes and then leaving again.

Clarisse called a friend who worked in social services, and the friend referred her to a drug and alcohol treatment center. When Brad returned home, somehow she was able to persuade him to go to the center with her. Brad placed all sorts of restrictions on the visit. They could only stay an hour, he was not going to abide by any restrictions, and he intended to keep his friends and go on drinking.

Clarisse credits the case manager who did the intake and followed their case with saving her family. The case manager was able to talk to Brad in a way that helped him to agree to an inpatient stay for two weeks. During Brad's stay the case manager met with Clarisse and her younger daughter, Allison. These family gatherings gave everyone an opportunity to talk about what was going on in the family. Later the family saw a therapist for family therapy and began to look at how the pattern that was evolving in Brad's behavior was similar to his father's. Brad went from blaming his father for his "genes" to taking responsibility for his behavior.

Brad's stay was extended another two weeks. Until almost the end of his stay, Brad insisted that he could go home and keep the same friends. In the end, however, he was able to see that keeping them would thrust him right back into the activities he engaged in before. Reluctantly he told his friends that he was not going to associate with anyone who was drinking or smoking marijuana. For awhile the friends continued to come around, but Brad held firm, in part because he was in fairly continual contact with his case manager who encouraged him and countered the arguments of his friends. Brad's best friend gave up drinking and smoking all together. The other friends drifted away.

Today Brad is on the honor roll at school, works with his new friends at a local truck stop, and is planning to go to college. He no longer sees his case manager, but he credits the case manager's support and the nonjudgmental attitude with helping him to overcome many of his misconceptions and negative behavior.

SPECIAL CONSIDERATIONS

Focus on Alcoholism

Much of the material available on addiction addresses alcohol addiction. In understanding the approach to alcohol addiction, one can gain an understanding of how all chemical addictions are addressed. The material contained in this chapter is based on information from several sources: *Introduction to Alcoholism Counseling: A Bio-Psycho-Social Approach* by Jerome David Levin (1995); the United States Center for Substance Abuse Treatment, Treatment Improvement Protocol (TIP) Series #7 (1995); and *Treatment of Alcoholism and Other Addictions: A Self-Psychology Approach* by Jerome David Levin (1991).*

Focus on Psychological Dynamics

In no other chapter will we look at psychological dynamics as thoroughly as we do here. That is because those suffering from substance abuse and addictions, unlike other populations we examine in this text, have some responsibility for their condition. Whether they have a biochemical predisposition to become addicted or have experienced biochemical changes as a result of prolonged substance abuse, the clients themselves have a part in the resulting condition. In addition, most have lost, in some measure, the ability to reverse the behavior that is inflicting so much damage upon them. To compensate for this loss, many use denial and other mechanisms to avoid dealing with the difficult task of changing their lives.

Work in the field of substance abuse and addiction is heavily focused, therefore, on how the client came to be addicted to drugs or alcohol and what the client needs to do to become clean and remain sober. This is, ultimately, a problem of individual responsibility. Although you are not the therapist, it is important for you to know how major researchers in this field explain substance abuse and addiction in terms of an individual's psychological dynamics. This will help you to know what therapists look for and what might be important to note in your assessment and records. In some cases, there may be no therapist currently treating your client, in which case your role in the client's life is even more important.

**Source*: Adapted from *Treatment of Alcoholism and Other Addictions: A Self-Psychology Approach*, by Jerome D. Levin. Copyright © 1991, 1987 by Jerome D. Levin. Reprinted with permission of Jason Aronson, Inc.

PSYCHOLOGICAL TREATMENT OF ALCOHOLISM AND ADDICTION

Treatment for chemical dependency (CD) often requires both medical and psychological interventions. Since abuse and addiction damage every aspect of the person's being, treatment must be comprehensive to be effective.

Psychological treatment aims to replace the addiction with a healthy relationship between the counselor and the client. This emotional bond is thought to produce integration and growth.

Treatment includes diagnosing the problem, educating the client about the problem, and then working to change the psychological and emotional problems that have resulted from the drug or alcohol use or have caused this use. It is important for you to understand the various mental and physical effects of addiction so you can help the client to understand them and so you can create a useful record and an effective service plan. The information you assemble helps the therapist be ready to confront the client's denial. This is not always easy. It must be done tactfully, and it must be timed well. Through careful listening, the counselor will understand the client's inner experience. Gradually the dynamics of the disorder will emerge and be understood by the counselor.

ADDICTION AS A DISTURBANCE OF SELF

Addiction might best be viewed as a form of self-destruction by self-poisoning. Self-poisoning is pathological behavior. This viewpoint posits that addicts have been unable to find a satisfactory way of loving themselves. As a result, they are self-absorbed.

There appears to be four separate kinds of pathology involved in addiction. First is the self-destructive behavior. Second, the client does not seem to have any way of caring for him- or herself or of maintaining his or her self-esteem; therefore, small slights and insults are devastating. Third, the addicted person is overly self-involved, often finding ways to mask or distract him- or herself from the psychological pain. Finally, the client's concept of who he or she is, that is, the client's self-concept, is fragile and unclear.

Alcohol Defined

Alcohol is both a chemical and a drug. It is found in many fermented fluids. The kind of alcohol that is used for drinking is called *ethyl alcohol* or *ethanol.*

Fermentation

Alcohol is produced by fermentation of substances that contain sugar. Yeast spores, present in the air, settle on the juice, producing enzymes. These enzymes cause the fermentation of the juice to produce ethanol.

Distillation

In the fifteenth century, distillation became popular as a means of producing alcohol for human consumption. Water was removed from the fermented beverage to increase the concentration of alcohol. Today we measure that concentration in terms of *proof.* A proof is half of a percent by volume, so pure alcohol would be 200 proof.

By-Products to Fermentation

There are a number of by-products to the fermentation process. As a group these are called *congeners.* Usually these by-products are present only in small amounts. Flavorings, colorings, and carbon dioxide are considered congeners.

PRODUCING THE HIGH

Graded Depression of Synaptic Transmission—An Important Definition

Graded depression of synaptic transmission is a term meaning that some parts of the central nervous system (CNS) are more sensitive than others. Therefore, some parts of the CNS will show the effects of alcohol sooner than other parts.

Pharmacology

Ethanol belongs to a category of chemicals classified as sedative-hypnotic. The classification is based on the effect these chemicals have on the CNS. All of these chemicals tend to depress the CNS. This means that increasing doses are increasingly sedative. Included in this classification are barbiturates and tranquilizers such as Valium.

Initial Response

Initially alcohol depresses inhibitions or the inhibitory synapses in the brain. This causes the seemingly positive reaction of excitement and lack of inhibition. At this stage alcohol appears to be a stimulant. The drinker appears to be full of fun, carefree and even euphoric. The drinker generally experiences reduced anxiety.

Continued Drinking

After continued drinking, the excitatory synapses are also depressed. At this point the drinker experiences sedation and may appear depressed. Certainly there is a reduction of the cheerful, devil-may-care behavior exhibited earlier.

Addiction

We can say that a person is addicted to alcohol when the drinker develops a *tolerance.* This means that he or she requires more and more alcohol to get the same effect. In addition, there are withdrawal symptoms after the addicted person stops drinking heavily or after a prolonged binge. The person will experience a disturbance of his or her normal sleep patterns. Most noticeably, there will be a reduced amount of time spent dreaming.

METABOLISM OF ALCOHOL

Metabolism takes place in every cell and tissue. Technically it is the sum of various chemical processes that produce an exchange of energy. Most of this work is done by the liver, which is particularly involved in metabolizing drugs and hormones.

Metabolism in the Liver

The metabolic steps take place in the individual liver cells. These cells are called *hepatocytes.* When a client is given Antibuse, the metabolism in the liver is blocked, causing an accumulation of acetaldehyde. This substance is highly toxic, has unpleasant physical effects, and can be lethal.

Heavy Alcohol Use

After a person has been drinking heavily for a long time, the normal biochemical processes of the liver become impaired, which leads to a number of diseases. Heavy drinkers of alcohol metabolize alcohol more rapidly because of these changes in the liver. This is what causes them to develop a tolerance for alcohol.

Tolerance

When we say a person has developed a tolerance, we mean that it takes more and more of the substance to produce a high. In some cases the person may develop a cross-tolerance, which means that once the person has developed a tolerance for alcohol, he or she will have a tolerance for other drugs, such as barbiturates and general anesthetics, as well.

Elimination

Ninety-five percent of all the alcohol is eliminated from the liver into the bowels. Carbon dioxide and water are eliminated from the lungs and the kidneys. Five percent of alcohol may be eliminated from the lungs and kidneys without ever being metabolized.

TOLERANCE, DEPENDENCE, AND WITHDRAWAL

This section discusses the neurological, psychological, and physical effects of prolonged, heavy drinking.

Tolerance

As noted, tolerance means that the person requires more and more of the substance to obtain the original high. In such a person, the nervous system has become less sensitive to the alcohol, and the liver is metabolizing more rapidly. This sets up an addictive cycle. A person who needs more and more alcohol to get high generally drinks more and more, which builds up further tolerance. In advanced alcoholism, the tolerance actually decreases because of severe liver disease combined with a lower rate of metabolism.

Psychological Dependence

A person can be said to be psychologically dependent on a substance when that person needs the substance to perform certain tasks. A person who needs a stiff drink to socialize is psychologically dependent on alcohol. Many people who are psychologically dependent on alcohol use it to relax, reduce anxiety, numb depression, perform in public, have sex, or function in social situations. Not all those who are psychologically dependent become physiologically dependent.

Physiological Dependence

A person who experiences withdrawal symptoms when he or she stops drinking is physiologically dependent on alcohol. This dependence develops when a person engages in prolonged, heavy drinking. The drinking depresses the central nervous system, and over time the CNS becomes used to functioning in a depressed state. Once the depressant is removed, there is a rebound effect. The CNS becomes hyperactive and the person experiences anxiety, tremulousness, and even hallucinations and convulsions. Severe withdrawal symptoms can cause the person to die.

Withdrawal

True withdrawal from alcohol depends on the duration of the drinking or the length of time the person has been binging and on the quantity of alcohol that was consumed during that time. Serious withdrawal, the type that is potentially dangerous, can occur after a person has consumed a pint of whiskey every day for 10 days. These symptoms can start anywhere from several hours to several days after the person has taken the last drink. In most cases the symptoms tend to peak sometime around the second to fourth day, with the third day commonly considered the worst. Acute withdrawal symptoms generally clear within one week.

WITHDRAWAL: A CLOSER LOOK

We should take a closer look at the withdrawal process. Sometimes a client will come to you and want to stop drinking after prolonged, heavy use of alcohol. To help such a client, you should be aware of what withdrawal may be like. Sometimes a client comes to you in acute withdrawal, in which case it is helpful for you to know the stage of the withdrawal process he or she is going through at the time.

Withdrawal Stage One

- *Mental/physical symptoms.* Feeling tremulous, restless, and jumpy. Clients describe feeling like they are going to jump out of their skin. They may be generally apprehensive.
- *Physical symptoms.* Clients may experience increased pulse and respiration rates.
- *Primary danger.* The person may begin drinking to relieve the pain.

Withdrawal Stage Two

- *Mental/physical symptoms.* The person may complain of the shakes inside, and anxiety and dread often intensify. Clients are usually oriented to time, place, and person, but they may be extremely frightened and need reassurance. If a client experiences alcoholic hallucinosis ("audiovisuals"), try to understand the meaning of the hallucination to the person.
- *Physical symptoms.* Pulse, blood pressure, and respiration continue to elevate; tremors are more severe; and grand mal seizures may occur.
- *Primary danger.* Clients are in danger of harm occurring during a seizure, and possibly in danger of falling into a permanent seizure condition that will not abate and will eventually lead to death.

Withdrawal Stage Three

- *Mental/physical symptoms.* Abject terror and hallucinations are not uncommon. Often clients experience tactile, visual, and auditory hallucinations (e.g., they may see and feel tiny bugs everywhere). Sometimes hallucinations are persecutory in nature. Orientation × 3 may be lost.

- *Physical symptoms.* These symptoms include intense psychomotor agitation, a continuing rise in pulse and blood pressure, and possibly fever.
- *Primary danger.* There is a significant mortality rate at this last stage.

DETOXIFICATION

Detoxification is a *medical treatment.* It almost always involves sedative drugs that are titrated down over several days to a week. Chlordiazepoxide hydrochloride (Librium) or diazepam (Valium) is often used. The treatment also includes vitamins and minerals to address deficiencies that have developed during the prolonged drinking. Some clients require anticonvulsant medication. During the detoxification process, the person will require close supervision, good nursing care, and strong emotional support.

Detoxification Dangers

How and where detoxification is carried out is a *medical decision.* Usually a physician who is experienced in the drug and alcohol field will make the decision. As the intake person, you would refer the client for a medical evaluation. The choices are fairly narrow: inpatient or outpatient treatment, with or without medication. The physical debilitation of the client will determine the length of the detoxification period and whether an inpatient medical unit is necessary.

Clients who have intact social support systems do better during the detoxification phase. It is important that the intake worker explore what social supports the person may have to help him or her through this process.

MEDICAL COMPLICATIONS OF ALCOHOL

In this section, we will look at each organ of the body and what happens to it as a result of prolonged use of drugs or alcohol.

Blood

Alcohol deranges the process by which the red blood cells (RBCs), the white blood cells (WBCs), and the platelets enter the bloodstream. Anemia, diminished resistance to disease, and increased risk of hemorrhage can occur. Anemia is most common.

Liver

Alcohol can cause the liver not to function properly and can change the structure of the liver.

- *Alcoholic fatty liver.* Alcoholism leads to a buildup of fat in the liver. There may be abdominal pain, swelling, and discomfort. The liver can repair itself if drinking ceases.
- *Alcoholic hepatitis.* This is an active inflammatory process that can cause permanent damage. The symptoms are swelling, jaundice, pain, and fever. These symptoms are serious and can be fatal.

- *Alcoholic cirrhosis.* Structural changes in the liver. A compromised metabolic function ensues. There are changes in the chemistry of the body. Treatment consists of a modified diet and total abstinence.
- *Hepatic encephalopathy.* This is a liver disease that causes toxins in the blood. The toxins come in as ammonia and cause drowsiness, total unresponsiveness, or confusion. The person may have a flapping tremor. This condition is treated with a restriction of protein intake.

Digestive System

- *Tongue, lips, mouth, pharynx.* All of these receive constant irritation that can lead to cancer. Heavy smoking makes the risk worse.
- *Tongue.* Alcohol lessens taste and lowers the appetite. A zinc deficiency will make this worse.
- *Esophagus.* The esophagus may hemorrhage as a result of blocked circulation or violent vomiting, and the risk of cancer is increased.
- *Stomach.* Gastritis or peptic ulcers are likely, and the risk of cancer is increased.
- *Small intestine.* The small intestine cannot function properly. There is malabsorption of minerals and of folic acid, vitamin B12, and fat. These effects increase the motility of the small intestine, leading to diarrhea.
- *Pancreas.* An uncommon complication involving the pancreas may appear as nausea, vomiting, and pain, and usually stops the drinking.
- *Chronic pancreatitis.* Functioning tissue is replaced with fiber, and continued drinking leads to death.

Skeletal Muscles

- *Acute alcoholic myopathy.* This involves tenderness, muscle pain, and swelling following binge drinking; it is usually felt in the muscles of the pelvis or shoulder area.
- *Chronic alcoholic myopathy.* In this condition, the person slowly wastes away without pain or tenderness. Progressive muscle weakness occurs, and recovery is usually slow.

Skin and Hair

- *Pellagra.* Skin lesions, often called "wine sores," appear due to nutritional deficiencies. Hair loss is another side effect.

Heart

- *Heart muscle.* Alcohol has a toxic effect on the heart muscle. The muscle is replaced with fat and fiber, enlarges, and becomes flabby. Treatment consists of complete abstinence and medical measures to guard against congestive heart failure.
- *Hyperlipidemia.* The body develops higher levels of fat in the blood, secondary to liver disease. This increases the risk of atherosclerotic cardiovascular disease, hypertension, and stroke. Normal blood pressure can return with abstinence.

Sleep

Problems with sleep occur during acute alcoholism and recovery. One problem is an inability to fall asleep. Restless, tormented sleep with anxiety-filled dreams is common, as is early morning waking. Alcohol disturbs the serotonin metabolism that provides for REM sleep; therefore, the normal sleep cycle is disturbed and REM sleep is reduced. After the last drink, the brain rebounds, making up for lost REM sleep, which causes excessive agitation and restless sleep.

Reproductive System

Drugs and alcohol are the most common cause of sexual dysfunction. Prolonged drinking can damage ovaries and gonads.

- *Impotence.* This can remit with abstinence, but a person may remain impotent or become impotent after sobriety if the person was using alcohol to perform sexually.
- *Feminization.* Enlarged breasts may occur in male alcoholics as a result of abnormally high levels of estrogen.

The Fetus

Ethanol crosses the placenta. Rapidly dividing cells are especially vulnerable to toxic effects.

- *Fetal alcohol syndrome.* Babies born to alcoholic mothers may have facial abnormalities and varying degrees of brain damage. These babies can remain gravely damaged. Risk seems related to dose. Two drinks a day can decrease birth weight. Children born to recovering alcoholics are not at risk.

Brain and Nervous System

- *Wernicke's syndrome.* This is an acute condition resulting from thiamin deficiency. Initially it causes confusion, delirium, and hyperactivity. Peripheral neuropathy sometimes occurs. This condition is reversible with administration of thiamin.
- *Korasakoff's psychosis.* A chronic condition that is residual to Wernicke's syndrome, this is a long-term result of brain damage. It involves severe short-term memory deficits. (The person may fill gaps in memory with confabulation to defend against anxiety about not remembering.) It often involves a lack of insight, impaired judgment, and general intellectual deterioration. Some fully recover with abstinence and thiamin, but some recover only partially or not at all.
- *Niacin deficiency.* This can cause psychiatric symptoms and brain damage.
- *Peripheral neuropathy.* Damage may occur to peripheral limbs due to nutritional deficiencies or the toxic effects of alcohol. Sensory abnormalities, gait disturbances, foot drop, and paralysis can all occur. Feet and legs are usually affected first. This is sometimes accompanied by muscle wasting. The treatment is abstinence and massive doses of vitamin B.
- *Avitaminosis.* This condition is caused by nutritional deficiencies. The tissue of the nervous system may become damaged, and an autoimmune response may be produced.

- *Alcoholic dementia or alcoholic degeneration.* Alcohol can cause a disruption in protein synthesis in the brain. Diffuse brain damage can develop from the clumping of red blood cells, and tiny capillaries in the brain may break, causing a series of microstrokes with cumulative damage. Dementia or degeneration may result in memory loss, confusion, and intellectual deterioration. There can be personality changes and emotional lability, and the person may become paranoid.
- *Trauma.* Heavy drinkers are prone to head injuries that generally result from fights, falls, and accidents. Trauma can result in slow intercranial bleeding or subdural hematomas, and can cause death or fatal brain damage if it goes undetected. The person may seem confused and have other symptoms that appear to be from withdrawal.
- *Blackouts.* Blackouts are alcoholic amnesia or memory losses. These can be partial or total. They are a common symptom of problem drinking. Blackouts disrupt the experience of the self and cause great anxiety.
- *Effects on learning.* Eventually there will be cognitive deficits and learning impairments that can persist long after the last drink. Neurons die as a result of prolonged drinking.

ASSESSMENT AND INTAKE

A good assessment and intake will cover the following major points:

1. Complete psychosocial profile of the person
2. All problem areas including drug and alcohol (D&A) use
3. Psychological, legal, and vocational problems
4. Family and other social relationships
5. Nutritional evaluation, regardless of how well the person appears

Promoting a Trusting Relationship

In the assessment interview, you want to begin to form a successful alliance with the client. There are three important ways you can begin to form this bond. First, tell the client about confidentiality and any other issues that might affect his or her case. In this way there are no surprises. In addition, try to arrange same-day involvement in a program, or at least involvement at the earliest opportunity. Finally, give plenty of encouragement and positive reinforcement for participation, and continue to do so as the relationship progresses.

Medical Problems or Instability

If, while doing the assessment, you find medical problems or physical instability, get an examination by a physician before admission. If you are the admitting worker and you find medical concerns, get a physical within the first few days of admission. When you write the intake report and develop a treatment plan, be sure you address the physical problems along with all the other problems. Part of every treatment plan should focus on medical problems and the plan for treating them. You may find that the medical problems of a client make him or her inappropriate for your facility. In such a case, it is the responsibility of your program to link the person with the appropriate care provider. You cannot simply choose whom you will serve and turn the rest away with no referral. Once a client who does not fit into your program comes to your attention, you must make an appropriate referral.

Enabling Families

Many families play a part in facilitating the addiction. For many spouses and children of alcoholics or drug addicts, admitting the severity of the problem can be much too painful, and so they minimize what the alcoholic or addict does and make excuses for the behavior. This is called enabling. It happens when another person does his or her best to make the alcoholic or addict look good, hiding what is really going on and giving plausible excuses for the behaviors and consequences of addiction.

According to Bill Milchak of the Penn State Milton S. Hershey Medical College, enabling has three stages:

1. *Denial.* The enabler tries to see the drinker's behavior as fun and rationalizes why the person is drinking (or using substances, in the case of an addict) as often as he or she does.
2. *Loss of self-respect.* This ensues when change has not occurred in spite of the enabler's exhortations, hostility, and even abuse. The family may turn in on itself, ashamed of the drinking or drug use and fearful of the consequences to the family as a group.
3. *Collusion.* The family excuses the drinker or addict and attempts to protect him or her from the negative consequences of the behavior. Generally, the whole family joins in this endeavor; they recognize that they are unable to effect a change, so they cover up the behavior for the good of all. As a result, the family or spouse can become isolated, fearing that close relationships will make them vulnerable to discovery of the problem. Sometimes family members hide incidents from each other so that the whole family is not facing the entire problem.

Life within the family can be unpredictable. Hope for a recovery or renewed abstinence is dashed by another round of drinking or drug use. Family members worry constantly about the behavior of the alcoholic or addict and what it will lead to. Some family members blame themselves for not being capable enough to force a change from the other person. A sense of inadequacy within the family or of failure is pervasive. Finally, some families develop elaborate rationalizations for why things are the way they are. Through the use of mutual support systems, often unspoken, the substance abuse is covered up and excused.

Not all families, however, reach that point. For some, enabling a substance abuser becomes extremely debilitating emotionally. Isolating themselves from other people, lest the problem be exposed, and focusing intensely on making sure the problem is not discovered take considerable energy. Eventually an enabling person may separate from others and withdraw emotionally. At this point the enabler may find that his or her moods are dependent on whether the drinker or addict is using or is doing well. It is easy to move into a desire to get away from the substance abuser, fantasizing his or her death. Enablers who remain with a substance abuser in spite of the extreme pain involved are often convinced that their only source of affection is from the addict or alcoholic; therefore, they continue to manipulate things on his or her behalf.

Enabling behavior is spontaneous. Most people want to help those they love, and at first enabling seems to be a loving and helpful thing to do. Some believe that by being helpful, they can help the alcoholic or addict stop his or her behavior. Under normal circumstances, help might produce such an effect, but with chemically dependent people, the help and reassurance of others just serve to convince them further that there really is no problem.

Following is a list of the kinds of well-meaning activities in which people engage to try to help the addicted person:

- Bailing the person out of jail
- Giving the person one more chance (and then another and then another)
- Ignoring the chemical use because the user gets so defensive when the subject is mentioned
- Using drugs or drinking along with the addict or alcoholic
- Joining the person in blaming other people for bad feelings or unhealthy behavior
- Lending the person money
- Lying or making excuses for the addict or alcoholic to friends
- Lying or making excuses for the person to his or her place of employment

In preparing the social history, it is important to get a sense of the degree of enabling that is going on within the family because this will give you a clue about the extent to which family problems need to be addressed as well.

Codependency

A word of caution is in order regarding the term *codependency.* Many enablers are given this label and treated for the condition by clinicians, and indeed enablers are often people who are scarred by long-term life with an addict or alcoholic and who have played a part, usually unwittingly, in the chemical abuser's continued chemical use. The problem stems from the fact that for the most part, there are no criteria for the condition known as codependency that have been rigorously researched for validity and reliability. The term has been defined primarily as a collection of behaviors—many of which are normal, caring behaviors that people (particularly women) have been socialized to do for the people they care about. The term most often has been applied to women, and generally it has been used as though it were a legitimate diagnosis requiring considerable treatment.

Agnes was going through a divorce when she sought help from a clinician to get through the emotionally wrenching aspects of this transition. Her ex-husband was not a drinker, nor did he use drugs, but he had been unable to hold a job and often engaged in fantastic schemes to make money rather than getting steady employment. None of the schemes amounted to anything. Agnes had filed for the divorce, arranged her affairs so that her ex-husband could not return, and had sought and gained a large promotion at her work in order to be able to better support herself and her children.

Agnes's therapist told her that her problem was codependency and gave her a list of books to buy on the topic. Rather than looking at all Agnes had done to set up a better life for herself and her children, the therapist focused on the fact that for awhile Agnes had earned the money and given her ex-husband a chance to make his schemes work. Agnes bought the first book and concluded that the list of "symptoms" making up the "diagnosis" were really pretty normal behaviors. Gradually she became incensed with the therapist's perceptions. Agnes walked away from therapy, but many women in her situation do not, being convinced that walking away would be a form of denial on their part.

Be extremely careful how and when you use the term *codependence* and about labeling someone as codependent. Be able to explain the way in which you use this term.

Client Education

Part of every intake procedure to a facility includes educating the client so that he or she can take the best advantage of the treatment being offered. Here are five areas to address in the admission procedure:

1. Policies, rules, and procedures
2. What the client has a right to expect and client rights
3. The program schedule
4. The results of noncompliance (i.e., use of D&A during treatment)
5. The role of toxicology screening results

Toxicology Screening

Most facilities for the treatment of drugs and alcohol will do a toxicology screening. You may be asked to see that one is done at the time of intake. The boxed text is a list of what you need in order to be able to do these screenings.

When Doing a Toxicology Screening

You will need the following in order to do a toxicology screening:

1. Written informed consent from the client
2. Who may be informed of the results (for instance, the court)
3. Written permission regarding anyone outside the program who may have access to the results
4. Client understanding that some consequences of positive results (e.g., return to jail, loss of employment) may be outside the control of the program
5. A program to do the screening that uses methods which meet the requirements for certification by the National Institute of Drug Abuse and the Clinical Laboratory Improvement Act
6. Supervision of a client providing a urine sample to reduce the risk of falsification of the sample, particularly if the results are to be used for legal or employment purposes
7. Knowledge of appropriate procedures for safe collection, handling, storage, and testing

TREATMENT GOALS FOR CLIENTS

Treatment goals should be established at the time of intake. If you are the case manager in a large case management unit, your job will be to do the initial assessment and decide on the treatment goals. Figure 5.1 provides examples of possible goals you might use for a client. Study these examples to make sure you understand the kinds of issues that are addressed in developing a treatment plan.

Examples of Treatment Goals

Withdrawal Potential

1. Specific withdrawal symptoms will be absent or reduced.
2. The severity of acute withdrawal symptom(s) will be reduced.

Biomedical Conditions

1. The client will retain a personal physician.
2. The client will identify any outstanding medical and dental problems.
3. The client will establish a treatment plan for outstanding medical and dental problems.
4. The client will develop a personal plan for health maintenance.
5. The client will develop a personal plan for wellness.

Emotional and Behavioral Conditions

1. The client's emotional and behavioral conditions will diminish in severity so that intensive management is no longer necessary.
2. The client will be able to appropriately express and process emotions.
3. The client will be able to identify and discuss feelings of shame and guilt associated with D&A use.
4. The client will recognize the association between D&A use and personal shame and guilt issues.
5. The client will identify problems that may require ongoing psychotherapeutic support.
6. The client will identify a plan for obtaining such support.
7. The client will manage anger and will learn specific anger management techniques.
8. The client will manage impulse and will learn specific impulse control techniques.
9. The client will learn cognitive techniques to diminish the symptoms of depression.
10. The client will learn assertiveness skills.
11. The client will demonstrate assertiveness skills.

Treatment Acceptance and Resistance

1. The client will recognize his or her inability to control D&A use.
2. The client will accept personal responsibility for recovery.
3. The client will understand the association between negative consequences and continued use of D&A.
4. The client will recognize that his or her relationship with D&A is self-defeating.

Relapse Potential

1. The client will understand the relationship between triggers, craving, and relapse.
2. The client will identify personal triggers for D&A craving and use.
3. The client will develop, integrate, and internalize skills and strategies for coping with triggers and high-risk situations.
4. The client will stop participating in high-risk behaviors and activities.
5. The client will discontinue high-risk relationships.
6. The client will develop D&A refusal skills.

Recovery Environment

1. The client will develop living habits that promote abstinence and recovery.
2. The client will develop community supports that specifically promote abstinent behavior.
3. The client will develop community supports that specifically promote a healthy lifestyle.
4. The client will develop the skills necessary to establish and maintain close interpersonal relationships.

5. The client will learn strategies and skills that enhance personal socialization.
6. The client will develop a plan for educational or vocational improvement.
7. The client will develop a spiritual or moral environment.
8. The client will plan a structured participation in a 12-step recovery program or a reasonable alternative.
9. The client will develop a plan for sustaining family recovery and achieving positive family relationships.
10. The client will identify community resources that may provide assistance for recovery.

Figure 5.1 Examples of treatment goals

LEVEL OF CARE

Once the intake assessment is completed, you will need to decide where your client should go for treatment. Clients who have acute medical complications may need inpatient care in a medical unit that serves alcoholics and addicts. A person in danger of serious complications from withdrawal of alcohol would be likely to be admitted to such a unit. Some programs will also admit a person who has overwhelming issues with relapse. Getting a person out of the environment that supports the substance abuse may be a good first step. For others, care may be outpatient, depending on the issues and the severity of the addiction. The outpatient program may be intense, requiring extensive daily contact, or less intense, where a client is seen less often and may also be attending AA. Most clients can be assigned to outpatient programs.

OUTPATIENT TREATMENT

Today as many of the drug and alcohol problems as possible are treated on an outpatient basis. This not only saves money, but it is also less disruptive to the person's life. It allows the alcoholic or addict to continue ties with his or her family, stay in school, and maintain his or her job.

The development of intensive outpatient programs is fairly recent. These programs attempt to keep the client focused on resolving the D&A problem during the time the client is not working or sleeping. In addition, these programs are comprehensive; they look at the total client and the problem areas in the client's life that are beyond the D&A abuse. In order to choose a good outpatient program for your clients, you need to know what components are considered core to any good program, and what additional optimal components might be included in a program.

Core Components of Intensive Outpatient Services

Program Leadership

Program leadership involves the following elements:

- Good planning with a mission, goals, and objectives for the program
- Coordination and evaluation of the delivery of services
- A recognition of the changing needs of the geographic area that is served
- Maintenance of links with referral sources
- A working environment that enhances staff productivity

Screening

This is the initial step for the client. Clients should be congratulated on taking it, since usually they are filled with reservations and anxiety at this point.

Nonclinical staff should not be asked to use clinical judgment. Screening is done for the following reasons:

- To know who is appropriate and who is not
- To determine the need for D&A treatment
- To ensure correct placement in the proper treatment program

Assessment and Intake

The goal of assessment and intake is to determine the individual needs of the client. You need a complete psychosocial profile. Include in the profile all problem areas. In addition:

- Use this time to promote trust.
- Inform the client about all informed consent and confidentiality issues.
- Strive for same-day involvement in the program.
- For medical instability, require a physician's evaluation.
- Educate the client regarding rules, regulations, and procedures.

Toxicology Screening

The goals of toxicology screening are to enhance accountability, to maintain a drug-free environment, and to help achieve the treatment goals. Toxicology screening involves the routine and random testing of body fluids for D&A use. Usually it is performed about once a week. Purposes of the screening include:

- Providing a structure for relapse prevention
- Fostering honesty about relapses
- Can serve as a measure of client progress

Treatment Planning

Planning is based on the following:

- Findings in the biopsychosocial assessment
- Client's expressed objectives
- Medical examination
- Toxicology screenings

Treatment planning establishes goals for an *individualized* master treatment plan, which contains *specific, measurable* goals that the client agrees to accomplish during treatment. The treatment plan is reviewed and updated regularly. A treatment contract containing specific behavioral commitments to which the client agrees can be used to provide structure and support to the client.

24-Hour Crisis Management Services

These services are useful because clients' problems do not conform to normal working hours. Such services include emergency services and counseling support.

Pharmacology Services

This is part of the medical management of withdrawal. Medications often used in the process are Methadone and Naltrexone. Medications may also be prescribed for the treatment of psychiatric disorders or medical problems, including HIV/AIDS. Medication should never be used as a stand-alone service.

Individual Counseling

Individual counseling may be used as a therapeutic attempt to help the client solve specific acute problems that bar successful D&A treatment. Multiple sessions are required, but brief counseling interventions are preferred. Such counseling provides a basis for a strong clinical relationship during treatment, and these sessions often become a place where the client can disclose issues related to shame and guilt.

Individual counseling can help to:

- Maintain client participation through continual review and clarification of treatment goals
- Reassure client about anxieties, which are expected in the behavioral change process
- Enhance client's retention by strengthening the client-counselor relationship
- Identify new and healthier responses and solutions to stressful situations

Group Therapy

Group therapy should be provided by a qualified clinician. Group processes and dynamics can be used to:

- Facilitate the process of recovery
- Orient all clients regarding appropriate group behavior
- Break down the isolating tendencies of D&A addicted clients
- Provide a place for exploring concerns about a drug-free lifestyle

Peer support and peer confrontation are important treatment tools. Group norms help to establish healthy recovery patterns. Ideally the group should be no more than 12 clients and 2 therapists.

Education Services

Education services include didactic presentations of information on addiction and recovery. The goal is to address core issues of human development and behavior associated with addiction and recovery. Information is most effectively delivered through small groups in highly interactive sessions. Presentations should include handouts, exercises, and writing assignments. Videos can be used to enhance the presentations. Time for client responses and discussion should always be provided.

Family Education and Counseling

The goal of family education and counseling is to educate family members about family dynamics and issues associated with addiction and recovery. The family program should include both didactic and experiential sessions. Family participation and engagement are critical. Family education and counseling can:

- Provide structure and support to stabilize the family
- Assist the family in making changes that support recovery
- Help the family understand the treatment and recovery process

Self-Help and Support Group Orientation

Self-help participation is the bridge between acute treatment and long-term recovery. It provides the client with extended support beyond the treatment episode. Clients should be encouraged to attend a support group and actively participate. Such encouragement should include the following:

- Providing clients with a directory of meeting places and times.
- Matching clients to an appropriate "home group" with members who have similar backgrounds, culture, and experience.
- Help clients explore reasonable alternatives if they resist AA.

The client should be acclimated to the "home group" before leaving treatment. Self-help effectiveness is based on the client's comfort level.

Case Management

The tasks of case management are:

- Make arrangements for services not delivered by your agency (e.g., vocational, rehabilitation, psychiatric, employment, education, etc.).
- Link the client with the services called for in the master plan.
- Manage the client's treatment plan.
- Obtain the client's legal consent to services.
- Monitor these services until the issue has been addressed.

All the issues raised in the biopsychosocial assessment should be addressed. An absence of critical services (e.g., child care, transportation, crisis management) can create barriers.

Discharge and Transitional Service Planning

The purpose of discharge planning is to make sure the recovery process continues beyond the intensive treatment program. Discharge planning should be done with the client early in the treatment program. *Continuing care plans* should specify what the client will need to maintain abstinence and a recovery-oriented lifestyle. Any issues left unresolved should be addressed in this plan. In planning for a client's discharge:

- Prepare the client for completion of intensive treatment.
- Develop plans for the client's ongoing support for recovery.

Transitional service plans may include, among other things, individual and family counseling, vocational assistance, group participation, and self-help participation.

Program and Outcome Evaluation

To determine the program's effectiveness, measure these factors:

- Completion rate
- Retention rate
- Abstinence
- Quality of life
- Employment and workplace stability
- Reduction or cessation of criminal behavior

The most important measurements are those of retention rates, completion rates, and variables related to these.

Retention rate refers to the number of clients who attend the program without dropping out. Agencies like to track when clients are most likely to drop out of the program and what factors might contribute to this, so that they can take steps to correct problems in the program and keep clients in it longer. Completion rate refers to the number of clients who actually complete the program, doing everything that is required of them successfully without dropping out. Most agencies track what it is about their program that encouraged those individuals to complete it and use this information to help strengthen their work with other addicts.

Program evaluation should include identification of negative versus positive outcomes. The purpose of evaluation is to develop new and innovative services based on your research. It should never be used to decide pay scales, merit pay, or for punitive purposes; rather, it should be used to determine staff training needs and to determine the best interventions.

Optimal Elements of Intensive Outpatient Services

Outpatient Withdrawal Management

The medical management of D&A withdrawal in an outpatient program can be done safely and cost-efficiently. The treatment program must secure and coordinate the appropriate medical resources. Withdrawal management involves daily or near-daily monitoring of withdrawal and includes individual, group, nursing, and physicians' services.

Family, Marital, or Couples Therapy

This type of therapy is used to address treatment and recovery issues related to family and relationship dysfunction. It should be conducted by appropriate professionals who are grounded in family dynamics, and it can coexist with individual therapy.

Parenting Skills Training

Training in parenting skills is particularly important for helping the spouses of addicts to keep their families intact (unless abuse or neglect is involved). This training allows the client to function in the family role during treatment.

Child Care and Transportation Services

Child care may be provided either on site or by arrangement. Transportation may involve bus, taxi, or staff drivers. These issues are important to address, as they can affect retention and completion.

Organized Recreation and Leisure Activities

A certified recreation therapist can teach clients recreation skills and leisure-time activities, as well as stress-reduction techniques, and explain the role these activities play in recovery. The client benefits from such teaching by:

- Learning social skills
- Learning cooperation and trust
- Experiencing healthy competition and teamwork
- Bonding with others
- Learning to have fun and relax without D&A

Physical activity can diminish stress, anxiety, and depression. It also increases the appetite and promotes healthy sleep patterns.

Transition and Continuing Care Services

These services are often referred to as *aftercare*. They provide a transition from the intensive treatment phase to nontreatment phases. Transiton services address treatment goals and objectives not met during the intensive treatment phase and provide clients with continuing support and opportunities to grow and develop. Such services may include:

- Case management
- Individual, group, or family therapy

- Liaison and advocacy services
- Monitoring and drug testing
- Social activities

The case manager can provide advocacy and liaison services between the client and the employer, union, judge, probation officer, and so on by documenting the client's participation and progress in treatment and providing this information to the appropriate agencies.

Alumni Activities

Alumni activities benefit both current and former clients. Those who have completed treatment maintain continuing contact with the treatment program and serve as role models and peer helpers for those who are still in the program. Such activities can also bring new clients to group meetings.

Alumni activities can include special social events such as picnics, parties, ball games, and drug-free outings. They provide clients with a continuing therapeutic milieu and give structure and support to recovery.

Outreach

It is often hard to engage clients in treatment. Outreach services should:

- Encourage potential clients to participate in screening and assessment
- Minimize barriers to program intake
- Provide interventions and education to families
- Motivate clients to engage in treatment

Outreach services may include satellite programs in accessible areas and visits by treatment staff to home, work, detention centers, inpatient units, and jails. The purpose of home visits is to encourage clients to come to the treatment site and to address client ambivalence.

Be sensitive to confidentiality issues, and be aware that under federal confidentiality regulations, individuals who have applied for treatment are considered clients, whether or not they actually follow through and attend the program.

Enhancing Intensive Outpatient Services

Intensive outpatient treatment programs often offer additional services that are thought to enhance the program and the recovery of the client. These services are not necessary elements of the program, but they are elements that might strengthen the program considerably. Some examples of such services are:

- Structured cognitive and behavioral interventions
- "Ropes" courses
- Psychodrama
- Acupuncture
- Biofeedback

EDUCATION PLAYS AN IMPORTANT ROLE

Most individuals working in recovery programs are asked to provide some educational programming. Following is a list of suggested topics for educational groups that you can use if you are asked to lead such a group. You can choose one of these topics and prepare a group presentation and discussion. Sometimes you might want to assign the research and delivery of one of these topics to a client to give him or her an opportunity to work with the information more closely.

Topics for Client Groups

The role and process of treatment and recovery
The dynamics of addiction and the addiction process
Medical aspects of addiction
The importance of abstinence from alcohol and all other drugs
Appropriate use of prescribed and over-the-counter drugs
Powerlessness and unmanageability of D&A use
Maximizing the use of self-help and support groups
Spirituality and the development of an externalized source of support
The roles of nutrition, exercise, leisure, and recreation
Experiencing emotions and feelings without D&A
Relationship skills
Sex and sexuality in recovery
Conflict resolution and confrontation skills
Family dynamics of addiction
Healthy relationships and family functioning
Relapse management skills
D&A refusal skills
Avoiding and defusing triggers for craving and relapse
Minimizing risks for HIV/AIDS and sexually transmitted diseases

Topics for Family Groups

The dynamics of addiction, treatment, and recovery in the family
Relapse and relapse prevention
Family issues common in addicted families
Enabling and denial
Healthy family detachment and "tough love"
Communication and problem solving in the family
Management of family social functions
Introduction to Al-Anon, Alateen, and other relevant support systems for family members

Considerations for Educational Programming

- Have mastery of the topic you are presenting.
- Be sure that what you present is accurate and relevant.
- Make sure videos are recent and of good quality.
- Be sure handouts are readable and are available before the presentation begins.
- Actual didactic material should be given in 20-minute segments.
- Be sure every exercise is followed by an opportunity for clients to process their reactions.
- Serve snacks for group cohesion.
- Try to avoid giving lectures in cold basements, with hard, cold metal chairs and shiny, cold linoleum floors.

RETENTION AND PROBLEMS OF RELAPSE

The Challenge

Clients must make a daily decision to return to treatment. There are three major factors that account for this. First, issues and conflicts in their lives may pull them away from treatment or seem more attractive than returning. In addition, clients often live and work in environments where substance abuse is a common behavior, and so slip back into old habits. Finally, the client may encounter environmental cues away from the treatment site that trigger drug hunger and increase the risk of relapse. Confronting these cues outside the structure of the treatment program may result in a serious relapse.

Factors Contributing to Dropout from the Treatment Program

Clients may feel some ambivalence about stopping the use of their primary drug of choice. They may lack a commitment to stop all D&A use. Some clients have good intentions, but leave the program because of a crisis occurring at home or at work that causes them to face responsibilities there. Even without a crisis, some clients have trouble participating consistently because of conflicts with their work schedule. In this case, coming to treatment may be more than the client can manage at the time. Many clients deny there is a problem or deny the seriousness of their problem. Some deny the adverse consequences of their D&A use.

Clients who are in the program may leave because they feel discomfort at being seen as a recovering person. This new identity may be uncomfortable for them. Others leave the program because they find it difficult to relate to others in a group setting.

In some cases, clients fail to return to treatment because they do not get support at home. Some families withhold support and encouragement; others actively discourage participation. Families can sabotage the treatment program by using enabling behaviors, protecting the client's D&A habit, and denying the need for treatment.

Clinical Response to Problems of Retention and Relapse

The problems of retention and relapse can be responded to clinically in a number of ways. Your program may give rewards for perfect attendance or excellent attendance. Rewards and ceremonial graduations may also be part of your program. Ceremonies and rewards can also be used for clients who have reached important milestones in treatment.

Making clients feel included is important. You need to facilitate group projects and social activities in which clients can participate together.

One effective way to obtain the cooperation of the client is to develop, with the client, a behavioral contract. This is a written agreement that he or she will complete the program. Some programs give points or tokens that can be redeemed for bus tokens or 12-step literature. These tokens are awarded to those who attend or reach certain goals. Tokens can be a part of the contract.

Because your clients will almost certainly encounter situations away from treatment that will be conducive to relapse, you need clearly defined sessions on relapse prevention. In these sessions, address the process of relapse and relapse-related thinking and behavior. Discuss thoroughly drug hunger, triggers, and subsequent responses. All clients should have practice in D&A refusal skills. There should be discussion of self-help, recovering peers, and professional services.

Frequent toxicology screening can also assist in preventing relapse and should be used if there is a history of relapse.

Unless the family supports the treatment, the client may not be fully committed. Aggressive encouragement of family involvement in treatment is important. In this way the family can own the treatment and recovery process with the client and give the client support. Your role is to help the family identify early warning signs of relapse and help them see the purpose of unifying to help the client avoid relapse.

In group and other sessions, prevent the client from giving "drugalogue" stories that glorify past D&A use. Instead, give your active support to the recovery process and recognize progress in that process.

At the beginning of treatment, obtain the client's permission to contact the referral source. This might be the employer, a judge, or a probation officer. That way you will be able to notify the referral source if the client leaves treatment against medical advice.

When a client does not arrive for a scheduled appointment, outreach should be initiated immediately. Such outreach must be conducted within the guidelines of confidentiality.

SCHIZOPHRENIA AND SUBSTANCE ABUSE

Fifty to sixty percent of people with schizophrenia experience an addiction. The typical age of onset for schizophrenia, late teens, is often the time when young people begin to experiment with drugs and alcohol. Schizophrenia often limits relationships, so using drugs or drinking may be a way of forming relationships. In some cases, people with schizophrenia use drugs or alcohol to self-medicate in the hope of relieving the symptoms, such as delusions or hallucinations, they are experiencing. Binging may be rationalized as necessary in view of the strange symptoms the person is experiencing.

A person with both a mental illness and a substance abuse problem is referred to as a person with a *dual diagnosis.* These individuals are hospitalized more often, stay in the hospital longer, and may be resistant to the effects of psychotropic medications.

To help the client recover, it is important to find ways to help him or her reduce the abuse of the substance or abstain. It is difficult to know which symptoms result from substance abuse and which are due to the schizophrenia. Another challenge with clients who have a mental illness is to help them form a healthy support system. Many clients have been rejected by their families for their bizarre behavior apart from their addiction or drug abuse. Yet family support is useful in both overcoming the addiction and preventing relapse of the mental disorder.

Dealing with individuals who are schizophrenic can be difficult because often they do not want to socialize or they lack the appropriate social skills. Also, not all recovery groups are supportive of people with a dual diagnosis. There are, however, 12-step programs for those who have a dual diagnosis, and generally those in AA are very accepting of the special issues confronting these clients.

In order to help clients maintain sobriety, you may have to arrange for any number of medication adjustments. They may need less medication to achieve the same effect as a person who is not addicted. In some cases, antipsychotic medications that are sedating may be used by clients to start a new addiction.

If you see the client regularly, pay attention to life stressors that might cause a relapse. Place the client in groups and programs where he or she can learn new coping and communication skills. In addition, see that the client's liver and thyroid function are monitored regularly and that a complete blood count is done. If possible, administer the entire treatment program from one agency or facility. Clients with a dual diagnosis will not be helped as much by a program that is fragmented, with one agency handling the mental illness and another the substance abuse.

ALCOHOL-INDUCED DEPRESSION AND ANXIETY

Depression

Alcohol is a depressant, so it will make depression worse. The initial euphoria the person feels is followed by a down. Alcohol produces an anesthetic effect that seemingly stops emotional pain. This may be one reason a person drinks, to self-medicate for depression. Extensive drinking is usually followed by guilt and increased depression. The person may continue to drink or drink for prolonged periods to mask the depression.

The hangover is often accompanied by the depressing effects of alcohol and by depression over the relapse. Continued drinking becomes less and less satisfactory as a means of masking depression. The pain does not subside and the original euphoria is gone. Nevertheless, the person is often inclined to continue searching futilely for both the original euphoria and a cessation of the depression. When occasional relief is found, it only serves to reinforce the drinking behavior because intermittent reinforcement is a powerful way to maintain behavior.

Anxiety

Alcohol tranquilizes and relieves anxiety when taken in small doses. Most people report that drinking is helpful in reducing anxiety, but their subjective reports do not fit with the objective measures of anxiety. The heart rate and the galvanic skin response of one who has drunk considerable quantities indicate anxiety. As a person drinks heavily over a long period of time, it takes more and more alcohol to reduce anxiety, and the tranquilizing effects of the alcohol wear off sooner.

Some studies have shown that three or more drinks can actually cause anxiety. This is a purely biomedical phenomenon. The alcohol causes the release of adrenalinelike substances, arousing the central nervous system (CNS). The person subjectively experiences this as anxiety and may continue to drink to relieve the anxious feelings, not realizing the feelings are actually caused by the drink itself. After prolonged drinking, there is a rebound effect on the CNS, which has been depressed. The result is to worsen anxiety following the binge.

OTHER CLINICAL CHALLENGES

You may encounter other challenges to treatment. It is important for case managers to be aware of these challenges and know the appropriate clinical responses to them. The six major challenges are spelled out in Figure 5.2.

Treatment Noncompliance

Challenge
Treatment noncompliance is a lack of compliance or feeble compliance with treatment goals.

Resistance to treatment is often manifested by:

intermittent attendance
minimal participation
refusal to attend self-help groups
avoidance of urine drug screens
refusal to sign consents
missed appointments

Clinical Response
Clearly delineate a list of expectations in the master plan.

Have the client sign the master plan.

Refer to these expectations throughout treatment.

Have peer helpers reinforce desired behavior.

Recognize desired behavior when it occurs.

Last Resort
Therapeutic discharge can be instituted, along with a means for the client to reengage in the program.

Employer Mandates

Challenge
Employer involvement is usually positive, particularly when there is an employee assistance program at work.

Employers can make demands and apply pressure in a counterproductive manner.

The employer may be unwilling to be flexible about the treatment schedule.

A lack of confidentiality at the worksite can make the client a target of discrimination.

Clinical Response
Involve the employer in treatment plan.

Education and frequent contact can make the employer an ally, especially if there is an employee assistance program.

If there is an employee assistance program, use it to enhance the treatment plan.

Listen carefully to clients who describe their employers as unsympathetic.

Clients with multiple positive drug screens may face termination and need to know that participation in the treatment program is not a protection from that.

Figure 5.2 Major challenges in drug and alcohol treatment *continued*

Unhealthy Relationships Between Clients

Challenge

Most clients have a history of unhealthy relationships.

Entering treatment does not necessarily end those relationships.

Unhealthy, disruptive alliances among clients in treatment, which are romantic and intimate, do evolve.

Treatment environments can be intense and emotional, and group therapy is inherently personal in nature.

Problems that result from these relationships include:

resumption of D&A use
covering up for one another
sexual relationships
conflicts
breaches of confidentiality
relapse for one or both

Clinical Response

The therapy group can be used to confront individuals.

Confrontation should be done in a sensitive and cautious manner.

Use the treatment contract to curb or prevent unhealthy alliances.

Last Resort

Therapeutic discharge may be instituted, but never before confrontation on a clinical level so that the clients gain a better understanding of their behavior.

Recidivism

Challenge

Some clients do not gain a healthy benefit from the treatment program.

Some clients never make a commitment to the goals.

Some live in externally chaotic, dysfunctional situations.

Some have particularly severe D&A problems.

Some would do better in a structured residential program, but few exist.

Clients with these needs are at greater risk for recidivism, often with multiple admissions to the same or different programs.

Clinical Response

Alter the treatment plan to meet individual needs.

Clearly defined admission and discharge criteria may give tighter clinical control.

Try using a contingency contract (a behavioral contract with clearly specified rules and responses described in specific measurable ways).

Schedule more frequent individual sessions.

Increase the involvement of the client's family.

Obtain more community support.

Examine your own program honestly to see if it is the right one for this client.

Arriving Intoxicated

Challenge
This is inevitable, given the lack of control the program has over the client's life outside the program.

Clinical Response
The initial treatment agreement should state that the client will arrive drug/alcohol-free and will not be allowed to participate in group or receive other services if intoxicated.

Request to hold car keys and arrange transportation home. (There may be liability issues if you allow a client to leave on his or her own while under the influence of a substance.)

Belligerent and threatening clients require:

- a staff trained to handle such a person
- advance contingency plans to contain such an individual
- plans that demonstrate a concern for the safety of others
- talk-down counseling in surroundings that are not stimulating, but also are not isolated
- possibly, a call for law enforcement

Family Conflicts

Challenge
Clients are often part of families that are loosely organized, dysfunctional, and characterized by anger and conflict.

These families generally have poor communication and coping skills and may be addicted themselves.

Some families refuse to participate in treatment and disavow any responsibility.

Families may offer repeated inducements to relapse or criticize (ridicule, shame) the client for attempts to get help.

Clinical Response
Family engagement and education should begin as soon as possible.

Clients should sign a document indicating which family members should be included in treatment.

Clients must also sign consent forms for the program to contact the family members (for confidentiality reasons).

Creative ways to engage families include:

- phone calls and home visits by family members of program alumni
- paid staff coordination of a network of volunteers who are family members of alumni, particularly spouses
- having volunteers invite family members to Al-Anon meetings and provide education
- having volunteers give families encouragement and friendship
- multifamily therapy groups, professionally led, that discuss real-life family issues

Figure 5.2 Major challenges in drug and alcohol treatment

Nakeesha and Darren had once worked for the same company, and both had been fired for coming to work intoxicated. When they found themselves in the same treatment facility some years later, they had much to talk about. They both tended to blame the company for being punitive rather than take responsibility for their part in the firing. Although Darren was married, he began to spend more and more time with Nakeesha. At one point, each of them began signing out to go home, but then they would secretly meet.

One evening both Darren and Nakeesha returned at different times, and both were intoxicated. The evening worker saw this at once and confronted each of them separately as they returned. In the course of the discussions with them, it became clear, although the couple tried to hide the fact, that the two had been together, and not with their respective families.

The next day in group, the situation was confronted. At first the couple denied it. Other group members described the unhealthy results of such an alliance that they could foresee. Nakeesha was indignant and remained indignant throughout the session, and even afterward. She posed questions such as, "What would you do if you fell in love with someone? Walk away?" At one point she asked the group belligerently how this was any of their business. Darren, on the other hand, was forced by his counselor to face the choice of going home where his family was supportive or give up the recovery he had made and move to a new drinking partner. When Darrren made the decision to begin working seriously with his family on the pain he had brought to them and on how they could construct a healthier family life, Nakeesha withdrew from treatment. When she left, she expressed bitter anger at the worker who had confronted the situation, telling the worker that "because you can't stand to see anybody happy, you miserable little man, you have to go around making other people suffer. Well, I am out of here. I'm not playing your sick little games."

Nakeesha's withdrawal from the program was unfortunate, but this case highlights how difficult it is for some clients to see the role they play in their own difficulties and to come to terms with their addiction.

DOING YOUR ASSESSMENT AND FOLLOWING YOUR CLIENT

You now have the information you need to develop a believable client. Use the assessment form to create a credible person who might come to you seeking services for problems of substance abuse. In the space for interviewer comments, elaborate on the problems the client has discussed. You can make a referral to a program you describe, giving the components in this program you feel will best serve your client. As you monitor your hypothetical client, you can draw from the information in this chapter to define the kinds of plausible problems and common setbacks your client is likely to encounter.

EXERCISES

Assessing Tolerance, Dependence, and Withdrawal

Instructions: In the vignettes that follow, see if you can identify tolerance, dependence, or withdrawal in each of these clients suffering from alcoholism.

1. Mr. Preston sees you for an intake for food and rent vouchers. During the course of the intake interview, he mentions to you that he "still drinks," only "I don't get high anymore." You ask if he is drinking more than he used to, and he admits that he is. Mr. Preston is probably suffering from:

2. Mrs. Borden is in the waiting room of a local outpatient clinic where you are the case manager. You take her into your office to do the intake. She is fidgeting and perspiring. You ask her if she will sit down, and she says she'd rather stand. While you talk to her, she paces and seems anxious to leave. She finally breaks down and says she feels like she will jump out of her skin at any minute. She has not had a drink for 24 hours. Mrs. Borden is suffering from:

3. Your team is called by an alcoholic's neighbors, and the police accompany you when you go out to do the intake and pick the man up. Mr. Lance is sitting in a corner of his room, moaning and covering his head. He is rocking, and sometimes he flails his arms. Occasionally he screams, "Get them off me! Get them out of here!" He appears terrified and unclear about who you are. Mr. Lance may be suffering from:

4. In a session with you, Mr. Horner tells you he rarely drinks. "Oh, I do whenever I go out with my girlfriend," he chortles with good humor. "It makes the evening more interesting. And besides," he says, winking at you, "I'm much more interesting when I drink!" Mr. Horner may be suffering from:

5. Mr. Carlson wants to stop drinking, but says he cannot do so. "Every time I stop, I get all fidgety and upset. I don't think I was like this as a kid, but now that I'm older it doesn't seem like me. I keep drinking so I won't have to feel that way. Every time I think about stopping I get kind of sick. My hands shake and I feel all nervous like something is chasing me, only it's not." Mr. Carlson is suffering from:

6. Mrs. Peral came into your detox unit after a particularly prolonged period of intense drinking. She seems to know that the bugs on the wall are part of her withdrawal. Nevertheless, she is frightened, and you feel you need to give her plenty of reassurance. She knows where she is and why she came to the hospital. She tells you, "I just feel like I'm going to pop out or something awful is going to pop out in my head." Mrs. Peral is suffering from:

Checking Physical Symptoms

Instructions: In the following vignettes, decide what other questions you should ask the client and what you think might be going on with the client physically. All of these individuals suffer from alcoholism. In some of these cases, you may suspect more than one problem.

1. Mr. Jones has been sober for 4 years after 25 years of acute alcoholism. He still smokes two packs of cigarettes a day. While sitting in your office, he tells you he wants to get the interview over so he can go out and "have a smoke." He also tells you that lately he has had trouble swallowing.

   You would ask him:

   You suspect:

2. Mrs. Pierce has just finished a long episode of binge drinking and is in your office to apply for a detox unit. She complains of swollen muscles in her arms and legs.

   You would ask her:

You suspect:

3. Anne is a teenager who is drinking a lot. She was referred to the unit where you work, which is a unit for teenagers with D&A problems. In taking the history, you note many infections, colds, and flu episodes in recent months.

   You would ask her:

   You suspect:

4. Mr. Kilborn is giving you a social history for a mental health problem. He is a transient and has recently taken up residence in a local shelter. He appears jaundiced and sickly to you. He says he drinks "well, a good bit, I guess you'd say." Today he is complaining of a stomachache.

   You would ask him:

   You suspect:

Develop a Treatment Plan for These Clients

Instructions: Look at the following two cases. These two clients are in your office for an intake. During the interview, you uncover problems and needs. Develop a treatment plan for each of these people.

1. Mr. Bonachia has been sent in by his employer to obtain help for his alcohol problem. He has been coming into work drunk more frequently during the last year. He has many friends at work. They drink a couple of beers when they take their lunch break, and they all go out after work to have a few more beers before going home. Mr. Bonachia's wife and children have left, and he claims that he really cannot understand why. He feels his wife always wanted more money and was never satisfied with the money he earned, which is why she left him, he believes. "She always did want more. Now she'll learn how hard it is to have all those material things." He is very thin and seems anxious. When asked what he does in the evenings, he replies, "Oh, you know, watch a little TV, sleep, have a few beers. I don't know." Your treatment plan includes:

2. Mrs. Krone is asking for help. She works at a UPS office and is well liked there. She is happily married and the mother of two children. She says she has been drinking socially for a number of years, but now feels as if she no longer can control it. Last week she put some whiskey into an empty cough medicine bottle and is keeping it at work. "No one knows how much I really do drink, and I have no one to talk to about it. My husband would die if he knew how often I am sneaking a drink just to get through a boring evening or a difficult meeting." She talks about how difficult her childhood was, how her mother drank in order to deal with an abusive husband and a lack of money, and how she started drinking in high school "just to keep up with everybody else." She claims she has not seen a doctor in years and does not eat much. "I cook for everyone else in the evenings, and then I just sort of make up an excuse, I'm tired from work or something, and I go to bed. But really I go up and have a drink and watch some TV." Your treatment plan includes:

Using the *DSM-IV-TR*

Instructions: Examine the following situations and discuss what diagnosis would be appropriate in each case. For more information on how case managers use the *DSM-IV-TR*, see Chapter 16 in *Fundamentals of Case Management Practice* (Summers, 2001). Also use the chapter on substance-related disorders in your *DSM-IV-TR*.

1. The client recently left a bar, is uncoordinated, has slurred speech, and is not able to focus on what you are saying to him.

   Dx:

2. The client appears to be withdrawing from alcohol. He has had one grand mal seizure and is seeing green bugs on the wall. He has tremors of the hands and feet and seems extremely frightened.

   Dx:

3. Katy is a teenager who has been using amphetamines for sometime. She is now on the unit for detox and therapy. She is having tachycardia and her pupils are dilated. She has asked for extra blankets and appears to be shivering.

   Dx:

4. Mr. Polar comes in from his bus route. He has been a successful driver with his company for 10 years. He tells you he feels sick and was unable to drive today, even though he started to this morning. He is restless and nervous, denies ever using drugs or alcohol, and complains of a racing heartbeat. You notice twitching of his facial muscles. He tells you he used to drive on the 10:00 A.M. to 6:00 P.M. shift, but a month ago they changed him to the 6:00 A.M. to 2:00 P.M. shift, and he "can't get adjusted." To get going in the morning, he drinks "a lot of coffee."

   Dx:

5. Mr. Lindsay has been a cocaine addict for about four years. He wants to stop and has come into the unit for help. He tells you that he has not used cocaine for about 36 hours. He tells you that "sleeping is hell" because of the bad dreams he is having. "I feel like I need to sleep. I mean I'm real tired, but when I do I have these nightmares!" In your office he is pacing and wringing his jacket between his hands. During the course of the interview, he eats nine pieces of candy from the bowl on your desk.

   Dx:

6. Mrs. Kippner has been on Valium prescribed by her physician eight years ago. When she decided that she did not need it anymore, she ran into severe problems. She has come into your unit for help. She admits that she increased her dosage in recent years and that she felt as if she needed more and more to "settle down." When she stopped the medication, she was unable to sleep and felt intensely nauseated. She is very upset at the possibility that she might be addicted. In your office she can barely sit still.

   Dx:

Evaluation for Drug and Alcohol Services
Wildwood Case Management Unit

GENERAL INFORMATION

Name ____

Current address ______________________________ Phone ______________

1. Agency ID number [ ][ ][ ][ ]
2. Social Security number [ ][ ][ ] [ ][ ] [ ][ ][ ][ ]
3. Date of first contact [ ][ ] [ ][ ] [ ][ ][ ][ ]
4. Date of assessment [ ][ ] [ ][ ] [ ][ ][ ][ ]
5. Time begun [ ][ ] : [ ][ ] [ ][ ]

   Time ended [ ][ ] : [ ][ ] [ ][ ]
6. Contact code [ ]

   1 = In person 2 = Phone
7. Gender [ ]

   1 = Male 2 = Female
8. Date of birth [ ][ ] [ ][ ] [ ][ ][ ][ ]
9. Race [ ]

   1 = White (not of Hispanic origin)
   2 = Black (not of Hispanic origin)
   3 = American Indian
   4 = Alaskan Native
   5 = Asian or Pacific Islander
   6 = Hispanic - Mexican
   7 = Hispanic - Puerto Rican
   8 = Hispanic - Cuban
   9 = Other Hispanic
10. Religious preference [ ]

    1 = Protestant
    2 = Catholic
    3 = Jewish
    4 = Islamic
    5 = Other
    6 = None
11. Have you been in a controlled environment in the last 30 days?

    1 = No
    2 = Jail
    3 = Alcohol or drug treatment
    4 = Medical treatment
    5 = Psychiatric treatment
    6 = Other

    How many days [ ][ ]
12. Assessment interviewer [ ][ ][ ][ ][ ][ ][ ][ ][ ][ ][ ][ ][ ]
13. Special [ ] 1 = Client terminated 2 = Client refused
    3 = Client unable to respond

MEDICAL STATUS

1. How many times in your life have you been hospitalized for medical problems? (Include ODs and DTs, but exclude detox.) [ ][ ]

2. How long ago was your last hospitalization for a physical problem? [ ][ ] Months [ ][ ] Years

3. Do you have any chronic medical that continue to interfere with your life? [ ]
   0 = No 1 = Yes ______________________________ Specify

4. Are you taking any prescribed medication on a regular basis for a physical problem? [ ]
   0 = No 1 = Yes ______________________________ Specify

5. Do you receive a pension for a physical disability? (Exclude psychiatric disability.) [ ]
   0 = No 1 = Yes ______________________________ Specify

6. How many days have you experienced medical problems in the past 30? [ ][ ]

Instructions: For the next two questions, ask client to use Client's Rating Scale.

0 = Not at all   3 = Considerably
1 = Slightly   4 = Extremely
2 = Moderately

7. How troubled or bothered have you been by these medical problems in the past 30 days? [ ]

8. How important to you *now* is treatment for these medical problems? [ ]

Instructions: For the next question, use Interviewer Severity Rating Scale.

Rate: 0 = No treatment necessary to
9 = Treatment needed to intervene in life-threatening situation

9. How would you rate the client's need for medical treatment? [ ]

Confidence Ratings

10. Is the above information significantly distorted by:

Client's misrepresentation? [ ] 0 = No 1 = Yes

Client's inability to understand? [ ] 0 = No 1 = Yes

Interviewer comments:

MEDICAL HISTORY

1. Have you ever had any problems with:

_____	Blood pressure	_____	Bowels
_____	Heart	_____	Back pains
_____	Stomach	_____	Hepatitis
_____	Liver	_____	Diabetes
_____	Kidneys	_____	Cancer
_____	Lungs	_____	Arthritis
_____	Skin	_____	Hypoglycemia

2. Any family history of these medical problems?
3. Do you smoke cigarettes? [ ] 0 = No 1 = Yes
   If yes, frequency ____________________
4. Have you ever had surgery? [ ] 0 = No 1 = Yes
   If yes, describe ____________________

Interviewer comments:

EMPLOYMENT/EDUCATION HISTORY

1. Employer ____________________ Wage __________
   Position ____________________ Dates employed __________

Reason for leaving ____________________

Instructions: For the next four questions, use this rating scale:

0 = Never 1 = Some 2 = Often

2. Did you ever drink/get high at work/school? [ ]
3. Did you ever drink/get high before work/school? [ ]
4. Did you ever miss work/school due to alcohol/drug use? [ ]
5. Have you ever lost a job due to alcohol/drug use? [ ]
6. Highest grade completed ______ School ____________________
7. Year graduated ____________________
8. Current educational/vocational program ____________________
9. Special training or skills ____________________

10. Longest period of employment ______ Where? ______________________

11. Are you unemployed? ______ How long? ______________________

Interviewer comments:

MILITARY HISTORY

1. Service branch ______________________________________

   Entry date ________________ Release date ________________

   Discharge type ______________________________________

2. Vietnam era veteran? [ ] 0 = No 1 = Yes

3. Was discharge due to: [ ] Alcohol abuse [ ] Drug abuse [ ] Neither

Interviewer comments:

EMPLOYMENT/SUPPORT STATUS

1. Education completed (GED = 12 years) [ ][ ] Years [ ][ ] Months

   Training or technical education completed [ ][ ] Years [ ][ ] Months

2. Do you have a profession, trade, or skill? [ ] 0 = No 1 = Yes

   Specify ______________________________________

3. Do you have a valid driver's license? [ ] 0 = No 1 = Yes

4. Do you have an automobile available for use? (No, if no valid driver's license) [ ] 0 = No 1 = Yes

5. How long was your longest full-time job? [ ][ ] Years [ ][ ] Months

6. Usual or last occupation ______________________________________

7. Does someone contribute to your support in any way? [ ] 0 = No 1 = Yes

8. If yes, does this constitute the majority of your support? [ ] 0 = No 1 = Yes

9. Usual employment pattern last 3 years [ ]
   - 1 = Full-time (40 hours/week)
   - 2 = Part-time (regular hrs)
   - 3 = Part-time (irregular day work)
   - 4 = Student
   - 5 = Service
   - 6 = Retired/disability
   - 7 = Unemployed
   - 8 = In controlled environment

10. How many days were you paid for working during the past 30 days? (Include "under the table" pay.) [ ][ ]

11. How much money did you receive from the following sources in the past 30 days?

    Employment (net income) [ ][ ][ ][ ][ ][ ]

    Unemployment compensation [ ][ ][ ][ ][ ]

    DPA [ ][ ][ ][ ][ ]

    Pension benefits or Social Security [ ][ ][ ][ ][ ]

    Mate, family, or friends (for personal expenses) [ ][ ][ ][ ][ ]

    Illegal [ ][ ][ ][ ][ ]

12. How many people depend on you for the majority of their food, shelter, etc.? [ ][ ]

13. How many days have you experienced employment problems in the past 30 days? [ ][ ]

Instructions: For the next two questions, ask client to use Client's Rating Scale.

0 = Not at all
1 = Slightly
2 = Moderately
3 = Considerably
4 = Extremely

14. How troubled or bothered have you been by these employment problems in the past 30 days? [ ]

15. How important to you *now* is counseling for these employment problems? [ ]

Instructions: For the next question, use Interviewer Severity Rating Scale.

Rate: 0 = No treatment necessary to
9 = Treatment needed to intervene in life-threatening situation

16. How would you rate the client's need for employment counseling? [ ]

Confidence Ratings

17. Is the above information significantly distorted by:

    Client's misrepresentation? [ ] 0 = No 1 = Yes

    Client's inability to understand? [ ] 0 = No 1 = Yes

Interviewer comments:

PATTERN OF DRUG USE

Instructions: Follow the codes in the box.

Drug Codes

02 - Heroin
03 - Methadone
04 - Other opiates
05 - Alcohol
06 - Barbiturates
07 - Quaaludes
08 - Tranquilizers
09 - Amphetamines
10 - Cocaine
11 - Pot/Hashish
12 - Hallucinogens
13 - Inhalants
14 - PCP
99 - Other

Frequency

0 - No use for past 6 months
1 - Constantly
2 - Every day
3 - Almost daily
4 - 3 to 4 days a week
5 - Weekends
6 - Less than once a week
7 - Once a month
8 - Less than once a month

How Taken

1 - Swallowed
2 - Smoked
3 - Snorted
4 - Sniffed
5 - Skin-popped
6 - Mainlined

Pattern of Use

1 - Alone
2 - With friends
3 - Alone with group
4 - No set style

Where Used

1 - Own place
2 - Bar/club
3 - Friend's place
4 - Street

Drug	Frequency	How Taken	Pattern of Use	Where Used	Age at First Use	Age at Last Use
[ ][ ]	[ ]	[ ]	[ ]	[ ]	[ ][ ]	[ ][ ]
[ ][ ]	[ ]	[ ]	[ ]	[ ]	[ ][ ]	[ ][ ]
[ ][ ]	[ ]	[ ]	[ ]	[ ]	[ ][ ]	[ ][ ]
[ ][ ]	[ ]	[ ]	[ ]	[ ]	[ ][ ]	[ ][ ]
[ ][ ]	[ ]	[ ]	[ ]	[ ]	[ ][ ]	[ ][ ]

1. Can you remember your first drunk/high? [ ] 0 = No 1 = Yes
2. Have you ever overdosed on drugs/alcohol? [ ] 0 = No 1 = Yes
3. If yes, what substance? ______________________________
4. Usual alcoholic drink? ______________________________
5. Longest period of time you have been drug- and alcohol-free __________

Instructions: Read the following statements, asking the client to choose which block best describes his or her response.

	Often	Sometimes	Seldom	Never
6. I seem to feel more at ease or less self-conscious around people after a few drinks.	[ ]	[ ]	[ ]	[ ]
7. I seem to spend a lot of time thinking about drinking or getting high.	[ ]	[ ]	[ ]	[ ]
8. People tell me I keep too much held inside.	[ ]	[ ]	[ ]	[ ]
9. I have lost my temper or argued with someone after getting high.	[ ]	[ ]	[ ]	[ ]
10. I have planned my day around using alcohol/drugs or I have gone to great pains to make sure it is available.	[ ]	[ ]	[ ]	[ ]
11. I must have what I want when I want it regardless of the consequence.	[ ]	[ ]	[ ]	[ ]
12. I feel bad or guilty about things I've said or done while under the influence.	[ ]	[ ]	[ ]	[ ]
13. I have gotten into physical fights/destroyed property while under the influence.	[ ]	[ ]	[ ]	[ ]
14. People have told me I'm a "different person" while under the influence.	[ ]	[ ]	[ ]	[ ]
15. In the past 5 years I have been drunk or high at least 2 days in a row.	[ ]	[ ]	[ ]	[ ]
16. If someone tries to keep me from drinking or from getting high I get angry or abuse them.	[ ]	[ ]	[ ]	[ ]
17. I use alcohol or drugs in order to have fun.	[ ]	[ ]	[ ]	[ ]
18. I have found that the more I get drunk/high, the worse my problems seem to be.	[ ]	[ ]	[ ]	[ ]
19. I think that I'm hurting those closest to me.	[ ]	[ ]	[ ]	[ ]
20. I have experienced feelings like craving when I am not drinking or getting high.	[ ]	[ ]	[ ]	[ ]
21. I have missed something important—days at work or time with friends, family, or children—because of my use of alcohol/drugs.	[ ]	[ ]	[ ]	[ ]
22. My alcohol/drug use has gotten in the way of my functioning.	[ ]	[ ]	[ ]	[ ]
23. I have tried to stop or cut down on my use but have been unsuccessful.	[ ]	[ ]	[ ]	[ ]
24. I have had to increase the amount of alcohol or drugs I use in order to get a "buzz."	[ ]	[ ]	[ ]	[ ]
25. I have failed in many goals in life, lost money, and given up social or occupational contacts because of my drug/alcohol use.	[ ]	[ ]	[ ]	[ ]

	Often	Sometimes	Seldom	Never
26. I have physically endangered myself or others while under the influence.	[ ]	[ ]	[ ]	[ ]
27. I wake up in the morning shaking or feeling like getting high.	[ ]	[ ]	[ ]	[ ]
28. I drink/use drugs in the morning before eating/going to work or school.	[ ]	[ ]	[ ]	[ ]
29. I have had a drink or gotten high when I feel:				
Angry or ticked off at someone/something	[ ]	[ ]	[ ]	[ ]
Depressed, upset, hurt feelings	[ ]	[ ]	[ ]	[ ]
Lonely, something to do	[ ]	[ ]	[ ]	[ ]
Happy, good mood, want to celebrate	[ ]	[ ]	[ ]	[ ]
Frustrated, bad day, things go wrong	[ ]	[ ]	[ ]	[ ]
Parties, get-togethers among friends, family	[ ]	[ ]	[ ]	[ ]
30. I don't remember things I've said or done when I'm under the influence.	[ ]	[ ]	[ ]	[ ]

Interviewer comments:

DRUG/ALCOHOL USE

1. Do you use more than one substance? [ ] 0 = No 1 = Yes
2. Which substances are you likely to combine? ______________________
3. How often do you combine these substances? ______________________
4. How long was your last period of voluntary abstinence? [ ][ ] Months [ ][ ] Years
5. How long ago did this abstinence end? [ ][ ] Months [ ][ ] Years
6. How many times have you:

   Had alcohol DTs [ ][ ]

   Overdosed on drugs [ ][ ]

   If overdosed on drugs, what substance? ______________________
7. How many times have you been treated for:

   Alcohol abuse [ ][ ]

   Drug abuse [ ][ ]

   Where were you treated? ______________________
8. How many of these were detox only? [ ]

9. How much would you say you have spent during the last 30 days on: [ ][ ] Alcohol [ ][ ] Drugs
10. How many days have you been treated in an outpatient setting for alcohol or drugs in the last 30 days? [ ][ ]
11. How many days in the last 30 days have you experienced: [ ][ ] Alcohol problems [ ][ ] Drug problems

Instructions: For the next two questions, ask client to use Client's Rating Scale.

0 = Not at all
1 = Slightly
2 = Moderately
3 = Considerably
4 = Extremely

12. How troubled or bothered have you been in the past 30 days by these: [ ][ ] Alcohol problems [ ][ ] Drug problems
13. How important to you now is treatment for these: [ ][ ] Alcohol problems [ ][ ] Drug problems

Instructions: For the next question, use Interviewer Severity Rating Scale.

Rate: 0 = No treatment necessary to
9 = Treatment needed to intervene in life-threatening situation

14. How would you rate the client's need for treatment for: [ ][ ] Alcohol problems [ ][ ] Drug problems

Confidence Ratings

15. Is the above information significantly distorted by:

Client's misrepresentation? [ ] 0 = No 1 = Yes

Client's inability to understand? [ ] 0 = No 1 = Yes

Interviewer comments:

LEGAL STATUS

1. Was this request for services prompted or suggested by the criminal justice system? (Judge, probation, parole officer, etc.) [ ] 0 = No 1 = Yes
2. Are you on probation or parole? [ ] 0 = No 1 = Yes
3. How many times in your life have you been arrested and *charged* with the following:

Shoplifting/vandalism	[ ][ ]	Assault	[ ][ ]
Parole/probation violations	[ ][ ]	Arson	[ ][ ]
Drug charges	[ ][ ]	Rape	[ ][ ]
Homicide, manslaughter	[ ][ ]	Forgery	[ ][ ]

Weapons offense	[ ][ ]	Prostitution	[ ][ ]
Burglary, larceny, B&E	[ ][ ]	Robbery	[ ][ ]
Contempt of court	[ ][ ]	Other	[ ][ ]

4. How many of these charges resulted in convictions? [ ][ ]
5. How many times in your life have you been charged with the following?

   Disorderly conduct, vagrancy, public intoxication? [ ][ ]

   Driving while intoxicated? [ ][ ]

   Major driving violations? (Reckless driving, speeding, no license, etc.) [ ][ ]
6. How many months were you incarcerated in your life? [ ][ ][ ]
7. How long was your last incarceration? [ ][ ] Months [ ][ ] Years
8. What was it for? ________________
9. Are you presently awaiting charges, trial, or sentence? [ ] 0 = No 1 = Yes
10. If yes, what for? ________________
11. How many days in the last 30 days were you detained or incarcerated? [ ][ ]
12. How many days in the last 30 days have you engaged in illegal activities for profit? [ ][ ]

Instructions: For the next two questions, ask client to use Client's Rating Scale.

0 = Not at all
1 = Slightly
2 = Moderately
3 = Considerably
4 = Extremely

13. How serious do you feel your present legal problems are? [ ]
14. How important to you *now* is counseling or referral for these legal problems? [ ]

Instructions: For the next question, use Interviewer Severity Rating Scale.

Rate: 0 = No treatment necessary to
9 = Treatment needed to intervene in life-threatening situation

15. How would you rate the client's need for legal services or counseling? [ ]

Confidence Ratings

16. Is the above information significantly distorted by:

    Client's misrepresentation? [ ] 0 = No 1 = Yes

    Client's inability to understand? [ ] 0 = No 1 = Yes

Interviewer comments:

PERSONAL INFORMATION

1. Place of birth ______________________________
2. Weight ______________ Height ______________
3. Present living arrangement ______________________
   (Note length of time client has lived in this area, instability in living arrangement, transient, etc.)
4. Does client attend church? [ ] 0 = No 1 = Yes

   If yes, where? ______________ How often? ______________
5. Religious preference ______________________________

FAMILY/MARITAL HISTORY

1. Month/year of marriage ______________ No. of years ________
2. Month/year of divorce/separation ______________ No. of years ________
3. Was separation/divorce related to client's alcohol/drug use? [ ] 0 = No 1 = Yes
4. How many children? ______________________________

   Names, gender, and ages:

	Name	Age	Address	Occupation
5. Spouse				
Father				
Mother				

No. of brothers ________ No. of sisters ________ Client's birth order ________

6. Describe relationships with family:
   (Is family supportive, nonsupportive, close, etc.?)

7. Family problems past/present: (Family deaths, separations, divorces, single-parent family, family history of drug/alcohol abuse, etc.)

8. Have any of your relatives had what you would call a significant drinking, drug use, or psychiatric problem—one that did or should have led to treatment?

Instructions: Place "0" in relative category where the answer is clearly *no for all relatives in that category*; "1" where the answer is clearly *yes for any relative within that category*; "x" where the answer is *uncertain or "I don't know"*; and "N" where there *never was a relative from that category.*

	Mother's side			Father's side		
	Alcohol	Drugs	Psychiatric	Alcohol	Drugs	Psychiatric
Grandmother						
Grandfather						
Mother/father						
Aunt						
Uncle						

	Siblings		
	Alcohol	Drugs	Psychiatric
Brother No. 1			
Brother No. 2			
Sister No. 1			
Sister No. 2			

Interviewer comments:

RELATIONSHIPS

1. Marital status ______________________________

2. How long have you been in the marital status? [ ][ ] Months [ ][ ] Years

3. Are you satisfied with this situation?

   [ ] 0 = No 1 = Yes 2 = Indifferent

4. Has your usual living arrangement for the past 3 years been: [ ]
   1 = With sexual partner and children
   2 = With sexual partner alone
   3 = With children alone
   4 = With parents
   5 = With family
   6 = With friends
   7 = Alone
   8 = Controlled environment
   9 = No stable arrangement

5. How long have you lived in this arrangement? [ ][ ] Months [ ][ ] Years

6. Are you satisfied with your living arrangement? [ ]
   0 = No 1 = Yes 2 = Indifferent

7. Do you live with anyone who: 0 = No 1 = Yes

   Has a current alcohol problem? [ ]

   Uses nonprescribed drugs? [ ]

8. With whom do you spend most of your free time? [ ]
   1 = Family 2 = Friends 3 = Alone

9. Are you satisfied spending your free time this way? [ ]
   0 = No 1 = Yes 2 = Indifferent

10. How many close friends do you have? [ ] [ ]

11. Would you say you have had a close, long-lasting personal relationship with any of the following people in your life?

Instructions: Place "0" in relative category where the answer is clearly *no for all relatives in that category*; "1" where the answer is clearly *yes for any relative within that category*; "x" where the answer is *uncertain or "I don't know"*; and "N" where there *never was a relative from that category*.

Mother	Father	Brother/sister	Sexual partner/spouse	Children	Friends

12. Have you had significant periods in which you have experienced serious problems getting along with: 0 = No 1 = Yes

	Past 30 days	In your life
Mother		
Father		
Brothers/sisters		
Children		
Other family member		
Close friends		
Neighbors		
Coworkers		

13. Did any of these people abuse you: 0 = No 1 = Yes

    Emotionally, by making you feel bad through harsh words? [ ]

    Physically, causing you physical harm? [ ]

    Sexually, through forced sexual advances or acts? [ ]

14. How many days in the past 30 days have you had serious conflicts:

    With your family [ ]

    With other people excluding family [ ]

Instructions: For the next two questions, ask client to use Client's Rating Scale.

0 = Not at all
1 = Slightly
2 = Moderately
3 = Considerably
4 = Extremely

15. How troubled or bothered have you been in the past 30 days by these:

    Family problems [ ]

    Social problems [ ]

16. How important to you now is treatment for these:

    Family problems [ ]

    Social problems [ ]

Instructions: For the next question, use Interviewer Severity Rating Scale.

Rate: 0 = No treatment necessary to
9 = Treatment needed to intervene in life-threatening situation

17. How would you rate the client's need for family and/or social counseling? [ ]

Confidence Ratings

18. Is the above information significantly distorted by:

Client's misrepresentation? [ ] 0 = No 1 = Yes

Client's inability to understand? [ ] 0 = No 1 = Yes

Interviewer comments:

PSYCHIATRIC STATUS

1. How many times have you been treated for psychological or emotional problems?

   In the hospital [ ] [ ]

   As an outpatient or private client [ ] [ ]

2. Do you receive a pension for a psychiatric disability? [ ] 0 = No 1 = Yes

3. Have you had a significant period that was not a direct result of drug/alcohol abuse in which you have experienced: 0 = No 1 = Yes

	Serious depression	Serious anxiety or tension	Hallucinations	Trouble understanding, concentrating, or remembering
Past 30 days				
In your life				

	Trouble controlling violent behavior	Serious thoughts of suicide	Suicide attempt	Taking prescribed medications for a psychological or emotional problem
Past 30 days				
In your life				

4. How many days in the past 30 days have you experienced these psychological or emotional problems? [ ] [ ]
5. Have you ever thought about hurting yourself or taking your own life? [ ] 0 = No 1 = Yes

Instructions: For the next two questions, ask client to use Client's Rating Scale.

0 = Not at all 3 = Considerably
1 = Slightly 4 = Extremely
2 = Moderately

6. How much have you been troubled or bothered by these psychological or emotional problems in the past 30 days? [ ]
7. How important to you *now* is treatment for these psychological or emotional problems? [ ]

Instructions: For the next question, use Interviewer Severity Rating Scale.

Rate: 0 = No treatment necessary to
9 = Treatment needed to intervene in life-threatening situation

8. How would you rate the client's need for psychological/psychiatric treatment? [ ]

Confidence Ratings

9. Is the above information significantly distorted by:

Client's misrepresentation? [ ] 0 = No 1 = Yes

Client's inability to understand? [ ] 0 = No 1 = Yes

Interviewer comments:

QUESTIONS FOR INTERVIEWER

1. At any time during the interview, was the client: [ ] 0 = No 1 = Yes

Obviously depressed/withdrawn [ ]

Obviously hostile [ ]

Obviously anxious/nervous [ ]

Obviously having trouble with reality testing, thought disorders, paranoid thinking [ ]

Obviously having trouble comprehending, remembering [ ]

Having suicidal thoughts [ ]

Severity Profile

	0	1	2	3	4	5	6	7	8	9
2. Problems (General overall severity of the problems as a whole)	[ ]	[ ]	[ ]	[ ]	[ ]	[ ]	[ ]	[ ]	[ ]	[ ]
3. Medical	[ ]	[ ]	[ ]	[ ]	[ ]	[ ]	[ ]	[ ]	[ ]	[ ]
4. Employment/support	[ ]	[ ]	[ ]	[ ]	[ ]	[ ]	[ ]	[ ]	[ ]	[ ]
5. Alcohol	[ ]	[ ]	[ ]	[ ]	[ ]	[ ]	[ ]	[ ]	[ ]	[ ]
6. Drugs	[ ]	[ ]	[ ]	[ ]	[ ]	[ ]	[ ]	[ ]	[ ]	[ ]
7. Legal	[ ]	[ ]	[ ]	[ ]	[ ]	[ ]	[ ]	[ ]	[ ]	[ ]
8. Family/social	[ ]	[ ]	[ ]	[ ]	[ ]	[ ]	[ ]	[ ]	[ ]	[ ]
9. Psychiatric	[ ]	[ ]	[ ]	[ ]	[ ]	[ ]	[ ]	[ ]	[ ]	[ ]

Interviewer's Summary of Interview: Impressions and Recommendations

Interviewer comments:

Chapter 6

Case Management with Individuals with Mental Illness

INTRODUCTION

When John and Belinda were married, John had already suffered two episodes of mania, periods of extreme activity, restlessness, and grand, unrealistic plans. Belinda had known John since they were in college in the music program together. She played the piano, but stopped playing professionally in order to raise a family. John, on the other hand, was an accomplished musician and played in a local symphony orchestra. Soon after the couple were married, they moved to a new city so that John could accept a position in the orchestra there. Shortly after the move, John suffered another manic episode and, at that time, was referred to mental health services where he was assigned a case manager.

John liked his case manager, a young man about John's age, and stopped in to see him each time he visited the psychiatrist to have his medication checked and his prescriptions renewed. In addition, they had regular visits during the year just to make sure things were working well for John.

One afternoon the case manager received a call from Belinda. John had been up most of the night before and had gone out early that morning. He was carrying his violin case and seemed irritable. The case manager asked Belinda to call him when John returned and told her that if John would not come out to the mental health center, he would make a home visit. Early the next morning, Belinda called the case manager and reported that John had come home only long enough to get his tuxedo for that night's concert. She said he was disheveled and irritable, and he "couldn't stop talking to me, just talking and talking. I couldn't get him to stop. He was just going on and on about music he had been writing all night in his head down at the bus station, of all places. I think he was down there all night."

The case manager decided steps needed to be taken to have someone see John. It sounded as if he was in another manic episode, and the case manager was worried that John might get into a situation that would be dangerous to him because of his seemingly impaired judgment. Belinda came to the center that morning as soon as the children had gone to school. She signed commitment papers, which the case manager took to the crisis team that would attempt to find John. When the team did not locate him during the day at any of the places Belinda suggested they check, the crisis team went to the auditorium with the case manager where the concert was to be played that night.

The case manager saw John enter the auditorium, carrying his violin case and dressed in his tuxedo. Turning to the crisis team, the case manager asked that they hold off giving John the commitment papers until after the concert. "If he can play in the concert tonight, I don't want to go in there and present these to him in front of his friends and colleagues. We can give him the papers when he comes out to his car."

That night John played beautifully. Orchestra members noted that he was irritable and rushed and talkative, but did not think it was extremely unusual. The team waited by the car, and when John came out after the concert, the case manager talked to him, showing him the papers and asking him to come with the team to the hospital to be examined by a physician. John went willingly, primarily because of the good rapport he had with his case manager. At the emergency room, the physician talked to John at some length.

Seeing him in his tuxedo and knowing he had just completed a long and difficult concert with the symphony orchestra, the doctor declined to execute the commitment, saying he felt John was tired and run down, but not in need of hospitalization. John's case manager thanked John for coming to the hospital and told him he was free to go home, but the case manager felt uneasy. It had been a long day and the case manager went home also.

The next afternoon a security officer called from one of the government buildings in the city. He claimed that John, still dressed in his tuxedo, had been playing his violin all night and all that day, first in the parking lot, later outside office doors, and finally in court rooms until he was eventually ejected from the building. "He's playing good stuff. You know, Beethoven and Bach. At least that's what he says he's playing. Sounds good to me, but he won't leave and he won't stop." The case manager called Belinda to let her know where John was, and then joined the crisis team to once again talk John into going to the hospital emergency room.

The case manager was shocked when he saw John at the government building. John was disheveled, with his tuxedo rumpled and torn, and playing furiously. Unlike previous times they had met, John was rude and even loud with the case manager, saying he needed to play this music here and now and calling the case manager "a low-class dude who wouldn't know adagio from allegro." Alarmed at the deterioration, the case manager signed commitment papers and, with the help of the crisis team and the security officer at the government building, managed to get John to the emergency room once again. This time another physician took one look at John and saw clearly that he was experiencing a manic episode and needed hospitalization. After trying unsuccessfully to talk to John, who talked over everyone else and sang loudly when he could not play, the case manager signed the paper to have John hospitalized. John was taken upstairs just after Belinda arrived with the children.

It only took a few days to establish what happened. John had been feeling well, better than usual, he said. He decided that he did not need his medication anymore and had stopped taking it. Soon after that he became ill again and needed the help of his case manager. After his stay in the hospital, John came back to the office to see his case manager and to apologize for the "things I might have said." John's case manager pointed out to John that he was not himself that night and that it was fortunate he was able to go to the hospital and be stabilized on medication again. They talked at length about the need to stay on the medication and the need for John to let the case manager know the next time he felt like going off his medication. John went on to play many more concerts with the symphony orchestra and to benefit from regular contacts with his case manager.

SPECIAL CONSIDERATIONS

Addressing Brain Disorders, Not Emotional Problems

This chapter will only address several of the more common brain disorders you are likely to encounter if you work in mental health. There are many reasons people seek treatment in mental health facilities that are not related to abnormalities in their brain chemistry or brain structure. Going though a divorce, seeking support to parent a difficult child, or working in therapy on the feelings caused by sexual abuse in childhood are all good reasons to seek help, but in those cases, the person seeking the help is rarely mentally ill. Usually the person's response is normal under the circumstances.

Research is giving us more and more information about brain chemistry and structure, and this research has led to more effective treatments and a better understanding of mental illness than in the past. Conditions that were once thought to be related to bad mothering, like schizophrenia, or to a poor attitude, like depression, are now understood to be the result of abnormalities or chemical imbalances in the brain. We will look primarily at these illnesses in this chapter. There are many other diagnoses in the *DSM-IV-TR* with which you will become acquainted when you begin to work in this field.

What You Are Likely to See

In this chapter we will look at common mental illnesses, but it is important to note that individuals with mental disorders often have a multitude of other problems. For example, many individuals coming for mental health services may also have drug and alcohol problems. Sometimes people have used these substances to self-medicate, or substance abuse itself has led to mental health problems such as depression. For more on mental illness and drug and alcohol abuse, consult Chapter 5.

In addition to mental problems, many individuals have been involved with the law. Sometimes they have committed petty crimes such as prostitution or shoplifting, but you may see clients who have been convicted of more serious crimes. Many mental health clients are arrested for behaviors that are a direct result of their illness. Law enforcement and communities are less tolerant of inappropriate behavior now that more individuals with mental disorders live among us. Sometimes these crimes were committed for financial support. Clients who are awaiting trial or who have a criminal background are best served by a case manager who acts as a liaison between the criminal justice system and the mental health system. In some cases, the probation and parole office may have an officer who is also an expert in mental health issues.

We will look at the most common mental disorders, but you need to be prepared to see additional problems in the lives of your clients.

Taking Things Personally

People who are contending with a mental illness are likely to say things to you that under the norms of normal social interaction would be considered insulting or hurtful. Depression and mania are often accompanied by high levels of irritability. People whose thinking is disturbed by schizophrenia are likely to say things that are patently untrue and may be hurtful, but these are simply a product of the distorted reality they are experiencing. In addition, families who feel frightened by their family member's illness or overwhelmed and possibly even guilty may seem unpleasant and demanding to you.

It cannot be stressed enough that you must learn to understand the underlying fears and concerns of your clients and their families and not take these comments or demands personally. Deal with the comments matter-of-factly, and continue your relationship with the client and family. Some workers who are not skilled in this area or who lack good communication skills actually punish such clients and families by refusing to take or return calls, becoming irritable and unpleasant themselves, or withholding treatment that is needed. You may hear your coworkers complain about the remarks and behavior of clients whom the workers have found offensive. Often such workers act as if they had no idea clients could behave this way. They do not understand that the behavior is not a personal attack but is a symptom of the illness. *Do not fall into the trap of taking hurtful or demanding remarks by your client or your client's family personally!*

National Alliance for the Mentally Ill (NAMI)

This chapter was written with the cooperation of the National Alliance for the Mentally Ill (NAMI), which provided numerous resources and information. NAMI advocates for better treatment of those with mental illness, including better and more realistic insurance coverage. NAMI has four major focuses, all of which may be helpful to the case manager.

1. *Support.* One of the charges of this organization is to give support to "persons with serious brain disorders and their families." This means that you should look for support in your state and community. There are many local chapters of NAMI, and this support is what families and clients need to see them through the rough times. By getting in touch with your nearest NAMI office, you can obtain all kinds of material on various psychiatric diagnoses that families and clients will find enormously helpful.
2. *Advocacy.* As you work in the mental health field, you will see many areas that need to be changed to benefit clients. NAMI advocates for clients and their families on the state and federal levels. Joining NAMI's efforts will help you to change some of the regulations that currently make it hard for clients and their families.
3. *Research.* NAMI has funded and supported research to better understand mental illness and to find more effective treatment.
4. *Education.* NAMI hopes to educate the general public in order to reduce the "pervasive stigma toward severe mental illness." You can team up with NAMI to work on reducing stigma in your own community.

Probably most important is the fact that case managers can obtain support and resource material for their clients and their families from NAMI and also from the Mental Health Association. You will encounter stigma, discrimination, ignorance, fear, and indifference while working in the mental health field, but you will have resources to help you counter those in your own community.

DSM-IV-TR

This chapter relies heavily on information found in the *DSM-IV-TR*. For more information on how case managers use the *DSM-IV-TR*, read Chapter 16 in *Fundamentals of Case Management Practice* (Summers, 2001). There you will learn the language of the *DSM* and how it is used, enabling you to better participate in discussions concerning diagnosis.

Stigma

Because of the unpredictable nature of many mental illnesses and because there has been, until recently, very little real understanding of what causes mental illness, people who suffer from a mental illness generally are shunned by their families and communities, even in the present day. People with mental illness experience all kinds of discrimination and rejection. The more severe the illness, the less people are willing to associate with the person who is ill. Part of your work is to be there for people who have few or no resources for support and to help them negotiate a system that is often hostile to them. Another important part of your work is to lessen the stigma of mental illness with every opportunity you get. This means educating employers, landlords, families, and others in the community about the biochemical nature of mental illness, that is, the fact that it is a disease and can be treated.

Mental Health and the Media

Among those who stigmatize the mentally ill is the media. Articles and stories about people with mental illness are often written in a breathless or frightening manner and serve to preserve the notion in the mind of the public that people with a mental illness are dangerous and unpredictable. For you, the problem will be how to deal with the media.

One afternoon in October Goldie was traveling from one city to another on the train. During her ride she became disturbed and difficult to manage. The Amtrack officials concluded that she posed a danger to others and put her off the train in a city along the route, notifying the police in that city. The police picked Goldie up and took her to the police station. It was obvious to the police that Goldie was mentally disturbed, and they immediately called mental health workers to come and make an assessment.

Two workers went to the police station and interviewed Goldie. They went with her to the hospital where she was given medications that seemed to soothe her and greatly diminish her disruptive behavior. They called her family in the city to which Goldie was traveling and learned that they were waiting for her to arrive and would be glad to meet her on the next bus. Family members informed the workers that Goldie had recently begun to "act crazy," but up until now she had been just fine, holding a job she loved and mothering two children well. The workers talked to the bus company and arranged for Goldie to travel to her family, only an hour away.

By now Goldie was entirely calmed down and doing well. The police promised to look after Goldie and see that she got on her bus. The workers got a dinner for Goldie and continued on to another emergency situation. Sometime before Goldie's bus arrived, Goldie finished her dinner, got up and left the police station, and jumped in the river, committing suicide. No one could have predicted this, based on her history or what was observed. Immediately the media reported the story, accusing mental health workers of "allowing" this woman to jump in the river. The paper wrote a scorching story about the inability of the mental health workers to predict the suicide and concluded that anyone should be able to know when a person is that ill. Many times the paper called the mental health center for an interview. Workers were not able to acknowledge the case in any way because of confidentiality regulations. Each time the paper reported that "mental health had no comment." This led many in the community to conclude that mental health was hiding something and Goldie's case was mishandled.

Particularly frustrating is your inability to talk to the media about sensational cases because you are bound by the law and by the ethics of your profession not to reveal information about a client to anyone. This often makes you look as if you have something to hide.

Another common interaction case managers have with the media occurs when the media contacts the case manager and asks him or her to bring a client to a TV studio or newspaper for an interview. They will say they are doing a story on schizophrenia or obsessive-compulsive disorder and need a client of yours to be a part of the story. In these situations, you need to tell the media, warmly, to find a person for the interview themselves. Although we all appreciate any efforts to promote an understanding of mental illness, asking a client to do something that reveals the client's situation, which is generally one that is stigmatized in the community, is unfair. Clients may feel they need to do this for you and may waive their right to privacy, thinking they are doing you a favor. Placing clients in this position is unethical.

Finally, if the media in your community seems uneducated about mental illness and reports situations in a skewed or biased manner, your agency can talk to the media about services and illnesses to better educate them.

BACKGROUND

Up until World War II, individuals with mental illness were housed in large state institutions, away from their communities and families. During World War II, men who were conscientious objectors were assigned to work in the state hospitals. Largely as a result of their documentation and advocacy on behalf of those suffering from mental illness, Congress and the American people began to take a closer look at conditions within these hospitals.

Large state institutions were used to house the mentally ill for several reasons. First, people believed that this would make persons with mental illness less of a burden on society. Second, mental illness carried with it a negative stigma, and families who tucked their family member with a mental disorder into a state institution far from home could avoid daily reminders of that stigma. Another reason for these institutions was that there were no medications that could control the symptoms of mental illness. Procedures to calm people with mental illness and to control symptoms included insulin shock, electroconvulsive therapy, hot and cold baths, and restraints.

In the 1950s the first medications came on the market for general use in treating the symptoms of mental disorders such as schizophrenia and depression. With these new drugs it became feasible to let clients return to their communities. This seemed like an advance in treatment, a more enlightened way to treat individuals who suffered from these disorders.

Problems soon followed, however. In many states, the money to treat clients in their communities was not made available by state legislatures. Meanwhile, state institutions saw their populations dwindle and, in some cases, their doors close even as they continued to receive considerable funding. In many communities, individual case managers struggled with huge caseloads in an attempt to organize services and keep *clients* (formerly called *patients*) from deteriorating. Many clients went off their medication and could not find services to occupy them or help them find employment. Many lost their living arrangements due to the untreated symptoms of their illness.

Today the situation is not much better in many states. Case management for the mentally ill is inadequate, and case managers are overwhelmed. Many case managers receive new cases of clients who have been in treatment with private psychiatrists or psychologists until their insurance coverage ran out. These clients are then dropped by the private provider and become clients of the public system. In addition, managed care provides little or no financing for many services. Clients find themselves in revolving situations as they get funding for only so many days of hospitalization or partial hospitalization and emerge into the community barely stabilized, only to relapse again. Those working in the mental health field see the short-sightedness of such policies and work to revise them continually. Many case managers note that by not giving the longer-term care that would truly stabilize a person with a severe mental illness, the system actually spends more in repeatedly using only short-term fixes that do not have a lasting effect.

Case managers, clients and their families, and others are currently seeking to pass laws that will require insurance companies to fund the treatment of mental illness in the same way they fund the treatment of other illnesses. The term for this is *parity*. For example, according to the National Alliance for the Mentally Ill (NAMI), epilepsy and schizophrenia have about the same prevalence in the general population, but health insurers cover epilepsy fully, while those with schizophrenia must turn to public programs for funding of much-needed medical care. In January 1998, a national law went into effect stipulating that if an insurance plan covers mental illness at all, the caps on what can be spent each year and over the course of the person's enrollment in the plan must be the same as the caps for all other illnesses. This only applies, however, to individuals who work for companies with 50 or more employees, and some insurers have shown a reluctance to honor this provision, changing the caps only when forced to do so.

For all these reasons, case managers play an extremely important part in the mental health system, giving support and direction to clients, and a voice to the problems facing the system today. Case managers working in mental health have become the best advocates for their clients and the system that serves them. In addition, case management in mental health is excellent preparation for advanced degrees in any of the helping professions primarily because case managers see so many different diagnoses and problems and work on so many different solutions.

Assignment

Look at the mental health services in your community and in your state. How many clients do case managers typically carry? What is the status of state institutions for those with mental disorders? What state legislation is there to fund services for those with mental illness? What specialized services exist in your community? How are these funded?

MYTHS

This section discusses some of the common myths that you will hear as you work in the mental health field.

1. *A person who has had a mental illness can never be a normal person again.* Like any other illness, a person can recover from mental illness and return to normal functioning. Today, with new medication, this picture is even more hopeful. These medications with more effectiveness and fewer side effects give people a better chance than ever at normal functioning over periods of time. Even those who have what we call "recurring episodes" will often be well and productive in between episodes. It is not realistic to assume that a person who has had a mental

illness is permanently "crazy." Yet you will hear that notion expressed as you work with landlords, neighbors, and employers on behalf of those with mental disorders.

2. *Mentally ill people are dangerous.* The number of dangerous individuals among the population with mental illness is about the same as the number of dangerous people in the population as a whole. People with mental illness who commit serious crimes and crimes of violence get extensive press coverage, which serves to strengthen the notion that all people with mental illness are dangerous.
3. *Mentally ill people are highly unpredictable.* There are certain mental disorders that cause individuals to act impulsively. For instance, a person in a manic state might act in ways that seem irrational and inexplicable. When the person has recovered, he or she generally behaves in a consistent and reasonable manner. Furthermore, there are many highly impulsive people who are not labeled as mentally ill.
4. *People who were formerly treated for mental illness make poor employees.* Those who have recovered from a mental disorder are no more likely to be poor employees than anyone else. Indeed, the illness may require the person to take sick leave, but so do many other disorders.
5. *Only case managers and doctors can talk to those who have been mentally ill.* People rarely say this openly, but people will often go to lengths to avoid having to talk directly with someone who has once been diagnosed with a mental disorder. Individuals who have been diagnosed with a mental illness are as able to talk with others as anyone else when they are well. A common observation made among those who work with clients of the mental health system, such as case managers, is that people avoid talking to their clients because they somehow think mental illness is a communicable disease and they might catch it.

The outlook for those diagnosed with mental disorders today is brighter than it ever was, due to new and better medications to treat the symptoms of mental illness. For that reason, many of these myths lodged in the public mind are outdated and unrealistic. Part of what you will encounter in this field are unfounded myths, and part of what you will do is help to reeducate the public and reduce stigma.

Lars worked successfully for a large architectural firm. He held several degrees in architecture and one in engineering and was highly successful in school and in his work. Several times after high school Lars had felt deeply depressed to the extent that he was not able to function. Generally these "spells" passed quickly, and he would move ahead with confidence again. When he was 38, Lars again suffered a severe depression. After several weeks he recognized that the depression was not lifting, it was affecting his work, and he would need to see someone for help. He got a referral from a friend and began to see a clinician who prescribed antidepressant medication.

Lars mentioned to a friend at work that he had been having problems and was seeing a psychiatrist, after the friend joked that Lars seemed to be "pretty sleepy lately." Lars explained that it was a side effect of the medication he was on, but that the symptoms were expected to diminish soon.

Several days later Lars was called into his boss's office and terminated. The boss did not use Lars's mental illness as a reason, but cited instead increased absences from work (none of which had exceeded the number of days allowed under company policy) and the slower pace of Lars's work in recent weeks. Nevertheless, it was clear that the real cause of the firing was Lars's recent bout with depression and the discomfort his boss and coworker felt when working with someone suffering from a mental problem. Today we hope that companies are more enlightened about mental illness and that Lars's experience would be less likely to be repeated.

Lars, however, now tells no one of his illness, fearing similar reprisals in the future. He is doing well on continued low doses of antidepressants, and he is again dynamic and successful in his work, having opened his own firm after he was fired. No one knows of his past illness. Because many successful and productive people hide their disorders, the myths about people with mental illness persist in our society.

WAYS OF VIEWING MENTAL ILLNESS

There are primarily four ways to look at mental illness. We will examine each of them in this section.

1. *Biomedical model.* This model views a number of psychiatric conditions as stemming from imbalances in the chemistry of the brain. In some cases, such as depression, depletions in certain neurotransmitters are considered a likely cause. In the case of schizophrenia, an overabundance of dopamine is thought to cause some of the more severe symptoms of the disorder. More and more research is being done to help us understand how the biochemistry of the brain affects mood and behavior. With the emphasis from managed care on short-term treatment for mental disorders, treatment using medications that rebalance the brain's chemistry are more attractive.
2. *Psychodynamic model.* In this model individuals are thought to have an illness that is derived from the way the person defends him- or herself from reality. When the person's defense mechanisms are used to the detriment of his or her functioning, the person seeks help. For instance, if a person tells lies to compensate for a life that seems less successful than it should be or if a person denies there are problems in certain situations in order to avoid dealing with real issues, the person might eventually need help. In the case of depression, the theory often looks at anger the person has that he or she cannot express; therefore, the person turns the anger inward onto him- or herself. Formerly people who underwent treatment under this model visited with a clinician numerous times, discussing issues and problems at length. The therapy could take years and was expensive. In today's short-term therapy climate, this type of therapy is provided only for those who can pay for it personally or through private insurance plans.
3. *Behavioral model.* People who view mental illness in behavioral terms are generally looking at disorders other than psychotic disorders and manic depression. For example, behaviorists think that behavioral theories are helpful in treating depression and personal adjustment problems that might arise as a result of more severe forms of mental illness, but not the severe mental illness itself. Behaviorists do not look at early personality development and tend to dislike attaching diagnoses to people. Their concern is with the behavior itself, believing that the person learned to respond this way for a particular reason and that the response is now detrimental to the person's well-being or adjustment. For this reason, treatment focuses on changing the behavior.
4. *Cognitive model.* Another particularly popular method of looking at depression and other forms of mental illness is the cognitive model. Here it is assumed that the way a person thinks causes and sustains the depression or other psychiatric

disorders, such as personality disorders. Another assumption with regard to depression is that the person has learned to feel helpless as a result of numerous negative events over which the person had no control. The person is likely, therefore, to give up efforts to create positive outcomes and events. This theory is not useful in the treatment of manic depression or schizophrenia because the illness is caused by chemical imbalances in the brain, and not by the person's thinking.

The best treatment is a bio-psycho-social approach. That is, biochemical problems are addressed through medication, while psychological and social problems are addressed through therapy. With the exception of long-standing illnesses, now well-controlled with the client functioning well, no case should be treated using only medications or only therapy.

MOOD DISORDERS

The *DSM-IV-TR* lists a number of mood disorders with which you will become familiar when you work in this field. We will look at the most common ones that you might encounter.

Major Depressive Episode

Depression has been referred to as the common cold of mental health. Records indicate that throughout history, many well-known people, such as President Abraham Lincoln, suffered from what was then referred to as melancholy. All age, racial, and ethnic groups experience depression. Studies indicate that it is more prevalent in women than men. NAMI estimates that 1 in 7 women will experience depression, while only 1 in 15 men will do so.

Depression should not be confused with normal feelings of being blue or sad from time to time. We all have bad days and passing feelings of unhappiness or dissatisfaction. Instead, depression is an illness, and as such it requires medical care.

Older People and Depression

NAMI estimates that for people over age 65, about 3 in every 100 people suffer from depression. It can be harder to spot in some older people because they may focus on vague pains and aches or on their illnesses and not really discuss feeling blue or hopeless. Often older people or their families mistake depression, especially severe depression accompanied by confusion or even delusions or hallucinations, for dementia and do not seek help because they believe this condition cannot be reversed. As older people experience the common symptoms of depression, such as memory problems, they may be convinced that these are signs of aging.

Older people are less likely to know that depression is a treatable illness. Some older people still subscribe to the notion that if they would change their attitude and "cheer up," the depression would subside. When all attempts to get over it on their own fail, they often feel guilty. In addition, mental illness is often a taboo subject for older people who worry about the stigma they might encounter if they were to seek help. Cost is another factor that keeps older people from seeking help.

The most important fact for you to remember is that depression in older people is often caused by a medical condition or a medication they are taking. Investigate this carefully as you take the history. Compile a record of medications and any medical problems or physical symptoms the person might be experiencing.

Causes

In the past, the person with depression was blamed for having a poor attitude. Those closest to the person would often cajole or scold the depressed person to just "cheer up." Today we know that regardless of what triggers a depressive episode, chemical changes seem to take place in the brain that relate to the way the person is feeling. There is still no absolute certainty, however, about the exact cause.

It is believed that a number of events or changes in a person's life may play a role in depression. Medical illness can trigger depression, as can some of the medications used to treat some illnesses. Psychological problems such as a great loss or disruption in life can cause some people to develop depression. Environmental problems such as living or working in hostile and difficult circumstances can trigger an episode of depression. Drugs and alcohol have an effect on mood. Some believe that a person's general outlook on life and habitual way of thinking also affect the way the person feels. Genetic factors may play a role in a person's predisposition to become depressed.

In looking at changes in the brain, three neurotransmitters appear to be involved. Neurotransmitters are the chemicals in the brain that help to transmit the electrical signals between the cells in the brain. The three neurotransmitters involved are norepinephrine, serotonin, and dopamine. If neurotransmitters are insufficiently available to the receptors on the nerve cells, depression is likely to occur. Many antidepressant medications, therefore, work to make these receptors more sensitive to the neurotransmitters in the brain.

Course and Symptoms

According to the *DSM-IV-TR,* Criterion A for Major Depressive Episode, the diagnosis is given when, during a two-week period, "five or more of the following symptoms have been present" and, in addition, these symptoms "represent a change from previous functioning." The *DSM* continues, "at least one of the symptoms is either (1) depressed mood or (2) loss of interest or pleasure." Following is the list of criteria:

> (1) depressed mood most of the day, nearly every day, as indicated by either subjective report (e.g., feels sad or empty) or observation made by others (e.g., appears tearful)
>
> (2) markedly diminished interest or pleasure in all, or almost all, activities most of the day, nearly every day (as indicated by either subjective account or observation made by others)
>
> (3) significant weight loss when not dieting or weight gain (e.g., a change of more than 5% of body weight in a month) or decrease or increase in appetite nearly every day
>
> (4) insomnia or hypersomnia nearly every day
>
> (5) psychomotor agitation or retardation nearly every day (observable by others, not merely subjective feelings of restlessness or being slowed down)
>
> (6) fatigue or loss of energy nearly every day
>
> (7) feelings of worthlessness or excessive or inappropriate guilt (which may be delusional) nearly every day (not merely self-reproach or guilt about being sick)

(8) diminished ability to think or concentrate, or indecisiveness, nearly every day (either by subjective account or as observed by others)

(9) recurrent thoughts of death (not just fear of dying), recurrent suicidal ideation without a specific plan, or a suicide attempt or a specific plan for committing suicide

In addition, the clinician must be sure that the symptoms do not better fit another depressive diagnosis, that these symptoms impair "social, occupational, or other important areas of functioning," and that the symptoms are not caused by a medical condition or a substance the person is taking. Finally, the diagnosis is not given for normal grief after the recent death of a loved one.

When a clinician gives the diagnosis of major depressive episode, he or she must rule out first any episode of mania in the person's history. You will ask clients if there have ever been times when they were extremely active and productive, felt elation, and experienced other symptoms of a manic episode. If a manic episode was ever present in the history, the diagnosis becomes one of the bipolar disorders, which we will examine next. If no manic episode can be documented, the diagnosis is major depressive disorder.

As a diagnosis, the term *major depressive disorder* is always followed by a comma and another term: either *single episode* or *recurrent.* Single episode means this is the first such episode in the person's life, while recurrent means the person has experienced other major depressions in the past.

Further, the clinician will specify the current clinical status and/or features of the disorder, indicating whether the current illness is one or more of the following:

Mild	Moderate	Severe
Chronic	Without psychotic features	With catatonic features
With melancholic features	With atypical features	With postpartum onset

The *DSM* gives a brief description of each of these to assist the clinician.

This gives you the *DSM-IV-TR* criteria for the diagnosis used by clinicians that are useful for you to know. Your clients, however, will come in complaining of such things as an inability to concentrate or remember, disturbed sleep, inactivity and lack of motivation, loss of interest in things they once found pleasurable, and loss of appetite. This is the subjective report mentioned earlier, which consists of the information the client brings. In addition, your own observations of the person's mood and affect are important. A lack of animation, a flat monotonous tone of voice, tearfulness, and a lack of hygiene are also part of the observable picture. Your notes on what the client tells you and what you observe will be important to the clinician who makes the diagnosis and works with you and the client to develop a service plan.

Depression and Other People

Depression almost always takes a toll on relationships, and the people in the client's life who are not depressed rarely have patience or understanding about why their family member is depressed or what to do about it. Referrals by you to family or couple therapy may be helpful, but it is also helpful for you to reassure people that these problems are part of the illness and do not necessarily signal a permanent disruption in the relationship. In *When Someone You Love Is Depressed,* Rosen and Amador (1996) list several ways in which depression affects relationships, which should be helpful to you as you work with families and with clients suffering from depression. Following are four problems noted by the authors.

1. *Sexual problems.* Clients who are depressed are often not interested in intimacy and withdraw from intimate partners, just as they often withdraw from other activities that were formerly pleasurable.
2. *Avoiding social contact.* Many depressed people avoid going out among friends and acquaintances. The whole idea of dressing up, going out, and interacting with others may be overwhelming to a person who is depressed.
3. *Getting into treatment.* Often those close to the depressed person know there are problems and want the depressed person to seek help. Depressed people may find this too difficult to undertake, or they may not believe there is any help for them. Some deny that there is anything wrong and may feel that seeing someone for treatment is a defeat of some kind. This can become an issue of contention in some relationships.
4. *Medication use issues.* Sometimes people go for treatment but will not comply with the medication regimen that is planned for them. A major issue is taking the medication "for the rest of my life." A partner may know that the medication makes a difference and become exasperated when the depressed person will not comply with the medication routine. It looks as if the person is unwilling to help him- or herself feel better.

Bipolar Disorders

There are two bipolar disorders, as described in the following text.

1. *Bipolar I disorder.* "The essential feature of Bipolar I Disorder is a clinical course that is characterized by the occurrence of one or more Manic Episodes or Mixed Episodes. Often individuals have also had one or more Major Depressive Episodes" (*DSM-IV-TR*). In other words, the person may or may not have had a major depressive episode, but the person has clearly had one or more manic episodes.
2. *Bipolar II disorder.* "The essential feature of Bipolar II Disorder is a clinical course that is characterized by the occurrence of one or more Major Depressive Episodes (Criterion A above) accompanied by at least one Hypomanic Episode (Criterion B)" (*DSM-IV-TR*). In other words, the most pronounced feature in this person's history is depression, but there have been symptoms of hypomania in the past.

What Is Mania?

A manic episode appears to be the opposite of a depressive episode. Here are the first two criteria for mania from the *DSM-IV-TR:*

> A. A distinct period of abnormally and persistently elevated, expansive, or irritable mood, lasting at least one week (or any duration if hospitalization is necessary)
>
> B. During the period of mood disturbance, three (or more) of the following symptoms have persisted (four if the mood is only irritable) and have been present to a significant degree:
>
> (1) inflated self-esteem or grandiosity
>
> (2) decreased need for sleep (e.g., feels rested after only 3 hours of sleep)
>
> (3) more talkative than usual or pressure to keep talking
>
> (4) Flight of ideas or subjective experience that thoughts are racing

(5) distractibility (i.e., attention too easily drawn to unimportant or irrelevant external stimuli)

(6) increase in goal-directed activity (either socially, at work or school, or sexually) or psychomotor agitation

(7) excessive involvement in pleasurable activities that have a high potential for painful consequences (e.g., engaging in unrestrained buying sprees, sexual indiscretions, or foolish business investments)

Individuals in a manic state are unlikely to tell you they need help. They will tell you they never felt better or that things have never gone so well. Most of the diagnosis is obtained by observation.

Phillip became depressed while in college. He managed to finish school with outstanding grades, but felt no interest in things he had once enjoyed. He was a gifted engineer and went on to work for a national company, eventually becoming the regional director. One day he was traveling in Kansas, checking on some jobs being completed by his company. He began to feel a sense of urgency that the tasks he had outlined be completed at once. He became agitated, his speech pressured, and he began to give directions to people in a hurried, hostile manner. Those who had known him were shocked by his behavior. When it became apparent that he was not sleeping but was staying at the company's headquarters going over records all night, and that many of the conclusions he had drawn made little sense, he was hospitalized. Eventually he lost his job and returned to his hometown where he was hospitalized. In time he was able to balance his moods with medication and supported himself successfully as the owner of several paint and wallpaper stores.

Ellie was a student when she first had a manic episode. She told her worker that it felt as if she could not land her plane. "I'm just up all the time and can't come down." Ellie's episode had come on very quickly. She had seemed agitated in class and seemed to have some pressure of speech, but otherwise she was appropriate. As the day progressed, Ellie felt an urgency to find a young man with whom she was doing her fieldwork. By evening she had found his apartment and placed lighted candles all around the house. In addition, she had rounded up a number of dogs in the neighborhood and placed them in the vestibule of the apartment building. Alarmed, the landlady and the young man called the police, who called a crisis team to go out and take Ellie into the hospital. When they found her, she was talking to her own reflection in a plate glass window and had lost her car.

We turn now to hypomania. According to the *DSM-IV-TR,* "Although Manic Episodes and Hypomanic Episodes have identical lists of characteristic symptoms, the mood disturbance in Hypomanic Episodes is not sufficiently severe to cause marked impairment in social and occupational functioning or to require hospitalization. Some Hypomanic Episodes may evolve into full Manic Episodes." In other words, many highly successful people may be subject to hypomanic episodes and come in to see you only when the hypomanic episode subsides or the person becomes depressed. There is always a feeling of loss when a person is no longer in a hypomanic state because during that time, the person's sense of well-being is positive and uplifting and the person's life is productive, even creative. Hypomania is not as readily observable. Others may simply envy or marvel at the seemingly boundless energy of this person.

SUICIDE

Suicide is the eighth leading cause of death, according to NAMI. Fifty percent of those who succeed in committing suicide were suffering from depression. A popular notion is that those who talk about suicide will not actually commit suicide. In fact, many people do discuss suicide with others before committing the act, often to indicate how grave their situation is or how deeply depressed and hopeless they feel.

Therefore, in talking with a person who is depressed, it is important to explore this topic with them. You may consider suicide a taboo subject in social conversations, but it must be addressed in your professional contacts with those who indicate they are depressed. You can ask the person, "Have you ever felt so sad that you have thought of suicide?" or "Do you just feel as if things are so hopeless you've thought about suicide?"

There are other important pieces of information, which we will consider next, that will help you to determine how serious a threat suicide is for your client.

If Your Client Has Considered Suicide

If a client tells you he or she has considered suicide, the client might be about to actually carry out the act. Remember, you are assessing where the client is today. Things can change for a person who is battling depression, and the suicide option can seem more or less attractive at any given time. What you want to know is where the client stands at this point. You learn this information by talking to the person about suicide directly, and with warmth and empathy. Begin with an open question such as, "Can you tell me a little more about that?" Here is what you need to know:

- Has the client ever thought about how he or she would do it?
- Does the client have the means to actually carry it out (e.g., a gun, medications)?
- Has the client planned when to carry this out?
- Has the client ever tried to commit suicide before?

If all of this information is not made clear in the client's answer to your open question, follow up with closed questions to obtain the rest of the information.

If you learn that the client has decided how to do it, has the means to complete it, has decided when he or she will carry it out, and has attempted suicide in the past, the risk that the client will commit suicide now is extremely high. Some workers feel uncomfortable about asking for this much information and so do not ask follow-up questions. Some mistakenly believe that if they discuss the subject, they will put ideas into the person's head. In reality, you are assessing the situation to determine the degree of risk. This assessment must be done.

Look at the Social History

A person's social history often contains clues that indicate whether this person is at greater risk for suicide than others might be. These risk factors should be noted when you are taking a social history. Here are some of those factors:

- The person sought help in the past but felt it was useless.
- The person has an unstable life with numerous ups and downs, and few things in his or her life remain stable and supportive.
- There is considerable stress at this point in the person's life.

- The person continually abuses alcohol, medications, or street drugs
- The person indicates that he or she has no one really close: no family, close friends, significant others, or confidantes.
- Few resources, such as money, abilities, and a supportive environment, are available to the person.
- The person is withdrawn from normal interaction and activities.
- In the past, the person has coped with difficulties in destructive, rather than constructive, ways.
- The person's ability to function on a daily basis is poor.
- The person tells you of previous suicide attempts (particularly note if these had a high probability of being successful and be doubly alert if you are seeing this person because he or she has just attempted suicide).
- There is a family history of suicide (e.g., a close relative or parent when client was at an early age).
- Others have been rejecting of the client's problems or symptoms.
- The client has no interest or belief in a religious or spiritual system. (This does not mean the person has to belong to an organized religion or attend church regularly; here you are looking for a spiritual belief system that sustains the person and gives him or her strength or hope.)
- The person has a chronic illness, a chronically painful medical condition, a life-threatening medical condition, or a severely disabling medical condition.
- The person has had a particularly long episode of depression.
- The person was previously hospitalized for psychiatric treatment.

Other considerations can increase the risk. For instance, the risk of suicide is somewhat more likely in:

- Older (over 45) or elderly people than in young adults
- Males rather than females (males are more likely to actually succeed)
- Unmarried people, as compared to those who are married
- Unemployed or retired people, as compared to those who are working

What Did You Observe?

What you observe when you are talking to the person is important. Here are some factors that you might observe that would alert you to the fact that the risk of suicide is present:

- The person came in alone.
- The person shows a severely depressed affect.
- You can see wrist scars from previous suicide attempts.
- The person has delusions that indicate persecution and external controlling factors.
- The person has hallucinations that command the person to commit some self-destructive act.
- During the interview, the person never relaxes or establishes any rapport. You feel as if no real communication is taking place.
- The person is extremely hostile (look for violence or rage in the history).
- The person refuses any help.

Your assessment in this area can save lives, so it is important to observe and record those things that might make suicide likely. All of the factors discussed here will not be present in any one person, and some factors will be more pronounced in one client than in another. It is your task to know what to note and when to alert others or take steps to protect the person.

An Ironic Fact About Suicide

An important point to remember about suicide is that many people commit suicide just when you think they are improving. Keep this in mind. As the depression begins to lift and the person feels more energetic, the energy to plan and carry out a suicide may be present. If your client is feeling better but still has ideas about suicide, there is an increased risk that suicide may occur. Certainly the overall risk of suicide is reduced with treatment, but there can be this window of increased risk when your client begins to feel better. It is important for you to be aware of this.

GRIEF

Grief, referred to in the *DSM* as bereavement, is not considered a mental illness, but rather a natural reaction to the death of someone close or meaningful in a person's life. You may see grieving people who find their grief difficult to tolerate. For instance, they may have insomnia, feel guilty about what they did or did not do for their loved ones before they died, or even feel that they would be better off dead themselves now that the loved ones are no longer in their lives. Their symptoms look very similar to a major depressive episode, but the diagnosis would be bereavement, a normal response to loss.

How people grieve and the length of time considered appropriate to grieve differs among cultures. For this reason, you want to understand the cultural norms associated with death in the cultures with which you work most frequently. You need to understand how those in the particular culture express grief and the length of time grieving is considered appropriate. For the most part, only those who are still showing considerable grief after two months would be given a diagnosis of major depressive episode.

ANXIETY

Some clients seeking mental health services may be suffering from anxiety. There are a number of disorders that are considered rooted in anxiety. According to the *DSM-IV-TR,* the following are considered anxiety disorders.

1. *Panic attacks.* These episodes are characterized by "the sudden onset of intense apprehension, fearfulness, or terror, often associated with feelings of impending doom" (*DSM-IV-TR,* p. 429). There are medical conditions that can mimic a panic attack. Because many individuals suffering from a panic attack, particularly the first time, seek medical treatment, medical personnel are in a position to differentiate between a panic attack and something medical. Common medical conditions that look like a panic attack are:

    - Hyperthyroid, which often causes anxiety, sweating, and increased heart rate
    - Hypoglycemia, which often causes dizziness, sweating, trembling, and anxiety

- A drug reaction to caffeine, cocaine, or amphetamines. In some cases, withdrawal from alcohol can cause intense anxiety
- Asthma, which can be caused by anxiety or can look like a panic attack

Panic attacks are enormously incapacitating. Clients complain of feeling as if they are suffocating, dying, or going crazy. Heart palpitations or a pounding, racing heartbeat are common during a panic attack. Other symptoms include chest pain or pressure, shortness of breath, trembling, nausea, sweating, chills, and hot flushes.

All individuals who have suffered a panic attack live in dread of suffering another one, and often they alter their lifestyles to avoid another such episode. For some individuals, an attack comes suddenly and with no explanation, while for others an attack may be triggered by a situation in which they find themselves or thoughts they have at a given time.

2. *Agoraphobia.* Agoraphobia can be a response to panic attacks, but not all those who suffer from agoraphobia also have panic attacks. Individuals with agoraphobia are fearful of leaving home, where they feel safe and protected. Leaving home can become associated with the fear of having a panic attack. This makes going away from home frightening and uncertain. Situations that commonly invoke anxiety and the desire to escape can include crowds, traffic, wide-open spaces, bridges, and being away from home alone.
3. *Phobias.* The *DSM-IV-TR* describes phobias as "characterized by clinically significant anxiety provoked by exposure to a specific feared object or situation, often leading to avoidance behavior" (*DSM-IV-TR,* p. 429). To someone without this condition, the fear or anxiety seems excessive and unreasonable. Generally the person is aware of how exaggerated his or her response is, but finds it impossible to control. Avoidance at all costs of those situations or objects that cause this response works for many. For others, the phobia can spread so that, for example, a phobia of snakes spreads to the same feeling around shoelaces, broken rubber bands, or other objects that are reminiscent of snakes.

   People with phobias of this magnitude find that the avoidance behavior and the anxiety aroused by the object or situation can impair their normal functioning. Some common phobias besides snakes are spiders, dogs and other animals, blood, injections and needles, flying, small spaces, storms, water, and heights. Common situations that cause a phobic reaction are flying, public speaking, and being alone in a hospital. It is important to keep in mind that the response is excessive and unreasonable. Many people are uncomfortable in very high places or around snakes, but they are able to tolerate the discomfort, which is minimal. For those suffering from a phobia, the response is intolerable, and they need to take steps, even drastic steps, to avoid contact with the dreaded object or situation.

Tameka was afraid of heights. She had been this way ever since she was little and her father had placed her on the wide concrete railing of a bridge so that she could watch a wreath being thrown into the river below in honor of sailors lost at sea. Even though her father held onto her, the distance to the water made her afraid, and she was relieved when he put her down. From then on, Tameka avoided heights.

As she grew older, she began to confront these fears and the way in which her avoidance behavior interfered with her work and activities. In college, Tameka never took a class on the second floor of the classroom buildings. This caused her to graduate a semester late because she needed to wait to get the right classes in the right room. Twice she left perfectly good jobs because the company was moving to a high-rise building. She could not go into town unless she was sure she would be able to find parking on the street. She never parked in a parking garage. When her mother was ill, family members had to go with her to see her mother on the eighth floor of the hospital, and Tameka's hands were sweaty and her heart racing when she finally left her mother's bedside after only a few minutes.

It was at this point that Tameka's family began to take her behavior seriously. Until then they had thought of her fear as an expression of some quirky preference, but they now saw that it was interfering with her ability to function normally. They talked to her about seeking help. Tameka agreed that the phobia was becoming more and more difficult to manage, and she did seek help. Through very gradual exposure to heights, beginning with imagining heights in the clinician's office, Tameka began to overcome her fear. She never felt entirely comfortable in high places, but she was able to tolerate them better, and eventually she could manage heights in the course of her normal activities.

Social phobia. Individuals who suffer from social phobia will become extremely anxious when exposed to "certain types of social or performance situations, often leading to avoidance behavior" (*DSM-IV-TR,* p. 429). Sometimes individuals who suffer from social phobia also suffer from low self-esteem. Parties, meetings, public speaking or giving public performances, engaging in conversation, eating or drinking in front of others, interviews, meeting new people, dating, and using public restrooms can all cause intense anxiety, an anxiety far greater and more incapacitating than the average person's reluctance to give a speech or meet a new person.

4. *Obsessive-compulsive disorder.* Obsessions are intrusive thoughts about something that is generally irrational. People with this disorder may repeatedly have thoughts that their hands are dirty and must be washed or that the groceries were handled by individuals with germs at the grocery store before they were bought and brought home. The person experiences tension between knowing the thoughts are irrational but fearing the consequences of ignoring them. Ignoring them or trying to make them go away can be a source of even greater anxiety.

   Compulsions are, according to NAMI, "repetitive rituals." Individuals may engage in excessive and ritualistic hand washing, or in scrubbing the canned goods brought into the house. Such activities may bring relief temporarily, but soon thoughts recur about unclean hands or unclean groceries, and the ritual must be repeated to bring renewed relief. NAMI lists a number of typical fears and behaviors that can characterize obsessive-compulsive disorder in some individuals:

   - The need to check things: Is the door locked? Did I really turn off the stove? Is my alarm set properly? Are the sheets really clean?
   - A fear of harming others: driving and fearing that every bump in the road may be a body; worry about harming children or pets
   - Feeling dirty or contaminated or fearing being contaminated: results in a constant need to clean and decontaminate oneself or objects
   - The need to arrange and order things in precisely the same way before moving on to the next activity: shoes in a perfect line, comb and brush

in exact places on the bureau, things laid out in precise order before one showers

- Excessive concern over imperfections in the body: engaging in precise routines to restore beauty, build muscles, or perfect the way the body looks
- An obsessive concern for numbers, believing some numbers represent good while others represent evil: results in counting steps taken, the number of steps in a flight of stairs, the number of steps it takes to go from the bedroom to the bathroom, the number of pieces of mail or peas on a plate
- An obsessive concern with being sinful, and engaging in activities that will assuage imagined guilt or purify the person in some way: constant praying, reading the Bible or the Koran, or performing religious rituals

5. *Generalized anxiety disorder.* The *DSM-IV-TR* states that this disorder is "characterized by at least 6 months of persistent and excessive anxiety and worry" (p. 429). The person is worried more often than not during this period, and generally about minor matters such as work or school, health and safety of self and others, or finances, relationships, and appearance. Many are worried about the world, the country, the environment, and other larger, more global issues. Irritability, fatigue, restlessness, the feeling of being on edge, and difficulty concentrating are all part of the disorder. Sleep can be disturbed, muscles can be tense, and the person may lose interest in things he or she once enjoyed.

   Many of us worry about things in our lives and even things going on in the world around us. The difference for people suffering from generalized anxiety disorder is that they are always worried about something, and the worry impairs their well-being and sometimes their ability to function.
6. *Posttraumatic stress disorder and acute stress disorder.* These disorders are covered in detail in Chapter 4 on rape and domestic violence. As noted in that chapter, these stress disorders can also result from witnessing any life-threatening or violent event, such as the death or murder of another person, and from living through a life-threatening event, such as a holocaust, tornado, violent crime, or accident.

ADJUSTMENT DISORDER

Case managers are seeing individuals who have been diagnosed with an adjustment disorder more often these days. Generally these individuals are responding to an event that has occurred in their lives, such as a move, a new job, the breakup of a significant relationship, a house fire, or a new baby. The reaction to this stressor must occur within three months of the event, and the distress, according to the *DSM-IV-TR*, "is in excess of what would be expected from exposure to the stressor." In addition, the *DSM* goes on to state that there is "significant impairment in social or occupational (academic) functioning."

Normal grieving is not considered an adjustment disorder. This would not be the diagnosis for someone who is grieving the death of a close relative.

If the symptoms persist for less than six months after the event or after the stressful circumstances have terminated, clinicians usually specify the adjustment disorder as "acute," while distress lasting six months or longer is usually specified as "chronic."

Adjustment disorders are responses that are excessive and out of the ordinary to stressful events or circumstances. Often they clear up in time and the person returns to

Peter and his lover Charles broke up after spending 12 years in a committed relationship. Charles found a new lover, which was the reason for the breakup, while Peter went on to live alone. Peter became very depressed and tearful. He stopped eating, going to work, and going out with friends. He spoke of his life as being over and told people there was "nothing left" for him. Friends took him to the hospital emergency room two weeks after Charles left, and there Peter was diagnosed with adjustment disorder with depressed mood.

Langley was diagnosed with adjustment disorder with anxiety after an accident at a local nuclear power plant. No one was injured, and there was no danger of radiation to the community, but by law the power plant had to report the accident to the local authorities and the media. From the time Langley read the article in the paper, he began to fret over the plant. He worked long hours to figure out how far he was from the plant "as the crow flies," studying maps and driving to the plant taking different routes. He stopped eating, listened to the news constantly, and felt edgy "about everything." He finally saw his family doctor a month after the accident and was diagnosed with adjustment disorder with anxiety.

normal functioning. Initially the person is thrown off-balance by the stressor and may need help to regain that balance.

SCHIZOPHRENIA

Schizophrenia is considered one of the most disabling of all the mental illnesses. According to the U.S. Department of Health and Human Services (Shore, 1986), about "1% of the population develop schizophrenia during their lives." The prevalence among men and women is about the same. Generally, a person with schizophrenia will show the earliest signs of this disorder in the late teens or early twenties, but the disorder can occur earlier or later. It is not unusual for women to first experience symptoms in their thirties.

According to NAMI (n.d.), "three-quarters of those with the disorder develop it between the ages of 16 and 25" (p. 4). NAMI also points out that the disorder tends to run in families, but for most people, the chances of having the disorder are extremely small.

Many people assume that those with schizophrenia are dangerous. In fact, although the behavior may be unpredictable and therefore frightening, people with schizophrenia are not inherently more dangerous than other people. The real danger comes from their inability to care for and protect themselves from exploitation or abuse by others when they are having acute symptoms. Many people with this disorder are withdrawn and shy.

Causes

Case managers should recognize that schizophrenia is not caused by bad parenting, and it is not caused by some sort of weak personal trait. They also need to make this point clear to family and friends of the client with schizophrenia who may misunderstand and blame themselves or the client for the condition. In addition, old notions about the illness referred to people with this disorder as having a "split personality," but this is misleading. People with schizophrenia do not have a split personality.

While there has been considerable research into the causes of schizophrenia, there is as yet no absolute certainty about the origins of the disorder. Some researchers have found abnormalities in the electrical impulses of the brain; other researchers have found structural abnormalities in the brain. There is research indicating that people with schizophrenia have impairment in memory, concentration, and problem solving. Some odd but interesting research results indicate that those with schizophrenia are more likely to have been born in winter or spring and are raised disproportionately in urban areas. Researchers also have found a significant number of difficult pregnancies and births for these individuals, possibly causing early brain damage that was not detectable at first.

Course and Symptoms

For some people with schizophrenia, the illness is preceded by behavior that seems worrisome, but not bizarre. Isolating themselves from others, appearing withdrawn or detached, expressing unusual ideas, and using unusual speech or behavior can all be part of their earliest symptoms.

When a person experiences the sudden onset of psychiatric symptoms associated with this disorder, the person is said to be psychotic and in an acute phase of the illness. It is not safe to assume that the disorder is schizophrenia until a thorough medical workup has been done. Many psychotic episodes, particularly in older people, can be caused by medical problems or be related to medications they are taking.

Psychosis

Psychosis is a term used to describe the most acute and obvious symptoms of schizophrenia. Psychosis is a condition that separates the person from reality. Many times the person can no longer tell what is real and what is not. These symptoms tend to be less severe in women. There are two common characteristics of psychosis: hallucinations and delusions. A person may have only one or both of them during an acute episode.

1. *Hallucinations.* Hallucinations cause the person to sense something in the environment through the senses that is not really there. For instance, the individual may hear voices; see objects, people, or animals and bugs; or feel like bugs are crawling over his or her body or like he or she is being touched by dozens of invisible fingers. Voices are particularly frightening to clients. Voices can carry on a conversation with the person, or they can warn of impending dangers and give directions that the person is afraid to follow. Some clients have reported feeling exhilarated at first upon hearing voices. They describe messages of omnipotence and a special relationship with the universe or God. Later, however, the voices can become more demanding and intrusive, greatly interfering with their ability to function. According to NAMI, in some cases people become extremely sensitive "to colors, shapes and background noises" and find it hard to distinguish between themselves and other people or objects in their environment.
2. *Delusions.* Delusions are beliefs the person holds that cannot be removed through the normal course of argument or contradictory evidence. One must be careful not to label a cultural belief or bias as a delusion. There are several types of delusions. In paranoid delusions, clients believe they are the intended victim of some negative plot or harassment. Clients may also feel they are being controlled by external forces. Some clients have grandiose ideas about who they are and what their mission should be, while others suffer from delusional guilt, believing erroneously that they are responsible for some tragedy. Clients may complain that

their thoughts are being broadcast or that their thoughts are being taken out of their minds by an external force.

When he was ill, Ralph believed that he was a frog. He had been an outstanding track star in high school and was used to sprinting away from a squatting position. When he was ill, he would often squat and hop to the mental health center. He often believed that the workers there were famous people. Ralph was well liked by the staff, and neighbors looked after him as well. When he was in an acute phase of his illness and presented a danger to himself by hopping into traffic, people made sure he got to the mental health center and that his medications were adjusted or he was hospitalized.

Carla was sure she was an employee of the FBI. She staked out a position at the federal courthouse and asked to go through the bags of those coming and going on business. Security tried to reason with her and to get her to leave, but eventually her behavior became intolerable to others and Carla was hospitalized. As she went to the hospital, she informed the security personnel at the courthouse that she was being taken into custody to protect her from the communists.

For a complete list of thought and perception problems, consult Chapter 17, The Mental Status Exam, in *Fundamentals of Case Management Practice* (Summers, 2001).

Other Signs and Symptoms

The following text discusses some of the other symptoms that people with schizophrenia can exhibit.

1. *Distorted reality.* Many people with schizophrenia see the world quite differently from those who are around them. Their perception of the world, while not psychotic, may seem unreliable and subject to drastic change. Of course, this is confusing and frightening.
2. *Preoccupation.* People with schizophrenia may appear at times to be detached and preoccupied. It may be they are listening to other voices, or that they are responding to a world that seems alien to them.
3. *Movement.* Sometimes a person with schizophrenia will sit rigidly and not move for a number of hours, while another person might be restless, even agitated, and move constantly. The same person may have different behavior on different occasions. Sometimes movement is slow and appears to be constricted. This may be due to medication in some individuals, but medication does not appear to account for all of it. Some people "repeat rhythmic gestures, or adopt ritualistic movements, such as walking in circles."
4. *Disordered thinking.* Clarity, logic, and comprehension may disappear for the person with schizophrenia. Some complain that their thoughts race through their heads and they are unable to "catch them." Thoughts become disorganized, spill over each other, and come in fragments. For more on disordered thinking, see Chapter 17 in *Fundamentals of Case Management Practice* (Summers, 2001). It is very hard for a person with disordered thinking to carry on a conversation because many people cannot follow or make sense of what the person is saying. This is one of the reasons people with schizophrenia are socially isolated.
5. *Emotional expression.* Some people with schizophrenia exhibit emotions that are inappropriate given the circumstances. This is generally referred to as

"inappropriate affect." Some people with schizophrenia are described as having a "blunt affect" or " flat affect." Such people do not express much or any emotion and often speak in a monotone. These people do not exhibit the normal animation people have when talking to one another.

6. *Lack of motivation.* Individuals with schizophrenia often show a marked lack of motivation and may have trouble completing daily tasks, preferring instead to sit and watch television or daydream.

Case Management and Prevention of Relapse

In this field, the prevention of relapse is a major focus for all the members of the treatment team. Because case managers see their clients more often, or may have better access to them, than other members of the treatment team, they are always looking for potential risks that could precipitate a relapse and for better arrangements that will avoid a relapse for their clients. Relapse often involves disorganization and disruption of the clients' lives, as well as considerable effort to reorganize after the acute phase has passed. In addition, in the age of managed care, insurers are unwilling to pay for countless hospitalizations but will fund programs and plans that appear to prevent a severe relapse requiring expensive medical care.

Lifestyle

Case managers, as we have seen, create treatment plans with the client. In working with individuals with schizophrenia, one of the most important considerations is the lifestyle these clients adopt because lifestyle will often prevent relapse. Following are some factors to consider in planning with clients how they will live. Alexander P. Hyde (1985) has outlined some lifestyle considerations in his book, *Living with Schizophrenia.*

1. *Sleep.* It is extremely important that people with schizophrenia get enough sleep. Usually they require more sleep than the average person. This means that clients need at least 8 hours of sleep, and perhaps more, every night. Extensive sleeping, however, when the hours are extreme, can be a sign the person is overmedicated. That is something that would need to be checked by a physician.
2. *Trouble falling asleep.* Some clinicians have found that difficulty falling asleep is a reliable early sign of a relapse. It may happen when individuals are excited or busy and have trouble getting settled down for the night. Helping clients find a slow, even pace so they can be more relaxed at bedtime is important. If you know that falling asleep is becoming a problem for a client, you may want to obtain a prescription for a sleeping medication that the person can use for several nights to get him or her back on track.
3. *Caffeine.* For many individuals with schizophrenia, only one cup of coffee can cause a sense of disorientation and disorganized thinking. In addition, caffeine can interfere with a good night's sleep. Caffeine is found in coffee, tea, cocoa, and soft drinks. Individuals with schizophrenia who use caffeine liberally have a more difficult time, often requiring more medication and experiencing a worsening of their symptoms. Water and juices are better drinks.
4. *Other stimulants.* Some over-the-counter pain medications, cold medications, and asthma preparations contain stimulants. Teach your clients to read labels and to

ask the pharmacist if they are not sure about the ingredients or effects of a medication.

5. *Alcohol.* Alcohol can make some people with schizophrenia feel relaxed and confident initially, but for many, according to Hyde (1985), the real effects set in days later when they are likely to feel "mildly depressed, listless, anxious, tense [and] irritable." Hyde states that this is "almost always followed by the overstimulated, nervous state," which of course can interfere with sleep. A person with schizophrenia may not associate these aftereffects with the alcohol taken days before, and because many do not get a typical hangover, they are likely to assume they can drink safely. Frequent drinking, say on a daily basis, can worsen the effects of the illness. Further, a person who drinks considerable quantities of alcohol at one time might develop hallucinations or delusions.
6. *Marijuana.* For most people with schizophrenia, marijuana can cause restlessness and paranoid thinking soon after it is smoked. Prolonged use of marijuana seems to cause a lack of motivation and irritability. The inactivity and lack of motivation can, in time, bring about a relapse.
7. *Nicotine and cigarettes.* Nicotine is a mild stimulant. Many people with schizophrenia smoke, with little effect on their illness. Nevertheless, nicotine is a stimulant, so for the person who is having trouble recovering, cigarette smoking may be part of the reason. In addition, nicotine tends to lower the blood levels of antipsychotic medications, making them less effective. This may require the physician to prescribe higher dosages to counteract the effects of nicotine.

Environment

1. *Home environment.* All families and people in relationships have difficult times, and disagreements are not uncommon. A person with schizophrenia who lives in a home where there is always an underlying tension and hostility, however, is likely to feel anxious and tense. A person with schizophrenia who lives in a home where there is constant activity and bustle may find it hard to relax and concentrate, as the atmosphere may be too stimulating. Individuals with schizophrenia need privacy, quiet, and time to relax and be quiet. Helping to arrange these within the family environment may be important for your client.

Lola lived with her mother, who was elderly. A younger brother and his girlfriend moved into the basement and converted it to an apartment. They brought with them a young puppy. Lola walked the puppy several times a day because no one else would. The puppy chewed things and was destructive in the way that puppies are. There was constant tension among the members of the household. The brother refused to pay rent and borrowed liberally from his mother, who seemed unable to set any limits. Lola could see the exploitation of her mother but was helpless to prevent it. There were often loud arguments and slamming doors. Lola always seemed distressed, and often appeared close to having another acute episode of schizophrenia. Eventually Lola's case manager helped Lola find a personal care home where she could have more privacy and a quieter atmosphere. The routine of the home helped her to feel secure as well.

A common source of tension in some families is the fact that the relative with schizophrenia cannot work while everyone else is working or has something to do. Some families find it difficult to think that their family member may never work, and some families find that they all need to pursue their own activities for a time. A family member who never goes out and is always involved in what is going on at home can be stressful to other family members. Day programs are often helpful when the person is not recovered enough to work. In most day programs, the person is able to get support and make friends away from the family for part of the day.

2. *Work environment.* Work can be extremely stressful for people suffering from schizophrenia. Jobs that have a fast pace, deadlines, and details that must be in order at all times do not allow the person to calm down and relax. This overstimulation is not helpful. In addition, it is common for people with this disorder to fret about doing the job well and to become tense and anxious over the pressures of the job. This sort of atmosphere can cause a relapse. Looking for work that is less intense and where the person has less emotional involvement might be helpful for some clients.

Juan worked in a bureau of vital statistics where he filed birth, death, and wedding certificates. Juan had a college degree and had been hired as a disabled person under a state program to employ the disabled. Juan's supervisor, however, had little understanding of his illness or of his needs. She was often impatient with his pace and with his reluctance to take on more responsibility, which she felt he could easily handle if he "would just stop focusing on himself." As the bureau took on an increasing amount of work and was moved to larger quarters, Juan began to feel overwhelmed. He felt as if his thinking was becoming disorganized, and he was sleeping less and less. Eventually he left his job, recognizing that the atmosphere there was likely to induce a more acute phase of his illness.

Diagnosis of Schizophrenia Using the *DSM-IV-TR*

A senior clinician, such as a psychiatrist or psychologist, will ultimately make the diagnosis. Nevertheless, you will participate in numerous conversations in which diagnosis is discussed and deliberated. It is important that you be able to follow these discussions and understand how the diagnosis is reached. For a detailed look at how case managers use the *DSM-IV-TR*, see Chapter 16 in *Fundamentals of Case Management Practice* (Summers, 2001).

The *DSM-IV-TR* states that the diagnosis of schizophrenia may be given if several criteria are met on the first set of criteria, referred to as Criterion A. The client must have two of the following symptoms from Criterion A: delusions, hallucinations, disorganized speech, grossly disorganized behavior or catatonic behavior, or negative symptoms such as a flat affect. Only one of these criteria needs to be met "if the delusions are bizarre or the hallucinations consist of a voice keeping up a running commentary on the person's behavior or thoughts, or two or more voices conversing with each other" (*DSM-IV-TR*).

Following are some other factors that are considered in diagnosing a person who may have schizophrenia.

1. *Social/occupational dysfunction.* Look at the level of functioning in such areas as work, social interaction, and self-care before the onset of the symptoms. Is the person now functioning below that level?

2. *Duration.* Have there been continuous signs that this mental illness exists for six months or more? There only needs to be one month during the six that the acute symptoms were present. By acute symptoms, the *DSM* is referring to those that meet Criterion A. In other words, the person has to have exhibited signs of the illness continuously over a 6-month period, and during at least one of those 6 months, the person must have shown one or more of the five criteria listed in Criterion A. Common signs of the illness are flattened affect, loss of motivation, and disorganized behavior and speech.

In considering the diagnosis of schizophrenia, the clinician must determine that the person is not suffering from a mood disorder like depression, that the person is not suffering from a medical condition that would account for the disorganization, and that the symptoms are not caused by a developmental disorder like autism.

3. *Subtypes.* Not all episodes of schizophrenia are alike. The *DSM-IV-TR* makes distinctions leading to five subtypes of schizophrenia. They are discussed in the paragraphs that follow.

Paranoid type. Here the person's delusions or hallucinations are usually persecutory in nature. For instance, one person believed he was working for the FBI and terrorists were trying to get him for what he knew. In another instance, a woman believed her neighbors were intending to kill her and she barricaded her home and set numerous traps for anyone entering her home. Sometimes this diagnosis is given to a person who has wildly grandiose ideas, such as thinking he or she is an FBI agent when that is not the case, or to a person who exhibits extreme jealousy. For example, a man was certain that the success of his coworker was based on ideas taken from his own head by the coworker, which led him to a furious preoccupation with his coworker's presumed unfair advantage and with how the coworker did not deserve the honor he received. In some cases, the client may seek to harm or threaten to harm another for perceived injustices or as a means of protecting him- or herself.

Other delusions and hallucinations may relate to religious ideas. One woman believed she had offended the Virgin Mary and spent days in the church near a statue of the Virgin Mary, "conversing" with her and asking perpetually to be forgiven. The woman was deeply afraid of what would happen to her if the Virgin Mary declined to forgive her. Other people with schizophrenia become preoccupied with health and illness, which is referred to as somatization. In one situation, a man was sure that he was becoming ill because of a plot by some people in his church. He heard voices explaining to him how this had happened and what medical tests to seek to prevent these people from killing him with a disease or illness. He spent much of his time protecting himself and "feeling the disease" enter his body.

Disorganized type. This form of schizophrenia is characterized by disorganization in speech and behavior, and often by an inappropriate affect. The person's speech is fragmented and does not come together coherently. Often the mood expressed is not appropriate to what is being said. There may be silliness or laughter that seems unrelated to what is going on. The disorganized behavior is often exhibited by an inability to complete anything, including self-care, and a tendency to dart from one activity to another without finishing any of them. Even the delusions and hallucinations are disorganized.

People with this kind of disorder usually experience a slow, insidious onset of symptoms before they become ill. Often they have trouble relating to others or are withdrawn. For example, one man with this disorder was considered a "loner" when he was in high school because he had few friends. To his family he seemed moody. He did well in school, but refused to participate in activities in school or to speak in classes. In college these characteristics became more marked. He stayed in his room, and at first people assumed he was just eccentric. After holiday break, however, he seemed to be talking to others no one else could see, and he began to describe to his roommate ideas "that made no sense." The roommate told the counselor at the college health clinic where he went to seek help that "either he is a genius or he needs help. I can't follow anything he says." When the college health services finally could not ignore the pleas for intervention from the roommate and others in the man's dorm, they found the man in the college library. He had numerous books on unrelated topics spread out on the floor and tables, and he was jumping from table to table, talking and laughing, but no one was there. His explanations to the health personnel were incoherent, and he was easily distracted, rushing over to another table to talk to voices he was hearing.

Catatonic type. The most prominent feature of this type of schizophrenia is some disturbance in motor activity. For instance, some people with this type of schizophrenia may be excessively fidgety and move about purposelessly. Others may imitate all the movements of someone else (called echopraxia) or mimic what is said by another (called echolalia). Some people may be mute and not move at all. These people can sometimes hold a position in which they are placed for long periods of time (called catalepsy or waxy flexibility). Still others may be rigid, resisting any attempt to get them to move. Some people with this condition repeat the same action or set of actions over and over. For example, they may repeatedly twist a piece of their hair, or they may stand, wipe off the chair, and then reposition themselves repeatedly.

Undifferentiated type. According to the *DSM-IV-TR,* the "essential feature of the Undifferentiated Type of Schizophrenia is the presence of symptoms that meet Criterion A of Schizophrenia but that do not meet the criteria for the Paranoid, Disorganized, or Catatonic Type."

Residual type. This diagnosis is used when a person has had obvious symptoms in the past that meet the criteria for schizophrenia, but has no obvious acute symptoms at the present time. There may be negative symptoms present like a flat affect or little speech and activity. Or this diagnosis can be made if two or more of the Criterion A symptoms are present but not strongly pronounced: eccentric behavior, somewhat disorganized speech, odd beliefs, and hallucinations or delusions that are not prominent and do not cause strong emotional responses. According to the *DSM-IV-TR,* the "course of the Residual Type may be time limited and represent a transition between a full-blown episode and complete remission. However, it may be continuously present for many years, with or without acute exacerbations."

Other Psychotic Disorders

The *DSM-IV-TR* lists other psychotic disorders that are too numerous to describe here. The *DSM* makes distinctions according to the length of time a psychotic disorder is acute, as in schizophreniform disorder or brief psychotic episode. Schizophrenia accompanied by a mood disorder is called a schizoaffective disorder and has its own list of criteria. A person with nonbizarre delusions and no other criteria for schizophrenia might receive a diagnosis of delusional disorder. The *DSM* also distinguishes between psychosis caused by a medical condition and psychosis caused by a substance.

As you work in the mental health field, you will become familiar with these diagnoses and begin to see the distinctions between them, even if you are not the clinician who makes the diagnoses.

THE MENTAL STATUS EXAMINATION (MSE)

In mental health services, a good mental status examination, like a good social history, is important in pinpointing the problem. As we have seen, the *DSM-IV-TR* has numerous diagnoses that reflect variations of similar disorders. Your observations can clarify for the clinician what the diagnosis might be.

A good mental status examination is based on accurate observations by the worker as described in thorough notes. The observations that take place during the verbal interview cover the following areas:

General appearance	Cognitive functioning
Behavior	Intelligence
Thought processes and content	Reality testing
Affect	Suicidal or homicidal ideation
Impulse control	Judgment
Insight	

Most intake assessments or evaluations end with the case manager's impressions and recommendations. That is where the case manager notes the observations he or she made of the person that were outstanding and contribute to an overall understanding of the way the person thinks and approaches life. Your mental health intake form may ask for these observations throughout the evaluation form. For more details on exactly what the mental status examination is and how it is done by case managers, see Chapter 17 in *Fundamentals of Case Management Practice* (Summers, 2001). That chapter also contains the terms to be used and instructions on how to write up the mental status examination.

FAMILIES

The issue of involving families is delicate. There is plenty of evidence that many mental health clients who have had severe episodes of their mental disorder are ignored or cut off by their families when they become adults. Often families turn their backs because they do not have support or the knowledge of how to deal with the family member who is affected. Many community mental health programs are working to give families the support and information they need so clients can be integrated back into their families. On the other hand, confidentiality guidelines prohibit disclosure to the family or involvement of the family without the adult client's permission.

Kelsey suffered from manic depression. When she was 20 and in her second year of college, she suffered a manic episode and was hospitalized at the university hospital. The case manager asked if she would like the hospital to notify her family and if she would be willing to involve her family in planning sessions related to her discharge. Kelsey refused, telling the staff her family was her primary problem. During the course of her stay, she told stories of the family's unkindness and mental abuse. The staff believed her, and their plan for Kelsey involved independence from her family. The hospital had no knowledge of her prior manic episodes, and Kelsey did not reveal them. She was discharged after five days in the hospital, seemingly improved, but her manic state began to worsen. She rented a car and drove across the country, spending money until her credit cards reached their limit. Her family eventually caught up with her 1,000 miles away, hospitalized and severely depressed. There was every indication that she had been in a number of unfortunate encounters during her cross-country trip.

The real story was that Kelsey came from a particularly loving and supportive family who would have done whatever they could to help her when she became ill. They were familiar with her many episodes and knew how to help Kelsey through these. Kelsey's stories about them were a symptom of her illness, but to hospital workers they seemed plausible. For Kelsey's family, there was considerable anguish over their exclusion from her treatment planning and their subsequent inability to prevent the unfortunate cross-country trip.

When a family member suffers from a mental illness, it affects everyone in the family. Many parents of those with a mental illness blame themselves, but the illness is no one's fault. Some families tend to blame the ill family member and believe that if the person would just cheer up or stop acting crazy, everything could return to normal. For disorders that come from biological imbalances in the brain chemistry, there may be genetic factors that predispose a family member to have this disorder. Ordinary stress in life can ultimately trigger the symptoms in this person that it would not trigger in another person. Case managers who see family members need to educate families about mental illness and the fact that no one is to blame for the mental disorder.

Family Embarrassment

In many cases, families try to hide the fact that a family member has a mental illness. The stigma of mental illness and the general lack of understanding make this a natural reaction. Case managers may be the only people with whom a family can freely discuss what goes on at home, their own fears and concerns, and what they think might help their family member. For this reason, case managers should be open and warm with family members who need to talk about what is happening within the family. Their support may be all the family needs to carry on the task of supporting the family member with schizophrenia at home.

How Case Managers Hurt Families

In a booklet published by NAMI, Joyce Burland (1997) looks at ways in which professionals often hurt the families of their clients. Following are some of the ways in which case managers might be unhelpful or even harmful.

1. *Failure to listen.* According to Burland (1997), families have complained "about staff who seem impatient, . . . unavailable, judgmental, condescending or patronizing" (p. 2). She relates how families have told of feeling hostility from workers or being treated as if the family were not there while others discussed them and their problem. Rapport is the most important tool you can develop for the work you will need to do to support people who have a mental disorder. Rapport is ruined when a worker resorts to hostile communication. An entire section of *Fundamentals of Case Management Practice* (Summers, 2001) is devoted to developing empathic and supportive listening skills. Case managers who have learned these skills should be less likely to come across as insensitive and condescending.

In addition, many workers lack the skills to give genuine empathic responses to people who are experiencing grief and anxiety over the illness of their family member. Families have reported feeling utterly devastated while a worker took information in the cool, efficient manner of someone taking information to open a checking account. A simple question, such as "tell me what happened," or a simple empathic statement, such as "you all must be feeling so worried right now," goes a long way toward giving people the confidence that they are in the right place.

2. *Blame and stigma.* Families have reported that some workers make them feel as if they are to blame for their family member's condition. Of particular concern is the blame placed on women who are wives and mothers. They can be labeled with everything from "smothering" to domineering or rejecting. They are often described as aloof and cold or intrusive, even sabotaging. Such labels only serve to make family members feel guilty and ashamed. Also, as in Kelsey's case discussed earlier, workers may encourage clients to become independent of their families and totally ignore the family's willingness to support their family member. In other instances, support and concern may be seen as suspect by workers who are convinced that the family is somehow to blame for the client's condition.
3. *Traditional therapy.* Some case managers build traditional family therapy into their service plan for the client. The family may benefit from sitting down together to discuss ways they can cope and support one another. The case manager needs to be very careful that the referral is not to a therapist who uses family systems theory, family dysfunction theory, or communication deviance theory. Such a therapist is likely to inform families that they are part of the problem or look at the behavior that results from the family member's illness as a useful tool in "sustaining the family's dysfunction" (Burland, 1997). The danger here is that such therapy can cause clients to see their family as the root cause of their illness and turn away from the very people who might be able to give them support. As Burland points out, "In this way family therapy colludes with the patient's denial of illness. This outcome can irreparably damage family relationships and compromise the family support system."
4. *A lack of shared understanding.* Families looking for collaboration have reported finding very few case managers who have any idea about how to collaborate with a family. In addition, when families use terms related to mental disorders familiar to them, case managers appear not to understand the meaning of these terms. This makes it hard for families and case managers to work together because they lack a shared understanding. If you are the case manager for clients with mental disorders, it is important that you be able to collaborate with families and be able to speak and understand the terms that are frequently used.
5. *Stigma.* Some families believe they have encountered disdain on the part of workers for their family member with a mental disorder. For example, workers often think clients and their families should be completely cooperative and compliant. When clients do not conform, often due to the illness itself, workers lose patience and withdraw support. We addressed this phenomenon in Chapter 1. It is unrealistic to think that any person with considerable problems is going to always be predictable, pleasant, and cooperative.

Also, clients and families who protest policies or treatment are often "branded as trouble-makers" (Burland, 1997). This happens even in agencies that routinely give to new clients and their families a clients' rights brochure that provides the clients with procedures for requesting a change in treatment or case manager.

How Case Managers Help Families

The following suggestions will not only help families to cope with the illness of their family member, but will also help you as the case manager. Families can be an enormous source of support for the client, give early warning of relapse, and give support to a system that is trying to help.

1. Using the listening skills that you learned from *Fundamentals of Case Management Practice* (Summers, 2001), respond to the devastation and uncertainty a family is feeling about their family member's illness. Acknowledge the hardships and pain the family is feeling and the exasperation they feel when the illness is unmanageable, the client does not take medications as directed, or the client has numerous recurring episodes. In addition, whenever possible, refer the family to a support group for families with relatives suffering from a mental illness.
2. In planning for clients who are supported by their families, look at what is placing the greatest strain on the families' emotional resources. Make every effort to address these topics so that your clients will remain connected to their families for support and love. Whenever possible, involve the family in treatment planning and discharge planning so that everyone knows what is expected and what will happen. In this way, the family can support the efforts of the treatment team.
3. To reduce some of the mystery of mental illness for families, educate them. Do not sound gloomy and pessimistic, but give them realistic information about what they can expect for their relative with a mental disorder so they can plan realistically. This includes information on the diagnosis and the prognosis of the illness. It also includes information about the medication being prescribed, the symptoms this medication is supposed to address, and the side effects that might occur. In a private system, a physician would be expected to do this, but in the public system, physicians are rarely available for such sessions, so this responsibility often falls on the case manager. Be sure you have all the facts before you talk to a family.
4. Families often have problems coping with the bizarre and unusual behavior that results from mental disorders. Providing suggestions for coping or referrals to those who can make suggestions is extremely helpful to families. Sometimes the illness causes the person to become listless and inactive. Activities and social involvement are often important, but families rarely know how to motivate their family member to do these things. Again, making suggestions or providing a referral to those who have worked with these issues is invaluable to the family.
5. Be available to families. Most mental health facilities are affiliated with or have their own crisis intervention team. Families need somewhere to turn when they see signs their family member is about to relapse or when there is a crisis the family cannot manage.

There are always, in any population, families who are not supportive and in fact exacerbate the client's illness with their own problems or lack of concern. Some families never get past blaming the client for the illness and being punitive. Case managers generally can tell the difference between families who are genuinely concerned and those who are not. If a family seems genuinely concerned for their family member, you can often include the family in planning and in supporting the plan for the client. In other words, do not automatically rule out family involvement or ignore families when working with your clients.

The Older Client

Older clients can appear to have clear signs of a mental illness. If they have a history of mental illness and the symptoms you are seeing are recurrent in the person's history, it is likely that you are again seeing symptoms of this same mental illness. However, for many older people, physical problems can cause what symptoms that appear to be of a psychiatric nature. In some cases, the older person is reacting to medication, or even to medication given to treat the original psychiatric symptoms. If the underlying medical condition is not discovered and treated, the condition will continue and become permanent, which can lead to years of confusion or premature death.

Many individuals, including family members, are inclined to treat such symptoms in older people as normal signs of aging and consign the person to a nursing facility without ever looking at the physical health of the client. Be very careful in working with older adults to recommend a complete physical examination. Consult Chapter 8 for underlying causes and clues you might uncover in taking the social history.

MEDICATIONS AND TREATMENTS

Psychotropic medications, that is, medications used to treat mental illness, were first developed in the early 1950s. These medications had a shotgun effect on the brain. In other words, the medications often went to the brain and affected the problematic symptoms in a therapeutic way, but at the same time they affected other areas of the brain, causing unwanted side effects and even long-term problems. In recent years, drug manufacturers have developed medications that act more like a high-powered rifle, going directly to the part of the brain that is affected, and not affecting other parts of the brain. With many of these newer medications, side effects are minimal or nonexistent.

Now that medications have fewer side effects, people are more likely to comply with the medication regimens that are designed for them. With better compliance and fewer side effects, many people return to normal functioning, some for the rest of their lives. In the past, recurrence of mental illness was often due to clients not taking the medications that were prescribed for them. Once they stopped taking their medications, the symptoms of the mental illness would return.

Case managers need to know what medications are being prescribed for clients. Note in your history any medications your clients tell you they are taking or have taken in the past. This information will allow both you and the clinician to know what medications the person has been given to address what conditions.

Since you will need to include medications in your clients' histories, you will find it helpful to know the names of some of the more common medications. The lists provided in this chapter are not comprehensive. Every day drug manufacturers find new and more useful medications and introduce them to the market. It is important to keep learning the names of these mediations in order to address this topic thoroughly in your clients' histories. If you do not recognize the name of a medication or need more information about a medication, most mental health centers have a *Physician's Desk Reference* (*PDR*) available to case managers. NAMI has provided lists of common medications, as well as some comments about the categories of illness for which these are used.

Depression

"Of all the mental disorders, depressive illnesses are among the most responsive to treatment" (NAMI, n.d., p. 9). It is estimated that 80% of those who suffer from depression improve and are able to resume normal functioning. Depression will often recur, however, once the person discontinues the medication (NAMI, n.d.). Figure 6.1 contains a chart of brand names, with generic names in parentheses, of medications used in the treatment of depression.

Electroconvulsive therapy. This is commonly referred to as shock treatment. It is used when all other remedies have failed or a person is unable to take antidepressants. Generally it is used in severe cases of depression. The manner in which the treatment is administered causes little stress to the body, in part because the shock is not administered until the person is relaxed and asleep with anesthesia.

Psychotherapy. Psychotherapy is often paired with medication to address some of the issues that may have triggered the depression or that sustain the depression. Much of the psychotherapy is geared to help people recognize these triggers and find ways to prevent recurring episodes of the depression.

Bipolar Disorder

In treating bipolar disorders, the goal is to stop the cycling from high to low that characterizes this disorder. During a period of depression, an individual may require antidepressant medications. Some of these, however, can actually trigger a manic episode in some individuals. Getting just the right combination of medications, finding medications that have fewer side effects, and discovering the smallest dose necessary for each individual person are all somewhat complicated. In the case of lithium, for instance, regular blood tests are conducted to make sure the medication does not reach toxic proportions in the person's body and to determine the least amount of medication that will correct the problem. Common medications used in the treatment of bipolar disorders are listed in Figure 6.2.

MEDICATIONS FOR DEPRESSION

MAO Inhibitors

Nardil (phenelzine)
Parnate (tranylcypromine sulfate)

For Psychotic Depression

Asendin (amoxapine)

Tricyclics

Adapin (doxepin)
Anafranil (clomipramine)
Desyrel (trazodone)
Elavil (amitriptyline)
Endep (amitriptyline)
Norpramin (desipramine)
Pamelor (nortriptyline)
Sinequan (doxepin)
Surmontil (trimipramine)
Tofranil (imipramine)
Vivactil (protriptyline)

Selective Serotonin Reuptake Inhibitors (SSRIs)

Celexa (citalopram hydrobromide)
Luvox (fluvoxamine)
Paxil (paroxetine)
Prozac (fluoxetine)
Zoloft (sertraline)

Others

Effexor (venlafaxine)
Remeron (mirtazapine)
Serzone (nefazodone)
Wellbutrin (bupropion)

Figure 6.1 Medications used in the treatment of depression

MEDICATIONS FOR BIPOLAR DISORDERS

Cibalith-S (lithium citrate)
Depakene (valproic acid)
Depakote (divalproex sodium)
Eskalith (lithium carbonate)
Lithobid (lithium carbonate)
Tegretol (carbamazepine)
Topamax (topiramate)

Figure 6.2 Medications used in the treatment of bipolar disorders

Psychotherapy. Psychotherapy in the treatment of bipolar disorder is focused on the consequences of the illness, particularly the impairment in relationships and work. Manic episodes are often frightening to those who witness them, and there is little understanding that the person may very well return to normal functioning with treatment. Many lives are disrupted by this bewildering disorder. Psychotherapy is not directed at helping the person understand what personal dynamics cause his or her behavior, since this illness is clearly understood as a biochemical disorder.

Anxiety

Some anxiety disorders are well treated with antidepressant medications as well as antianxiety medications. For example, obsessive-compulsive disorder and panic disorder are often helped by a selective serotonin reuptake inhibitor (SSRI). Figure 6.3 lists some of the anxiety disorders and the common medications prescribed for them.

Psychotherapy. There are a number of therapies that are used to help people overcome panic disorder and obsessive-compulsive disorder. Many of these involve exposure to situations and objects that trigger the symptoms, allowing the person to slowly get used to these triggers. This kind of therapy is very effective with many individuals suffering from these disorders.

Benzodiazepines. Some medications used to treat anxiety fall into the category of benzodiazepines. These mediations are similar in chemical structure and are also used as muscle relaxants and to treat insomnia. They act swiftly, taking effect within hours. Generally a person is given a small amount of this medication at first, and then the doses are gradually increased until the symptoms appear to be under control.

The concern regarding this group of medications is that individuals can become dependent upon them, particularly when they are used over a long period of time. The person does not become addicted to the medication in the sense that we talk about a drug addict being addicted to a drug, but the person's body becomes used to the chemical compound, and sudden withdrawal can cause considerable discomfort, even seizures.

The best method of withdrawal for people who have been taking benzodiazepines over a long period of time is to withdraw from them slowly under the supervision of a physician. Some of the withdrawal symptoms look very much like the original disorder and can include "anxiety, shakiness, headache, dizziness, sleeplessness, loss of appetite" (NAMI, n.d.), and in severe cases seizures. You need to understand the results of the long-term use of benzodiazepines, and be sure to note such long-term use in your client's history. Your awareness and observations may prevent long-term dependence or unfortunate withdrawal problems. Figure 6.4 contains a list of the benzodiazepines.

ANXIETY DISORDERS AND MEDICATIONS

Anxiety	Obsessive-Compulsive Disorder	Panic Disorder
Ativan (lorazepam)	Anafranil (clomipramine)	Paxil (paroxetine)
BuSpar (buspirone)	Luvox (fluvoxamine)	Prozac (fluoxetine)
Centrax (prazepam)	Paxil (paroxetine)	Tofranil (imipramine)
Klonopin (clonazepam)	Prozac (fluoxetine)	Zoloft (sertraline)
Librium (chlordiazepoxide)	Zoloft (sertraline)	
Serax (oxazepam)		
Tranxene (clorazepate)		
Valium (diazepam)		
Xanax (alprazolam)		

Figure 6.3 Anxiety disorders and medications used to treat them

BENZODIAZEPINES

Brand Name	Generic Name	Brand Name	Generic Name
Ativan	lorazepam	Paxipam	halazepam
Centrax	prazepam	Restoril	temazepam
Dalmane	flurazepam	Serax	oxazepam
Halcion	triazolam	Tranxene	chlorazepate
Klonopin	clonazepam	Valium	diazepam
Librium	chlordiazepoxide	Xanax	alprazolam

Figure 6.4 Brand and generic names of benzodiazepines

Schizophrenia

As yet there is no cure for schizophrenia, but the symptoms can be controlled with medication. The medications used for schizophrenia are often referred to as antipsychotic medications or neuroleptics. The medications relieve hallucinations, delusions, and other thinking problems associated with schizophrenia. They appear to work by correcting a chemical imbalance in the brain. Today newer medications promise fewer side effects and therefore greater compliance in the medication regimen by the person. Early treatment, accurate diagnosis, and proper medication make it more likely that the long-term prognosis will be favorable. Common medications prescribed for schizophrenia are listed in Figure 6.5.

One of the common side effects of antipsychotic medications is stiff muscles. Anticholinergic medications are prescribed to counter this side effect; common ones are Cogentin (benztropine) and Akineton (biperiden).

Psychotherapy. In the treatment of schizophrenia, therapy should not be directed at changing the person in some way in order to avoid behaviors that are really symptoms of the illness. Much of the therapy that takes place can be done in a group setting and is directed at helping clients prevent psychotic episodes, make lifestyle changes, and accept and work with the illness.

Hospitalization. For many with schizophrenia, hospitalization is required, since that is the only way to regulate the medication under supervision and protect a person in a dangerous psychotic episode. Today, with the managed care requirements, individuals with schizophrenia are getting less and less of this stabilizing hospitalization. There are,

MEDICATIONS FOR SCHIZOPHRENIA

Typical Antipsychotics	Atypical Antipsychotics
Compazine (prochlorperazine)	Clozaril (clozapine)
Haldol (haloperidol)	Geodon (ziprasidone)
Haldol Decanoate (haloperidol)	Risperdal (risperidone)
Loxitane (loxapine)	Seroquel (quetiapine)
Mellaril (thioridazine)	Zyprexa (olanzapine)
Moban (molindone)	
Navane (thiothixene)	
Prolixin (fluphenazine)	
Prolixin Decanoate (fluphenazine)	
Serentil (mesoridazine)	
Stelazine (trifluoperazine)	
Thorazine (chlorpromazine)	
Trilafon (perphenazine)	
Vesprin (triflupromazine)	

Figure 6.5 Medications used in the treatment of schizophrenia

however, alternative settings, such as step-down units and partial hospitalization programs, that can bring structure and stability to the person's life while the proper regimen of medication is worked out.

Tardive Dyskinesia

The term *Tardive dyskinesia* is used to describe involuntary movements that appear late in the course of pharmacological treatment (treatment with medications). *Tardive* means late, and *dyskinesia* means movement disorder.

According to NAMI, about 15% to 20% of those who take antipsychotic drugs for several years will get these symptoms. The movements primarily involve the face, such as grimacing or twisting of the mouth, but often they also involve the arms and legs. The condition is thought to be the result of treatment with antipsychotic medication (neuroleptics) over a long period of time. The medications that control the symptoms of the schizophrenia can have adverse effects on the neurology of the person, causing the involuntary movements to eventually appear.

Some clients move continually, while other clients exhibit movements only occasionally. Some movements are subtle and barely noticeable, while others are obvious and extreme (e.g., licking one's lips, blinking, twitching the tongue). Sometimes the person simply taps a toe or hand. Extreme forms of this condition are rare, but in these cases the movements are more conspicuous, and the person may jerk, twist, and writhe. Sometimes the body stiffens or flexes, and sometimes the person rocks back and forth.

The question that always arises is why should a person take antipsychotic medication if the eventual side effects will be so debilitating. As we have seen, newer medications have fewer side effects and may be more efficient in affecting only the part of the brain in which the problem is found. The older medications, however, were the only ones available that would reliably clear up symptoms and prevent relapse when many older people first became ill, so some clients today will do better on those medications than on the newer ones. These neuroleptics that were first developed can cause the rapid onset of Tardive dyskinesia in older people, sometimes within weeks or months of starting the medication; therefore, they should be given only when there is absolutely no other medication available to help the older client regain mental health. Part of advocating for the older client is to inquire about alternative medications available that might work as well and to report any signs of Tardive dyskinesia to the prescribing physician immediately.

Some of the options available for dealing with the side effects include lowering the dosage, changing to a medication with fewer side effects for the particular person, and prescribing medication to offset the effects of tardive dyskinesia to some extent. Most physicians today look for the lowest dose of a medication that will allow the person to function well without a relapse.

Part of obtaining informed consent from clients involves giving the clients a risk-benefit ratio for any medication that is being prescribed. This is something the prescribing physician should do, but as a case manager, you may need to ask for that information on behalf of your client.

SERVICES

Services for those with a mental illness tend to be in the person's community and are varied in order to meet the needs of a number of clients. In the managed care environment, one of the major goals is to reduce the number of hospitalizations, as hospitalizing a person is costly. For that reason, many services are designed to prevent hospitalization or to intervene before hospitalization is necessary, At times, however, hospitalization is necessary to stabilize the person.

Involuntary Commitment

All states have laws regarding when a person can be hospitalized against his or her will. The purpose of such hospitalization is to obtain care for a person who is acutely mentally ill and who is unwilling or unable to seek that care him- or herself. Such commitments are generally referred to as involuntary commitments. In some states it is mandatory that the person pose a threat to him- or herself or to others. In other states a person may also be committed if there is a significant deterioration and the person can return to his or her usual level of functioning if care is given.

Efforts are being made by NAMI to make significant deterioration a reason for commitment in states where this is not currently used as a criterion for commitment. The argument on the part of funding sources is that hospitalization is too expensive and should be used only in the dire circumstances. The argument on the other side is that immediate care before the person deteriorates further will save money by preventing a more severe and costly episode later. Furthermore, many contend that waiting until a person presents a danger to him- or herself or others may mean that by then it will be too late to intervene.

Assignment

Look at the laws in your state and determine what kind of commitment laws exist. Look at both involuntary and voluntary commitment criteria. (Voluntary commitments are commitments in which the person signs him- or herself into a hospital for care, usually for a specific length of time.) Can a person who is experiencing a severe mental disturbance be committed even if he or she does not pose a threat to him- or herself or others?

Voluntary Commitment

Many hospitals require that a person who is able and willing to do so sign him- or herself into the hospital for care. Clients who sign themselves into the hospital make a contract with the hospital to stay a certain length of time and receive medical treatment for their disorder. Sometimes individuals who sign their own commitment papers change their minds. If they pose a threat to themselves or others at the time they change their minds and seek to leave the hospital, it may be necessary to file an involuntary commitment to keep the person in treatment.

Hospitalization

During hospitalization, individuals receive assessments and participate in therapeutic activities. In inpatient psychiatric units, people are encouraged to get dressed and be active, rather than lying in bed during the day. Group therapy, community meetings in which the unit as a whole takes care of issues and problems that arise, and recreational activities are all part of the regimen. In addition, the right medication is sought in order to clear up the symptoms and allow the person to function better. Various medical tests are conducted, particularly when the disorder appears to be attributed to a medical condition, such as an imbalance in electrolytes due to high blood pressure medication. Today insurance does not pay for extended stays in the hospital. As soon as the person appears to be stabilized, he or she is often discharged. Those who cannot go immediately back to independent functioning often go to a step-down unit.

Step-Down Units

Step-down units are very much like hospitals, but clients take more responsibility. The clients may prepare the meals and keep their rooms cleaned and their beds made. They are usually encouraged to take their own medications without being reminded. They also participate in the same activities that are offered in a hospital. The goal is to have clients move into more independent situations after they have practiced the skills needed for independent living.

Some step-down units are not locked. Others are locked, but as clients become more stable, they can move to an unlocked situation with more freedom of movement and off-site visits and activities. Some step-down situations function as a home. These units have a small number of residents who live in and take care of the home. The residents do the grocery shopping, prepare meals, and clean. Workers staff such facilities to give guidance to residents and to keep the routines on track.

Personal Care Homes

For some, leaving a sheltered environment like the hospital or a step-down unit is too stressful. On their own, these people tend to regress and become ill again. Personal care homes are places where residents live while pursuing activities with others in the home or going off-site for activities and visits. Some residents work and return to the home after work. Meals are provided for the residents in personal care homes.

Partial Hospitalization

Clients who need structure and treatment but who do not need to be hospitalized may be placed in a partial hospitalization program. These programs vary in type and quality. In one city, individuals who worked came to the partial program after work for dinner, medication reviews, and group or individual therapy sessions. In another location, a partial program designed to return long-term residents of a state hospital to independent living was open daily and offered medication checks, group and individual therapy, lunch, and recreation. Partial programs are good places for clients to be monitored for any signs of deterioration, and they are also good places for clients to learn independence and new skills.

Recreational Programs

Social life is often difficult for people with serious mental disorders. The stigma involved often makes others refuse to allow them to participate in recreational activities in the community. Whenever possible, find generic recreational opportunities for clients—recreational opportunities we would all use. Many clients find themselves left out and lonely. To counteract that, communities often establish recreational programs for clients. Usually there is a facility where clients can drop in, eat together, and talk. There are generally recreational activities, such as bowling, a trip to the movies, or card games. Trips are sometimes planned to go hiking, camping, or to the shore.

Drop-in Centers

Because insurance companies do not want to pay for partial hospitalization for long periods of time, many community mental health programs have established drop-in centers. Sometimes these are run by high-functioning clients or entry-level workers. These centers give clients a place to go rather than sit home alone. Generally these centers have a television, card games, and refreshments. People get together and put puzzles together or watch a favorite day-time soap opera. Drop-in centers are available as an alternative to sitting home alone.

Outpatient Treatment

Community mental health centers have outpatient facilities where a variety of services are offered to keep people stable and as independent as possible. Following are some of the services likely to be found at an outpatient facility.

- *Medication review.* Clients need periodic checks with a physician to renew prescriptions for medications and to monitor how well the medications are working for the clients. Changes in medication are also considered when appropriate.
- *Individual counseling.* Some clients benefit from individual counseling. Often issues arise as a result of the mental disorder, or issues exist that either caused or exacerbate factors in the illness. Because of insurance constraints, counseling tends to be short-term and goal-directed.
- *Group therapy.* Clients may join groups in which the group members discuss the problems and issues they have in common. Many clients do exceptionally well when they learn that others share their problems and viewpoints and when they have the support of a group as they grapple with their illness.
- *Family therapy.* Families as well as clients often need to be seen. For a client with a serious mental disorder, engaging the family in the client's life can be helpful in preventing hospitalization. Family members also may have issues

that need to be resolved among themselves. This is often done best when a therapist is present to bring an objective view to the difficulties.

- *Psychological assessments.* A clinical psychologist is often able to assess the degree of risk clients pose to themselves and others as well as administer tests and conduct interviews that give valuable information about a client's illness, personality, motivation, aptitude, and IQ. Often a psychological evaluation is used to plan more individualized services and to bring another dimension of insight to the client's problems.
- *Psychiatric evaluation.* Psychiatrists often staff outpatient facilities to evaluate clients for the best diagnosis and treatment, including medications that might be helpful. A psychiatric evaluation is also used to better plan for the client.

Case Management Services

All successful community mental health programs have good case management units. Case managers, as we have seen in *Fundamentals of Case Management Practice* (Summers, 2001), bring clients into the system with an assessment of what they need, develop an individual plan for clients, link clients to the appropriate services, and monitor clients' progress and changing needs. Case managers, who are often the most direct link between the clients and the mental health system, provide valuable information and observations to other members of the team.

Intensive case management. Some clients need intensive case management services in order to remain in the community. Intensive case managers carry smaller caseloads and give considerable support to their clients. The goal of intensive case management is to allow people to live successfully in their own communities without frequent hospitalizations. Intensive case managers assist clients in activities such as washing clothes at the Laundromat, balancing the checkbook, and shopping for groceries. These case managers are available to prevent difficult or stressful situations from escalating. For more information on intensive case management, see Chapter 2 in *Fundamentals of Case Management Practice* (Summers, 2001).

Crisis Services

The type of crisis services that are available vary from one community to the next. One type of service is the hot line, where individuals who are feeling desperate, hopeless, or suicidal can call and talk to an empathic listener. Another type of crisis service functions in much the same way, but is part of a hospital emergency room and is available to those who come into the emergency room in a psychiatric crisis.

The best crisis services are mobile and go into the community, including the emergency room, to assist in any psychiatric crisis. Often the crisis team is accompanied by the police. For instance, a mobile team might accompany the police to a hostage situation, to the home of a family who can no longer cope with a family member showing signs of becoming psychotic, to meet a person and his or her friends at the emergency room after the person took an overdose, or to visit an elderly wife who needs to commit her husband because he has become uncharacteristically violent. Such teams assist emergency medical technicians, police and fire departments, and the staff of emergency rooms.

Managed care looks at the quality of a crisis team because a strong crisis component in a community mental health program can make a considerable difference in preventing hospitalizations and offering alternative solutions.

DOING YOUR ASSESSMENT AND FOLLOWING YOUR CLIENT

You now have enough information to develop a believable mental health client. Use the assessment form to create a credible person who might come to you seeking services for mental health problems. Use the space for interviewer comments to elaborate on the problems the client has discussed. Develop an individualized plan for this client, providing the components that you think will best serve your client. As you monitor your hypothetical client, you can draw from the information in this chapter to define the kinds of plausible problems and common setbacks your client is likely to encounter.

EXERCISES

Assessing Suicidality

Instructions: Following are some brief notes on clients. Note all the warning signals you see in each case, and decide how much risk of suicide is present for each person. In your deliberations, decide whether the person can go home and be treated later in the week, or whether the person needs to be placed someplace outside the home.

1. Carl lost his job as a bank director 7 months ago. He was fired after bank examiners found irregularities in the bank's records. Carl insists that he did nothing with the money that was illegal or dishonest and that the irregularities were the fault of poor bookkeeping, not theft. The bank did not have evidence to prosecute Carl, so they fired him. Carl believes this is an enormous stain on his reputation and that he will also never be able to work in banking again, the only field in which he is something of an expert. At the time of his firing, there were articles in the paper, and he and his wife and children suffered enormous embarrassment. Carl has stopped going to church and has given up activities he used to enjoy. He is not eating and is having trouble falling asleep at night. His wife estimates he has lost 15 pounds since he left the bank. He was referred to intake by his family physician.

   When the case manager asked Carl if he had ever considered suicide as a way out of this difficult and embarrassing situation, Carl admitted that he had been considering suicide and that one of the reasons he had come in today was because that thought had occurred to him more and more recently. During further discussion Carl denied ever feeling like this or attempting suicide before. He said he had thought pretty carefully about how he would do it in the last week and concluded that he could use his handgun in the garage after everyone else had left for school and work. Carl talked about the enormous stress all of this has been for him. He discussed the fact that not being charged meant he would never have a chance to clear his name. Carl was accompanied to the interview by his wife, who appeared concerned for his welfare.

Warning signs you noted were:

What is your opinion of the risk of suicide here?

Would you let Carl go home at this point?

Why or why not?

2. Alisse has had a number of episodes of depression beginning when she was about 14 years old. She has not been into the case management unit nor sought mental health services for several years. She is seeing the case manager today because she is again suffering from depression. In taking the history, the case manager learns that Alisse's husband is leaving her. Alisse tells the case manager that her "whole life is going up in smoke." She has quit her job, is sleeping most of the day, and is not eating well. There is some indication that Alisse may be abusing alcohol as a means of self-medication. She tells the case manager that she has no close friends and no family in the area. In fact, Alisse came in today alone.

   In taking the social history, the case manager learns that Alisse's father committed suicide when she was 8 years old. Alisse has attempted suicide on two previous occasions, and the case manager notes wrist scars from one previous attempt. Further, she has been hospitalized for depression on six different occasions. Alisse has worked as a cleaning person for a local company, but recently she quit going to work. When the case manager asks Alisse if she has thought about suicide, Alisse answers that she has. She states that she has saved a number of sleeping pills, prescribed by her family physician, for suicide if and when she feels there are no other alternatives. Alisse tells the case manager she came in today to see if the case manager could help her. She says, "You all never did me much good in the past. I'm still depressed. Nothing has changed in my life."

Warning signs you noted were:

What is your opinion of the risk of suicide here?

Would you let Alisse go home at this point?

Why or why not?

3. Mac is a truck driver who was injured in a trucking accident about 4 months ago. Since that time, he has had two surgeries and considerable rehabilitation, but he says he remains in severe pain and is uncomfortable most of the day. Mac tells the case manager that he has thought about suicide a lot lately, but that he has no plans for exactly how or when he would do it. He says that he has a good friend who owns a sporting goods store and that he could easily buy a gun from his friend. Mac states he was never depressed before and that this is a new and terrible feeling for him, almost intolerable.

   Only 2 months before the accident, Mac's wife died after a long battle with cancer. Mac says that the two events have "just sent me over the edge." He admits to eating very little, mostly junk food, and states that he sometimes does not dress for days at a time. In fact, he says he found it a relief to have to get dressed and go someplace today, even if it was to the case management unit. Mac has stopped most of the activities he used to enjoy, like bowling and making furniture, mostly because they are too painful. "I can't bend over the lathe any more," he tells the case manager. Mac never did go to church and says he never believed "that stuff about God and a higher being or whatever. Just never could believe in anything like that."

   Recently the company talked to Mac about retiring on disability. "That scares me because I won't know what to do with myself," Mac says. He appears to be severely depressed and to be choking back tears throughout most of the interview. Asked if he has any close friends or family nearby, Mac answers that he has a brother who is not very considerate of his condition. "He's probably right. He tells me I am making myself feel like this. He doesn't really want me around him or his family until I get a grip and cheer up. He thinks I'm doing this to myself." Mac says he has lost touch with friends since the accident. "Most of my friends were people I worked with, you know."

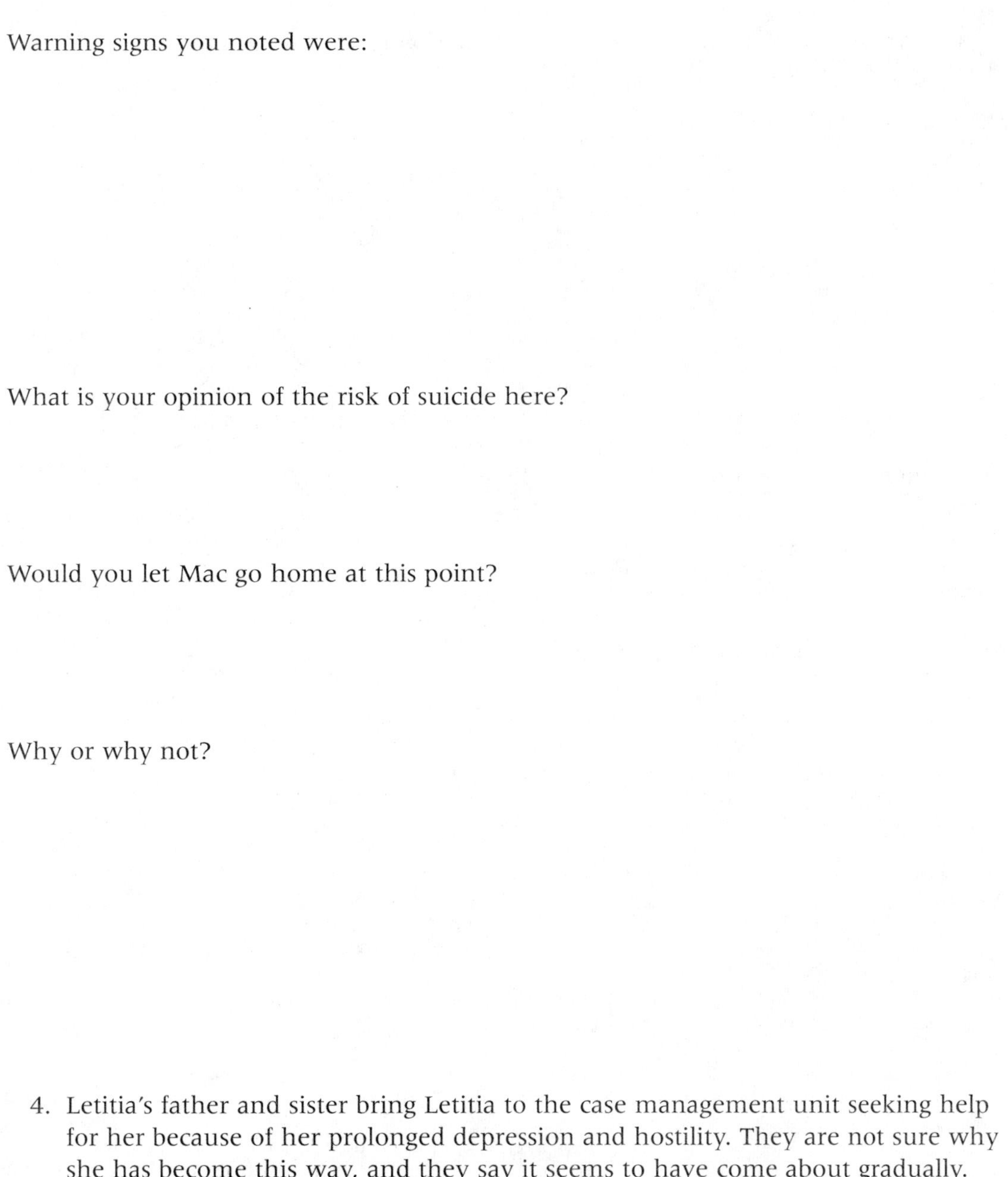

Warning signs you noted were:

What is your opinion of the risk of suicide here?

Would you let Mac go home at this point?

Why or why not?

4. Letitia's father and sister bring Letitia to the case management unit seeking help for her because of her prolonged depression and hostility. They are not sure why she has become this way, and they say it seems to have come about gradually. Letitia is hostile during the interview, admitting freely that she is considering suicide and has several means by which to do it. She says this in a challenging manner to the case manager. When asked what those means are, Letitia is vague. Throughout the interview Letitia remains angry and sarcastic.

   The case manager learns that Letitia lives alone and works for a transcription service, doing much of the transcription at home. She has wrist scars, and there are other scars that lead the case manager to believe she has engaged in self-mutilation in the past. Letitia is angry with her family for bringing her in and at the case manager for thinking that the case management unit can help. She tells the case manager, "I've seen dozens of you people and you all are alike. Think you have answers to everyone's problems. Well, you never have for me, and you never will."

   Letitia's mother committed suicide when Letitia was 12 years old. Letitia denies having any close friends and is not close to her family. The family appears to want to help, but she is rejecting of them, saying she came in today "to do them a favor. Now maybe they will leave me alone."

Warning signs you noted were:

What is your opinion of the risk of suicide here?

Would you let Letitia go home at this point?

Why or why not?

Using the *DSM-IV-TR*

Instructions: Read the cases that follow and see what diagnosis you might assign the person. Remember that this is only an exercise. Try to come up with as accurate a diagnosis as possible, but you might find that several fit. For more information on how case managers use the *DSM-IV-TR,* look at Chapter 16 in *Fundamentals of Case Management Practice* (Summers, 2001). Use the chapter in your *DSM-IV-TR* on anxiety disorders.

1. Lily is depressed following the birth of her first child. She denies ever being depressed previously and tells the case manager that she does not know what has "gotten into me." She is tearful during the interview, and she complains of not being able to eat and of waking up early in the morning, worrying about the baby and her ability to take care of her. She seems listless and complains of being tired every day. She tells the case manager that she is uncertain she can take care of her

baby because, "I just am not that good at things I do. I just don't feel I should be the one to raise a child."

Your tentative diagnosis:

Because:

2. Gordon has had several episodes of terror when he was alone. On several occasions, he was out running errands, and on several others he was at home by himself. He had such an episode about 2 months ago, and his wife finally insisted that he see someone for help. Gordon tells the case manager, "My wife wanted me to get help because she feels I am overly upset over these attacks. I am really worried I'll have more of them, and I know she feels that I am planning my whole life around trying to avoid having them. I do think about it a lot, but really I can't tell you when I will have one. I just feel like I'm going crazy, and one of these days I think I may be permanently crazy if they don't stop." Gordon describes his last attack in which his palms got cold and sweaty and he felt like he was choking. "I felt like I couldn't breathe and that my chest was getting tighter and tighter. It always feels as if I am about to die or something worse. I can't get any air, and I start to shake all over."

Your tentative diagnosis:

Because:

3. Biranda is seeking help for a problem that she describes as "getting out of hand." She says that some months ago she began to be concerned about whether everything was in order. She claims these worries began after she saw a television documentary on people who died leaving things out of order. "They were talking about people dying with no will or insurance to take care of their families, and I went right out and got my will up-to-date and made sure I had enough insurance. But then I started to think that if I were to die, there would be other things out of order, like my checkbook wouldn't be balanced or my stove clean or food for the family to eat or, I don't know—you name it, and I worried about it."

   Today Biranda describes having constant thoughts about dying. She has tried to ignore these thoughts. She tells the case manager that she realizes she probably is not going to die, but she just cannot "put the thoughts aside until I fix up everything." This has entailed cleaning, balancing and rebalancing her checkbook, and counting the numbers of different food products and replacing them. "I go to the store every day because I want 8 rolls of toilet tissue in each bathroom, or I want 14 frozen dinners in the freezer, so if someone eats a dinner or uses up a roll of toilet paper, I have to go and replace that." Sometimes, in order to sleep that night, she will go to the store late at night, so everything will be in order, "you know, in case I die overnight."

Your tentative diagnosis:

Because:

4. Charles comes into the case management unit complaining of depression. He has been referred by his family doctor after the doctor found that Charles seemed depressed. Charles has all the symptoms associated with depression. He feels sad, even tearful at times. He has dropped out of all the activities he used to enjoy. He is unable to sleep and has lost weight. He tells the case manager that his life is "a waste," even though he holds several graduate degrees in engineering.

   In taking the history, the case manager learns that Charles has had periods of joy and productivity in his life. He tells the case manager that during those times, he has felt "on top of the world. I feel like I can do anything I put my mind to, and my company is always promoting me because I do accomplish a good bit during those times." He says that there have been times when he has been "so in love with my work" that he has worked around the clock to get things done. "I like those times. I can have a dozen new ideas in an hour, and they are all good ones. I bring together a team of the people under me, and we can make most of the ideas happen." He says the team is always telling him, "We wind up, and we wind down." I know it is hard on them, but it is hard on me, too. To have felt that good, and now be reduced to this."

Your tentative diagnosis:

Because:

EVALUATION FOR MENTAL HEALTH SERVICES
WILDWOOD CASE MANAGEMENT UNIT

Date ______________________ Intake worker ______________________________

Giving information ____

Relationship to client ____

IDENTIFYING INFORMATION

Client name ____

Address ____

Phone: Home ______________________ Work _____________________

Social Security No. ___________________ Date of birth (DOB) _______________

Gender: [ ] M [ ] F Veteran status ______________________________

Primary source(s) of income ____

Primary language _______________________________ Need interpreter? _______

Maiden name/Name at birth __________________________ Marital status _______

INSURANCE

Coverage by ____

[ ] Uninsured and no medical assistance or Medicare

OTHER AGENCY INVOLVEMENT

Name of agency

____

____

____

DESCRIPTION OF PRESENTING PROBLEM

____

____

____

____

____

____

____

____

____

____

EDUCATION/WORK

Highest grade completed ______________________________

Currently employed? [ ] Yes [ ] No

If yes, where? ______________________________

Type of work performed ______________________________

Currently a student? [ ] Yes [ ] No

If yes, where? ______________________________

For: [ ] GED [ ] College degree Other ______________

Vocational rehabilitation office involved? [ ] Yes [ ] No

Vocational rehabilitation referral needed? [ ] Yes [ ] No

HOME

Who lives in your home?

Name	Relationship to client	Age

Significant others not living in the home

Name	Relationship to client	Age

How would you describe your home and home life?

____

____

____

____

____

Pets [ ] Yes [ ] No Type ____________________

TRANSPORTATION USED

[ ] Car [ ] Bus/taxi [ ] County transportation [ ] Bicycle [ ] Walking

SOCIAL/RECREATIONAL

[ ] Religious [ ] Sports

Clubs ____________________

Hobbies ____________________

Interests ____________________

Activities with friends ____________________

Other ____________________

Interviewer comments:

____

____

____

____

____

____

____

MEDICAL HISTORY

Primary care physician ____________________ Phone ____________________

Date of last physical examination ____________________

Medical conditions (other than psychiatric)

____

____

____

____

____

Medications (other than psychotropic)

Medication	Dosage instructions

PSYCHIATRIC HISTORY

Is there a commitment for outpatient? ____________________

Has client received psychiatric services before?

Where When Termination date

____

____

____

____

____

Suicidality

____

____

____

Panic attacks

____

____

Previous diagnosis (if known) ____________________

MENTAL STATUS EXAMINATION

[ ] Oriented x 3 If not, describe

____

____

Appearance

[ ] Appropriate [ ] Disheveled [ ] Unconventional [ ] Other

Interviewer comments:

____

____

[ ] Depression
____ Looks sad
____ Tearful/cries a lot
____ Irritable
____ Withdrawn
____ Sleep problems
____ Decreased appetite

[ ] Anxiety
____ Panic attacks
____ Social avoidance
____ Persistent worry
____ Uncomfortable leaving home
____ Somatic complaints

[ ] Mania
____ Euphoric
____ Agitated

[ ] Suicidal
____ Vague death wish
____ Thoughts without plan
____ Thoughts with plan
____ Gestures
____ Attempts
____ Self-attempts

[ ] Homicidal
____ Thoughts without plan
____ Thoughts with plan
____ Gestures
____ Attempts

[ ] Other ______________________________________

AFFECT

[ ] Appropriate [ ] Restricted [ ] Flat [ ] Inappropriate [ ] Labile

Interviewer comments:

____

____

IMPACT OF PROBLEMS

[ ] Health [ ] School [ ] Work [ ] Relationships [ ] Other

Interviewer comments:

____

____

____

____

____

PSYCHOSIS

[ ] Hallucinations
_____ Auditory
_____ Name calling
_____ Command
_____ Vague
_____ Visual
_____ Other

[ ] Delusions
_____ Paranoid
_____ Grandiose
_____ Erotomanic
_____ Jealous
_____ Persecutory
_____ Somatic
_____ Guilt
_____ Mixed
_____ Other

[ ] Thought broadcast [ ] Thought withdrawal [ ] Thought insertion

THOUGHT PROCESS

_____ Perseverative Re: ______________________________
_____ Preoccupied Re: ______________________________
_____ Flight of ideas
_____ Distractible
_____ Clang associations
_____ Illogical
_____ Neologisms
_____ Blocking
_____ Tangentiality
_____ Racing thoughts
_____ Clear/coherent

SPEECH

[ ] Normal
[ ] Impoverished
[ ] Overly talkative
[ ] Under talkative
[ ] Pressured
[ ] Loose associations

MEMORY

[ ] Adequate [ ] Impaired

Interviewer comments:

____

____

INSIGHT

[ ] Good [ ] Fair [ ] Poor

Interviewer comments:

____

____

INTELLIGENCE

[ ] Above average [ ] Average [ ] Below average

Interviewer comments:

____

____

MOTIVATION

[ ] Good [ ] Fair [ ] Poor

Interviewer comments:

____

____

OTHER BEHAVIORS

[ ] Restless [ ] Poor hygiene [ ] Peer problems

[ ] Fire setting [ ] Tics [ ] Compulsive behaviors [ ] Other

Interviewer comments:

____

____

PRESENT MENTAL HEALTH TREATMENTS

Diagnosis ____

Hospitalizations ____

Medications ____

Therapy ____

PAST MENTAL HEALTH TREATMENTS

Diagnosis ____

Hospitalizations ____

Medications ____

Therapy ____

Interviewer comments:

____

____

CHEMICAL DEPENDENCY ISSUES

Present treatment for ____

Where ________________________________ Since ________________

Client's assessment ______________________________

Past treatment for ______________________________

Where ______________________________ When ______________

Client's assessment ______________________________

Interviewer comments:

____

____

LEGAL ISSUES

Present legal issues (describe)

____

____

Client's assessment ______________________________

Past legal issues (describe)

____

____

Client's assessment ______________________________

Interviewer comments:

____

____

ABUSE ISSUES

[ ] Physical abuse

When ______________ By whom ______________

Reported [ ] Yes [ ] No

Comments:

____

____

____

[ ] Sexual abuse

When ______________ By whom ______________

Reported [ ] Yes [ ] No

Comments:

____

____

____

[ ] Neglect

When ______________ By whom ______________________

Reported [ ] Yes [ ] No

Comments:

____

____

____

[ ] Witness to violence

When ______________ By whom ______________________

Reported [ ] Yes [ ] No

Nightmares [ ] Yes [ ] No Flashbacks [ ] Yes [ ] No

Comments:

____

____

CLIENT'S FAMILY

Chemical Dependency Issues

____

____

____

Legal Issues

____

____

____

Mental Health Issues

____

____

____

Family Response to Client's Problems

[ ] Good [ ] Bad [ ] Indifferent [ ] Hostile [ ] Avoidant

[ ] Guarded [ ] Cooperative [ ] Uncooperative

Interviewer comments:

____

____

CLIENT RESPONSE TO INTERVIEW

[ ] Good [ ] Bad [ ] Indifferent [ ] Hostile [ ] Avoidant
[ ] Guarded [ ] Cooperative [ ] Uncooperative

IMPRESSIONS AND RECOMMENDATIONS

____
____
____
____
____
____
____
____
____
____
____
____
____
____
____
____

GAF ______________ Level of case management ______________

Signature of case manager completing evaluation

____

Chapter 7

Case Management and Mental Retardation

INTRODUCTION

Mr. and Mrs. Gonzales waited nervously for the doctor to come to the conference room. They were there on that late October day to learn the findings from a series of tests performed on their daughter, Anna Marie, 2 years old. When Anna Marie was born, she seemed to be a normal, healthy baby. For the first six months she appeared to develop normally, but then her parents noticed that she was failing to develop. In the first year she began to lose some of the skills she had acquired earlier. She had been saying a few words, but now she said nothing. She had begun to pull herself up in her playpen, but she had stopped doing that. By the time the tests were complete, she was actually having difficulty sitting up.

Dr. Creider entered the room with a chart under his arm. He introduced the young man who accompanied him. "This is Stephen Gessner. He is a case manager here at the center." The diagnosis, according to the doctor, was Rett syndrome. He went on to explain that it affects only girls (male fetuses are presumed to die before birth if they have the syndrome) and that, after normal development, the cerebrum begins to atrophy, causing problems with coordination, movement, and balance. Anna Marie's inability to use her hands purposefully had been one of the first things Mr. and Mrs. Gonzales reported to their pediatrician; the doctor now confirmed that the problem is one of the symptoms of Rett syndrome. Later the parents had seen Anna Marie wringing her hands and making hand-to-mouth movements that seemed to be purposeless and repetitive. This is a later symptom, the doctor explained. He told them that the prognosis was not favorable. Seizures and breathing difficulties could develop later, and although their daughter might grow to adulthood, the parents might see periods in which their daughter was entirely unresponsive. The cause is unclear, he told them, but it seems that it is due to a dominant gene on the X chromosome.

Mr. and Mrs. Gonzales were given an opportunity to ask questions. When they had exhausted all their concerns, Dr. Creider turned the meeting over to the case manager. "Mr. Gessner is here to help you plan for your daughter. He will work with you as she grows and help you put together a package of services that Anna Marie and your family will need."

During the course of the next hour, Stephen Gessner proceeded to help the family identify the services they needed to maintain Anna Marie at home. They explored day-care options, in-home assistance, and medical devices to help Anna Marie become more mobile. Stephen explained the various services that were available and gave information about services the Gonzales family might need in the future. He even arranged for the couple to attend, at the hospital, a support group of parents going through similar difficulties. Throughout the interview, he asked the parents what they preferred for their daughter and what services the parents felt were most important to the family.

The diagnosis and the poor prognosis devastated this family. They had held out hope that there was some sort of cure, that their daughter was suffering from some temporary setback that could be corrected with medication or stimulation. The best reassurance they had was in not being alone in this difficulty. Their case manager would walk through this with them, helping them to address each new problem as it arose and putting them in touch with others. Mrs. Gonzales reported several years later that she did not know how they would have gone on without their case manager. "We didn't have any idea what to expect. The doctor told us, but that was all so clinical. On a day-to-day basis Stephen gave us valuable advice and assistance that allowed us to keep Anna Marie in our home and a wonderful part of our family."

SPECIAL CONSIDERATIONS

Terms and Expressions

In the social work field, you will often hear the terms *developmental disability* and *mental retardation* used interchangeably. Although mental retardation is indeed a developmental disability, it is not the only one. There are a number of other developmental disabilities that have nothing to do with intelligence. For instance, a person could have a learning disorder and still have a perfectly normal IQ. The *DSM-IV-TR* uses the term *mental retardation* to refer to "significantly subaverage general intellectual functioning." That is the condition that is the focus of this chapter; hence the term *mental retardation,* rather than *developmental disability,* will be used. Nevertheless, when you begin to work in the field of mental retardation, you may find that your agency prefers to use the term *developmental disability* because it sounds less pejorative.

Things to Think About

In this chapter you will learn only the most basic information about mental retardation. The unique considerations for this population are broad. They cover many aspects of the person's life.

First, you need to think about the safety and well-being of your clients, as they are usually unable to do that entirely on their own. In addition, you must consider any medical needs your clients may have, as many individuals with mental retardation also have physical problems. Further, you should look for programs and placements that will enhance your clients' lives and allow them to reach their full potential.

As a case manager, you will also work with parents and families to help them come to terms with what the disability will mean to all of them in the long run. You should give assistance to help them cope with their family member's disability, and you should provide support and instructions that will minimize the effects of the disability and allow the family to better include the disabled member. Finally, you will help parents with long-range planning for the care of their disabled family member when they are no longer able to provide that care.

The Need to Control

Because of your clients' impairment, you may be tempted to view them as needing your control. Some poor case managers actually behave as if their clients belong to them. Families, too, view their disabled family member as belonging to them. When the person wants to leave home or makes other independent moves, the family may try to have him or her declared incompetent. They may call the case manager and ask to have their disabled family member picked up. They may believe that you have control over your clients and can tell them what to do.

You can talk to clients about the decisions they make, but it is important that you support their decisions. The fact that your clients have mental retardation does not necessarily make their decisions worse than the decisions of supposedly normal people. Many people live lifestyles that are unusual, make bad decisions, and engage in poor relationships. Only if you feel your client is in real danger would you interfere, but you are not a social control agent.

In one situation, a case manager did everything she could to discourage her client from dating. Her client, Angela, had met a young man in a sheltered workshop. They went for walks together, and occasionally to the movies when family members drove them. Their families included them at family picnics and holiday gatherings. The case manager felt that the couple might decide to marry and this "wouldn't be in anyone's best interest." She was warned by her supervisor to stop interfering in the lives of these two people, but she continued to actively discourage them from seeing each other and denigrated one to the other when she was with each of them in the hope that she could break up the relationship, which she described as "much too close for comfort." Eventually the families complained to the director of the agency, and the case manager was disciplined. Although she refrained from interfering after that, she continued to talk to her coworkers about how "inappropriate" the relationship was.

WHAT IS INTELLIGENCE?

Three general areas that are considered when defining intelligence:

1. *Problem-solving ability.* Finding practical solutions to common problems; being able to think through a problem and arrive logically at a good solution
2. *Verbal ability.* Being able to express emotions and ideas verbally; understanding verbal communication of others
3. *Social intelligence.* The ability to read social cues; adapting one's behavior to fit the social situation; having the skills to interact and participate in social groups and activities

For all of these specific capacities, there is the underlying ability to learn new facts and new appropriate behaviors. According to Baroff (1999), "Intelligence is seen as the ability to learn and to profit from experience, to acquire knowledge, to reason, to cope with changing conditions, and to motivate oneself to accomplish what needs to be done."

WHAT IS MENTAL RETARDATION?

People with mental retardation have been found to have impaired general intelligence. This in turn leads to some degree of difficulty handling their lives. The amount of difficulty in carrying out normal responsibilities is very much related to the amount of intellectual impairment a person has. For example, people with mild retardation may have the most difficulty with scholastic achievement, while those with a greater degree of retardation may have difficulty negotiating nearly every aspect of their lives. These individuals are unable to assume the degree of personal responsibility that might be expected for their chronological age.

Characteristics of Mental Retardation

The three chief characteristics of mental retardation are:

1. Significantly subaverage intelligence
2. Discovered or diagnosed before age 18; it must occur during the period of mental development and prior to the beginning of adulthood
3. Accompanied by a diminished ability to handle two or more of 10 adaptive skill areas related to everyday living (see list in next section)

A diagnosis of mental retardation must be made before the person is age 18. Nearly all cognitive growth takes place between birth and age 18. In a child with mental retardation, that growth is slower than in the normal child, and there is a difference in the ultimate level of cognitive growth between the two. Those with the diagnosis of mental retardation are viewed as quite different from other members of their families. These differences lead to variations in how that person is treated from an early age, and often to problems with acceptance.

Brain Injury

Certainly people can become retarded after age 18. This can happen when a person suffers a severe head injury or an illness that damages the brain in some way. Such people, however, are considered to be brain-injured, and not retarded, because the injury took place *after* a normal period of cognitive development. The brain-injured person can be distinguished from the person with mental retardation by the acute onset (e.g., after an accident or stroke), followed by problems with memory and organization. Some brain-injured people have trouble maintaining attention or concentrating, and these characteristics are often accompanied by changes in personality that may appear as emotional instability.

In the long run, brain-injured individuals may eventually use the same services as those with the mental retardation diagnosis. Acceptance and concern by friends and family are often more forthcoming with brain-injured people than with those who have mental retardation.

WHO ARE THOSE WITH MENTAL RETARDATION?

Baroff (1999) determined that about 1% to 3% of the population has mental retardation. According to Baroff, there tend to be two distinct groups of people with mental retardation:

1. Those whose impairment is mild, who have no physical abnormalities, who come from a lower socioeconomic group, and who have other family members with a similar mild degree of retardation and no physical abnormalities
2. Those whose form of retardation is more severe, often with physical abnormalities or complications, and whose condition is unique or unusual within the family; these individuals are found in all socioeconomic levels in about equal numbers

DIAGNOSING MENTAL RETARDATION

Awareness of a Problem

Diagnosis generally begins with the awareness that a person is functioning with substantial impairments compared to others at the same chronological age. We might say such people lack the normal capacities that would be expected given their age. As pointed out earlier, this awareness that there is a significant problem must occur before the individual is 18 years old.

Testing to Confirm

Intelligence tests are used to determine whether a person suspected of having mental retardation actually does have it; in fact, the diagnosis cannot be given without testing first to confirm it. A score on one of these tests is called an intelligence quotient (IQ). Mean IQ is somewhere around 100. Using statistical equations, the designation of mental retardation is assigned when a person's IQ falls two standard deviations below 100, or at about 68 on the Stanford-Binet test and 70 on the Wechsler scales. In 1973, using this method, a chart was devised to determine the degree of retardation as follows:

Mild retardation: IQ 52–69
Moderate retardation: IQ 36–54
Severe retardation: IQ 20–39
Profound retardation: IQ 0–24

Since 1983, the ceiling for IQ can be as high as an IQ of 70, and these four levels of retardation have been largely dropped. This was done to include those who need services due to additional impairments, as well as to block workers from locking people into a certain level of IQ and having no further expectations for them.

In this chapter, we will continue to refer to these levels as descriptive of the degree to which people are able to handle their lives and responsibilities. The *DSM-IV-TR* still lists the four levels of retardation, as well as the category "mental retardation, severity unspecified."

Intelligence quotient can also be used as a way of measuring the rate of mental growth. A low IQ can indicate how well people will do in school, but not how well they can learn to adapt to and handle everyday activities. Those with IQs near 75 have academic problems but generally can function independently. A person's IQ and ability to handle everyday challenges are assessed to determine the degree to which he or she will need services.

Assessment of Adaptive Skills

Finally, for the diagnosis to be made, there must be a minimum of impaired functioning in at least two adaptive skill areas. Baroff (1999) lists 10 adaptive skill areas:

1. *Communication.* Understanding and using spoken language
2. *Self-care.* The ability to feed, dress, handle toileting, grooming, and personal hygiene
3. *Home living.* Housekeeping, clothing care, cooking, budgeting, safety, property maintenance
4. *Social skills.* Handling interpersonal interactions, understanding social cues and emotions, recognizing and participating in reciprocity, controlling impulses
5. *Community use.* Using public transportation, shopping, obtaining and using services
6. *Self-direction.* Exercising choice, initiating activities, planning, using problem-solving and appropriate assertiveness
7. *Health and safety.* Exercising caution, recognizing and responding to one's health problems, ability to protect oneself
8. *Functional academics.* Reading, writing, and arithmetic skills as they are applied to activities of daily living
9. *Leisure.* Assuming responsibility for recreation and leisure activities
10. *Work.* Ability to maintain full-time or part-time work (Baroff, 1999, pp. 19–20).

These impairments cannot be due to some other condition, such as mental illness, substance abuse, a physical disability, or an illness, and the impairments cannot be related to a lack of familiarity with the language or culture. This last point is important to remember in order to prevent large numbers of immigrant children from being diagnosed as retarded when in fact they are normal children struggling to learn a new language.

A person whose IQ is borderline and whose only area of impairment is in functional academics would most likely be diagnosed as having a learning disorder, rather than mental retardation. Individuals with more severe intellectual impairment generally have additional impairment in more than two of the adaptive skill areas. Case managers look at both the IQ and the adaptive skills of the person to determine the amount of support he or she is likely to need.

DOCUMENTING A FULL ASSESSMENT

In order to plan for the best interests of a client, a thorough assessment must be done. Case managers who assist families and individuals with mental retardation assemble documentation from a number of sources. One type of documentation is that of other practitioners who have evaluated the person with mental retardation. This documentation is often supplemented by case managers through their own observations and intake histories, which round out the picture of the client and his or her circumstances. Based on the documentation, families and the clients themselves can work with case managers to choose the best services to meet their needs and fit their circumstances. The following text discusses the four major areas to be investigated.

Intellectual Functioning and Adaptive Skills

Psychologists and others qualified to administer IQ tests will supply case management with a written report of the individual's score on an intelligence test and a description of the client's strengths and weaknesses, particularly as they relate to the 10 adaptive skill areas. It is important to keep in mind the limited time these practitioners have been with your client. Their work is important in making the diagnosis, but is not the whole picture.

Psychological and Motivational Considerations

Psychological reports generally outline any significant behavioral problems. The case manager's assessment should document parents' concerns in this area. It is estimated that about one third of those with mental retardation do have some behavior problems (Baroff, 1999).

Etiology Considerations

Etiology refers to the origin or cause of the condition. If known, the etiology can play an important role in treatment and prevention. Some conditions can be prevented from becoming more severe, and certain medical treatments can prevent mental retardation if they are applied early enough. Both the social history and the medical history become important in uncovering possible etiology. Baroff (1999) lists four possible causes for mental retardation.

1. *Biomedical.* This refers to biological conditions that affect the brain. Often these conditions are present before birth.
2. *Social.* There is growing concern that home environments that do not provide enough stimulation for an infant to develop properly can be the cause of mental retardation. Often case managers evaluate the home and the understanding of parents about the crucial need in developing children for a stimulating environment.
3. *Behavioral.* This refers to possible prenatal activities engaged in by the mother. Heavy drinking of alcohol or drug addiction, and even legal prescription medication, affect the baby before birth.
4. *Educational.* Early verbal stimulation and stimulating preschool environments make a large contribution to children's intellectual development. In an assessment, the case manager is often able to document the activities in the home, the parents' understanding of the parenting role, and their ability to provide what is needed for the developing child.

Environmental Considerations

An evaluation is made to determine if the client is provided with an environment that meets his or her psychological needs. Following are some issues to consider when making an evaluation.

1. *Basic needs.* The case manager might begin by looking at the degree of attention or neglect the person is receiving, noting such things as whether the person is fed, clean, and provided with health care and a safe environment.
2. *The need for love and affection.* The case manager should examine to what extent, if any, the parents or caregivers seem resentful of the client, consider the client a burden, or withhold affection and pride.
3. *The need for inclusion.* Case managers look at whether the client's need to be included in a group and in the larger community is being met. To what extent, if any, do parents or caregivers seem embarrassed by the person with retardation and seek to limit contact with the larger community? To what extent, if any, do they hold low expectations that prevent the person with mental retardation from participating in stimulating and enriching activities?

4. *The need for some control.* Case managers seek to give their clients and clients' families as much choice in areas of treatment and support as possible. In programs where clients receive treatment, this may be as simple as allowing the client to choose what to wear or what activity to pursue next. Everyone wants to feel that he or she has some control over the direction of his or her life.
5. *The need for structure and stability.* The case manager needs to examine the stability of the environment in which the client lives and functions, including school and work sites. Do these environments have predictable routines? Do they provide a structure that promotes well-being? For a person with mental retardation, constant unpredictable changes in routine are often very disorganizing, producing considerable anxiety.

DEVELOPING THE PLAN FOR SERVICES AND SUPPORTS

In the assessment, the specific needs of the individual are uncovered and documented. In the next step before monitoring, the service plan is created. This is always done with as much input as possible from the client and the client's parents or caretakers, who have needs of their own and desires for their child. This type of planning is referred to as person-centered planning. The budgeting of money for a particular case is referred to an individualized budget. Baroff (1999) points out that in general, the plan should be created to address the following issues:

1. *Personal productivity.* Clients should be provided with school or work opportunities that allow them to produce, gain experience, and feel pride.
2. *Integration.* The plan should include ways to integrate the client into the community and into groups that consist of both normal individuals and those with disabilities.
3. *Life satisfaction.* Does the person have an opportunity to enjoy his or her life? Built into the plan are opportunities to have fun, grow, and meet others.
4. *Natural environments.* There has always been a tendency to try to keep all those with disabilities together, isolating them from those without obvious disabilities. The plan should include elements that will place the client in general community settings.
5. *Needed supports.* Access to tutors in school, job coaches at work, and personal aides to facilitate living in a group home or at home can make the difference in the amount of integration a person with mental retardation is able to achieve. The plan should specify the type of activity to be supported, what support will be needed for that activity, and how long the support will be needed. Baroff (1999) describes four levels of intensity for support services:

   Intermittent—as needed
   Limited—constant, but not permanent
   Extensive—constant and not time-limited
   Pervasive—constant, not time-limited, and in all environments

In dealing with people with mental retardation, the shift is away from a focus on IQ and toward a consideration of the deficits in adaptive skills. Case managers focus on creating plans that will provide the services and supports necessary to address these deficits so that the client can better live as a member of the community.

PERSON-CENTERED PLANNING

All over the United States, services for mental retardation are engaging in person-centered planning. During this process, case managers and others closely associated with the person develop a plan that spells out what the person wants in his or her life. The plan reflects how the person wants to live, not how the case manager and other professionals assume the person should live.

In addition, the plan looks at those elements in the person's life that are working well. For instance, close relationships are enhanced and protected. This way of planning respects a person's right to live with people he or she likes, be cared for by people who treat him or her with dignity and respect, and receive services that the person feels will be most beneficial.

Problems with Person-Centered Planning

The four major problems that may arise during the development of a person-centered plan are:

1. The person may want to do something that is not entirely safe, such as living alone. Many arrangements can be made that come close to living alone. For instance, a person might share a space with another person, but lead a wholly independent life, or the person might have an apartment in an apartment cluster where staff is readily available.
2. The person may want to be with people who do not want to be with him or her. It then becomes the case manager's responsibility to help the person seek another good alternative.
3. The person may want to do something that is too expensive or will take a lot of planning and changes. In such a case, the goal then becomes a long-term goal, something the person can work toward. The case manager, however, needs to really help the client work toward that goal, and not simply say it can be done "someday."
4. Case managers and administrators and even funding sources may say they are using person-centered planning with their clients when, in reality, the system is too brittle to change to creating new supports where they are needed and getting the community involved in helping individuals live the way they want to live. You may encounter a social service system that values uniformity and predictability, and in which the case managers are reluctant to view clients as unique individuals or to create new services for a few. In such systems, you may hear that person-centered planning is taking place, but you will notice that clients are expected to fit into existing services and that the services are not particularly responsive to the clients.

The plan focuses on the typical everyday arrangements the person indicates are desirable. It is not about making fantastic dreams and wishes come true. Case managers are responsible for integrating safety and health issues with the person's stated desires. A committed case manager can find ways to meet both concerns. This process involves preventing communities from segregating and congregating those with mental disabilities. A case manager who genuinely values each client's uniqueness and is committed to person-centered planning can break down barriers and make such a system work.

MENTAL AGE

Intelligence quotient (IQ) tests, administered to thousands of children in every age group, give us an understanding of where children should be in their development at a certain age. We use the collective scores on these tests to tell us where most children are at a certain age, or what is considered normal development. With mental retardation, a child's score and thus his or her mental age may be behind his or her actual chronological age.

Development for all children is expected to take place primarily from birth to about 18 years of age. Children with mental retardation develop at a slower rate during that time than normal children, and therefore, by age 18, they are at a permanent disadvantage. There are, however, many variations:

- In some types of severe retardation, mental development may take place in a shorter number of years. Children with this sort of severe retardation may complete development before age 18, developing only as much as their disability allows and no further.
- In some types of mental retardation, a child develops slowly from the beginning. For instance, most normal infants are able to suck at birth, but a child who is slow in developing may have trouble sucking at birth and only gradually develop this ability.
- Some children, like Anna Marie, develop normally at first, but then begin to slow in their development later, after the first year or so.
- Other children may be slow in most areas of mental growth, but develop normally in a few select areas. Some children develop normally in most areas and have trouble in only a few select areas; these children are commonly diagnosed with learning disorders, but not mental retardation.
- Adults with mental retardation can learn new adaptive skills throughout most of their lives, and some increase their verbal abilities in adulthood.
- Some children who appear to be slow in the beginning may actually catch up if placed in the right environment or stimulated to grow in new ways.

It is important to understand that tests indicating a child's mental age only indicate the child's ability levels at a particular time during his or her developmental years. Knowing where the child is in relation to what is considered normal gives information about what remedial steps might be taken. These tests do not necessarily indicate where the child will always be, nor can these tests always predict accurately where the child will be when the developmental years end.

MENTAL RETARDATION AND COGNITION

Cognition means thinking. Thinking involves an assessment of situations and people, planning, and making decisions. It includes developing strategies, being able to foresee consequences, and using imagination. We will look at some general findings about people who have mental retardation and how that condition often impacts the way a person thinks.

Visual Learning

For many people with mental retardation, visual learning works better than verbal learning. If they can see a task being performed or actually work the problem, they will remember it better than if someone explains it to them. This has translated into teaching techniques that stress visual learning and focus on concrete or practical problem-solving tasks.

Suggestibility

Mental retardation appears to increase suggestibility. Because the person with retardation may be more sensitive to external clues than to inner thinking on a matter, he or she may be left open to exploitation. Those who work in this field have been concerned in recent years about several areas of exploitation.

First, young girls with mental retardation are sometimes sexually exploited by their male peers. Children with mental retardation have been exploited by adults who prey on young children.

Another area for potential exploitation is in the criminal justice system. Here people with mental retardation are often coerced into confessing to acts they did not commit or agreeing to accusations that are not entirely accurate. In many communities, a liaison between the criminal justice system and the service system for people with mental retardation seeks to prevent this sort of exploitation. The liaison serves as an advocate for the client and a consultant to the criminal justice system so that the client receives fair treatment.

Exploitation can happen at any age. Margaret lived in her own apartment and was considered by case management to be fairly independent. One day Margaret came to her case manager looking emaciated and unkempt. She was crying and upset. The case manager learned from the conversation that Margaret had fallen in love with a man who professed to love her. She had allowed him to move into her apartment a month ago. Two weeks after he moved in he changed the locks and refused to let Margaret back into her apartment. Margaret said she went by every day, asking him to let her in, but he refused. Today she found that he had moved another woman and the other woman's young son into the apartment. Needless to say, case management was able to have the man removed from Margaret's apartment, but Margaret still believed the man loved her and felt bad that the case managers had treated him "so bad."

Passivity Rather Than Strategizing

Many people with mental retardation appear passive in the face of difficult situations. Often they are not able to develop strategies to help them to cope with problems. They are also often unable to develop the strategies, such as rehearsing information or establishing routines, that help people to remember things.

Difficulty with Foresight and Planning

People with mental retardation have trouble looking ahead to possible consequences or occurrences and planning. Thinking about what might happen is difficult, as the person is more likely to focus on exactly what is.

Allen lived in an apartment with two other men, all of whom had varying degrees of mental retardation. One night Allen found a kitten and brought it home. The case manager, Harold, helped the men buy litter for the kitten and showed the men how to feed and care for the kitten. In addition, Harold found an inexpensive plan to neuter the kitten. The kitten and the men lived together well, but some time later Allen found another cat and brought that one into the home also. Some weeks later the cat had kittens. The case manager was not aware of the additional cats before several of them produced more litters of cats. Harold had been seeing the men on a regular basis at the sheltered workshop where they worked and so was unaware of the situation at their apartment.

Eventually the management of the apartment house called Harold, asking that he help to clean up a terrible mess he had discovered on a routine visit to Allen's apartment. By the time Harold arrived, there were 16 cats and a litter of 5 nursing kittens. The cats were underfed, and there was no cat litter. Allen and his roommates seemed overwhelmed by the turn of events and obviously had not been able to see that rescuing several homeless cats would result in such a proliferation. Harold was able to place the cats in an adoption program, help the men clean up the apartment, and review the care of cats with them. At present the men have only the original cat.

Concreteness and Rigidity

When we categorize things, we see the similarities among items or situations that are not identical. When asked how a chair and a bench are alike, a person with mental retardation may very well focus on what is different about them; for example, the chair is inside, while the bench is outside. The person would ignore that both are objects on which people sit. Abstract thinking, the type used to interpret proverbs, is also very difficult for people with mental retardation.

Speed of Thinking

People who have mental retardation appear to have a slower reaction time, even on skills that are well practiced. Recent research indicates that there is a slowing of the ability to process information. For instance, the person may discriminate between two letters correctly, but take a bit longer to do so than the average person.

Limited Creativity and Imagination

Some people with mental retardation have excellent artistic ability or are able to perform interesting and unusual cognitive feats. In general, however, most people with the condition are limited in their ability to create imaginatively. In tests where individuals with mental retardation were asked to look at a picture and tell a story about what was happening in it, the individual usually described the picture, rather than using the picture as the basis for a story.

MENTAL RETARDATION AND ADAPTIVE FUNCTIONING

The diagnosis for mental retardation requires significant impairment in at least 2 of the 10 adaptive skill areas. As you may recall, these skill areas are:

Communication	Self-care
Social skills	Community use
Health and safety	Functional academics
Work	Home living
Leisure	Self-direction

The Need for Services

Impairment in the 10 adaptive skill areas is affected by life experiences as well as by mental development. This fact must be considered in understanding the person's condition. According to Baroff (1999), "many of the adjustment problems found in mental retardation are *not* intrinsic to the disability. Rather they are the *expected* emotional and behavioral consequences of the *absence* of services essential to the fulfillment of legitimate aspirations and basic psychological needs." In other words, some of the problem behavior we see in people with mental retardation is not necessarily the result of the retardation, but is often the result of inadequate services that have prevented these people from meeting the needs and goals they, like all people, have for themselves.

Billy was diagnosed as having mild mental retardation when he was about 4 years old. His situation was brought to the attention of a school psychologist after Billy had trouble in kindergarten. The teacher noted that Billy had trouble with some basic concepts like numbers and shapes. In addition, she found that he was disruptive and did not listen well, often doing as he pleased. The psychologist gave Billy a standard battery of tests and talked extensively with the family and with Billy.

The IQ tests showed once more that Billy was only mildly retarded. What the family picture revealed was that the family was neglectful of Billy, on the one hand, and overly punitive with him for slight infractions on the other. This atmosphere at home, not the mental retardation, was seen as the main contributing factor to Billy's behavioral problems. The psychologist made some recommendations to the teacher about ways to help Billy learn and feel included at school, and met with the parents and referred them to parenting classes to ameliorate the situation at home.

Certain factions in our society argue against special services or entitlements for those who are different, including people with mental retardation. Every one of us, however, should be given the opportunity to maximize our real potential. There are any number of ways people can do this. We are all different, so having different services makes it more likely that all of us will have that opportunity.

It makes little sense to deny those with mental retardation good service because they have limited potential. In the long run, each of us has limitations. If people criticize the services you provide, the answer is to point out that differences among us are really commonplace, not exceptional. There may be a continuum of abilities and capacities along which each of us falls. All of us expect that our need to develop to our full potential will be met; others should not be denied that opportuntiy just because they fall on a different place along the continuum.

What to Expect

Those with mental retardation generally experience a slower rate of growth in all areas of development in early childhood. This includes motor abilities, language development, cognition, self-care, and social skills with peers.

As these children enter school, they have poorer academic achievement. The older child who is becoming aware of self begins to perceive the problems and differences he or she has in relation to peers, particularly in coping skills. By adolescence, the person usually becomes aware of the often-negative reaction of others to the disability, as peers may exclude him or her socially.

Adolescence is a turbulent time in the life of any child. Restrictions, personal limitations, and social problems with peers make it particularly difficult for the young person with mental retardation. For that reason, behavior problems are not unusual at this age.

Pietra was 17 and the oldest daughter in a family of three girls. As the other two girls reached puberty, they began to date and to have friends over. When Pietra's sister, Amilee, was 16, she got her driver's permit. Pietra chafed under restrictions that prevented her from going out independently. Because of seizures, she was denied the right to drive. Her poor performance in school, lack of friends, and difficulty with age-appropriate activities made her especially resentful.

Pietra's sisters took time to do things with Pietra. They often included her in activities with their own friends, but not all the time. Pietra felt left out and resentful. By the time she was 17, she was screaming at her parents, often appearing out of control. She was also prone to tears. In addition, Pietra would leave the house in the evening when no one was looking and be gone for hours. At those times, the family scattered across town looking for her, fearing she might be confronted with situations she could not handle or people who might exploit her desperate need to feel included. Finally the family went for family therapy as a group, and Pietra was also seen individually. These sessions, short-term medication for depression, and new activities recommended by the therapist helped this family to all cope better with Pietra's situation.

In young adulthood, the person must face the fact that the disability is permanent. Those with severe mental retardation may be less aware of its permanence than their parents, who must look ahead and plan for lifelong supervision. Yet, many people who are diagnosed with this condition do hold adult roles in life. They become good friends to others, often hold jobs responsibly, and even marry and parent children. It is useful, therefore, to think of mental retardation as a condition of slower development, and not as a condition of no development at all. Baroff (1999) looks at development over the life span.

PRESCHOOL ADAPTIVE FUNCTIONING

Motor Development

Both gross motor and fine motor skills are likely to develop slowly in the early years, particularly if the origin of the condition is related to genetics or brain structure. Sometimes the rate of development can be increased through programs of intensive motor training and stimulation that help the child to use all of his or her potential. As the child grows, these problems are often reflected in hand-eye skills and in general coordination.

Not every child who has a delay in motor skills is mentally retarded. For instance, a child with cerebral palsy may have normal cognition and a lesser known condition, hypotonia. This is a muscle disorder that delays motor development but is unrelated to mental retardation. Be careful about assuming that children you see for intake who are delayed are also mentally retarded until all tests have been concluded.

Language Development

There are two aspects of language development. First there is receptive language, which refers to the ability to understand what is being said, and then there is expressive language, which refers to the ability to speak coherently and to use language correctly. Problems with speech, or expressive language, are extremely common in people with mental retardation. Speech is generally slower to develop than in other individuals. In expression, the person with mental retardation is likely to have problems clearly articulating a point and may do so in short utterances. Speech is likely to be very concrete and literal, not especially abstract or imaginative.

Self-Help

Young children are taught gradually to manage basic self-care skills such as feeding themselves, getting dressed, toileting, and grooming. Those with mental retardation have a slower rate of accomplishment in learning such tasks, which can lead to several problems. The child who is slow to learn bowel training may give his or her caretakers problems, leading them to be harsh and to feel negatively toward the child. Some parents are overly solicitous and make very few demands on the child. Although mental retardation may increase dependency somewhat, the parent who makes few demands may make a child more dependent than necessary and add to the problems created by the disability.

Jude was the fifth child of seven children. The family was close, and older siblings had responsibilities for younger siblings and household chores. When Jude was diagnosed with mental retardation, the family was devastated. From the beginning, the parents were determined to keep him at home, in spite of the common practice at the time of institutionalizing children. Each family member was given a responsibility for Jude's care and well-being. Since the parents were fairly well off, they were able to devote time and attention to Jude's care and needs.

At no time was Jude ever disciplined. He was never encouraged to speak or to use good toileting practices. His urination on the furniture and other difficult behaviors were explained away by the parents as part of his condition, and all the children were told that Jude was a blessing in their home, a wonderful cross to bear. The father particularly insisted that he knew and understood "this precious child" better than anyone else. For that reason, no therapists were allowed in the home, and Jude never attended any sort of educational program.

As Jude grew older and the other children left home, his parents found him increasingly difficult to manage. He was bigger and had become insistent, to the point of striking out, on having his own way. He tore up furniture, urinated routinely in an antique grandfather clock, and screamed. When the father died, the mother was no longer able to manage him. Jude was placed in an institution, and later in a group home. The slow process of teaching Jude how to live with others was begun. In time, Jude learned to be more civilized and was able to live well among others. In their well-meaning attempt to deal with Jude and their own guilt, his parents neglected important lessons that almost cost Jude a life in his own community.

Cognition

By school age, children are aware of and understand the concepts of color, shapes, sizes, textures, tastes, odors, space, time, and quantity. Mental retardation tends to slow the understanding of these concepts. A 5-year-old child may still be where a 2-year-old would be, unable to recognize a color or which of two items is bigger than the other.

Social Skills

Intellectual impairment often affects the child's ability to relate to others. This skill is one of the most complex of all the adaptive skills. Two results are that the child is unable to fully understand social situations and that the child's social behavior is immature for his or her age. These things affect the child's play with other children. Often children with mental retardation spend more time playing alone, in part because such children may be less responsive to children their own age, and sometimes because their disruptive behavior causes other children to avoid them.

In general, children with mental retardation who have been raised in loving, accepting homes show more confidence in new social situations; they are more receptive to new social situations and more trusting of others. In families where the child has not been accepted and the child's condition is a disappointment, the child may be wary of others and new situations, and perhaps even antagonistic. Compounding the problem is the child's need to avoid rejection and ridicule. Children who have received both from family, teachers, or peers are likely to avoid putting themselves in situations that are painful to their self-esteem. The quality of a child's home life is something to note as you gather information.

SCHOOL-AGE ADAPTIVE FUNCTIONING

During the time a child with mental retardation is in school, he or she will have a slower educational progress than peers in the same age group. Most of the services to those with mental retardation are given in educational settings. Whether these children are placed in special classes or included in regular classes (known as mainstreaming), they need special assistance in educational endeavors.

The goal for all children with mental retardation, regardless of the degree, is to prepare them to live in their own communities, rather than being placed in an institution far away from family. This means that the education provided to such children should prepare them to live as independently as their potential will allow. Many skills taught in educational programs for children with mental retardation are geared to their being able to function in the community. Being able to read a newspaper, take the bus, cook a meal, and manage money are functional skills learned in school that assist those with mild retardation to live without supervision.

Loosening Ties to Family

In the normal teenager's life, the adolescent begins to pull away from family and turn to peers for validation. For children with mental retardation, who experience much the same stresses as other teenagers, there are added problems. First, the young person begins to understand the meaning of "retarded." In adolescence, it becomes more apparent that the person is different and that this difference can have a negative affect on friendships and relationships with people the same age. Second, the adolescent, like all teenagers, wants more independence and may be frustrated in that desire. Normal siblings may be given more independence at an earlier age, causing frustration and anger.

Preparing to Work

Most teenagers are preparing to go on to college or vocational school as they approach graduation or they have made some decisions about working after graduation. Vocational preparation is limited for the teen with mental retardation because of academic limitations. In addition, the teen may be blocked in the choice of work by communication problems, physical health problems, motor difficulties, and even emotional and behavioral problems. Finding realistic goals may prove frustrating.

Nevertheless, school is crucial in the future success of those with this condition. School teaches them skills and values needed to hold a job, such as persistence, reliability, and accepting supervision. In many schools, this phase of the person's education is referred to as transition planning.

Schools are supposed to develop an individualized education plan (IEP) for children with special needs. Many parents are unaware of their rights with regard to their child and may be given a plan to sign that is not in the child's best interests. Many of these plans are much the same for all the children with special needs in that particular school or school district, and many of them lack any real transition planning. In such a case, parents must take the initiative to request a more suitable plan for their child, and the case manager should support the parents in this action. Case managers assist parents who object to current planning for their child because it is limiting, and may help them determine what other elements to request in their child's plan.

ADULTHOOD ADAPTIVE FUNCTIONING

Several issues must be considered for adults with mental retardation.

Unsupervised Living

Those with mild mental retardation seem to do fairly well living with minimal or no supervision. The quality of their adjustment to community living may be marginal. They may not take full advantage of all the community has to offer. Difficulties often center around the management of money, problems finding employment, and using leisure time. In difficult circumstances or emergencies, these adults may need to rely on others for assistance. In cases where the condition is more severe, there will always be some level of dependency on others.

Patty lived in a neighborhood with her mother who was elderly and in need of assistance. Neighbors worried about what would happen to Patty when her mother died because she had been diagnosed as mentally retarded years before. They also marveled at the way in which Patty cared for her mother's everyday needs, helping with bathing and dressing and running errands. Patty did not drive, and eventually a homemaker service did come into the home to assist in her mother's care. When the mother died, neighbors were sure that Patty would have to move into a group home, but the will was such that Patty was able to stay in the home.

As time passed, it became apparent that Patty was doing pretty well. She kept her home clean and continued with many of the housekeeping routines she and her mother had observed for years. Some days Patty could be seen walking her little poodle or walking from the nearest supermarket laden with bags. Neighbors began to offer her rides when they went to the store. One man offered to help her with taxes and insurance. Another neighbor took Patty to church with her. Patty remained a part of her neighborhood and had people to whom she could turn when she had questions. Case management was involved and gave oversight to bill paying and spending money when that was needed, and Patty had a court-appointed payee. She is still living on her own and occasionally earns a little money by helping out at neighbors' homes.

Reproduction

Early in the twentieth century, there was considerable fear that those with mental retardation would reproduce children who were themselves retarded, thus infecting the general population with this condition. This sometimes led to institutionalization and even to sterilization programs in some places.

Today it is understood that those with mental retardation can and do benefit from birth control information and do not reproduce more children than the average population. Individuals with mental retardation, however, are often poor parents, and for this reason steps are taken to either assist them if they have children or to help them avoid parenthood altogether. Professionals working in this field now acknowledge that those with mental retardation have sexual feelings, rather than deny it as they once did.

Employment

Many individuals with mental retardation engage in competitive employment, usually in unskilled jobs. With the decline in unskilled work, many are working in service sector positions.

Carla and Maurice both had mental retardation. After they finished school, they were placed in a program to learn janitorial skills. Neither could drive. Both of them had considerable trouble in school, not advancing much beyond third grade. Nevertheless, at the end of their training, their case manager looked for a good placement for each of them. A local college employed both of them in the custodial department. There they were responsible for the grounds, each one taking a half of the campus. During the day, pushing a cart with the equipment they needed, they picked up cigarette butts and paper dropped on the ground, cleaned outside ashtrays, and straightened up around outdoor benches. Now each of them has worked there for over 10 years, and each is considered highly reliable. The college community knows them well, and they join in college activities, ranging from lunch with the staff and faculty in the cafeteria to attending plays and recitals.

When the economy is good and workers in unskilled positions are hard to find, those with mental retardation are often tapped to work in areas such as cleaning, dietary services, hotel maid services, and so forth. Their general reliability and willingness to perform repetitive tasks well make these individuals who are employable an asset to many companies. On the other hand, when the economy is not strong, these jobs, being the least secure, are most vulnerable to layoffs and terminations. In addition, not all individuals with mental retardation want to do repetitive tasks; some may find them boring.

Developing an employment strategy for your clients, where that seems useful, is one of the considerations you will address in planning for your clients with mental retardation.

Social Roles

Our intelligence influences our behavior in a variety of social situations. Each role we play, from student to parent, friend, or spouse, has specific behavioral expectations that are related to the culture in which we live. Our intelligence allows us to understand how each of these roles is different. Mild retardation does not preclude a person from functioning in all of the adult roles. Generally, however, those with mental retardation may appear to be more socially isolated than those who do not have this condition. Certainly if a person is more than mildly retarded, he or she will have trouble meeting the expectations for various roles. With more severe retardation comes extreme difficulty in participating in any relationship that requires reciprocity, or give and take.

For these reasons, many individuals with mental retardation are socially isolated. Loneliness is one of the concerns of people with mental retardation and of their families. In planning for the person with this condition, you need to assess the degree to which the person can participate in relationships, and develop social contacts for your client if they are needed.

In a small town, an elderly man died of a heart attack. At the funeral parlor, two uniformed firefighters stood at attention by the casket. The entire fire department came to the funeral in uniform. The fire chief gave the eulogy, during which he mentioned the devotion to the fire department this elderly man had shown most of his life. The fire trucks then proceeded to the cemetery, leading and following the hearse. The department laid a large wreath on the grave.

The elderly man who died had lived for many years in a group home around the corner from the firehouse. His case manager, learning of his love for the firehouse and the men there, arranged it so his client could go there to visit. Occasional visits hosted by uncertain firefighters turned gradually into complete acceptance. The man began to take meals with the firemen. He helped to fold hoses and fed the Dalmatian. In the years before he died, he was there everyday, doing odd jobs and enjoying the company of the firefighters. He participated in all fund raising activities, and the men at the station house found innovative ways to get him involved as part of their team. This is an example of good planning on the part of the case manager, and a wonderful example of what can happen when the community is encouraged to accept people with disabilities.

Community Adjustment

Mental retardation can greatly affect a person's ability to follow the social mores of the community. The areas that receive the most attention, according to Baroff (1999), are sexuality and criminality.

1. *Sexuality.* The three areas that seem to be of greatest concern are as follows.

   Inappropriate sexual behavior. The concern is whether or not the person will act on sexual impulses or be able to apply appropriate restraint. Restraint happens when the individual understands the accepted behavior in society and the consequences of unacceptable behavior.

Vulnerability to exploitation. On occasion young women with mental retardation are used sexually by their peers. Certainly children with mental retardation are more easily exploited than other children by pedophiles. As those with mental retardation move about independently in the community, the potential for exploitation sometimes becomes a reality. It is one of the reasons parents of children with mental retardation are so protective.

Fulfillment of parental roles. Often when those with mental retardation become parents, they are unable to apply the kind of early stimulation their child will need to grow and develop normally. People with mental retardation who are parenting may need considerable assistance just to handle the survival needs of their infant and child. Very often communities lack that kind of intense service. Case managers take all of this into consideration when planning for clients.

2. *Criminality.* Those with mild mental retardation do commit crimes that can lead to imprisonment and execution. Often they seem to be unaware of the consequences. Usually these crimes are crimes against persons. At any given time, a percentage of the prison population is mentally retarded. Research has indicated the percentage to be as high as 10% and as low as 2% (Baroff, 1999).

Now there is a greater awareness of the need to protect those with mental retardation when they come into contact with the criminal justice system. Education for those who work in the system, such as the police, district attorneys, and advocates, revolves around the protection of the person's constitutional rights, which is a complex concept that someone with mental retardation might not fully understand. Thus such a person might, for example, waive his or her Miranda rights. Another concern is in the person's ability to confess appropriately. Many with mental retardation can easily be intimidated into confessing to crimes they did not commit or to playing a greater role in a crime than they actually did. This can happen in the courtroom when they go to stand trial.

The thorny question for those in the criminal justice system is the extent to which a person is culpable. People with mental retardation may have a vague idea that what they did is wrong, but have no understanding of why it is wrong and what the ramifications of the behavior will be for themselves and others. Much of the criminal activity of those with mild retardation, the group most likely to come into conflict with the law, has an impulsive quality; in other words, the crimes are usually committed without thought.

GROWING OLDER

Many people with mild retardation live normal life spans. They experience the same decline in health, loss of close friends and relatives, and inability to work with reduced income. They may find themselves isolated with little to do. People with a more severe degree of mental retardation have probably had assistance throughout their adult lives, but those with mild retardation will need renewed assistance to manage.

Planning with your client for growing older is important, as is helping parents and family to plan for the time when they are no longer able to care for their family member with considerable retardation.

Living Arrangements

You may encounter parents who refuse to plan for their own eventual decline and their subsequent inability to care for their family member with mental retardation. They often assume a brother or sister will simply take this person into their own home or that the county will arrange automatically for a group home placement. You may find yourself caught in the middle of a family situation in which the parents are telling you the siblings will care for the person with mental retardation while the siblings are calling you to find out what alternatives are available.

Older parents often fear that planning with you will mean that their child will be dumped in an institution after the parents have died.

In one situation, a case manager was called to take care of a person who was wandering around the neighborhood. Both parents had died, and the son with mental retardation, who never received services before, was being looked after by neighbors. They became concerned when he seemed unable to take care of eating on his own and was wandering around the neighborhood. In another case, the death of the parents broke the family apart. The mother of a woman with mental retardation had steadfastly refused to plan for her daughter. When she died, the father did not feel he should go against the mother's wishes. When he died, each daughter thought the other should take in the sibling who was disabled. The case manager arranged for emergency respite care and then permanent placement, but because the mother had been so adamant that this woman be cared for by family members, the family fell apart at the time of the mother's death because adequate planning had not been done.

Financial Arrangements

Another area of concern as clients grow older is finances. Parents often leave large sums of money to a child for their care. Parents, however, need advice on estate planning so that their child remains eligible for government programs. The laws vary from state to state, but generally an irrevocable trust within the will works to your client's advantage. This is the kind of information you will give to parents who are planning for their child's future after the parents are gone.

MENTAL RETARDATION AND THE FAMILY

Initial Impact

Sometimes mental retardation is evident at birth, as in the case of Down syndrome. Other times the disorder gradually becomes evident, usually by age 2, as the child fails to develop. In either case, the understanding that their child has mental retardation is likely to devastate parents, who usually are not prepared for a child with problems. It is at this time of shock and devastation that parents are most likely to want to place their child outside the home.

In the past, placement in an institution was thought to be a relief to parents, and this was encouraged as a way of helping parents to handle the fact that the child was mentally retarded and there was no medical intervention to change this. Today, however, many services are available to help parents keep their child at home, and parents are less interested in institutions as an answer to caring for their child.

As a case manager, you will offer services to help parents with caregiving decisions regardless of the diagnosis. The options you offer will be designed to help the child reach his or her own potential. Keeping a child with mental retardation at home is somewhat more hopeful than it was once because of the array of support services available to parents today in their own community. You will become involved in helping parents plan for services that will assist them in raising a child with mental retardation.

Many of the parents you talk to will feel guilty or ashamed about their child with disabilities, as if the child in some way reflects negatively on them. You need to listen to parents' concerns and give accurate information where it is needed. Sometimes guilt and shame keep families from seeking the services and assistance they really need. Often the impulse is to hide the problem. You may be asked to give services long after the family recognized there was a problem because the needs have become so acute that they have no choice but to seek help. Again it is important to establish rapport and listen.

Early Intervention Programs

Most states have early intervention programs (often referred to as EIP). These programs are generally a collection of services typically offered to parents of newborns or toddlers who seem to be at risk for developmental delays. The services provide thorough assessments of what each child needs, with considerable input from parents. Programs to enhance the child's development, vision and hearing assessments and care, and medical needs are usually available as well. These service plans are intense and address many of the child's needs. The goal is to minimize delays or prevent them altogether. In some cases, services may assist a child to catch up with peers in the same age group.

For parents who are very young and inexperienced, or parents who are not aware of ways to help their child develop well, early intervention services can provide education, nutritional planning, and preschool programs that stimulate a child's normal development. Special case managers who work in these programs identify very young children at risk, work with the parents to develop individual service plans, and monitor the service and the children's progress.

Continuing Impact

Mental retardation is a condition that can lengthen the childhood period of dependency into a lifetime. Siblings often take on the role of surrogate parents to help out, and sometimes they are the only playmates the child with mental retardation has.

Parents of preschoolers are most concerned with the medical needs of their child. To a lesser extent, behavior problems and physical disabilities are also concerns. As the children grow up, the families continue to be concerned with medical problems. Hyperactivity and behavioral problems are also of concern where they exist. In addition, parents have concerns about the education of their child. When the child is older, parents become concerned that their child have a social life and recreational outlets. As the child reaches puberty, there are concerns about the child's growing sexuality.

Family Ability to Cope

Part of the case manager's assessment involves evaluating the family's ability to cope with these problems. Look at the parents' ability to solve problems. Are they able to make good decisions? Look at the kind of support they receive from other people, such as relatives and friends. Do they appear able to take advantage of the services you offer, or do they seem reluctant? Look at their own sources of enjoyment. Are the parents totally focused on the problems created by their child with mental retardation, or do they have enjoyable activities they continue to pursue?

Planning for Growing Older

As mentioned earlier, as parents age, they need to think about the ultimate care of the child with mental retardation. Helping them plan for the child's living arrangements, the activities in which the child will participate, and financial support is crucial to the child's future well-being.

Case Managers and Judgment

Sometimes parents do not participate in planning, and sometimes siblings fail to come to meetings about the sibling with mental retardation. It is easy for a case manager to judge such a family as uncaring. Instead, case managers should try to put themselves in the family's shoes. Perhaps the parents are exhausted from years of caring for the child with mental retardation. Siblings may feel they have given all they can and must turn to their own growing families. The person with mental retardation may have caused the family considerable embarrassment because of behavior problems that brought shame or law enforcement into the picture. At this point, the family may feel that case management has the situation well under control and want to back away.

Case managers dealing with families like this need to assume that the family cares, but that they may have reached their limit, at least for now, as to what more they can handle. Keep the family informed, and always invite their participation, but refrain from negative judgments.

CAUSES OF MENTAL RETARDATION

There are any number of reasons why a person is diagnosed with mental retardation. These causes fall into three broad categories:

1. Biological factors having to do with abnormalities of the genes or chromosomes
2. Biological factors unrelated to genes and chromosomes
3. Psychological factors

In each of these categories, a number of separate conditions can occur. Mental retardation is a prominent feature, but there are features that distinguish the conditions. In the next sections, we will look at some of the most common types of mental retardation.

Biological Origins: Genes and Chromosomes

This section examines chromosome and gene abnormalities. It is estimated that 10% of all mental retardation is biological in origin. According to Baroff (1999), chromosomal abnormalities occur fairly often, but most of them are not compatible with life and usually lead to a miscarriage sometime early in the pregnancy. Prenatal testing for some disorders allows parents to know whether the child they are expecting may have a developmental disorder. Some parents may elect to terminate the pregnancy, some may wish to place the child for adoption, while still others will want to keep and raise their own child. When parents decide to parent a child with a developmental disability, you may be the person who assists them in understanding the condition and all that it involves. They may need your help to prepare to parent the child with this condition.

Down Syndrome

Down syndrome is probably the most common of the chromosomal difficulties. Technically it is referred to as Trisomy 21. The cause of the syndrome is a third chromosome 21, meaning the person has 47 chromosomes instead of the normal 46. Older mothers in their late 30s and 40s are most at risk for having babies with this condition.

Prenatal Detection A screening blood test is used to detect Down syndrome, but this test can miss 20% of the cases. If this test indicates the baby has Down syndrome, amniocentesis or a chorion biopsy can be used to confirm the diagnosis. Because the blood test can be unreliable, amniocentesis is generally offered to all women over age 35.

Common Clinical Features Present to varying degrees are:

- Any number of joint and muscle difficulties
- Organ abnormalities (nearly half have congenital heart disease)
- Skeletal abnormalities
- A shortened hand with a curved little finger is common
- Poor muscle tone
- Hearing and visual problems
- Thyroid problems (It is important to check for hypothyroidism early.)

Behavioral Characteristics These children have always been viewed as amiable and affectionate. They appear to enjoy social encounters and generally are not shy about interacting with others. As children, they are usually obedient and easy to control. From the research it appears that these children are less likely to have conduct disorder, attention-deficit disorder, or even problem behaviors like stubbornness. They appear to have a diminished sexual drive as well, particularly the males who are considered to be sterile. Genital abnormalities are common in both sexes. There may be some sexual activity, however, often of a masturbatory nature.

Early Aging and Alzheimer's Disease Individuals with Down syndrome usually start to age earlier than the general population. Decline related to aging is usually seen after age 50. Dementia is seen as early as the 40s in about 9% of those with Down syndrome. The percentage increases to nearly 55%, according to some studies, in the 60s. This dementia is often accompanied by apathy and withdrawal. The life expectancy for individuals with Down syndrome is reduced after age 50 (Baroff, 1999).

The link between Alzheimer's and Down syndrome is a genetic one. There is an inherited form of Alzheimer's disease, and individuals who have Alzheimer's disease appear to have an increased risk of having relatives with Down syndrome.

Developmental Difficulties Evidence of developmental delay appears during the first year. The child does not develop at the normal rate, but lags behind. After the first year, the rate slows progressively.

Speech. One delay will be in speech. These children begin to speak later and speak less, generally with fewer gestures, than other children their age. They usually have some difficulty imitating words they have heard. Commonly their speech is unclear and poorly articulated. According to Baroff (1999), there is "a significant disparity between the ability to understand language and to express it." Often they understand better than they are able to speak.

Intellectual development. Children with Down syndrome often grow unevenly, having periods of time, referred to as plateaus, when there is no intellectual growth at all. Although these children develop at the level of mild retardation through their third year, it is common for their IQs to decline as they grow, meaning that many will be in the severe mental retardation range by 17 or 18. There is no explanation for why this slowing occurs. Nevertheless, there is a good bit of variation in intellectual development among children with Down syndrome. Some children are higher functioning than others with the same condition. The years between 8 and 11 are often a time when there is no increase in the complexity of speech. From about 13 to 17, there may be some growth once more, but these children remain behind developmentally.

Motor development. Motor development occurs at a more normal rate than intellectual development. Because children with Down syndrome often learn best visually rather than orally, they have less trouble imitating sequences of movement they have witnessed. By age 5, they are usually able to run, walk, and have adequate eye-hand coordination.

Self-help skills. They may be slow to learn to dress, feed, and clean themselves.

Fragile X

Fragile X is the most commonly inherited form of mental retardation. It is so named because one of the arms of the X chromosomes is prone to breakage and loss. The fragile site is caused by a specific dominant gene. Female relatives of children affected by this condition can be carriers of this gene, so early identification is very important.

Clinical Features This condition disproportionately affects males. The main characteristics are retardation and enlarged testes (usually at puberty). Other features are narrow face and protruding ears. There is hyperextensibility of the joints. Often attention deficit, hyperactivity, and impulsivity are present, and the person usually experiences difficulty with changes in his or her routine. Females with the condition are free of physical abnormalities and have a milder form of retardation or just a specific learning disability. One third of females show no effects, and another third are likely to have personality disorders.

Developmental Difficulties There is generally a delay in language skills and often marked hyperactivity and attention deficit in males. These children frequently have trouble making eye contact. They often display unusual hand movements. Touching is difficult for many of them; sometimes these children display sensitivity to touch and defend against being touched. Often this sensitivity extends to noise and light as well. As the children grow older, they are known to be impulsive.

The clinical picture shares some of the characteristics of autism, but fragile X children enjoy social activities and seek close relationships far more than children with autism. Only about 7% of the autistic population is also fragile X (Baroff, 1999, p. 141). Autistic children and fragile X children both persevere in questioning; that is, both tend to latch onto one subject and go at it over and over. The fragile X child tends to have rapid speech, while the autistic child may have little or no speech or be uncommunicative.

Intellectual Development Intellectual development tends to vary. A few males may be unaffected, but most of the children will have some impairment. The common pattern is some intellectual delay early in life that typically leads to mild retardation. This slowing and delay are evident by 5 years of age. As these children grow, they slow down in their ability to acquire new skills and lose IQ points. Some researchers believe these children may actually lose previously held skills.

Affected males typically have considerable trouble with short-term memory. Their strength appears to be in their overall alertness and ability to grasp things visually.

Educational Considerations Children with this condition are usually visual learners. Some higher-functioning males do well with basic reading and spelling. These children do better in smaller classes where there are fewer distractions. Speech and language therapy are often essential components in the child's education if the speech difficulties are severe. Sign language may be an option. A few fragile X children have good musical ability, and that should be explored and developed if this is found to be so. Some of the children may need physical therapy as part of their educational program.

Medical Treatment Much of the medical treatment for these children is to curb hyperactivity. This usually involves medication. Often folic acid is prescribed as a vitamin supplement, as it seems to help both hyperactivity and irritability. In addition, about a fifth of the children have epilepsy, ranging from petit mal to grand mal seizures. Chronic ear infections are commonly seen and require treatment in fragile X children.

Adaptive Behavior There is a steady growth of skills until adolescence, followed by a decline in skills, particularly in communication and social skills. Skills for daily living, such as self-care, seem to remain pretty much intact, probably because they are learned early and practiced every day.

Nongenetic Biological Contributors

Any number of events during pregnancy, birth, and immediately following birth can contribute to problems for a child's developmental capacity. These three periods can be categorized as: (1) prenatal, meaning before birth; (2) perinatal, meaning at birth; and (3) postnatal, meaning immediately following birth.

Prenatal

About a third of the cases, including the most severe cases, occur because of difficulties experienced in the prenatal period. The fetus is most vulnerable during the first trimester. Here are a few of the problems that can occur in the prenatal period:

- The mother suffers from an infection such as rubella, AIDS, or syphilis.
- Toxins such as prescribed medications, cocaine, nicotine, caffeine, and alcohol are ingested by the mother.
- Radiation is experienced by the mother and therefore by the fetus.
- Health problems of the mother, such as high blood pressure or diabetes, affect the fetus.

Fetal Alcohol Syndrome This syndrome is caused by impairment to the blood flow in the umbilical cord, leading to a lack of oxygen for the fetus. Even moderate drinking can cause some abnormality. A single binge can be as harmful as small amounts of alcohol spread over time. The fetus is most vulnerable in the first trimester. Later in the pregnancy, alcohol increases the risk of low birth weight.

Developmental progress. Babies with fetal alcohol syndrome are generally small and thin at birth and remain stunted in growth and head circumference. At birth they are often irritable, unable to suck well, gain weight slowly, and have poor reflexes.

During childhood, motor development and speech are delayed. The child may talk but lack appropriate content of speech for his or her age. Usually the child appears as alert and friendly with a strong desire for body contact. Hyperactivity is common, causing adjustment problems throughout school. Some seem impervious to verbal restrictions.

Toward puberty many of the physical features related to the condition begin to disappear. These children have problems in school, ranging from learning disorders to obvious mental retardation as indicated by psychological testing. Testing often shows that these children do better on performance than on verbal tests. Arithmetic in particular seems to be a problem, and there are problems with attention deficit and impulsivity.

In young adulthood, all of these people have some difficulty functioning independently, although for some the problems are minor. Structure seems helpful. Later problems can affect memory and cause difficulty in orienting accurately to time and space. Judgment is often faulty as well. For some, the impulsivity of the early years persists and may result in the person turning to criminal activity and having difficulty with relationships.

Treatment. Most of the treatment involves education of the at-risk mother in an effort to prevent alcohol fetal syndrome. Counseling coupled with education about the potential problems of drinking while pregnant can be useful. Many workers in entry-level positions work with groups through programs designed to help addicted mothers remain clean during their pregnancy and deliver a healthy child.

Perinatal

At the time of birth, there can be hazards to the infant. For example:

- Brain injury at birth causing prolonged lack of oxygen
- Bleeding in the brain (intercranial hemorrhage) caused by trauma
- Lung disorders that can curtail oxygen
- HIV acquired in the birth canal
- Herpes simplex acquired from the mother's genitalia
- Severe jaundice (kernicterus) in the first week of life

Any condition that restricts the flow of oxygen can cause brain damage. The extent of the damage depends on the extent of the oxygen deprivation. Children who suffer from brain injury during birth may recover in three to five days, signaling a good prognosis. Others may take longer and have permanent central nervous system damage involving motor difficulties. Infections can cause lesions in the eye, blindness, and brain inflammation. If severe jaundice results from an incompatibility of blood types between the mother and infant, the baby may have trouble sucking, may cry a lot, and may show abnormal motor behavior such as involuntary writhing. Generally if mental retardation occurs, it is not severe and can be corrected at birth by vigilant medical practitioners.

Postnatal

Conditions following birth may give rise to mental retardation. These include infections such as meningitis or encephalitis, head injury, brain tumor, poisons such as lead and mercury, and malnutrition.

Lead and Mental Retardation Children appear to be particularly at risk for lead poisoning. Lead is found in many places in our environment. Most children with lead poisoning show no signs of the problem and thus go undiagnosed and untreated. Lead poisoning can certainly be prevented. In 1971 federal legislation was passed to set standards for the amount of lead allowed in paint and toys. In many places, prevention programs actively diagnose, with routine screening, and treat lead poisoning, as well as seek out sources of lead, such as paint and lead water pipes in older houses, and eradicate them. The lead content in gasoline has been reduced considerably, and consequently there have been reduced levels of lead in the blood of children and adults. Poor families are at greater risk for lead poisoning because of the type of housing they can afford.

Lead appears to affect both physical and cognitive development. Infants and children who have eaten flaking lead paint over a period of time may develop a severe disease known as lead encephalitis. The symptoms are visible and include stupor, coma, and seizures. Children who survive are likely to have stunted growth and cognitive deficits. In recent years, with legislation and prevention, this condition is relatively rare.

There is plenty of evidence to support the idea that lead will diminish a child's IQ and thus the child's ability to learn. Even at lower levels this appears to be true. Children with blood levels of μ l/dl of 9 are considered at risk, but researchers have never been able to establish a concrete threshold below which children are not be affected by lead. Diets low in fat and high in iron, calcium, and vitamin C can reduce the amount of lead the body absorbs. Such a diet is often recommended for children who show no symptoms but who do show elevated blood levels.

Malnutrition An inadequate diet, particularly one low in the protein needed for growth and development, can cause mental retardation. Protein is especially linked to brain and cognitive development. A lack of iodine also can lead to mental retardation. Malnutrition, in order to prevent permanent effects, must be corrected and addressed before 2 years of age. There are degrees of malnutrition:

1. *Severe malnutrition.* This takes two forms:

   Marasmus is a severe calorie deficit. In this form, the tissue wastes away, and the child fails to grow physically.
   Kwashiorkor is a severe protein deficit. This often occurs after the child is weaned from his or her mother's protein-rich milk and given a diet high in starch and low in protein. The child fails to grow and shows edema as the tissues fill with water. This condition causes skin sores and colorless hair.

2. *Moderate malnutrition.* Here we see stunted growth and some cognitive impairment. School feeding programs high in protein often offset the effects of malnutrition.

Psychological Contributors

The way in which a child's maturing brain encounters the environment has, in the long run, a tremendous effect on later intellectual development and capacity. Children who are exposed to new and varied experiences are stimulated and grow intellectually as they develop physically. The primary psychological reason for mental retardation is psychological deprivation.

In the worst cases, which are comparatively rare, children are kept in closets or tied to beds or confined to a single room and neglected. These are the shocking examples we read about from time to time in the news. More common are children raised in large institutions, such as orphanages, where varied and stimulating activities are not available and all the children receive is the care needed to survive, such as feedings, a clean bed, and bathing. Play time is not varied or interesting. Children with only a mild developmental disability, one that might be corrected if the child were properly stimulated, may end up in institutions for the mentally retarded where there is little or no attempt to stimulate intellectual growth.

In other cases, the child may be reared by parents who cannot provide a stimulating intellectual environment, either because of disabilities or a lack of understanding of what is needed to stimulate good intellectual growth. Sometimes parents are themselves mentally retarded, or they may be too young to know what is needed for sound development. They may not be able to interpret what their child needs and respond appropriately. These parents often lack outside support, are most likely to neglect their children, and are most likely to use abuse as a means of control. They are often overwhelmed by the child's needs and may have unrealistic expectations about children at any given age. The risk is increased when there are several children in the home.

These children may appear to be physically intact. They have normal sensory perception and no abnormal neurological deficits. Because of the environment, however, they are delayed and may suffer permanent retardation if the situation is not corrected early.

Needed in the ideal environment (Baroff, 1999) are:

- Good nutrition
- Good health care
- Stimulating activities
- Freedom to explore the immediate environment
- Guidance that includes limits and structure
- Love and caregivers who respond to what the child needs
- Access to activities that are fun and rewarding
- The ability to affect the environment in some way, usually through play

In such an environment, parents or caregivers often engage in verbal exchanges with children and allow the children to take the lead in the games and activities in which the parent enthusiastically participates.

When children are reared in environments that are not stimulating, cognitive development suffers, but so does social and emotional development. Where there has been minimal verbal exchange, verbal skills are delayed. Some of the resulting delay can be reversed with intense caregiving and stimulation in a loving and responsive environment.

CONDITIONS COMMONLY SEEN WITH MENTAL RETARDATION

Cerebral Palsy

Baroff (1999) describes cerebral palsy as "a disorder of movement, balance, and posture that results from a nonprogressive lesion in the brain areas that control muscles and maintenance of posture" (p. 184). About half of these children have cognitive impairment, but a quarter of them have average or above-average intelligence. For many, IQ increases as they mature. Low birth weight babies, babies whose weight is less than 5.5 pounds, appear particularly susceptible to this condition (Baroff, 1999).

It is thought that a perinatal brain injury such as asphyxiation or intracranial bleeding is responsible for the condition, although prenatal and early childhood injuries also can produce cerebral palsy. In the prenatal period, infections and exposure to toxins can cause the condition. In the postnatal period, infections such as meningitis and encephalitis, brain abscesses, or head trauma can cause cerebral palsy. Many of the brain traumas are the result of physical abuse.

There are several types of cerebral palsy:

1. *Spastic cerebral palsy.* This is the most common type. Movement for those affected is slow and takes effort. The range of motion is restricted. Individuals with this

condition move in an uneven, jerky manner with explosive movements. Attempts to extend the limbs are usually thwarted by contracting muscles. The arms and legs are affected. There are mild forms where there is simply more difficulty with fine motor activities and an awkward gait. In the more moderate form, speech and most motor activities are affected. The person can usually handle activities of daily living. In severe forms, all movement and speech are affected adversely, and for some sitting or even holding up one's head is impossible. Braces, wheelchairs, and crutches can assist the person to be more independent.

2. *Ataxic cerebral palsy.* This is primarily a disorder involving lack of coordination. The person will have trouble balancing.
3. *Extrapyramidal cerebral palsy.* This refers to one of two different nerve tracks in the brain that control movement. When this track is affected, it results in a variety of impairments, including poor muscle tone, rigidity of muscles, and abnormal postures. Movement is affected, and the individual has uncontrolled movements that intensify under stress, writhing, spasticity, and tremors.

Associated Disorders

Speech impairment often accompanies cerebral palsy. The person may have trouble pronouncing words, making certain sounds, or controlling his or her breath so as to speak clearly.

Perceptual difficulties can accompany this condition. For example, some children with cerebral palsy are unable to distinguish colors, shapes, and sounds.

Attention-deficit and hyperactivity, as well as learning abilities, are seen in some people with this condition.

Treatment

Physical therapy is used to promote a better posture and to prevent muscle deformities. Such therapy should begin by the age of 2. Speech therapy and occupational therapy are also used. Orthopedic surgery can be done to lengthen or release muscles, and bone surgery can be done to correct deformities. Orthopedic devices may enable the person to function. Medication has not been particularly successful. Muscles relaxants may cause oversedation.

PREVENTION

Programs to prevent mental retardation address known causes that can be eliminated through changes in behavior and the environment. According to Baroff (1999), such programs commonly address the following:

- Reduction or elimination of drug and alcohol intake during pregnancy
- Genetic screening
- Good prenatal care
- Targeting of premature and low birth weight babies for possible developmental delays
- Early screening for metabolic abnormalities, and prompt institution of medical and nutritional programs to offset the effects
- Immunizations
- Good nutrition
- Avoidance of exposure to lead and other toxic substances

- Well-baby examinations on a regular basis
- Car seats and later bicycle helmets to prevent head injury
- Home maintenance to prevent accidents and injury

SERVICES FOR INDIVIDUALS WITH DEVELOPMENTAL DISABILITIES

Communities across the United States have come up with innovative and interesting ways to bring persons with mental retardation out of institutions and into their communities. These services and programs seek to make the community more inclusive of people with developmental disabilities and allow those who are developmentally disabled to live successfully in their community.

Diagnostic Services

IQ testing. As stated earlier, before a person can be diagnosed as mentally retarded, diagnostic tests must be done, usually by a psychologist. Once the person's IQ is established through testing, the diagnosis can be made.

Occupational testing. This is done to determine the extent to which a person can live independently and the extent to which he or she can work. Such testing provides information about the amount of support a person will need to fulfill these roles.

Physical evaluations. Any number of physical conditions can be evaluated by physicians and therapists. Orthopedic physicians often evaluate individuals who have orthopedic difficulties that may need correction, and physical therapists can evaluate the need for muscle building and decide how that will be done. For children with muscle weakness or motor difficulties, such evaluation can be very helpful.

Speech evaluations. The need for speech therapy can be evaluated by a speech therapist.

Employment Support

Sheltered workshops. Clients who can work may need a sheltered workshop situation where the work is brought into a central location and performed with the help of support staff. Most of this work is routine and repetitive, but some sheltered workshops provide services such as small catering services and janitorial work under the supervision of support staff.

Supported employment. Here clients work in the community at routine jobs such as dishwashing, maid service, or janitorial service and are supported in this work by a teacher or supervisor, who often begins by actually performing the work with the person and gradually turning more of it over to the person as he or she learns how to handle the job.

Educational Services—Preschool

Infant stimulation. These services identify infants at birth who are at risk for mental retardation. Often staff is located right in the hospital, or they make regular visits there. Infants placed in this program are given considerable stimulation to increase intellectual and cognitive development. Parents who themselves may be developmentally disabled or extremely inexperienced receive support in stimulating their infant to grow.

Home-based services. Workers make periodic visits to the home to assist parents of young children in the stimulation programs devised for their children.

Day-care programs. These programs appear to prevent the decline of cognitive abilities in children with Down syndrome, at least during the period that the children are in the service. In other children, modest gains may be made from such programs, but they do not provide major acceleration of cognitive growth except in cases where children can benefit from early stimulation.

Combination programs for young children. Some of these programs combine in-home and center-based services so that children and their families receive individual attention, but the child is also in a program with other children outside the home. Another combination that is used is programs for children with additional programs for parents, giving them instruction and support in the stimulation of their young child.

Integrated education. This is often referred to as mainstreaming. Children with developmental disabilities are placed with children who have none. This benefits the handicapped child in developing social skills, but it often requires additional effort on the part of the teacher. Children with disabilities often isolate themselves from peers on the same developmental level, and interactions need to be encouraged. This includes helping normally developing children to initiate interaction and become comfortable with children who are different.

Educational Services—School-Age Children

Special education. In recent years the focus has been on what the child will need in order to live independently. The purpose of the program is to maximize the child's competency to live in the community. Depending on the degree of retardation, children may be in special classrooms in regular schools, or in special schools set aside for the purpose of providing this education. Generally the material is appropriate for the children's age, and the children move from grade to grade as they would in a school for nonhandicapped children.

Mainstreaming. This appears to work better for children in elementary school and for children whose developmental difficulties are mild. In middle school, the curriculum begins to be focused on college preparation. For the child with mental retardation, skills acquisition is important at this point, and it can be done in special settings.

Individualized education plan (IEP). This plan is required by law. It must stipulate what will be included in the child's educational program. The IEP includes:

- Current level of educational attainment
- Prevocational and vocational skills
- Annual educational goals
- Short-term educational objectives
- Psychomotor status
- Social adaptation and skills
- Self-help skills
- Specific needs, such as speech therapy, hearing aids, or physical therapy

Speech therapy. This is given to make the child's speech more intelligible and to improve articulation.

Augmentative communication. Methods (e.g., sign language) and devices (e.g., communication boards) are used to help the child speak when speech is extremely impaired. Computers are also useful in helping children to communicate.

Task analysis. This is a process that breaks tasks, such as dressing and undressing, into small steps, so the child can be taught to perform each step in a chain. This technique is useful in severe retardation.

Self-help skills training. Many techniques are used to teach self-help skills to those with severe forms of mental retardation. These techniques may involve repetitive instruction and transfer of the techniques to real-life situations. The following skills are usually addressed:

Dressing	Grooming	Toilet training
Feminine hygiene	Tooth brushing	Hair combing
Showering	Some cooking	Self-feeding

Sex education. Sexual development in those with mental retardation generally proceeds at the usual biological rate. Because these individuals have normal sexual interests and desires, it is important to provide them with sex education. Of particular importance is instruction about the difference between public and private behavior, the various ways we express affection, and the appropriate ways to deal with genital feelings. You may encounter resistance to this sort of education for those with mental retardation, even though they very much need it to function appropriately.

Recreational Services

A wide variety of recreational services exist for those with mental retardation. These include physical activities, music, arts and crafts, and camping. All activities should be age-appropriate.

Physical activities. These are engaged in to promote better coordination and strength. Balance and flexibility are also goals. For those with more severe handicaps, activities to extend the head, neck, and limbs (e.g., reaching and upward stretching) are useful. Children with cerebral palsy can increase the interaction between impaired and unimpaired limbs and can increase eye-hand coordination.

Arts and crafts. These activities give people a chance to express themselves and take pride in what they achieve. Materials that have color, texture, weight, and even odor are useful. Drawing, cutting, pasting, folding, and stitching, all of which require dexterity, can strengthen fine motor skills.

Camping. This is an intense recreational experience that provides skills for living embedded in games and camaraderie. Many of these skills serve the person for a lifetime.

Special Olympics. All 50 states and 110 countries have Special Olympics with more than 20 individual and team events. The Special Olympics increases social skills and provides children with athletic opportunities, an avenue for achievement, and a group with whom the children can identify. Travel to games increases independence. Since its inception, the Special Olympics has served to integrate handicapped and nonhandicapped athletes in their communities, often on the same team.

Bowling. This is another popular way to integrate team members into the community, increase the skills they need to function independently, and provide avenues for achievement. The bowling alley is a place to mingle with nonhandicapped persons, learn to order snacks, and have a group activity with others.

Water play. This is particularly therapeutic for individuals with cerebral palsy, as it helps them to flex their muscles, move more easily, and relax the body. It provides both exercise and fun.

Music. As recreation, this allows participants to sing, play musical games, play rhythms, and dance. All of these are a means of self-expression and provide real pleasure.

Family Support Services

Respite care. This service allows parents and families to take a break from the often arduous task of caring for the family member with multiple handicaps. It is used, for example, when the family is going on vacation or when a family member becomes ill and is unable to care for the person with disabilities.

In-home care. Providing health equipment, such as wheelchairs, hospital beds, and oxygen, along with services to assist the family often gives the family the support they need to keep a family member at home, rather than placing the individual in an institution or group home.

Specialized foster care. This service allows a child to be placed in a foster home specifically set up to care for the person with multiple handicaps. Many parents see this as preferable to a group home or institutional care.

Group care. This service is usually reserved for children with severe retardation. The residents have 24-hour nursing care, and basic self-care needs are met. These services are often referred to as ICF-MRs in planning meetings, which stands for intermediate care facilities for individuals with mental retardation.

Residential Options

Institutions. This option is rarely used anymore, and large state institutions are being phased out. Some families who can afford it send their family member with disabilities to a private institution that specializes in the care of the mentally retarded, but this is less common than it was in the 1960s when institutions were the living arrangement of choice. The discovery of abuse and inhumane living arrangements largely contributed to the end of these institutions.

Community-based residential settings. Considered a more "normal" living arrangement, these programs are located within the community and give the residents more choices. They provide opportunities to socialize, engage in community and residential recreational activities, and increase skills in self-care and home care. Group homes generally have three to five residents ranging in age from 22 to 63. The degree of cognitive impairment is moderate, not severe.

Supported independent living. These arrangements are available for individuals who need less supervision. Often these people live together in apartment clusters with two or three individuals to an apartment. They receive assistance with managing their finances and resolving social and health problems.

Nursing homes. Placing younger individuals with mental retardation in nursing homes is controversial. Federal legislation now restricts such placement of individuals with mental retardation to those who have medical needs.

Integrated communities. Several groups have set up integrated communities within the United States, but not many of them exist. These are communities in which individuals with mental retardation function side by side with nonhandicapped individuals. Often these communities are self-sustaining, providing farm work and craft work to the members.

Behavioral Services

In some cases, individuals with mental retardation also have behavioral problems that make it difficult for them to live compatibly with others. The following are common problems:

- *Aggression.* Biting, kicking, and hitting others
- *Self-injurious behavior (SIB).* Head banging, hand biting, drinking excessive liquids, eye gouging, placing objects into body orifices, eating inedibles
- *Stereotypes.* Repetitive movement disorders such as rocking, swaying, hand waving
- *Trichotillomania.* Pulling out one's hair so that there is noticeable hair loss
- *Dyskinesia.* Involuntary movements generally caused by long-term use of psychotropic medications
- *Acathisia.* Extreme restlessness
- *Obsessive-compulsive disorder.* Obsessive thoughts driving the person to compulsive actions, usually repetitive and ritualistic and done in order to reduce anxiety
- *Problematic sexual behavior.* Public masturbation, exposure of genitals, inappropriate touching or verbal expressions

Psychotropic medications. These medications can be given to control behaviors such as aggression and self-injury, to reduce anxiety with conditions such as obsessive-compulsive disorder and trichotillomania, or, as in the case of Ritalin, to increase concentration and reduce distractibility. Antidepressants are helpful in stabilizing moods and seem to assist in repetitive movement disorders and anxiety. Medications can also help with hyperactivity and irritability.

Applied behavioral analysis. This technique operates on the assumption that behavior is repeated because the consequences of that behavior reinforce it. First the behavior to be increased and the behavior to be decreased are stipulated. Reinforcers for desired behavior are developed, and the unwanted behavior is punished in some way or ignored in favor of the desired behavior. These plans are usually developed by a behavior specialist, who then teaches the worker how to implement them. The plans are highly individualized for each person and each behavior, and they may need to be adjusted several times before the proper remedy is found.

DOING YOUR ASSESSMENT AND FOLLOWING YOUR CLIENT

You have information now to develop a believable client with mental retardation. Use the assessment form to create a credible person who might come to you seeking services or whose family might contact you on the client's behalf. Use the space for interviewer comments to elaborate on the problems that were discussed during your intake and assessment of this client. You can make a referral to programs and services you think will best serve your client. As you monitor your hypothetical client, you can draw from the information in this chapter to define the kinds of plausible problems and common issues your client and those closest to your client are likely to encounter.

EXERCISES

Developing Service Plans

Instructions: Develop a service plan for each of the individuals described in the following vignettes. In each plan, demonstrate that you have consulted with the client and the family, if that is appropriate, and that you have taken their wishes into consideration.

1. Mrs. Rodriquez brings 8-year-old Jose into the office. They have recently moved here from another state, and she is seeking services for Jose. She tells you he has been diagnosed as having both mental retardation and cerebral palsy. Jose's movements are slow and appear to be difficult, and his range of motion is restricted. He is in a wheelchair for mobility. His speech is unclear, and you are concerned that he may be able to communicate more than he does now. Jose has not been enrolled in any programs at this point. His mother brings along psychological tests from his previous records showing Jose's IQ as 60.

2. Karen is 43-year-old woman who has been diagnosed as having mental retardation. Her IQ is 53 according to the psychological tests in her chart. Her mother, with whom she lived all her life, has recently died, and Karen is now living with her youngest sister. Karen's sister is married and has three young children. She feels Karen is more than she can handle, but fears "putting her somewhere." The sister tells you that Karen is "easily led." She says, "Mother kept an eye on her all the time because she was afraid she would go off with strangers or something." Karen never worked outside her mother's home.

3. Sachiko is a 3-year-old living with her parents in very poor housing in an older part of town. Her parents come to you at the suggestion of church members who sponsored the family when they immigrated to the United States. They are concerned because the child is frail and seems to be failing to grow. She also seems to be cognitively delayed and listless.

4. John is a 52-year-old who is coming into your community after spending years in an institution. He has been classified as having moderate retardation. He tells you he likes to sing and wants to have a dog. His parents are elderly and do not seem able to have him in their home. They would like to see him often, however, and are pleased that he is returning to the community. He went to the institution when he was a baby. His parents tell you, "The doctors told us that was the thing to do for him because he could never have a normal life. We never saw him as often as we wanted to. The place was so far away, and we had two other children. It was hard, you know, to get up there and see John."

5. Annette is pregnant and was referred to you by her physician. She has a drinking problem, and she is concerned about the health of her unborn child. She says, "I need help to stop drinking. You'd think I just would, but I can't seem to stop even though I know it could hurt my baby."

6. Helena is 13 and seems lonely. She has been diagnosed as having mild retardation, and her mother is concerned about the treatment she is receiving. She has difficulty articulating clearly, and her mother believes this makes people think she is less intelligent than she really is. Helena tells you she would like to have friends. She also likes to draw and paint.

7. Bud and Christy are 17 years old. Last spring Christy became pregnant, and Bud is the father. The baby was born prematurely this week. The couple married hastily at the insistence of their parents, and they appear to be very close and supportive of one another. Nevertheless, neither of them seems prepared to take on the tasks of caring for a baby with special needs. They tell you they want to take the baby home with them, but you sense they are not clear about the amount of work needed to care for the baby. Christy is planning to take a year off from high school so Bud can finish school and go on to the community college.

8. Mr. and Mrs. Peterson are in their 80s. Recently Mr. Peterson had a stroke that required him to go to a nursing home. Randy, their son, has lived at home all his life. He has mild retardation and has never worked outside the home. Mrs. Peterson tells you that her husband always resisted making any plans for Randy after their death because he thought it was morbid to dwell on such unpleasant things. Now Mrs. Peterson is unsure what will become of Randy. She seems very anxious about this. The social worker at the nursing home where Mr. Peterson is staying puts Mrs. Peterson in touch with you. She comes to see you, accompanied by her daughter, Alice, and her other son, Carl.

Using the *DSM-IV-TR*

Instructions: Look at the situations below and discuss what diagnosis would be appropriate in each of these cases. For more information on how case managers use the *DSM-IV-TR,* look at Chapter 16 in *Fundamentals of Case Management Practice* (Summers, 2001). Use the chapter in your *DSM-IV-TR* entitled "Disorders Usually First Diagnosed in Infancy, Childhood, or Adolescence," as that is where information on mental retardation and developmental disorders can be found.

1. Belinda, 14 years old, does well at school in math and science when the problems are not presented as written descriptions. Her reasoning and problem-solving abilities have been judged to be normal. She seems to have considerable difficulty with reading and comprehending what she has read. This inability to read is holding her back in school.

2. Billy is 3 years old. His family physician referred him for a psychological examination. Billy never makes eye contact with those around him. He plays alone and avoids contact with his siblings, stiffening if they try to hold him or touch him. When they talk to him, he appears not to reciprocate or, in some instances, to even notice. His development has been slow, with very little verbal ability at this point. If the daily routine is at all disrupted, Billy becomes extremely upset, which is demonstrated by crying and rigidity of posture.

3. Yollie had a normal birth and appeared to do well immediately following her birth. She developed normally until she was about 6 months old, when she began to use hand motions that were no longer purposeful. She has never developed speech, and her gait is extremely unsteady.

4. Bertie is 7 years old. By all accounts, he was a normal 2-year-old child. He seemed to be doing well, but gradually it appeared that he was falling behind. He no longer seems able to do things that he could do, like tying his shoes and maintaining bladder control. He also was able to play with certain toys that he now seems no longer able to master. The parents are alarmed and are seeking a way to reverse whatever is happening to their son.

5. Pedro is 15. He has been tested by a psychologist, who gave him an IQ of 36. Pedro has communication skills and can perform simple tasks, such as helping to set up for lunch in the school cafeteria, under supervision. He has mastered the activities of daily living, and he reads on a 2nd-grade level.

6. Arnold is 2 years old, and his mother complains that he eats "all sorts of things." She tells you that he picks at the paint on the windowsill by his crib in the bedroom and ingests the flakes he picks off. She has caught him eating pieces of plaster, and even pieces of string. Arnold's family lives in run-down housing, and both parents work. Arnold is not under the best care during the day, and you are concerned that there may be some neglect.

INTAKE AND ASSESSMENT FORM FOR CONSUMERS WITH MENTAL RETARDATION

Wildwood Case Management Unit

Case manager ______________________ Date taken ______________________

Name ______________________
Address ______________________
Phone number:
Home ______________________
Work ______________________
____

Agency # ______________________
Intake date ______________________
Referral source ______________________
Social Security # ______________________
Birth date ____________ Age ____
Marital status ______________________
Sex [ ] M [ ] F
Case manager ______________________

1. Emergency contacts
____
____
____

Phone number:
Home ______________________
Work ______________________
Relationship ______________________

2. Emergency contacts
____
____
____

Phone number:
Home ______________________
Work ______________________
Relationship ______________________

INCOME TYPE

Wages $ ______________________
SSI Amount $ ______________________
SSA Amount $ ______________________
Other source ______________________
Amount $ ______________________

Representative payee ______________________
Address ______________________
____
____

Is there a burial trust (irrevocable)? ______________________ Amount $ ____________
Life insurance ______________________ Cash value amount $ ____________
Other assets ______________________ Amount $ ____________
(Stocks, bonds, inheritance, savings accounts, home, automobile)

This information was reported by ______________________
____

ELIGIBILITY CRITERIA

Documented ______ Documentation requested ______ Date of request ______

Level of mental retardation

02 Mild (317.00) ______

03 Moderate (318.00) ______

04 Severe (318.10) ______

05 Profound (318.20) ______

06 Unspecified (319.00) ______

19 Dually diagnosed ______

Evaluator ______

Evaluation date ______

Method ______

Mental health diagnosis ______

Date of diagnosis ______

By whom ______

Review of eligibility

Date ______ Reviewing psychologist ______

Recommendations: ______

______

______

______

______

______

LIVING ARRANGEMENTS

Own home ______ Relative ______ Family living provider ______

Community home program ______ MR institutiton ______

MH hospital ______ Nursing home ______ Domicilliary care home ______

Other ______

EMPLOYMENT STATUS

Full-time ______ Part-time______ Unemployed ______ Student ______

Homemaker ______ Retired ______ Disabled ______

PRIOR HOSPITALIZATION

Yes ______ No ______

If yes, where ______ When ______

WHAT IS IMPORTANT TO ME (AND MY FAMILY)

(Include likes/dislikes; things I do for fun, activities I am involved with or would like to be, places I go and how I get there, any specialized routines and/or rituals I prefer, and celebrations I like. Include those things for which I have a positive reputation and what I am good at doing.)

What others who support me need to know:

COMMUNICATION

Language I speak/understand ______________________________

My family speaks/understands ______________________________

My way of communicating includes ______________________________

____

____

(Include signs, gestures, verbal, written, assistive device, adaptive equipment, etc.)

MOBILITY

__________ Walk independently

__________ Walk with assistance

Walker ______ Cane ______ Brace ______ Wheelchair ______

Need assistance on steps only ______

Transfer skills (from wheelchair to bed or chair, into tub or shower)

Assistance needed ______________________________

____

____

SELF-CARE

I am able to care for myself:
(This includes personal hygiene, dining, etc.)

___________ With assistance

___________ Need total support

___________ Independently

Assistance needed (verbal and/or physical) ________________________________

____

____

SELF-PRESERVATION SKILLS

I am able to read	Y	N
I am able to use a telephone book	Y	N
I am able to identify money	Y	N
Coins ______ Bills ______		
I am able to write a check	Y	N
I know my name	Y	N
I am able to provide my name	Y	N
I know my address	Y	N
I am able to provide my address	Y	N
I know my phone number	Y	N
I can provide my phone number	Y	N

Knowledge of procedures in the event of an emergency

Independently ______ Physical/verbal assistance ______

Total assistance ______

AWARENESS OF DANGER AND SAFETY PRECAUTIONS

Type of Danger	No Awareness	Somewhat Aware (Please comment)	Adequately Aware
Poisonous material			
Traffic crossing streets			
Strangers threatening people			
Hot water			
Hot oven or range			
Fire, open flame			
Water, swimming pool			
Getting lost or separated			
Other			

Any other information regarding safety:

INVOLVEMENT IN THE CRIMINAL JUSTICE SYSTEM

(Past and present) **Y** _____ **N** _____

Describe:

NOTABLE INFORMATION SHARED AT INTAKE

(Family, social, educational, or work history)

IMPRESSIONS AND RECOMMENDATIONS

____
Case Manager

SERVICE PLANNING

Name ______________________________ Fiscal year ______________

Type	Provider/ Contact	Address/ Phone	Frequency/ Duration	Authorized
Case management				
Residential setting				
Day/ education services				
Educational work program				
Other				
Special Therapies				
Physical				
Occupational				
Behavior				
Visual				
Visiting nurse				
Other				
Other Special Services				
Psychotherapy/ counseling				
Advocacy				
Structured recreation				
Vacation program				
Respite				
Other				

Allied Health Service				
Primary dental				
Primary vision				
Podiatry				
Nutrition/diet				
Nursing				
Other				
Medical Services				
Primary medical				
Emergency medical				
Gynecology				
Seizure management				
Other neurological				
ENT				
Psychiatry, medicine management				
Patrial program				
Mobile therapist				
Behavior therapist				
Therapeutic support staff				
Other				

Signature ______________________________ Date ______________

Parent or guardian signature (if necessary) ______________________________

Request copy of plan: Y N

Plan received Y N

Case manager ______________________________

Supervisor ______________________________

Next review date ________________ Entered into computer ________________ ,

Participants in this plan:

Chapter 8

Case Management with Older People

INTRODUCTION

Agnes, 86 years old, had four daughters and was living alone at the time of the first "episode." Agnes described it as "unbearable anxiety." She became irritable and extremely negative, which alarmed her daughters because Agnes had always been even-tempered and cheerful. A visit to her family doctor indicated that Agnes's electrolytes were out of balance. Potassium was given by mouth to try to make up for a potassium deficiency. The doctor then put Agnes on new blood pressure medication, stating he felt it was the blood pressure medication that had caused the problem with the electrolytes. He made it clear that it was not the blood pressure medication that was causing the mental confusion and anxiety because Agnes had been on this medication for nine months with none of these symptoms.

Agnes did not improve. In fact, she grew worse. She began to sit up at night rocking and crying. She begged her daughters to get her help, saying, "This isn't me. I'm not myself." At last the doctors consulted a psychiatrist. He said that Agnes was both depressed and anxious and prescribed both an antidepressant and an antianxiety medication. At times these medications seemed to work, but for the most part Agnes continued to deteriorate.

Her daughters were upset for their mother. Only a month before she had been actively doing her own shopping, singing in the choir, and acting as a poll watcher in her local precinct. She had been independent, up-to-date on news and politics, and had a good sense of humor. Now all of that was gone. Agnes became more and more convinced that no one was safe and that terrible things were about to befall her. The daughters took turns staying with her and eventually called the county Office of Aging services.

The case manager who came to the home took a complete social history. She was struck by how recently Agnes had been independent and cheerful. With Agnes's permission, the case manager contacted the psychiatrist and described Agnes's worsening condition. To the case manager's dismay, the psychiatrist replied, "The daughters are just going to have to baby-sit her. She is looking for attention at this point. Double her medication for now, and have her see me next week." The psychiatrist made it clear during the conversation that the case manager should begin preparing the family for institutionalization of Agnes.

When the case manager finished the call, she was not satisfied with the explanation given by the psychiatrist. Why, she asked herself, would Agnes want attention now when she had never sought it before, and why was she so well only a month before? The case manager knew that when a history shows that a person has changed quickly or suddenly, the condition is often reversible. The case manager shared with the daughters her concern that Agnes's condition might very well be a medical or physical problem, and not a behavioral or mental one as the psychiatrist had suggested. With the daughters' permission, the case manager arranged for Agnes to enter the geriatric unit of a large teaching hospital.

Agnes was not pleased. She accused her daughters of abandoning her and entered the hospital in an angry mood. In the admission interview, the resident reassured Agnes and her family, telling them they had come to the right place to address Agnes's problem. During the next 48 hours, a thorough workup was done, and Agnes was removed from the medications the psychiatrist had given her. An IV was given to immediately balance the electrolytes. Within a few days, her daughters found Agnes smiling and discovered her sense of humor had returned. "Agnes is back," she told them jokingly.

A conference with Agnes's doctor revealed that her electrolytes had been badly out of balance. In addition, Agnes had been given doses of the psychotropic medications that were too much for her. The antianxiety medication had calmed Agnes for only a short time before it wore off; thus, a toleration for the medication had developed rapidly, more rapidly than it would have in a younger person. The antidepressant medication had been too strong, causing Agnes to feel anxious and agitated. On new, lighter doses that were gradually lowered until the medication was discontinued, Agnes did fine. Finally, the doctor explained that just because an older person does well on a medication for a time does not mean the person will not have problems with it later on. "As we grow older," he told the daughters, "our metabolism changes. Doses of medication that worked before may now prove too strong and no longer useful."

In this case, the thoughtful approach of the case manager and the case manager's willingness to look at other possible causes for Agnes's change of personality saved Agnes's life. Not only did she return home and resume her independent lifestyle again, but she also was able to pick up new interests and develop new friends well into her 90s.

SPECIAL CONSIDERATIONS

Case management with older people requires paying particular attention to details. This chapter is designed to help you become a competent case manager for older people. You will learn about the social and medical problems that commonly affect older people. You will discover what clues to look for and what pieces of information to further develop for other professionals who may work with your clients later. You will also learn the components of a good assessment of an older person and the ideal services for their problems and issues. In the process, you will become better able to understand how older people feel as their bodies and their social worlds change, often in ways they find uncomfortable.

One inescapable fact of life is that for every year we live, we grow older. After age 65, and in some cases after age 55, people become more at risk for problems that develop specifically as a result of growing older. Some of these problems have to do with physical changes that occur as we age. Other problems are related to the social adjustments that must be made in a society that is not entirely comfortable with aging and older people. This collection of potential problems is the focus of both social service and medical professionals. Physicians who specialize in medical problems most often associated with aging are called gerontologists, and their field is referred to as gerontology. Others who specialize in working with older people are engaged in a field referred to as geriatrics. There are, therefore, geriatric social workers, intake workers, case managers, and psychologists, to name a few.

The two most important facts with which to start are these:

1. Growing older is not a problem. It is a normal part of life. The problems arise when either the society or the person cannot handle the accompanying changes, which places the older person at risk. That is when social service and medical personnel may become involved.
2. The involvement of social service and medical personnel does not necessarily indicate that the older person is emotionally unwell, completely incapable, or befuddled. Older people usually bring to their difficulties enormous resources grounded in the experience of years of living, that you, as the worker, need to respect, document, and access as you plan with older persons or their families.

MYTHS

In popular culture, certain beliefs about older people persist, in spite of the fact they are unfounded. Large numbers of people subscribe to these ideas, and this affects their interaction with older people. Here we will examine five of these myths.

Senility

It is commonly believed that all older people will at some point become senile and that being senile accounts for their behavior or thinking, particularly when that behavior or thinking seems odd to a younger person. The assumption is that senility is an untreatable, permanent condition. Therefore, there is no imperative to help the older person, if one assumes that person would not appreciate or know the difference anyway. Many believe that there is no really useful intervention once a person is deemed to be senile. In reality, most older people remain mentally active and aware.

It is important to know first that there is no diagnosis of "senile" or "senility." In this chapter we will look at cognitive disorders and their correct names, and you will learn the clues to reversible cognitive disorders. For now, however, you need to be aware that when anyone uses the term *senile,* including medical and social service professionals, you should inquire about what symptoms have been observed or what the person means by the term, because it is not a legitimate diagnosis.

Particularly frustrating are family members who refuse to entertain the fact that some cognitive disorders are reversible. Often they will not support the tests or treatments that might reverse a cognitive disorder.

In one family, the mother, 87, had been living with her daughter. She was fine until suddenly one summer, she appeared to be confused. Although the family consulted a social service agency, they refused to follow through on tests to determine the cause of the mother's confusion. The mother became harder to manage, and they hired in-home health services to help the daughter handle the situation and her own family. A health worker suggested that the condition might be reversible, but the daughter and her husband brushed off the idea, explaining that the mother was, after all, 87, and therefore she was just "senile." In late August, the mother jumped into a nearby farm pond, apparently disoriented and agitated, and drowned.

Many cognitive disorders are reversible if caught in time. Your role is to help sort out what exactly the client and the family have been experiencing.

Tranquility

Some people believe that all older people sit around doing nothing, without any cares or concerns. They think that old age is an idyllic, carefree time. The reality is that many older people have financial concerns or medical problems they did not experience in their younger years. In addition, many older people are involved in volunteer projects, their communities and families, and even in new personal growth activities.

Productivity

Many people assume that older people cannot be productive or creative, that they have outlived their usefulness. In fact, many older people remain employed longer than in previous generations, and those who are not actively employed are often actively involved in life and activities in useful and creative ways.

Resistance

"You can't teach an old dog new tricks" is a phrase used to explain older people's resistance to change. Resistance to change, however, is often the result of poor health and other changes that have led the older person to feel that too many things are changing too fast. In addition, some older people, just like some younger people, are resistant to change as a personality trait they have always had. For the most part, older people can be as flexible as those in other age groups.

Gender and Growing Older

Growing older is somewhat similar for both sexes, since both genders have bodies that age and new challenges to face. Women, however, tend to have a longer life expectancy than men, they are more likely to be the caregiver of a spouse with a long-term illness, and they are more likely to suffer elder abuse. In addition, while men are considered distinguished and experienced as they age, women often feel a need to hide their age because women are usually judged for their youthful good looks. When men are widowed, it is acceptable for them to marry younger women who will outlive them and perhaps take care of them as they grow older. It is not acceptable for women to marry men much younger than themselves.

Today, as the population grows older, it is possible that people are becoming less likely to subscribe to these myths. The Baby Boomer generation is taking a strong stand to dissuade social service and medical personnel from applying these myths to all older people without thinking. As older people mingle with the rest of the population, they demonstrate the many different ways people age.

A COMMON MISTAKE ABOUT CHRONOLOGICAL AGE

It is common for children of older people, and perhaps even for social service workers who are unfamiliar with the aging process, to underestimate the competence and capabilities of a person they consider old. Common assumptions about older people are that they can no longer live alone, that their homes are too big for them to handle, that they are unable to handle their pets any more, and that they should drop out of certain activities that are seen as too demanding. Sometimes these are accurate assessments, but in far too many cases they are based on preconceived notions about what elderly people can handle.

In one apartment complex for senior citizens, a social service worker ran a workshop titled "How to Handle Your Well-meaning Children." Older people in the complex flocked to the workshop, sharing stories and ideas, often with humor, about intrusive decisions younger people had made for them, including their young doctors. They told of being pressured to give up their homes or cherished activities. They told of younger people who rushed to take over their parents' affairs, assuming that the first serious illness was the beginning of senility and incompetence.

In fact, people age at different rates while having the same chronological age. For example, Carmen is 74 and in a nursing home. Her son placed her there after she appeared to be unable to get around because of arthritis. She requested more and more assistance with the management of her home and her affairs, and she seemed unable to handle even a small apartment he found for her near his house. After several falls, the son placed her in a situation where she is largely responsible for dressing and bathing herself, but has her meals and other activities planned and provided for her.

Dorothy, on the other hand, is 92, a widow, and living in the home in which she raised four children. She has a dog, and recently she adopted a kitten from the Humane Society. The kitten knocks over things on the mantle and leaps around the room on the furniture. Everyone would like to assume that this is too much for Dorothy to handle, but she has expressed humor about the antics of her kitten. In addition, she remains active, filling bird feeders every day, attending symphony concerts, going on bus trips to museums with younger friends, and entertaining nieces and nephews who come through with their children during summer vacations. When one of her children pointed out that she should get a home all on one floor, Dorothy shot back that it was the stairs that kept her legs strong and she had no intention of moving out of her home.

Chronological age is less important than other elements you explore, such as attitude toward growing older, physical abilities, cognitive abilities, recent stress, and the degree of support the older person has. You will probably be younger than the people whose histories you are taking. Your education and understanding of the aging process will help you to refrain from making the common assumptions discussed here, and will give you the tools to help the family look at the older person's situation more realistically.

EMOTIONAL WELL-BEING AND GROWING OLDER

Most of the literature, and therefore the common view, holds that older people are an irritable and unpleasant group of people, growing more so as they age. In fact, older people run from pleasant to unpleasant, just like any other segment of society. For the most part, older people remain much as they have been all of their lives. People who have been good-natured and had a good sense of humor tend to remain that way, and those who have been argumentative and difficult tend to go on being so in old age.

When taking a social history, determine whether there has been a change in the person's way of relating to others. If so, you will want to note whether this is a change in the person's personality and document when that change occurred. These are important clues to what may be underlying problems.

People who are aging may have reasons for acting unpleasant, reasons they may not be able to articulate. For instance, they may not feel well, and whatever is wrong with them may have gradually crept up on them. They may have experienced one or more losses that they found devastating. As friends and relatives die, older people face unexpected and unwanted changes in their social life. They may have trouble sorting out those changes and what the changes mean for the future. In any assessment that you do where a person seems to be sad and angry, try to determine whether this is a recent change in the person's personality or whether it is the person's habitual way of relating.

A HEALTHY OLD AGE

Emotionally healthy older people have often been blessed with good health as they age. There are many older people suffering from chronic conditions or terminal illnesses who maintain a positive outlook, but it is harder to do when a person is struggling with extreme changes and physical pain.

Emotional health, however, does seem to be most obvious in individuals with a number of common characteristics. You need to know these characteristics in order to know what to look for in developing a social history of the person because these are strengths you may be able to access as you and the client plan for services. These characteristics are as follows.

Sense of Purpose

Look in the social history for evidence that the person has always found something useful to do or has always had projects he or she was working on. Listen for evidence of goals the person developed and completed. Look for a sense of not having enough time to do all the things that interest the person. Many older people will laugh about how they can never do all the things they would love to do before they die.

Good Planning

In taking the social history, look at the way in which the person prepared for growing older. Did he or she plan for retirement? Was he or she able to think ahead about what might be needed? Is he or she planning ahead now? You will find that a person who prepared for growing older may be less burdened with problems than a person who suddenly faced diminishing capacities and fewer financial resources.

Support

Look in the social history for evidence of social support. Are there close friends and relatives? Is there someone the older person talks to regularly? Is your client included in activities with others? Does the person have a pet? Support contributes enormously to emotional health in old age.

Experimenting

As you collect information, notice times in the history when the person took chances or risks. Look at times of crisis and how the person coped. Generally an older person has been through more than one crisis in his or her life. A divorce, the death of a child, the loss of a job, a home burning down, and the death of a spouse are examples of such crises. Often when people face a crisis, they find ways to handle it in a creative and personal manner. Explore these times with the person as you take the history and learn how he or she managed them.

Faith

Many older people have developed, through years of living, a certain degree of faith. It may be expressed through the practice of an organized religion, regular church attendance, and attendance at church functions. Many, however, have faith in a higher power that is practiced in ways that are more solitary and personal. Discuss with older people their feelings about a higher being. A sense of faith is a part of good emotional health.

Cheerfulness

How does the person seem to you? Does the person seem cheerful? Does the person appear to be approaching aging with humor? Do you sense that he or she is pleased for the most part with the way life turned out? These are indications of emotional health or strength. If the person seems to be sad, angry, regretful, or afraid, note this in your assessment and try to pinpoint with the person why he or she might be feeling this way.

IMPORTANCE OF THE HISTORY AND ASSESSMENT

With this background, we are ready to turn to taking the history. The social history you take for an older person is extremely important. In many cases, the elderly are unable to give a complete history because of cognitive difficulties, and it may be hard to find someone to help you fill in the information you need. Your history, however, is the fundamental document on which additional assessments and planning will be developed. In some cases, you will need to be a detective in tracking down the information you need.

You also must be a keen observer as you take the history, watching for signs of cognitive and medical problems that others might not detect. This can be critical and even life-saving for the elderly. Illnesses and conditions left undetected and untreated can pose life-threatening situations for older people and eventually lead to death. Catching these early often prevents unnecessary suffering and pain.

When taking the social history, you may need to get most of the information from a spouse or some other person close to the client. Try to speak with that person alone, without the client being present. Often people are reluctant to give a description of the symptoms in front of the client. For example, an elderly man was brought in for a history by his wife. It was not until the wife was alone with the case manager that she told about his incontinence and intermittent confusion. She explained to the case manager, "I just didn't feel comfortable telling you all that in front of him. It is hard enough for him and, well, some of this is embarrassing."

THE SOCIAL HISTORY

By social history, we refer to aspects of the older person's life and current circumstances. When you take the social history from older people, look at their childhood, middle adult years, and work and education history, just as you would for any other client. Focus as well on the following important factors.

1. *Current living arrangements.* In assessing the current living arrangements, you assess the degree to which these arrangements are helpful to the client or a hindrance to the client. Can your client manage in this environment?
2. *Physical layout.* Look at the physical layout of the home in the light of any physical barriers the older person might be experiencing. Does the layout of the home support or curtail independence?
3. *Condition of the home.* Look at the condition of the home for clues about the person's ability to maintain it. Many older people live with clutter they find comforting. It is not as important to them as it once was to have everything picked up and put away. On the other hand, you may find that the home is extremely dirty and that common daily tasks have been neglected.

Current living arrangements can give valuable clues to the person's needs. Arla, for example, had lived alone since being widowed 10 years before. At 78, she suffered from a mild heart condition, but was active. Daily she visited friends in a nearby nursing home and made a run to the local super market. In both places, she was well known to employees and enjoyed the regular contacts with these people. Her case manager monitored her situation, and for many years Arla ate regularly, remained active, and managed the housekeeping of her small apartment.

One day the case manager came to the house and discovered that there were no sheets on the bed. Instead, Arla seemed to be sleeping on a mattress pad that appeared soiled. In addition, Arla had a body odor that indicated she had not washed herself recently. The case manager understood at once that these were clues to be further explored because this situation was not in character for Arla.

As they talked, the case manager learned that Arla had severe diarrhea. She was not eating regularly because she did not feel like cooking, and when she did eat, "it runs right through me." In this situation, the case manager made a medical appointment, and it was discovered that medication was causing the diarrhea. The doctor made a medication adjustment. Because Arla had lost weight, the case manager also arranged for Meals-on-Wheels. In addition, he developed with a home health agency a plan for a person to come once every two weeks to dust, run the vacuum cleaner, and change the bed.

The keen observation of the worker, the prompt medical assessment, and the interventions to prevent further deterioration or medical complications allowed Arla to remain in her home and somewhat independent much longer.

4. *The neighborhood.* Look at the neighborhood and assess the person's ability to cope or be safe in that environment. Some older people want to remain in neighborhoods that are likely to have crime and delinquency and seem to be able to handle living there. Others are no match for the danger and resort to remaining behind locked doors, afraid to go out.
5. *The marital relationship.* Look at the marital relationship. Couples often do not get along as well after they are retired and have time on their hands. In some cases, cognitive impairment may lead to actual abuse by one spouse of the other. Just because a couple has been together for a number of years does not mean they cannot have marital problems in later life.
6. *Substance abuse.* Loneliness, former habits with regard to drugs or alcohol, and self-medication are all reasons why substance abuse might become more extreme as a person becomes older. Ask about the use of street drugs and alcohol.

Mattie and Ezell were married nearly 50 years when Ezell moved out to a small apartment of his own. Neighbors were worried about the situation. Ezell seemed angry at Mattie for not letting him smoke, even though he had been warned that smoking was taking a toll on his heart. Mattie told neighbors she could not stand the cigarette smoke any longer and if Ezell was going to smoke he would have to leave. She was concerned about second-hand smoke and the effects it was having on her own breathing problems. Ezell told the social worker he missed Mattie, but he intended to smoke. After Mattie had a fall, she was tearful as she told the social worker that she missed Ezell, but she said she was not prepared to take him back as long as he smoked.

In this situation, case managers were able to help the couple reconcile and also help Ezell to stop smoking. The problem had only become prominent in the relationship after Ezell retired and the couple was together all day. In the end, the couple celebrated 50 years together and invited neighbors and friends and their case managers to their party.

7. *Current support.* When taking the history, look for current support the person has. You are, in a sense, assessing the degree of isolation. Isolation is a risk factor for depression, suicide, lack of adequate care, and, when needed, lack of supervision. The more active and involved an older person is, the less at risk he or she is for depression and loneliness.

- *Friendships.* Begin by looking at friendships, daily phone contacts, and contacts with neighbors, if there are any.
- *Siblings.* Check to see where the person's siblings are, and ask about the amount of contact the client has with them. Sometimes siblings are deceased or live too far away to visit.
- *Children.* Examine the contact the person has with his or her children. In some cases, children no longer live in the area, and the client's contact with them may be limited.
- *Organizatons.* Find out whether anyone from a synagogue, church, or mosque visits the person regularly.
- *Regular activities.* Ask about activities outside the home. Bus trips, senior center activities, and church involvement are common, but also look for evidence that your client is able to get out and shop or go to the doctor when needed. If she is not able to drive, ask about her access to rides when she needs them.

8. *Recent stress.* Of particular importance are recent events in the person's life that have been stressful. For older people, it is common to find that a number of losses have occurred recently. Following is a partial list of losses that are most likely to occur as people grow older.

- *Death.* The death of a spouse is thought to be one of the most stressful events a person can encounter, and we will look more closely at grief later in the chapter. Other deaths may have occurred as well, such as the death of a child, pet, or close neighbor. Cousins and other family members of the person's generation may have died. Good friends age and die. Some older people find themselves being one of the last survivors of a long-term group of friends.

- *Retirement.* Retirement is often viewed as a loss of status and relevance. Older people who have stopped working often feel they are no longer productive and useful. Many take other jobs or do volunteer work to overcome these feelings.
- *Independence.* As people grow older, they find themselves becoming more dependent on others for help. Perhaps they are not as able to do housework or yard work, even though that may be something they enjoyed doing and did well. An older person may require help in navigating banking and insurance or tax systems.
- *Mobility.* When the time comes to give up the car keys, many older people see their lives growing smaller. The inability to drive and get out is part of losing independence. An older person may have arthritis and be unable to walk as well as he or she once did. Shopping and other errands become painful. Older people find they must pace themselves, doing less than they used to do.
- *Sensory.* A loss of any of the five senses can diminish the pleasure a person takes in life. Vision loss and hearing loss can limit the person's participation in simple things like family conversations and happy occasions like weddings and graduations, where it is hard to see or hear what is going on. The way older people adapt to such losses is often mistaken for the beginning stages of a cognitive disorder. Someone who cannot hear well, for example, may appear to respond inappropriately. A person whose hearing and vision are limited may be passive or appear to be confused.

Rita lived alone in the city. What had been a quiet middle-class neighborhood when she and her husband purchased the house 52 years before was now close to the heart of the city. Traffic and pedestrians streamed by the house at all hours. Rita began to hear people attempting to break into her house. On several occasions, she called the police, complaining of noise near the back door. Each time the police checked and could find no evidence of any attempt to break in. After the third call, the police contacted mental health, saying they believed Rita was hallucinating.

A worker who spent some time in Rita's home taking a social history recognized almost at once that Rita had some hearing loss. During the interview, Rita heard the sounds again and indicated to the worker that someone was breaking in. The worker checked on the sound and found that it was being made by a branch rubbing against the side of the house in the wind. Not only did Rita's poor hearing cause her to hear the noise as coming from a different direction, but it also caused her to hear a noise that seemed more like someone breaking in than like a branch rubbing on the side of her house. The worker arranged for several assessments as well as a hearing test. The test indicated considerable hearing loss. All other tests were negative, and a thorough psychiatric evaluation showed that Rita was not suffering from any cognitive disorder. A hearing aid was purchased. Rita told the worker some months later that she believed her hearing was more accurate, particularly in regard to the direction from which sounds came.

There are other sensory losses as well. Sometimes older people complain of a loss of appetite, which may be caused by a loss in the sense of taste and the resulting lack of pleasure in eating. A loss of smell and feeling also limit the pleasure a person finds in everyday life.

When you are doing an assessment, be sure to note if the person uses hearing aids, glasses, or dentures. Also note whether these devices were being used at the time you interviewed the person. If they are not being used during the assessment, do two things:

1. *Make a note of that in your assessment.*
2. *Inquire about the absence of the devices.*

Be sure to note any unwillingness to use the devices on the part of caretakers, as this constitutes neglect. In addition to noting it in your record, the matter of this reluctance should be taken up with your supervisor.

Individuals may forget to use their devices or may be unable to. Because of cognitive difficulties, a person may have lost the item or be unaware of the need to use it. In addition, caregivers, even in nursing homes and hospitals, often fail to help the person use these devices, either because of time pressure, the belief that the older person is confused and the devices will not make a difference, or the items have been misplaced. Many times an older person enters a nursing facility with working hearing aids, but no one ever replaces the batteries when they need to be replaced, leaving the older person unable to hear and participate in conversations and decisions regarding their care. Failure to give people their dentures can result in them becoming malnourished and eventually can lead to a weakened state and death.

MEDICAL HISTORY AND CURRENT MEDICAL STATUS

It is important to document a complete medical history covering three areas:

1. *Past medical problems,* including surgeries, diseases, and short-term illnesses. You want to know about the onset of chronic illnesses, falls, and any recent illnesses with a fever.
2. *Present medical condition,* including any limitations and prostheses (such as artificial hips or knees), the current state of any chronic illnesses, and current mobility.
3. *Medications currently being used by the person,* including nonprescription medications. (For instance, Tylenol PM and Benedryl, both of which are over-the-counter medications, can cause confusion in some older people.) Ask about vitamins and herbal remedies the person is using. Also ask about alcohol and illicit street drugs.

Information about common problems with medication can be found later in this chapter in the section on delirium.

There are two major reasons for taking the medical history in meticulous detail.

1. *Assessment of independence.* You want to document the current level of independence and the current need for assistance. Conditions the person was once able to manage well, such as insulin injections, may now be difficult. Even a partial inability to care for oneself can threaten an older person's life. For that reason, conditions should be noted, as well as the older person's ability to handle them.
2. *Assessment of the origins of cognitive problems.* Many times you will be asked to do assessments of older people who are exhibiting some degree of confusion. In a number of these cases, the confusion will be recent and can be traced to medication problems or to an underlying medical problem. Once that problem is uncovered and documented, there is a very good chance that the confusion can be reversed. This is why careful documentation of medical conditions and medications is important.

COGNITIVE HISTORY AND CURRENT COGNITIVE STATUS

Cognition has three separate parts: perception, thought, and memory. Disorders of cognition seem to affect people over 75, with a sharp rise in the incidence of cognitive disorders after 80.

An adequate evaluation of a person who appears to have a cognitive disorder is extremely detailed, in part because there is always the possibility of an underlying medical condition that is the cause. A social history, often taken by the case manager or intake worker, becomes the basis for further studies conducted by other professionals. Medical and psychological personnel follow up with other tests and evaluations such as:

- Medical history and physical
- Neurological assessment
- Laboratory studies: complete blood count (CBC); electrolyte panel; screening metabolic panel; thyroid function studies; vitamin B12 and folate levels; syphilis serology; urinalysis
- Electrocardiogram
- Chest x-ray
- CAT scan or MRI (not needed by all clients; used only where indicated)
- Psychological evaluation
- Psychiatric evaluation

ASSESSMENT FOR COGNITIVE DISORDERS

Good assessment becomes crucial in prolonging life and reversing or arresting conditions related to cognitive functioning. Because some diagnoses are difficult to determine, the social history is often a richer source of information than the medical examination. You are the one who will collect and write up that social history.

Where cognitive difficulties exist, older people may not be good historians who are able to relate their background to their current situation. They may be guarded, deciding not to tell you things that they find embarrassing because they want to leave you with a certain impression. They may not recognize there is a problem, and thus be unable to describe it accurately. They may distort the history, particularly if their ability to remember and reason is poor. Because of their age, there may not be any reliable sources to tell you about early background that would be helpful.

You can begin, with permission, by talking to the people who have known the older person the longest: the spouse, children, or friends. If those people are unable to relate the details you need, you can, with permission, check old medical records. For example, the children may say to you, "Oh yes, Mother did have a nervous breakdown about 10 years ago," and this may be all they can or will tell you. You need to know more than that, however, to determine whether the client's current condition is a condition that occurred before, a condition that started some time ago, or a completely unrelated condition.

Important Points to Cover

In obtaining the needed information, ask the client first. If he or she cannot fill in the details, try family, friends, and even doctors to see if they can provide some help. It is important to obtain information about:

- *A history of the present illness*
- *What is the chief complaint?* Find out why the client is seeking help. The older person may not be the one initiating the contact with you. Often it is a caretaker who cannot handle the situation any longer who is seeking the help.
- *When was the client last in his or her usual state of mind?* This is a key question in determining if the condition might be reversible.
- *How did it start?* You want to know whether the condition began suddenly, developed over a few weeks, or caused an insidious decline that was hard for those closest to the client to detect at first.
- *How does the person function in his or her usual environment?* Common behavior that causes family and friends to seek help is leaving the stove on, wandering and getting lost, forgetting to pay bills, becoming assaultive, being incontinent, or losing interest in things that once were important or enjoyable.
- *Family history of cognitive disorders.* Because some major psychiatric diagnoses and cognitive disorders tend to run in families, ask if there is a family history for these disorders.
- *Past psychiatric history.* You want to know if the client had any periods of significant psychiatric disability. The diagnosis given at the time is not as important as how the person behaved—what symptoms he or she exhibited and what he or she complained of. Years ago there were fewer diagnostic categories, and people with a variety of symptoms were likely to be given a similar diagnosis.
- *Medical history.* Look particularly at medical conditions likely to exacerbate or cause cognitive dysfunction. A history of strokes, high blood pressure, Parkinson's disease, or even cancer would be important for you to note carefully.

When the Family Gives the History

Families may give a false history. For instance, a son may tell you that his father got worse on January 12th. "He didn't recognize me," he tells you. In reality, the father may have been getting worse for some time, but there was enormous anguish for the son when his father no longer recognized him. That first lack of recognition may cause the son to think his father suddenly grew worse on that particular day, when actually the father has a slowly progressing cognitive disorder.

Family members may tell you the client was suddenly worse on a particular holiday or after a bad fall. They may not have seen their family member since the previous holiday, or they may have had no contact with him or her for awhile before a bad fall occurred. Coming into contact again with the older person, they notice the deterioration and then date it from this point of contact. If a person tells you the client grew suddenly worse at a specific time, find out what contact the person had with your client before that time.

Another common mistake that can distort the history is to date the sudden deterioration from a family event. For example, suppose a family has a grand wedding, and family members take the father to the wedding and reception. After this event, they seek your help saying the father became suddenly disoriented. What actually may have happened is that the father, who may have a slowly progressing cognitive disorder, became more disoriented at the wedding, in a new place with lots of excitement, many new and unfamiliar people, and perhaps a glass of wine. He may have become more disoriented in this environment than he would have been at home in familiar surroundings. Go back before that event and find out whether anyone noticed any previous changes.

Documentation

Your impressions are also important. Unless the person is in a coma, you can observe much about the person. Following are some important items to note in your assessment.

- *History giving.* When the client gives the history, note whether he or she was able to give a coherent, relative account. Was the client aware of the difficulties that brought him or her to you? Was the client able to follow the conversation and describe things chronologically?
- *Mental status.* Look at the client's general appearance for signs of neglect. Are the client's clothes stained with food or urine? If so, is the person upset about that or unconcerned? Is the mood and demeanor appropriate to the situation? Does the person interact with you spontaneously? Does he or she seem confused, or is he or she slightly inappropriate? Subtle social inappropriateness is often a first sign of dementia.
- *Psychomotor activity.* How active or inactive is the person, even when seated or unable to get out of a wheelchair? Does he or she appear to be restless or move about normally?
- *Verbal output.* As you conduct the interview, note the rate, inflection, volume, and content of the client's verbal output. Be sure to note any suicidal content, as well as anything that looks like an aphasia. Sometimes aphasia, which is always the result of a neurological disease, is misdiagnosed as psychosis. Some clients with aphasia seem to be struggling to speak a language they do not know even when it is their native language, while others speak fluently but there is no content. For you it would be like listening to someone speaking a language you do not understand. For more information on aphasias, see other textbooks, the *DSM-IV-TR,* and *Fundamentals of Case Management Practice* (Summers, 2001).
- *Level of arousal.* Does the person seem reasonably alert? Is he or she attentive or easily distracted?

The *DSM-IV-TR* outlines several cognitive disorders. We will look at these briefly here, but it is recommended that you become familiar with these disorders as they are spelled out in the *DSM-IV-TR* under the heading "Delirium, Dementia, and Amnestic and Other Cognitive Disorders."

Delirium

According to the *DSM-IV-TR,* delirium is "a disturbance of consciousness that is accompanied by a change in cognition that cannot be better accounted for by a preexisting or evolving dementia" (p. 136). There is "a reduced clarity of awareness of the environment" (p. 136). The person usually has trouble focusing on what is immediately taking place. It is hard for the person with delirium to sustain attention to any one thing and to shift attention appropriately to something else. In addition, you might notice some memory problems or fluctuating levels of arousal, and sometimes these clients show disorientation and language disturbance. For all deliriums, "the symptoms . . . develop over hours to days although in some individuals they may begin abruptly (e.g., after a head injury)"

(*DSM-IV-TR,* p. 138). There may be periods when the client is lucid, followed by periods of confusion. You may notice a mild aphasia, such as an inability to name things. Other features you may see, according to *DSM-IV-TR,* are "restlessness, anxiety, irritability, disorientation, distractibility, or sleep disturbance" (pp. 138–139).

Onset

It is important to recognize delirium when you see it, and not to mistake it for depression, psychosis, or dementia. *The key to recognizing delirium is the sudden onset.* Delirium is an acute condition with three possible outcomes. The person can make a full recovery, particularly if the origins of the condition are found and corrected early in the course of the problem, or the condition can result in permanent disability and, finally, in death when left undiagnosed and untreated. It is your responsibility to document all information carefully for those who will actively seek an underlying cause for the delirium. Document conditions reported by family doctors, family, and others, as well as the medications the person is taking.

Common Causes

The primary reasons for delirium are declining organ function, increasing medical illness, multiple medications, sensory deprivation, and physical, emotional, and environmental losses. Delirium can be caused by an underlying medical condition. Many conditions have been known to cause delirium in older people, although not all older people with these conditions exhibit delirium. Conditions you might see as the cause of delirium are:

diabetes	stroke	heart problems	hyperthyroidism
colds or flu	anemia	dehydration	constipation
kidney stones	glaucoma	pain	infections
blood clot	hepatitis	a fall	vitamin B12 deficiency
broken bones	pneumonia	vision loss	heart attack
urinary retention	renal failure	gallstones	depression
Parkinson's disease	hearing loss	appendicitis	allergies

This is only a partial list. For some older people, any medical condition may induce delirium. You may not see the usual signs of illness. For instance, older people often do not run a temperature when they have an infection. Some do not feel pain when they are experiencing a heart attack. Problems with endocrine glands are common, as glands become less active with age. An older person who complains of being cold all the time may have developed a low thyroid later in life. Another older person who appears disoriented may have developed low blood sugar, possibly because of erratic eating habits.

Medication Problems

Delirium can also be caused by medications or other substances. Older people often face problems with medication that younger people do not face. An older person, because of changes in metabolism, may require less medication than the average middle-aged adult. Yet a physician may prescribe the medication at the normal rate, without taking into account body weight and size. A person can be on a medication successfully for some time, but then need the medication dosage reduced as his or her metabolism changes. Some older people have trouble remembering when they last took their medication, or if they took it at all, which can result in taking double doses or missing several doses. Taking medication in this manner causes uneven amounts of the medication in the bloodstream and can lead to confusion in some cases.

An older person who is seeing more than one physician or is being treated for more than one condition may be given medications that have a negative interaction with each other. Some older people keep track of 10 to 12 medications every day. A doctor may add a new drug to combat the side effects of another drug without realizing that the symptoms are side effects of the other drug. In other words, the physician treats the side effects as though they are symptoms of a new condition the client is developing. Sometimes finances cause older people to skip doses of their medications in order to save money; thus, these people take far less than the prescribed amounts. Also in an effort to save money, older people may self-medicate with over-the-counter medication, and some over-the-counter medication interacts badly with prescribed medications.

Common problem medications are sedatives, digitalis drugs, diuretics, and antihypertension medications. All of these can cause symptoms resembling depression or delirium in some older people. In addition, psychotropic medications can cause symptoms that look very much like the onset of Parkinson's disease. Over-the-counter antihistamines can cause people to be unsteady or confused.

These are some of the reasons why you may see medication problems in older people. Part of every evaluation should be a review of any medications the client is taking. Have your clients take all their medications to the physician doing the evaluation. Clients should tell the physician exactly what medications they are taking and how often, so that the physician can determine if there are any medication problems.

Dellamarie had been on a medication for high blood pressure for nearly a year. When she began to exhibit symptoms of delirium, her physician contended that it could not be the medication because she had been taking it successfully for nearly 12 months. A blood test revealed that Dellamarie was low in potassium, a side effect of the medication. The doctor prescribed potassium tablets, but during the next few weeks, Dellamarie's condition worsened. She had periods where she was lucid and knew something was wrong, but at other times she appeared confused and agitated. Finally she was admitted to the hospital. There doctors removed her from the blood pressure medication, started an intravenous medication to rebalance her electrolytes, of which potassium is one, and gave her another type of blood pressure medication. Within 48 hours, Dellamarie had regained her normal disposition and good humor and was able to talk about the extreme confusion she had experienced.

Medications can throw off the physiology of the person just enough to impair his or her ability to function well cognitively. In other cases, a medication can exaggerate the signs of aging, causing physical slowing and mental confusion. Medications that are often involved in delirium or the rapid development of symptoms of aging are digitalis, steroids, diuretics, sedatives, most psychotropic medications (medications given for mental conditions), analgesics, and oral diabetes medication. This is just a partial list, as any medication can have a negative effect for some older people.

Other Considerations

Many illegal street drugs, such as cocaine and amphetamines, can overwhelm some older people, even when they have taken these drugs for much of their lives. Delirium can also result when an older person stops taking a medication; for instance, the sudden withdrawal from a medication such as prednisone (a steroid) can result in confusion in some people.

Delirium can result from several medical conditions or from a medical condition and a drug interaction. As with all diagnostic categories in the *DSM*, there is a diagnosis that can be used when delirium is present but there is insufficient evidence to pinpoint exactly what is causing it. The diagnosis in such a case would be "delirium not otherwise specified."

Always take a careful and history, document the information well, and seek an immediate medical evaluation if you see signs of delirium.

Dementia

According to Robert Butler et al. (1998), "between 2% and 5% of the population over the age of 65 has some form of dementia," and the likelihood increases with age (p. 129). Whereas delirium is characterized by a disturbance in a person's consciousness, dementia is characterized by a number of problems and involves memory disturbances, such as loss of long- or short-term memory. In fact, problems with memory may be the most noticeable sign of this condition.

Think of the three As when looking at dementia:

1. *Aphasia.* The inability to understand what is said or to express oneself
2. *Apraxia.* The inability to accomplish purposeful movements required to care for oneself
3. *Agnosia.* The inability to comprehend sensory data even though the senses are intact; for example, the inability to recognize common objects

In addition, the person may have trouble with executive functioning, that is, with making decisions and taking care of the details of daily living.

People with dementia sometimes have trouble taking care of themselves. They may not be able to handle simple tasks, even though they do not appear to have any motor impairment. They may be unable to make simple decisions. You might find that simple math is now difficult or impossible for a client who has competently balanced his own checkbook for years. Sometimes people with dementia have trouble expressing themselves. They may be unable to think of words or use confusing phrases. They may also have difficulty understanding what is said to them.

Family and friends are likely to complain that clients with dementia are forgetful. They may not be able to name familiar objects. It is not unusual for them to repeat the same story or the same question. Sometimes they misplace things and get lost in places they should know well.

Many older people jokingly refer to having a "senior moment" because they forgot a familiar name or misplaced something important. Such incidents do not necessarily indicate the person is in the beginning stages of dementia or delirium. For the case manager, however, these can be early signals and bear further observation and inquiry. In other words, what family and friends can dismiss, the case manager would make note of and continue to observe or investigate.

Other Possible Symptoms

Many times people suffering from dementia appear depressed. The family may report that the client has lost interest in things that used to be important or that the person seems to have withdrawn. You might also hear that the person's personality has changed. For instance, he or she may have become tactless, blurting out socially inappropriate comments or snapping at others. Any combination of these symptoms usually brings the person into contact with social services, since they often impair the person's ability to function independently, socially and occupationally.

Onset

The onset of dementia is a slow, gradual course. When you take the history, people close to the client with dementia will describe a gradual decline in mental functioning.

Libby began to have problems remembering insignificant details in her 60s. She would joke about her inability to recall names and phone numbers. Gradually she began to have trouble with small routines. Instructions from her bank about a new credit card made her anxious and seemingly confused. Her daughter found her unwilling even to read the information thoughtfully. In more and more instances, Libby's daughter began to manage small tasks her mother had managed competently in the past. At times they both dismissed Libby's failure to understand and handle things as normal aging or "the world has just gotten too complicated."

On several occasions, however, Libby's daughter noticed that her mother was not fully following the conversation. Libby appeared not to be able to recall fully what was said only minutes before, and she did not participate spontaneously, often sitting by and looking straight ahead. It was after a Christmas gathering that the daughter brought Libby in for tests and an evaluation. Medical tests were inconclusive, but Libby's decline worsened. New surroundings confused her. New demands or changes in routine made her anxious and afraid. She stopped elementary routines such as dressing in the morning and eating regular meals, something she had always done.

The daughter took Libby home to live with her and placed Libby in a day program for individuals with Alzheimer's. In time Libby was unable to remember information given to her just minutes before. She failed to recognize her grandchildren and did not remember their names. Her speech became garbled, and she was frequently disoriented in surroundings other than the day program or her daughter's home.

Common Causes

There are a number of causes of dementia that you can find listed in the *DSM-IV-TR*. These causes usually can be diagnosed through laboratory tests and imaging. Some common underlying medical causes are:

strokes	HIV disease
Parkinson's disease	Huntington's disease
head trauma	other medical conditions

Characteristics of Dementia

Dementia of the Alzheimer's type is a diagnosis of exclusion. If no underlying cause can be found for the client's deteriorating cognitive functioning and all suspected causes have been ruled out after extensive medical testing, then dementia of the Alzheimer's type is generally the diagnosis given. There are two subtypes: *with early onset,* if the deterioration began before age 65, and *with late onset* if the deterioration began after age 65.

To understand the difference between normal forgetfulness and the memory loss of dementia, take the example of misplacing your car keys. Normally you can retrace your whereabouts and remember where you might have left them. The person with dementia, however, has absolutely no memory of where he or she has been. As another example, while the normal person might forget certain details of a family reunion but remember them when prompted, the person with dementia will never remember the details even when others remind him or her about them.

One difficulty you will face as a case manager is the tendency of family members and even medical personnel to diagnose many older people suffering from delirium or dementia as having Alzheimer's. You may know that significant medical testing could turn up causes for a person's problem that, if addressed, might reverse or arrest the condition. In such a case, you will need to advocate for the best interests of your client.

DEPRESSION AND GROWING OLDER

Depression is not always associated with growing older, but you may encounter family and friends who are not inclined to seek help or an explanation for it, assuming that it is a normal part of aging and of becoming "senile." In fact, depression may be a condition your client has contended with earlier in life. It can also be a response to stress or loss in a person's life, regardless of age. Signs of depression, or what appears to be depression, may occur from a loss of hearing or vision that prevents the person from participating in normal conversation and activities. Depression may also be a part of delirium or dementia where cognitive problems have caused the person to withdraw from social contact.

Depression in the elderly can be a sign of other difficulties as well, for instance, loneliness and isolation, or in some cases endocrine or hormonal imbalances. Drug and alcohol abuse may be the cause. Clients also may use drugs and alcohol to self-medicate the depression. Depression in older people also can result from the many losses they have suffered.

Older people, particularly older men, have a higher risk of suicide when depressed than do younger people. According to the Pfizer U.S. Pharmaceutical Group (Jefferson & Greist, 1996), "Older people make up about 12% of the population in the United States, but account for 20% of all suicides." Long-term illness, chronic pain, and being all alone can contribute to making an older person a greater risk for suicide. In addition, there is some evidence that if depression is left untreated for a long period of time, dementia may follow.

Always take signs of depression seriously. Seek the medical evaluations needed to find out why the person is depressed. Include a psychiatric evaluation and medical tests that might indicate an underlying medial condition. Look at recent stressors you might be able to address in your care plan, and find ways for the person to relieve loneliness. Older people may not know how to relieve their depression, but your intervention can restore them to better functioning and richer, fuller lives.

ASSESSMENT AND SUPPORT FOR THE CAREGIVER

When you are assessing the situation of an older person, it is very important to look carefully at the caregiver's situation as well. According to the National Family Caregivers Association's (1997) survey of caregivers, 82% of all caregivers were female. A large number of them were caring for a spouse, usually with no children at home. Eighty percent of the caregiving was done at home. Although the caregivers felt they had discovered inner strength and learned new skills, many of them (67%) also felt considerable frustration. Forty-one percent of the respondents said they had more back pain, 51% more sleeplessness, and 61% more depression. This gives us a picture of what we are likely to find in a home assessment where one spouse is caring for another and both are elderly.

Caregivers are likely to become drained, and sometimes may be barely able to carry on adequately. Both the caregiver and the client may be at risk and require intervention.

Many caregivers (43%) reported feeling isolated because of their caregiving responsibilities. This is one area you need to explore with caregivers, looking for any support they might have and supplying support where needed as part of your plan. Seventy-six percent of the respondents to the survey said that a major difficulty for them was not having consistent help from family members. This means that even when you find some support among family and friends, it is likely to be unpredictable and insufficient. It should not be considered the only support for the caregiver.

Lack of support and assistance are primary reasons for the abuse of older people by their caretakers.

One evening after a local baseball game, an old man was still sitting in the grandstand in his wheelchair. The stands were cleared of fans, and after waiting for some time for someone to come and take the man home, the stadium personnel called the local police. That evening the man was taken to the nearby hospital, and then transferred to the county nursing home while authorities and social service workers looked for his family. He appeared to be well cared for and was adequately dressed for the cool evening. He also looked like he had been well fed.

In time it was discovered that his wife had taken him to the game as a treat, but feeling utterly overwhelmed and exhausted with her caretaking responsibilities, she had walked away, assuming correctly that someone else would take over. Once she was located, it was discovered that she had been caring for her husband around the clock for six years as he had grown more and more dependent. He refused to consider transfer to a nursing facility when she approached the subject, and she had no idea about where to turn for help. She was unaware of the services available to her in the community. Finally, in desperation she had abandoned her husband.

What workers found significant about this situation was that the caregiver appeared to be in somewhat worse shape than her husband. She looked worn and thin, with some signs of self-neglect. Examination revealed that she was dangerously underweight, suffered from chronic lower back pain, probably from lifting, and was depressed.

Probably the most difficult part of dementia for families and caregivers to deal with is the personality change that occurs in the person with dementia. Such changes can be devastating for the caregiver and those closest to the person.

Alice and her father had been close all her life. He had given her a keen wit and a good sense of humor. When she decided to go to law school, he supported her decision, and he was there for her as a loving support when her first child died. When her father began to show signs of dementia, Alice wrote them off as normal aspects of aging. She took her father home to live with her in order to give him the supervision he needed, and as he grew worse, she hired a homemaker during the day to take care of him.

Gradually, however, his personality changed. Alice's father began to call her a slut and a tramp. He accused her of going through his things. When she came home late, he accused her of running around with other men. He did not seem to recognize his grandchildren anymore, roaring at them to get out of his room and acting as if they frightened him. Alice and her husband were devastated. On rare occasions, she and her father were able to resume their close relationship, but these moments became fewer and fewer.

Eventually Alice placed her father in a nursing home, in part because his ranting at her was so upsetting. Alice's husband confided to the case manager that Alice needed help with her feelings about her father's personality change. The case manager was able to refer the couple and their children to a family therapist, where they all sorted out what had happened in order to put his behavior into the perspective of his illness.

ELDER ABUSE

Why Does It Happen?

There are several reasons elder abuse happens. When these reasons are present in the history you take, they should alert you to the possibility that the older person is, or may be in the future, at risk for abuse by those responsible for the person's care or involved in the person's life in some way.

One of the primary reasons for abuse is the stress of the caregiver. Some caregivers take care of a person for 24 hours a day, often contending with the person's incontinence and interruption of the caregiver's sleep, in addition to physical strain from lifting. Finances may be limited or dwindling as a result of a long illness. The caregiver may have physical problems and very little support from others. If older people are frail or disabled, their greater dependence places them at greater risk for abuse, particularly if they are unable to control or escape from a situation that has grown abusive.

Sometimes older people are in the homes of children with unsettled personal problems of their own that make their lives disruptive. This can cause the caregiver to be more impatient and intolerant of the added stress of caring for the older person. Older people who require considerable assistance and are unable to take steps to protect themselves may experience abuse in such situations. In addition, a family that has always had violence as part of the way family members relate to one another will often use violence while caring for an older relative.

Defining Elder Abuse

In one state, the law defines abuse as "the infliction of injury, unreasonable confinement, intimidation or punishment with resulting physical harm, pain or mental anguish; or the willful deprivation of necessary goods or services to maintain physical or mental health; or any sexual act, harassment or placing one in reasonable fear of bodily injury" (AARP, 1992). The American Association of Retired Persons (AARP) lists several kinds of abuse:

- *Passive neglect.* Here the caretaker does not intend to inflict harm or distress on the older person, but does so through unintentional failure to adequately care for the person.
- *Psychological abuse.* The older person is subjected to demeaning comments, name-calling, insults, or humiliation. The older person is ignored, frightened, threatened, or isolated. The result is mental anguish and distress.
- *Material and financial abuse.* In this situation, the person is exploited, either illegally or unethically. Generally funds and property belonging to the older person are taken for the personal gain of another person. Often these are obtained under false pretenses.
- *Active neglect.* Here the neglect is intentional, and the result is usually physical and emotional stress and even injury to the neglected person. Abandonment,

denial of food or medication, and refusal to tend to the older person's personal hygiene are considered intentional.

- *Physical abuse.* With physical abuse, the older person is subjected to physical pain or injury through "physical coercion, confinement, slapping, bruising, sexually molesting, cutting, lacerating, burning, restraining, pushing, or shoving, etc."

Reporting Elder Abuse

Some states have laws requiring that those who are aware of elder abuse report it to a state or local protective unit. Whether or not reporting is required by law in your state, you are ethically responsible for reporting such abuse and for helping to place the person in a protected situation.

Never ignore such things as bruises, burn marks, and broken bones when you see them on an older person. Older people do have accidents, and they may be more likely to fall than younger people. Nevertheless, remain alert to the possibility of abuse, even from individuals who appear to be pleasant and willing caretakers. Everyone, including seemingly dedicated caregivers, can reach the end of their rope at some point. Question the caregivers, and follow up on any suspicions of abuse you might have.

Assignment

Find out what the law is in your state regarding reporting of elder abuse. Find out whether reporting is voluntary or mandatory, and to whom reports should be made.

Clues

Obvious clues such as broken bones and bruises are noticeable. Here are some other clues to note:

In the Older Person

- Abrasions on both arms or wrists, or elsewhere, from being restrained
- Poor hygiene
- Malnourishment or dehydration
- Glasses or dentures missing
- Over- or undermedication
- Confusion, anxiety, being withdrawn or timid, or depression
- Seldom or never seen

In the Older Person's Family or Caregiver

- Neglects medication or medical care when needed
- Fails to keep the older person properly dressed and clean
- Displays violent or excessive anger toward the older person
- Is verbally abusive
- Has a history of personal problems
- Gives conflicting stories abut what is happening to the older person

Potential Financial Exploitation

- Sudden bank account withdrawals or closures
- Abrupt change in the older person's will
- Older person lives in poverty or without proper care in spite of adequate financial resources
- Strangers accompany the older person to the bank
- Caregiver displays sudden newly found wealth
- Sudden transfer of property

CASE MANAGERS' HELPFUL INTERVENTIONS

Case managers can help older people and their caregivers in many aspects of their lives. Following are some of the ways case managers can be particularly helpful.

Helping Families Cope with Dementia

Often case managers can help the family see that the personality change in the older person with dementia is a symptom of the illness, and not something to be taken personally. You can show the family how to respond sympathetically. Teach the communications skills you learned in *Fundamentals of Case Management Practice* (Summers, 2001) that validate the person, rather than confronting or scolding the person. Help the family use distraction with their older member, such as looking at old photographs or movies or reminiscing about other times. Sometimes folding wash or doing other repetitive chores can have a calming effect. You might want to model these approaches when you visit in the home.

Helping Clients Cope with Grief

As noted, loss is one of most common features of growing older. Grief should be understood as a journey through intense pain. The most important thing you can do is let people talk and give them permission to grieve. Let people feel what they feel. They are in transition, and what they feel today may not be what they feel tomorrow. Grief is the way a broken heart is healed.

Begin by asking open questions about the person who died or the item that was lost. You can say, "Tell me a little about your husband" or "Tell me something about your friend." Your client will welcome the chance to tell you how important the life of their friend or spouse was to them. If your client was a caretaker for a long period of time, his or her feelings for the person who died may have diminished as the caregiver ultimately became tired or angry. You can validate those feelings for your client by saying something like "You must have been exhausted" or "It must have been so stressful to have these long nights when you got no sleep at all."

Next help the person establish significance. Not every relationship is a happy or loving one. Sometimes needs are met, and sometimes they are not. It is finding the balance, a realistic and accurate understanding of the significance of the relationship, that is important. What did the deceased mean to your client? What, in their daily life together, did your client take for granted? When a mate dies, the client has to provide things for him- or herself that the mate formerly provided. As days pass, your client will find more and more things he or she took for granted. The loss grows, and so does the personal pain. As the person talks about the relationship, these should become evident (Manning, 1993).

Expect your clients who are in grief to feel all alone. They often say there are a million things they would like to tell the deceased person. You might help your clients plan a memorial or funeral for the deceased person, during which you would help them to include friends and relatives. It is helpful for your clients to know how much the deceased person meant to others.

After the death of Maria's husband, her case manager was there. The case manager had worked with Maria and the family through her husband's long and difficult final illness. Everyone needed to talk and establish significance. The case manager met with the family the night before the funeral. They sat at the funeral home together, and the case manager encouraged everyone to talk about the father and husband who was no longer among them. They told stories about him, and they laughed and cried together. Each of them remembered special moments in their relationship with the deceased. This wise case manager was able to help a grieving family establish significance at a crucial point in their grieving.

Once you have done the initial work of establishing the significance of the loss, your clients can move more easily into the grieving process.

Helping Clients Cope with Guilt

Guilt and self-blame are often a part of growing older. People think of things they wish they had done differently or things they think they should have done. Regrets and sorrow may be a part of your clients' concerns. There are two kinds of guilt: unrealistic and realistic.

Unrealistic guilt happens when people are too hard on themselves. They may take a very human mistake and blow it up into criminal proportions. At the time a spouse dies, the surviving spouse may chastise herself for not doing more, for not giving better care, or for her feelings of annoyance and impatience. Help clients to see that we all have room for improvement and that all of us could have loved better, done more, and acted more wisely. In the actual moment, however, we all pretty much do our best, given our limitations. One of our limitations is that we cannot predict what will happen in the future.

Then there is realistic guilt, the kind that happens because a person really is responsible for a death or an accident. Clients will tell you it would have been easier to be the victim than to have been responsible because of carelessness. Help clients to see that all of us are negligent at some point in our lives, but not every negligent act turns out tragically so we do not always remember those times. We live the best way we can, and being negligent at times is very human. Most of us do not deliberately set out to harm another person.

People who are suffering from realistic guilt need to be allowed, at some point in their lives, to move on. Allowing others to attack them personally is not helpful. Instead, assist them in getting the help they need to resolve the issues surrounding the guilt and to avoid self-destructive behavior, such as drinking or taking drugs. Provide continuing acceptance of your clients. Sometimes people act as if they should have known what was going to happen when they had no real way of doing so. Ask about the guilt using an "I" message, such as "I guess where I'm having trouble is understanding how you could have known that before it happened. To me it sounds as if you are relying on hindsight, which you couldn't have had at the time." Many times people blame themselves entirely for what happened, acting as if the other person had no choice and no responsibility in the matter. An "I" message you could use with these clients is: "I can see as you talk to me about this that you feel very responsible for what happened. Where I am having some trouble is where the other person fits into all this. From my point of view, I think he had some choice in the matter. What do you think?"

Life Review

Ask your clients to tell you about their lives or some aspect of their earlier lives. Listen to them carefully, asking questions and expressing an interest. Older people tend to reflect on and review their lives, a tendency that is thought to be universal. It is not always possible, however, to do this alone and still obtain real therapeutic value from it.

The life review serves a purpose at the end of life. It allows people to return to and resolve old conflicts; they can put events into perspective and come to see that they did their best. They also can take pride in all they accomplished, and decide what to do with the time left as they prepare to die. Although younger people often have trouble listening to these reflections, careful listening is important. This process is enormously healing, allowing the older person to prepare for death with greater peace of mind. It should be part of the mental health care of all older people.

Leaving a Legacy

Older people often want to leave something of themselves behind when they die. Their legacy may be their children, their grandchildren, a work of art, or a garden. It may include personal wisdom for those who come after them. You can help older people leave this type of legacy by helping them to develop ways of sharing their ideas and opinions. For instance, you might buy a notebook and invite the older person to write letters to grandchildren that the children will receive after the person dies. The letters or notations would contain the thoughts and opinions the older person believes are important to share. Another idea is to take an oral history. These tapes are then preserved for the next generations. If older people want to discuss what material possessions to leave to others, listening supportively can help them sort that out. (It is, of course, illegal and unethical for case managers to take anything from an older person.)

Providing Opportunities for the Elder to Function

Encourage older people to take the role of guiding and sponsoring younger people. Sometimes, because of lack of contact with others, the professional serves in this capacity. Older people have a natural propensity to want to share with younger people the knowledge they gained from all their experiences and the challenges they faced. Giving guidance to younger people enhances self-esteem and allows older people to feel connected to the next generations. Older people find being ignored or denigrated by younger people a devastating experience. Some older people view younger people with envy and distrust. The elder function is not an option for them. For those who seem interested in younger people and appear to want such a relationship, it is helpful to develop opportunities for the elder function to take place. Assisting in schools and acting as a tutor, coach, scout leader, or mentor are some of the ways this can be accomplished. Look for programs in the community where your clients can serve.

Pets

Although case managers do not provide pets, and generally it is not part of the case manager's responsibilities to help care for a pet, it is important for case managers to respect their clients' need for a pet. Research is quite clear that those with a pet have fewer illnesses, lower blood pressure, and tend to remain more active and independent. The dependence of pets on older people and the love shared between people and their pets should not be underestimated or dismissed. If your client simply must give up a pet, you should make every effort to see that the pet is placed in a situation where it is not likely to be euthanized. If an older client appears to need a pet and is able to take care of one, you should encourage your client to obtain one that is easily managed.

COMMON SERVICES AVAILABLE FOR OLDER PERSONS

As with any case management position, case managers who work with older people should become familiar with what is in their community for older adults. Piecing together a variety of services may make the difference between an older adult being able to stay in his or her own home or going into an institutional home of some sort. Following is a discussion of the common services available in most communities. As a case manager, it would be your responsibility to find out who in your community offers these services and to look for additional, useful supports your community might offer. The services discussed here are formal services. The good case manager would supplement these with informal supports in the family, neighborhood, and community.

In-Home Care

For some older people, care in their home will extend the time they can remain in their home. In-home care could be several sessions a week with a physical therapist or a pulmonary technician. It might be a number of sessions with an occupational therapist who helps the client learn again to navigate in his or her home after a stroke or a fall. It might be several mornings a week with a nursing assistant who helps clients bathe and tend to other personal activities.

Visiting Nurse Association

Nurses from visiting nurse associations come to the home to perform nursing responsibilities such as caring for a wound, checking on a pacemaker, or following up on oxygen or an IV line. Their work is more sophisticated than a nursing assistant's work would be.

Homemaker Services

Homemakers come to a person's home at regular intervals to do light housework and assist in meal preparation. The frequency of the visits generally is related to the person's insurance coverage, what the person can afford to pay, and what is covered in public programs for senior citizens. In one situation, a woman who broke her arm had homemaker service for two hours in the morning and two hours at night. In the morning, the homemaker helped the woman dress and make her bed, and she prepared breakfast and a lunch before she left. In the evening, she prepared dinner, cleaned up the kitchen, and helped the woman get ready for bed. The cost for this service was covered by the client herself and lasted only as long as it took for the client to adjust to working with a broken arm.

Meals-on-Wheels

Some older people are unable to prepare a meal or do not eat regularly because they are alone. Meals-on-Wheels provides regular meals for such people, and often sends out extra prepared food people can use on weekends or when it snows and delivery cannot be made. This program provides one hot meal a day so that older people do not need to prepare that meal themselves.

Senior Centers

Older people often enjoy one another's company at centers set up for them to socialize. Many senior centers serve a hot noonday meal. Often they are open five days a week, but some open only once a week. They can be provided by a public agency or by churches or civic groups. In addition to meals, a variety of activities are provided. Many of them are useful to the community, such as helping out at a nearby elementary school. Square dancing, bus trips, bingo, self-help workshops, support groups, and choruses are just some of the many activities that a senior center can provide. Some centers are staffed by a director, but some are run by the seniors themselves.

Transportation

Many communities set up transportation services for senior citizens and the disabled. These small buses or vans pick up and deliver people right at their doors. Transportation services help older people keep doctors' appointments and do light shopping.

Low-Income Plans and Senior Discounts

Some states and local governments have plans for individuals who are older and on low, fixed incomes. For instance, many states have developed prescription plans or discounts for certain services. In addition, merchants, banks, and restaurants often have discount offers for senior citizens.

Adult Day Care

This service is provided for families who do not feel comfortable leaving an older person at home alone. Individuals showing early signs of dementia often benefit from going to adult day-care centers. These centers feed people and dispense medication as part of the daily regimen, and they also provide activities that stimulate memory.

Lifeline

The lifeline is an emergency response system. Older people can wear a call device around the neck, or attach it to themselves in some other way, and use the device to call for help if they fall or have any other emergency. Sometimes these are provided by a public agency for low-income clients to help them stay in their own homes.

Personal Care Home

Personal care homes are places where older people live. For the most part, the residents in these homes take care of themselves, but activities are planned for them and meals are provided. Generally residents have rooms or small apartments.

Assisted Living

Assisted living arrangements are, for the most part, the same as personal care homes. The person is largely responsible for activities of daily living, but joins other residents for meals and activities. In addition, there may be supervision of medication.

Domiciliary Care

In this situation, an older person is placed in the home of a family who takes the older person in as part of their family and provides the supervision that may be needed. The family is generally paid for their services. Individuals who want to remain in the community but are lonely or in need of minor supervision can benefit from such a placement.

Nursing Home

When a person cannot manage at home, nursing homes become a useful alternative. Helping clients adjust to leaving home is a lengthy process that cannot be rushed. The transition should move at a comfortable pace to help the older person accept the need for the move. Family members may be in denial or be reluctant to spend the money for a nursing home. They may not be able or willing to spend the time needed to keep the older person in his or her own home, but they may feel considerable anguish about the person going to a nursing home, especially if at one time they promised the client he or she would never have to go to a home. In many cases, it takes time for everyone to accept a nursing home as the solution. Case managers need to be patient during this time when clients and family members are changing the way they think about the situation.

Palliative Care

Palliative care is care that assists the person who is dying to die comfortably. It is most often provided by hospice services in communities, but hospitals and nursing homes often provide it as well. In some instances, the dying person can be moved to a hospice facility. In other situations, the person is cared for at home, and family members are given considerable support in providing this care and preparing for the death.

Protective Services

Protective services are designed to protect older people who are unable to protect themselves from abuse, neglect, exploitation, or abandonment. Typically an older person comes to the attention of an agency when he or she, or someone close to that person, reports possible abuse to the agency. In many states, human service and medical personnel are obligated by law to report suspected abuse. The agency handling protective services will investigate and take steps to protect the older person.

DOING YOUR ASSESSMENT AND FOLLOWING YOUR CLIENT

You have information now to develop a believable older client. Use the assessment form to create a credible older person who might come to you seeking services or whose family or close friends might contact you on the client's behalf. Use the space for interviewer comments to elaborate on the problems that were discussed during your intake and assessment of this client. You can make a referral to programs and services you feel will best serve your client. As you monitor your hypothetical client, you can draw from the information in this chapter to define the kinds of plausible problems and common issues your client and those closest to your client are likely to encounter.

EXERCISES

Making Good Assessments

Instructions: In the following vignettes, jot down those points you would include in your case notes for each client and those points you would recommend for further investigation. In each case, note what your hunch is about what might be going on with the client.

1. Mr. Pierce is seen in his home by you, his case manager. You find he has definite psychomotor retardation. Worried about his condition, you ask him to do some simple arithmetic and find that he cannot do the calculations. He tells you that his neighbor, Potter Blain, was over to see him last night. In fact, Potter Blain, another older client, was moved to a nursing home eight days before. All along Mr. Blain's deteriorating condition and his apparent need to move upset Mr. Pierce greatly. During this interview, Mr. Pierce tells you that you are asking him far too many questions and says vaguely that one cannot be too careful who one talks to these days. This seems unusual to you because only two weeks before, Mr. Pierce sought your help in preparing to take his taxes to the accountant, and he showed no suspiciousness of you then or at any time before. You know he has been taking methyldopa for hypertension and that, several weeks ago, Mr. Pierce's doctor gave him haloperidol (a popular tranquilizer) to help him feel better about the failing health of his good friend, Mr. Blain.

Your case note would read:

You would recommend the following be investigated further:

Your hunch about what might be wrong here:

2. Mrs. Rodriquez helps out at a senior center as a volunteer. She has been visiting the center ever since her husband died. She is efficient and has a good sense of humor. She went to the doctor for a medical checkup when she caught a bad cold that would not go away. She was treating her cold with an anticongestant. The doctor discovered at that time that she had high blood pressure and put her on medication for hypertension. About a week later, she returned to the center, but she was not herself. Center personnel called you, and you went out and met with Mrs. Rodriquez. She seemed unsteady and unsure of herself. Tasks she was used to doing easily seemed to perplex her, although ultimately she did perform them with some coaching. The center director confided to you that Mrs. Rodriquez had been working on an inventory of the game closet. Today when she went to type up the lists she had made, she did not recognize her own handwriting. "Did I type those?" she asked, while looking at what she had written. While you are talking to her, Mrs. Rodriquez gives you the impression she believes she is at home, and not at the center when she informs you that she is going next door to feed her neighbor's cat.

Your case note would read:

You would recommend the following be investigated further:

Your hunch about what might be wrong here:

3. You are called to the emergency room and told to do something with an elderly man lying on a litter. He was found lying on the street along a curb. He had slurred speech and jerky, unsteady movements. Sometimes he seemed to briefly lose consciousness. The emergency room personnel are recommending that he go to a detoxification center because he is obviously intoxicated. You note the man is well dressed and was found one block from a high-rise apartment building for senior citizens. The man tells you, in a somewhat garbled way, that he was going out to dinner at the diner across the street and he "got this feeling in his head." After spending time with him, you are not convinced that he has been drinking.

Your case note would read:

You would recommend the following be investigated further:

Your hunch about what might be wrong here:

4. You are asked to visit Mrs. Perkins because the mail carrier reported that she seemed sick when he saw her this morning. You find Mrs. Perkins lying under a pile of blankets even though it is a hot July day. She has her heat on and tells you that she is cold and just cannot warm up. The neighbor looks in and tells you that

Mrs. Perkins has recently "gone daft." The neighbor strongly recommends that you have Mrs. Perkins placed in a home. To you, Mrs. Perkins seems fine except for her need to keep warm.

Your case note would read:

You would recommend the following be investigated further:

Your hunch about what might be wrong here:

5. Mr. Baldini gets out of bed angry every morning, which upsets his family. He lives with his daughter's family in a small apartment over the garage and appears to be quite self-sufficient. The family has a number of young children. Some days they drop in to see Mr. Baldini, and some days they do not. In the last few months, he has been surly and uncooperative in the morning and not inclined to get dressed or follow his usual morning routines. The family notes that as the day progresses, he seems to recover somewhat, particularly if he comes over for a meal or two with them. The next morning he is the same. The family tells you they think it is a ploy on Mr. Baldini's part to get to see more of the family, and they express guilt over how busy they are and how they have let him follow his own routines and interests quite apart from them. You are not sure that this is manipulation on Mr. Baldini's part.

Your case note would read:

You would recommend the following be investigated further:

Your hunch about what might be wrong here:

6. Mr. Cramer is sitting in his living room when you arrive to see how he is doing. You are stopping by in response to a neighbor's telephone call. The neighbor told you that Mr. Cramer has stopped coming out to talk to the neighbors the way he always did in the evening, and that the evening before, Mr. Cramer was rude and weepy and told her to "Just leave me alone!" When you see him, he answers your inquiries in monosyllables, but he does say that he does not know what has "gotten into" him. Gradually he tells you, "I can't see the TV, and I can't see things in the yard like I did. I don't go down in the cellar anymore because I can't see the stairs." It looks like he has been sleeping on the sofa rather than in his bed, and he confirms this. He says, "What's the use of going up to bed? I wake up at 3:00 in the morning and can't get back to sleep." He tells you that he cannot remember when he ate last. His clothes are dirty, and he appears not to have washed recently.

Your case note would read:

You would recommend the following be investigated further:

Your hunch about what might be wrong here:

Using the *DSM-IV-TR*

Instructions: Look at the situations that follow and discuss what diagnosis would be appropriate in each of these cases. For more information on how case managers use the *DSM-IV-TR,* look at Chapter 16 in *Fundamentals of Case Management Practice* (Summers, 2001). Use the chapter in your *DSM-IV-TR* on anxiety disorders.

1. Mrs. Jackson began taking a new prescription for inflammation of her joints. The medication was a cortisone product. Several days later, Mrs. Jackson seemed confused and restless. She was not sleeping; instead, she was wandering around the house at night. Her confusion seemed more severe at times but faded at others. At times, she seemed unaware of what was going on around her.

2. Mr. Bigelow was found wandering in the streets by the city police. He was well-dressed, but confused. He did not seem to understand that the police wanted to help him. Police officers spoke to neighbors and learned that Mr. Bigelow had been living independently in a high-rise apartment building for senior citizens. He was president of the residents' council. At the hospital, Mr. Bigelow was found to have appendicitis and a fever.

3. Over the years, Miss Booth seemed to lose interest in the things around her. She was slightly forgetful, but after retirement and in the years that followed, there was a gradual deterioration. A niece told the case manager that Miss Booth seemed to just gradually become more and more forgetful. It also became hard for her to find her way to familiar places. She began to need more help to accomplish chores and tasks she had carried out competently before. For instance, she made minor mathematical errors in balancing her checkbook that made no sense. After having always cooked for herself, she seemed confused about the stove and how to make a meal. "None of this happened overnight," the niece told the case manager. Just little by little she went downhill. Medical tests were done, but the results were not conclusive.

Assessment for Senior Citizens
Wildwood Case Management Unit

PERSONAL INFORMATION

Client name ______________________

Address ______________________

____

____

____

Social Security # ______________________

ID # ______________________

Birth date ______________________

Phone ______________________

Language assist needed for assessment?
Yes [ ] No [ ]

Referred by ______________________

Emergency contact ______________________

Presenting problem ______________________

____

____

____

____

____

____

____

____

____

____

____

____

Requesting ______________________

____

____

Location of interview ______________________

Present for interview: Client [ ] Significant other [ ] Other [ ]

Names ______________________

____

____

MEDICAL HISTORY

Does the client have any of the following conditions?

Eyes

Glaucoma Yes [ ] No [ ] Receiving medical attention [ ]

Cataracts Yes [ ] No [ ] Receiving medical attention [ ]

Vision Good [ ] Fair [ ] Poor [ ] Vision aids [ ]

Last exam ______________________

Clinician ______________________

____

____

Ears

Wax buildup Yes [ ] No [ ] Receiving medical attention [ ]

Hearing Good [ ] Fair [ ] Poor [ ] Hearing aids [ ]

Last exam ______________________

Clinician ______________________

____

____

Nose

Deviated septum Yes [ ] No [ ] Receiving medical attention [ ]

Polyps Yes [ ] No [ ] Receiving medical attention [ ]

Nose bleeds Yes [ ] No [ ] Receiving medical attention [ ]

Postnasal drip Yes [ ] No [ ] Receiving medical attention [ ]

Last exam ______________________

Clinician ______________________

____

____

Throat

Dysphagia Yes [ ] No [ ] Receiving medical attention [ ]

Aphasic Yes [ ] No [ ] Receiving medical attention [ ]

Snoring Yes [ ] No [ ] Receiving medical attention [ ]

Speech Good [ ] Fair [ ] Poor [ ] Hearing aids [ ]

Last exam ______________________

Clinician ______________________

____

____

Mouth

Missing teeth	Yes [ ]	No [ ]	Receiving medical attention [ ]
Dentures	Yes [ ]	No [ ]	Receiving medical attention [ ]
Gum disease	Yes [ ]	No [ ]	Receiving medical attention [ ]
Dentation	Good [ ]	Fair [ ]	Poor [ ]

Last exam ______________________________

Clinician ______________________________

____

____

Neck

Laryngectomy	Yes [ ]	No [ ]	Receiving medical attention [ ]

Last exam ______________________________

Clinician ______________________________

____

____

Lungs/Breathing

Tuberculosis	Yes [ ]	No [ ]	Receiving medical attention [ ]
Bronchitis	Yes [ ]	No [ ]	Receiving medical attention [ ]
Chronic obstructive pulmonary disease	Yes [ ]	No [ ]	Receiving medical attention [ ]
Emphysema	Yes [ ]	No [ ]	Receiving medical attention [ ]
Allergies	Yes [ ]	No [ ]	Receiving medical attention [ ]
Orthopnea	Yes [ ]	No [ ]	Receiving medical attention [ ]
Dyspnea	Yes [ ]	No [ ]	Receiving medical attention [ ]

Last exam ______________________________

Clinician ______________________________

____

____

Heart

Angina	Yes [ ]	No [ ]	Receiving medical attention [ ]
Irregular heart rate	Yes [ ]	No [ ]	Receiving medical attention [ ]
Congestive heart failure	Yes [ ]	No [ ]	Receiving medical attention [ ]
High blood pressure	Yes [ ]	No [ ]	Receiving medical attention [ ]
Heart attack	Yes [ ]	No [ ]	Receiving medical attention [ ]

Last exam ______________________________

Clinician ______________________________

____

____

Circulation

Leg ulcers	Yes [ ]	No [ ]	Receiving medical attention [ ]
Edema	Yes [ ]	No [ ]	Receiving medical attention [ ]
Vericosities	Yes [ ]	No [ ]	Receiving medical attention [ ]
Vascular disease	Yes [ ]	No [ ]	Receiving medical attention [ ]
Cerebral insufficiency	Yes [ ]	No [ ]	Receiving medical attention [ ]
Thrombosis	Yes [ ]	No [ ]	Receiving medical attention [ ]
Embolism	Yes [ ]	No [ ]	Receiving medical attention [ ]

Last exam ______________________________

Clinician ______________________________

____

____

Lymph Nodes

Enlarged	Yes [ ]	No [ ]	Receiving medical attention [ ]

Last exam ______________________________

Clinician ______________________________

____

____

Extremities

Paralysis	Yes [ ]	No [ ]	Receiving medical attention [ ]
Missing limbs	Yes [ ]	No [ ]	Receiving medical attention [ ]
Weakness	Yes [ ]	No [ ]	Receiving medical attention [ ]

Last exam ______________________________

Clinician ______________________________

____

____

Gastrointestinal

Ulcer	Yes [ ]	No [ ]	Receiving medical attention [ ]
Bleeding	Yes [ ]	No [ ]	Receiving medical attention [ ]
Colitis	Yes [ ]	No [ ]	Receiving medical attention [ ]
Intestinal problems	Yes [ ]	No [ ]	Receiving medical attention [ ]

Diverticulosis Yes [ ] No [ ] Receiving medical attention [ ]

Jaundice Yes [ ] No [ ] Receiving medical attention [ ]

Gall bladder Yes [ ] No [ ] Receiving medical attention [ ]

Last exam ____________________

Clinician ____________________

____

____

Hernia Yes [ ] No [ ] Receiving medical attention [ ]

Last exam ____________________

Clinician ____________________

____

____

Genitalia Male

Prostate problems Yes [ ] No [ ] Receiving medical attention [ ]

Last exam ____________________

Clinician ____________________

____

____

Gynecological

Posthysterectomy Yes [ ] No [ ] Receiving medical attention [ ]

Disease of uterus/cervix Yes [ ] No [ ] Receiving medical attention [ ]

Prolapse of uterus Yes [ ] No [ ] Receiving medical attention [ ]

Ulcers of cervix Yes [ ] No [ ] Receiving medical attention [ ]

Last exam ____________________

Clinician ____________________

____

____

Anorectal

Hemorrhoids Yes [ ] No [ ] Receiving medical attention [ ]

Prolapse Yes [ ] No [ ] Receiving medical attention [ ]

Fistulas Yes [ ] No [ ] Receiving medical attention [ ]

Fissures Yes [ ] No [ ] Receiving medical attention [ ]

Last exam ____________________

Clinician ____________________

____

____

Blood Disease

Anemia Yes [ ] No [ ] Receiving medical attention [ ]

Leukemia Yes [ ] No [ ] Receiving medical attention [ ]

Last exam ________________

Clinician ________________

____

____

Musculoskeletal

Effects of fractures Yes [ ] No [ ] Receiving medical attention [ ]

Congenital impairments Yes [ ] No [ ] Receiving medical attention [ ]

Osteoporosis Yes [ ] No [ ] Receiving medical attention [ ]

Osteoarthritis Yes [ ] No [ ] Receiving medical attention [ ]

Rheumatoid arthritis Yes [ ] No [ ] Receiving medical attention [ ]

Contractures Yes [ ] No [ ] Receiving medical attention [ ]

Condition of feet Good [ ] Fair [ ] Poor [ ] Hearing aids [ ]

Last exam ________________

Clinician ________________

____

____

Skin

Dry Yes [ ] No [ ] Receiving medical attention [ ]

Fragile Yes [ ] No [ ] Receiving medical attention [ ]

Rashes Yes [ ] No [ ] Receiving medical attention [ ]

Psoriasis Yes [ ] No [ ] Receiving medical attention [ ]

Open areas Yes [ ] No [ ] Receiving medical attention [ ]

Excoriated areas Yes [ ] No [ ] Receiving medical attention [ ]

Pressure sores Yes [ ] No [ ] Receiving medical attention [ ]

Burns Yes [ ] No [ ] Receiving medical attention [ ]

Bruises Yes [ ] No [ ] Receiving medical attention [ ]

Last exam ________________

Clinician ________________

____

____

Nervous System

Effects of stroke Yes [ ] No [ ] Receiving medical attention [ ]

Parkinson's disease Yes [ ] No [ ] Receiving medical attention [ ]

Cerebral palsy	Yes [ ]	No [ ]	Receiving medical attention [ ]
Muscular dystrophy	Yes [ ]	No [ ]	Receiving medical attention [ ]
Multiple sclerosis	Yes [ ]	No [ ]	Receiving medical attention [ ]
Polio history	Yes [ ]	No [ ]	Receiving medical attention [ ]
Seizures	Yes [ ]	No [ ]	Receiving medical attention [ ]
Epilepsy	Yes [ ]	No [ ]	Receiving medical attention [ ]

Last exam ______________________________

Clinician ______________________________

____

____

Endocrine (Glandular)

Diabetes	Yes [ ]	No [ ]	Receiving medical attention [ ]
Thyroid	Yes [ ]	No [ ]	Receiving medical attention [ ]
Spleen	Yes [ ]	No [ ]	Receiving medical attention [ ]
Pancreas	Yes [ ]	No [ ]	Receiving medical attention [ ]
Liver	Yes [ ]	No [ ]	Receiving medical attention [ ]
Metabolic disorders	Yes [ ]	No [ ]	Receiving medical attention [ ]

Last exam ______________________________

Clinician ______________________________

____

____

Kidney/Urinary Tract

Urinary retention	Yes [ ]	No [ ]	Receiving medical attention [ ]
Infection	Yes [ ]	No [ ]	Receiving medical attention [ ]
Kidney failure	Yes [ ]	No [ ]	Receiving medical attention [ ]
Urgency	Yes [ ]	No [ ]	Receiving medical attention [ ]

Last exam ______________________________

Clinician ______________________________

____

____

Dementia

Alzheimer's disease	Yes [ ]	No [ ]	Receiving medical attention [ ]
Multi-infarct	Yes [ ]	No [ ]	Receiving medical attention [ ]

Last exam ______________________________

Clinician ______________________________

____

____

Communicable Diseases Yes [ ] No [ ] Receiving medical attention [ ]

Type ______________________________

Last exam ______________________________

Clinician ______________________________

____

____

Cancer/Tumors Yes [ ] No [ ] Receiving medical attention [ ]

Last exam ______________________________

Clinician ______________________________

____

____

Recent Surgeries Yes [ ] No [ ] Receiving medical attention [ ]

For ______________________________

Last exam ______________________________

Clinician ______________________________

____

____

Other Disabilities, Health Problems

Specify ______________________________

Last exam ______________________________

Clinician ______________________________

____

____

Substance Abuse

Alcohol Yes [ ] No [ ] Receiving medical attention [ ]

Tobacco Yes [ ] No [ ] Receiving medical attention [ ]

Drugs Yes [ ] No [ ] Receiving medical attention [ ]

Type ______________________________

In treatment? Yes [ ] No [ ]

Clinician/program ______________________________

____

____

Interviewer comments on medical issues:

____

____

____

____

CURRENT MEDICATIONS

Prescription Medications

Medication	Dose/Frequency	Route	For

Over-the-Counter Medications (If Frequently Used)

Medication	Dose/Frequency	Route	For

Date of last medication review by doctor ____________________

Help needed with medications Yes [ ] No [ ]

Setup [ ] Administration [ ] Verbal reminding [ ]

Information [ ] Regular monitoring of effects [ ]

Allergies to medications Yes [ ] No [ ]

Medications ____________________

____

____

THERAPIES, TREATMENTS, AND OTHER SKILLED SERVICES

Service	Ordered	Received
Overall evaluation of care plan		
Overall management of care plan		
Patient education services		
Injection		
Parenteral fluids		
Tube feeding		
Suctioning		
Catheter		
Sterile irrigation		
Decubitus or extensive skin care		
Sterile dressings		
Therapeutic heat treatments		
Initial phase of oxygen or inhalation therapy		
Rehabilitative nursing services		
Therapeutic exercises		
Therapeutic activities		
Gait training or evaluation		
Range of motion exercises		
Ultrasound		
Shortwave or microwave therapy		
Hot packs		
Hydrocollator		
Infrared treatments		
Paraffin baths		
Whirlpool treatments		
Speech therapy		
Audiology		

Interviewer comments on medications, therapies, and treatments:

____

____

ACTIVITIES OF DAILY LIVING

Activity	Independent (no assistance needed)	Uses Assistive Devices (takes long time, great difficulty)	Needs Some Help (setup, coaxing, cueing, supervision)	Maximum Help Needed (or does not do at all)
Teeth care				
Bathing				
Dressing				
Undressing				
Grooming				
Eating				
Getting out of bed				
Getting out of chair				
Toileting				
Bladder management				
Bowel management				
Other				

Medical restrictions that impede activities of daily living:

____

____

____

____

Interviewer comments on activities of daily living:

____

____

____

____

____

____

____

MOBILITY

Activity	Independent (no assistance needed)	Uses Assistive Devices (takes long time, great difficulty)	Needs Some Help (setup, coaxing, cueing, supervision)	Maximum Help Needed (or does not do at all)
Walk indoors				
Walk outdoors				
Climb stairs				
Wheel in chair				
Other				

Impairment is likely to be:

Temporary [ ] Long-term [ ] Permanent [ ] Unknown [ ]

Is client at risk of falling? Yes [ ] No [ ]

Has client fallen recently? Yes [ ] No [ ]

Does client need assistive devices (cane, crutches, braces)? Yes [ ] No [ ]

Does client currently use assistive devices? Yes [ ] No [ ]

Medical restrictions that impede mobility:

____

____

____

____

Interviewer comments on mobility:

____

____

____

CLIENT RATING OF HIS OR HER HEALTH

How is your overall health? Excellent [ ] Good [ ] Fair [ ] Poor [ ]

Compared to a year ago, your health is: Better [ ] About the same [ ] Worse [ ]

How much do your health problems limit your daily activities?

[ ] None [ ] Some [ ] A great deal

INDEPENDENT LIVING

Activity	Independent (no assistance needed)	Independent with Great Difficulty	Assistance of Helper	Unable to Do (helper does)
Preparing meals				
Doing housework				
Doing laundry				
Shopping				
Using transportation				
Driving				
Managing money				
Using the telephone				
Doing home maintenance				

SUPERVISION

How long can client routinely be left alone?

[ ] Indefinitely (client does not need supervision and is independent)

[ ] An entire day and overnight (occasional checking needed)

[ ] Eight hours or more a day or night (checking needed daily)

[ ] Eight hours or more only during the day (checking needed daily)

[ ] Short periods of time (needs regular daily supervision)

[ ] Cannot be left alone (needs constant supervision)

Who gave this information? Client [ ] Family [ ] Friend [ ] Medical record [ ]
Case record [ ] Physician [ ]
Staff of agency/facility [ ]

Interviewer comments on living independently and need for supervision:

____

____

____

____

____

____

NUTRITION

Appetite: ______________________________

Three meals a day:

Typical breakfast ______________________________

____

____

____

Typical lunch ______________________________

____

____

____

Typical dinner ______________________________

____

____

____

Food allergies ______________________________

Special diet (describe) ______________________________

____

____

____

Special nutritional needs ______________________________

____

____

Is client able to follow diet? Yes [ ] No [ ]

Is client able to chew without problems? Yes [ ] No [ ]

Is client able to swallow without problems? Yes [ ] No [ ]

Food client does not eat: ______________________________

____

Food client cannot eat: ______________________________

____

Physically: Overweight [ ] Underweight [ ] Normal [ ]

Weight change last 6 months? Yes [ ] No [ ]

Pounds ______________ Gained [ ] Lost [ ]

Reason ______________________________

____

SOCIAL ACTIVITIES

Does client work? Yes [ ] No [ ]

Occupation

Current employment status

Did client work outside the home? Yes [ ] No [ ]

Occupation

Is client retired? Yes [ ] No [ ]

Highest grade completed

Activities Client Enjoys

Solitary	Yes [ ]	No [ ]
With friends	Yes [ ]	No [ ]
With family	Yes [ ]	No [ ]
With informal groups	Yes [ ]	No [ ]
With clubs	Yes [ ]	No [ ]
Educational	Yes [ ]	No [ ]
Travel	Yes [ ]	No [ ]
Hobbies	Yes [ ]	No [ ]

Other activities enjoyed

How often does client leave the residence?

How often does client leave the residence for some activity?

Would client like to be more [ ] or less [ ] active? Explain.

Does client have pets? Yes [ ] No [ ]

Will pets need consideration in planning care? Yes [ ] No [ ]

Explain

Optional Questions (Make certain client knows he or she does not have to answer these.)

Religious affiliation

How involved

Church, mosque, or synagogue

Clergy person

Clergy person's phone #

COGNITIVE FUNCTIONING

Is client comatose? Yes [ ] No [ ]

(If so, skip this section.)

	No Problem	Some Problems	Major Problems
Is client oriented to:			
Time			
Place			
Person			
Memory			
Recent memory			
Distant memory			
Verbal instructions			
Written instructions			
Judgment			
Safety			
Consequences of decisions			

If cognitive impairment:

Did impairment increase gradually? Yes [ ] No [ ]

Did impairment increase rapidly? Yes [ ] No [ ]

Has client been evaluated for a medical condition that might reverse impairment? Yes [ ] No [ ]

Explain ______________________________

____

Can client communicate needs? Yes [ ] No [ ]

Who gave this information? Client [ ] Family [ ] Friend [ ] Medical record [ ] Case record [ ] Physician [ ] Staff of agency/facility [ ]

Interviewer comments on cognitive functioning:

____

____

____

____

____

MENTAL HEALTH AND BEHAVIOR

Recent stressful events ______________________________

____

____

Client response (note anger, withdrawal, adapting well, accepting changes) ________

____

Recent illness/disability events ______________________________

____

____

Client response (note anger, withdrawal, adapting well, accepting changes) ________

____

Emotional strengths client or others see (note good coping, cheerfulness, accepting, etc.)

____

Emotional difficulties client or others see (note poor coping, demanding, hostile, negative, etc.)

____

Motivation: High [ ] Average [ ] Low [ ]

Has client received mental health treatment or counseling in past year? Yes [ ] No [ ]

Where ______________________________

With whom ______________________________

Has client had psychiatric hospitalization in past year? Yes [ ] No [ ]

Diagnosis ______________________________

Where ______________________________

Is client on psychotropic medications? Yes [ ] No [ ] (see medication list)

Does client feel:

[ ] Anxious [ ] Worried [ ] Abusive physically

[ ] Irritable [ ] Easily upset [ ] Abusive verbally

[ ] Lonely [ ] Lethargic [ ] Fearful

[ ] Suspicious [ ] Depressed [ ] Hopeless

Does client have:

[ ] Hallucinations [ ] Delusions [ ] Suicidal thoughts

[ ] Suicidal behavior [ ] Problems wandering [ ] Sleep disturbances

Other unusual behavior ______________________________

Interviewer comments on mental health and behavior:

____

____

____

INFORMAL SUPPORTS

Does client have informal supports? Yes [ ] No [ ] (If no, skip this section.)

Name, location, and phone # of each: 1. ______________________

____

____

____

2. ______________________

____

____

____

3. ______________________

____

____

____

Help provided ____

____

____

Does client have a primary informal caregiver? Yes [ ] No [ ]

Name ______________________________

Address ______________________________ Phone ____________

Describe any problems with continuing to give care ____________

____

____

Does caregiver feel constrained by caregiving? Yes [ ] No [ ]

Is caregiver feeling:

Not burdened [ ] Somewhat burdened [ ] Very burdened [ ]

Does caregiver desire service or support? Yes [ ] No [ ]

Describe ____

____

____

Is caregiver: [ ] In poor health [ ] Lacking in skills [ ] Living at a distance

[ ] Disabled [ ] Providing care to others [ ] A substance abuser

[ ] Employed [ ] Not reliable [ ] Under financial strain

[ ] Dependent in some way on client

[ ] In a poor relationship with client

Interviewer comments on caregiver situation:

____

____

FORMAL SUPPORTS

Does client have formal supports? Yes [ ] No [ ] (If no, skip this section.)

	Currently	Past 6 Months	Ordered/Not Yet Received
Adult day care			
Attendant care			
Case management			
Center services			
Congregate meals			
Financial management counseling			
Home health aid			
Home support			
Job counseling/ vocational rehabilitation			
Legal services			
Nursing services			
Occupational therapy			
Partial hospitalization			
Personal care			
Physical therapy			
Protective services			
Respite care			
Speech therapy			
Transportation			
Other			

Interviewer comments on informal and formal supports:

____

____

____

____

____

____

ASSESSMENT OF PHYSICAL ENVIRONMENT

Currently living in:

[ ] House

[ ] Apartment

[ ] Mobile home

[ ] Subsidized housing

[ ] Private care home

[ ] Domiciliary care

[ ] Group home

MH [ ] MR [ ] Other [ ]

Type ___________________

Client: Owns [ ] Rents [ ]

Client lives with:

[ ] No one, lives alone

[ ] Spouse

[ ] Children

[ ] Other relatives (relationship)

____

____

____

[ ] Other (describe)

____

____

How long has client lived at this address? ___________________________________

If less than one year, previous address ___________________________________

____

Reason for move ___________________________________

Can client remain in this living arrangement? Yes [ ] No [ ] Uncertain [ ]

Explain ___________________________________

Is client satisfied with current living arrangement? Yes [ ] No [ ]

Explain ___________________________________

Condition of home. There are problems with:

[ ] Building (unsound) [ ] Furnishings (unsafe) [ ] Stairs or other barriers

[ ] Running hot water [ ] Health hazards [ ] Electricity

[ ] Heating system [ ] Cooling system [ ] Toilet facilities

[ ] Bathing facilities [ ] Refrigerator [ ] Stove

[ ] Telephone [ ] TV/radio [ ] Food preparation area

[ ] Washer/dryer

Home is accessible to:

[ ] Banking [ ] Pharmacy [ ] Recreational/social activities

[ ] Laundry [ ] Doctor and clinics [ ] Shopping

Interviewer comments on neighborhood and usual means of transportation:

____

____

____

FINANCIAL RESOURCES

Client may refuse to answer these questions. Did client refuse? Yes [ ] No [ ]

____

Monthly income $______________________

From (list sources such as social security, pension, IRA, welfare, VA benefits, rental income, interest and dividends, wages, or other)

____

____

____

____

Is client in a subsidized program for:

[ ] Prescriptions [ ] Fuel [ ] Medicare
[ ] Transportation [ ] Housing [ ] Meals (such as Meals-on-Wheels)
[ ] Weatherization [ ] Medical assistance

Are there programs for which client might qualify that should be explored?

Yes [ ] No [ ]

They are ________________________________

____

____

Does client have health insurance? Yes [ ] No [ ]

Type ______________________________ # ______________

Type ______________________________ # ______________

Does client have a savings account? Yes [ ] No [ ]

Does client need assistance with legal and financial matters? Yes [ ] No [ ]

Is one of the following currently helping? [ ] Guardian [ ] Lawyer
[ ] Representative payee
[ ] Power of attorney
[ ] Informal helper

Name of above ______________________________

Address ______________________________

____

Prepaid funeral: Yes [ ] No [ ] Living will: Yes [ ] No [ ]

Does client feel income is adequate? Yes [ ] No [ ]

Interviewer comments on resources and assistance needed to manage:

____

____

____

____

PREFERENCES

What services does client want? What does client say he or she needs?

____

____

____

____

____

____

____

____

What services does family want for client? What does family say client needs?

____

____

____

____

____

____

____

____

ASSESSMENT SUMMARY

Directions: Summarize your findings and conclusions, paying special attention to unmet needs.

Physical Health

Activities Of Daily Living

Nutrition And Mobility

Independence

Social Activites

Mental Health And Cognitive Functioning

Informal And Formal Supports

Physical Environment

Financial Resources

Risk Factors For Protective Services

IMPRESSIONS, RECOMMENDATIONS, AND OUTCOME

Impressions and Recommendations

Case manager ______________________ Date __________

Service Plan Developed in Service Planning Conference

Service	Service Provider

Case manager ______________________ Date __________

Case management supervisor ______________ Date __________

SUMMARY OF CLINICIANS, FACILITIES, AND SOURCES

Family Physician Yes [ ] No [ ]

Name ______________________________

Address ______________________________

____

____

Phone ______________________________

How long? ______________________________

Specialists (currently or recently treating)

Name ______________________________

Address ______________________________

____

____

Phone ______________________________

How long? ______________________________

Treating for ______________________________

Name ______________________________

Address ______________________________

____

____

Phone ______________________________

How long? ______________________________

Treating for ______________________________

Name ______________________________

Address ______________________________

____

____

Phone ______________________________

How long? ______________________________

Treating for ______________________________

Ambulance membership? Yes [ ] No [ ]

Where ______________________________

Hospitalized past year? Yes [ ] No [ ]

Dates of hospitalization ______

Where ______

For ______

Dates of hospitalization ______

Where ______

For ______

Dates of hospitalization ______

Where ______

For ______

Nursing facility past year? Yes [ ] No [ ]

Dates ______

Where ______

For ______

Who gave this information? Client [ ] Family [ ] Case record [ ]
Friend [ ] Physician [ ] Medical record [ ]
Staff of agency/facility [ ]

Name ______

Facility/agency (if applicable) ______

Address ______

______

Phone ______

Relationship to client (if applicable) ______

Interviewer comments:

______

______

______

______

Placement Assessment Tool
Wildwood Case Management Unit

Directions: Use this form if client needs placement. The information below is used to develop an appropriate placement for the client.

Client name ______________________ Social Security # ______________________

Address ______________________ ID # ______________________

______________________ Birth date ______________________

______________________ Phone ______________________

______________________ Language assist needed for assessment?

Yes [ ] No [ ]

Is client able to:

Write	Yes [ ]	No [ ]
Read	Yes [ ]	No [ ]
Tell time	Yes [ ]	No [ ]
Find way home	Yes [ ]	No [ ]
Count	Yes [ ]	No [ ]
Find outside door	Yes [ ]	No [ ]
Follow verbal instructions	Yes [ ]	No [ ]
Manage toileting	Yes [ ]	No [ ]
Handle activities of daily living	Yes [ ]	No [ ]
Drive	Yes [ ]	No [ ]

Is client MR? Yes [ ] No [ ]

If yes: Profoundly [ ] Severely [ ] Moderately [ ] Mildly [ ]

Have MH/MR assessments been obtained (if appropriate)? Yes [ ] No [ ]

Behavior or conditions that might affect client placement:

____

____

____

____

Client preferences and special needs:

Would you share a room?	Yes [ ]	No [ ]
Would you live in a home with pets?	Yes [ ]	No [ ]
Would you live in a home with children?	Yes [ ]	No [ ]
Do you drink alcohol?	Yes [ ]	No [ ]
Would you live with someone who drinks alcohol?	Yes [ ]	No [ ]
Do you smoke?	Yes [ ]	No [ ]
Would you live with someone who smokes?	Yes [ ]	No [ ]
Do you have a boyfriend/girlfriend?	Yes [ ]	No [ ]
Do you have pets we should consider?	Yes [ ]	No [ ]

Is there a specific area in which you want to live? ______________________________

In seeking placement, describe what would be ideal: ______________________________

____

____

____

____

Participating in planning were ______________________________

____

____

____

____

Taken by ______________________________ Date ______________
CASE MANAGER

Abbreviations and Definitions

activities of daily living (ADL) activities that have to do with self-care, such as brushing teeth, dressing, feeding oneself, and taking care of hygiene needs; does not refer to work or leisure activities

ADL activities of daily living

BID two times a day

BSU base service unit (often where case managers work and where intakes to the mental health system take place)

CASSP children and adolescent service system program; a program, funded and defined by the federal government, that sets forth guidelines for services to children, seeking to coordinate the services and individualize service plans

CD chemical dependence

CMU case management unit

contratures a condition in which the muscle tissue shrinks, often as a result of injury to or inflammation or disuse of the muscle

D&A drug and alcohol

decubitis ulcer commonly referred to as a bedsore; "an ulcerated area of the skin caused by irritation and continuous pressure on a part of the body: a hazard to be guarded against in all bedridden (especially unconscious) patients" (*Bantam Medical Dictionary,* 1990)

diverticulosis refers to a state where *diverticulum* (small pouches that push out from the walls in a weak digestive track) are present but are causing no current problems; once these pouches become inflamed and possibly infected, the condition is referred to as *diverticulitis*

DOB date of birth

domiciliary care (dom. care) a living arrangement in which the client lives in another's home; usually arranged for people who need housing and perhaps minor supervision

DPA department of public assistance

DTs delirium tremens; a condition often experienced by heavy drinkers when they have stopped drinking that may include anxiety, tremors, sweating, and vivid visual and sensory hallucinations

Dx diagnosis

dysphagia "a condition in which the action of swallowing is either difficult to perform, painful, or in which swallowed material seems to be held up in the passage to the stomach" (*Bantam Medical Dictionary,* 1990)

dyspnea condition in which person cannot breathe easily or is having trouble breathing

encropresis "the essential feature of encropresis is repeated passage of feces into inappropriate places (e.g. clothing or floor)" (*DSM-IV-TR*)

enuresis "the essential feature of enuresis is repeated voiding of urine during the day or at night into bed or clothes" (*DSM-IV-TR*)

excoriated where the surface of the skin has been scraped, removing the surface or removing the tissue covering an organ

GAF global assessment of functioning (see *DSM-IV-TR*)

GED general educational development; an academic award given in place of a high school diploma to people who did not or were unable to complete their high school education and who have completed the requirements for this equivalent to the high school diploma

IM injection of fluid or medication is made into the muscle (intramuscular)

IV injection of fluid or medication is made into the vein (intravenous)

MSE mental status examination; for all the words found in mental status sections of intake evaluations, see *Fundamentals of Case Management Practice,* (Summers, 2001, chapter 17)

myocardial infarction the death of heart tissue following the termination of blood to that tissue, experienced as a heart attack

ombudsman a person, either in the agency or appointed by an outside authority, who looks into clients' concerns and complaints and seeks to resolve them

orthopnea "breathlessness that prevents the patient from lying down so that he has to sleep propped up in bed or sitting in a chair" (*Bantam Medical Dictionary,* 1990)

OTC over the counter; generally used to refer nonprescription medications

parenteral administered other than by mouth

PCH personal care home; a home where individuals live together and take care of themselves, but in which meals often are provided

PRN medication or treatment as needed

protective services services that seek to protect victims of abuse or exploitation within vulnerable populations; such services for elderly and children are supported by legislation (in most states) or are provided within programs funded by the state

psychotropic medications prescribed for mental disorders

QD once a day

QID four times a day

QOD every other day

rape kit a tool used in the forensic investigation of a rape; contains precise instructions and items needed to collect specimens or samples and prepare them for the investigating officer

representative payee (rep. payee) a person appointed by the Social Security Administration, based on a medical decision, to administer the client's social security funds; this person may also administer funds from other income at the client's discretion, but the Social Security Administration does not make a decision about any income aside from social security benefits

respite care care given to a client to relieve the full-time caregiver; not available in all communities or for all populations in communities that have such care. Examples include care for individuals with mental retardation while the families take vacations, for elderly persons whose caregivers are exhausted and need a break, and for children whose parents are angry and afraid that, without separation, they might harm the children

RTC residential treatment centers

SO significant other

SSI supplemental social insurance

subcutaneous beneath the skin

TID three times a day

Tx treatment

VA benefits benefits given to veterans by the Veterans Administration

vericosities "veins that are distended, lengthened, and torturous. The superficial veins of the legs are most commonly affected." This can be an inherited condition or can be caused by a lack of blood flow to the legs. "Complications including thrombosis, phlebitis, and hemorrhage may occur" (*Bantam Medical Dictionary,* 1990, p. 458)

References

American Academy of Pediatrics, Committee on Adolescence. (1994). Sexual assault: The adolescent. *Pediatrics, 94*(5), 761–765.

American Association of Retired People (AARP), Criminal Justice Services. (1992). *Domestic mistreatment of the elderly: Towards prevention—Some dos and don'ts.* Washington, DC: Author.

American Association of Retired People (AARP). (1995). *Spouse/partner abuse in later life: A resource guide for service providers.* Washington, DC: Author.

American Psychiatric Association. (2000). *Diagnostic and statistical manual of mental disorders,* 4th ed., Text Rev. Washington, DC: Author.

Baroff, G. S. (1999). *Mental retardation: Nature, cause, and management.* Philadelphia: Brunner/Mazel.

Barrientos, T. (1995, November 26). Rejecting the violence. *Philadelphia Inquirer,* Final edition, Features/Life Style section, p. 1.

Berry, D. B. (2000). *The domestic violence sourcebook.* Los Angeles: Lowell House.

Brandeis University, Center for Human Resources. (1989). *A guide to case management for at risk youth.* Waltham, MA: Author.

Brandenburg, N., Friedman, R., & Silver, S. (1990). The epidemiology of childhood psychiatric disorders: Prevalence findings from recent studies. *Journal of the American Academy of Child and Adolescent Psychiatry, 29,* 76–83.

Burland, J. (1997). *What hurts/what helps* (4th ed.). Arlington, VA: National Alliance for the Mentally Ill.

Butler, R. N., Lewis, M. I., & Sunderland, T. (1998). *Aging and mental health: Positive psychosocial and biomedical approaches* (5th ed.). Needham Heights, MA: Allyn & Bacon.

Caplan, G. (1964). *Principles of preventive psychiatry.* New York: Basic Books.

Castillo, P. S. (n.d.) But why does she put up with it? In *Domestic violence in the Latino community.* Harrisburg, PA: National Resource Center on Domestic Violence.

Correia, A. (1999). *Housing and battered women: A case study of domestic violence programs in Iowa.* Harrisburg, PA: National Resource Center on Domestic Violence.

Craven, D. (1996, December). *Female victims of violent crime.* Washington, DC: Bureau of Justice Statistics, Office of Justice Programs, U.S. Department of Justice.

Davies, J. (1998). *Building opportunities for battered women's safety and self-sufficiency.* Harrisburg, PA: National Resource Center on Domestic Violence.

Davies, J. (1999). *The new welfare law: Child support enforcement.* Harrisburg, PA: National Resource Center on Domestic Violence.

Downs, S. W., Moore, E., McFadden, E. J., Costin, L. B. (2000). *Child welfare and family services: Policies and practice* (6th ed.). Needham Heights, MA: Allyn & Bacon.

Finkelhor, D., & Browne, A. (1988). Assessing the long-term impact of child sexual abuse: A review and conceptualization. In L. E. Auerbach (Ed.), *Handbook on sexual abuse of children: Assessment and treatment issues.* New York: Springer.

Ganolf, E. W. (1995). Batterer programs: What we know and need to know. Unpublished manuscript submitted to *Journal of Interpersonal Violence.*

Greenfield, L. A. (1995). *Prison sentences and time served for violence.* Washington, DC: Bureau of Justice Statistics, U.S. Department of Justice.

Greenstone, J. L., & Leviton, S. C. (2002). *Elements of crisis intervention.* Belmont, CA: Wadsworth.

Hammeal-Urban, R. (1999). *Using housing vouchers to assist battered women move from welfare to work.* Harrisburg, PA: National Resource Center on Domestic Violence.

Hanson, M., Anderson, C., Harbaugh, S., Lindblad-Goldberg, M., & Marsh, D. (1999). *Child, family and community core competencies.* Harrisburg, PA: Pennsylvania CASSP Training and Technical Assistance Institute.

Harlow, C. (1991). *Female victims of violent crime.* Washington, DC: Bureau of Justice Statistics, U.S. Department of Justice.

Hart, B. (1990a). Assessing whether batterers will kill. *Seeking Justice,* sec. 5. Harrisburg, PA: Pennsylvania Coalition Against Domestic Violence.

Hart, B. (1990b). Why she leaves, why she stays. *Seeking Justice,* 8–9. Harrisburg, PA: Pennsylvania Coalition Against Domestic Violence.

Hart, B. J. (1995). *The violence against women act: Identifying projects for law enforcement and prosecution grants: Fiscal year 1995 funding.* Harrisburg, PA: National Resource Center on Domestic Violence.

Herman, J. (1992). *Trauma and recovery: The aftermath of violence from domestic abuse to political terror.* New York: Basic Books.

Hodas, G. R. (1996). *What makes wraparound special: Understanding and creating unique experiences for children and their families.* Harrisburg: Pennsylvania State University, Pennsylvania CASSP Training and Technical Institute.

Hyde, A. P. (1985). *Living with schizophrenia.* Chicago: Contemporary Books.

Jefferson, J. W., & Greist, J. H. (1996). *Depression and older people: Recognizing hidden signs and taking steps toward recovery.* Pfizer U.S. Pharmaceutical Group.

Jones, A. (2000). *Next time she'll be dead: Battering and how to stop it.* Boston: Beacon Press.

Kaplan, Harold I., & Benjamin J. Saddock. (1998). *Synopsis of psychiatry: Behavioral sciences/clinical psychiatry* (8th ed.). Baltimore, MD: Williams & Wilkins.

Kilpatrick, D. G., Edmunds, C. N., & Seymour, A. (1992). *Rape in America: A report to the nation.* Arlington, VA: National Victim Center.

Knitzer, J. (1982). *Unclaimed children.* Washington, DC: Children's Defense Fund.

Lissette, A., & Kraus, R. (2000). 7 steps to taking your life back: Free yourself from an abusive relationship. Berkeley, CA: Hunter House.

Levin, J. D. (1991). *Treatment of alcoholism and other addictions: A self-psychology approach.* Northvale, NJ: Jason Aronson.

Levin, J. D. (1995). *Introduction to alcoholism counseling: A bio-psycho-social approach.* Philadelphia: Taylor & Francis.

Manning, D. (1993). *Establishing significance* (Special Care Series, Book 1). Oklahoma City, OK: In-Sight Books.

McCauley, J., et al. (1995, November). The battering syndrome: Prevalence in primary care internal medicine practices. *Annals of Internal Medicine, 125*(10).

McClellan, J., & Trupin, E. (1989). Prevention of psychiatric disorders in children. *Hospital and community psychiatry, 40,* 630–636.

National Alliance for the Mentally Ill (NAMI). www.nami.org

National Alliance for the Mentally Ill (NAMI). (n.d.) *Understanding schizophrenia: What you need to know about this medical illness.* Arlington, VA: Author.

National Alliance for the Mentally Ill (NAMI). (n.d.). *Understanding major depression: What you need to know about this medical illness.* Arlington, VA: Author.

National Alliance for the Mentally Ill (NAMI). (n.d.) *What you need to know about benzodiazepines* (Publication No. R107). Arlington, VA: Author.

National Crime Victimization Survey. (1996). Washington, DC: Bureau of Justice Statistics, U.S. Department of Justice.

National Family Caregivers Association. (1997). *Member survey 1997: A profile of caregivers.* Retrieved August 11, 2000, from http://www.nfcacares.org/survey.html

National Institute of Mental Health (NIMH). (1999, November 8). *Brief notes on mental health of children and adolescents.* Retrieved February 19, 2002, from http://www.nimh.nih.gov/publicat/childnotes.cfm

National Safe Workplace Institute. (1995, April). *Talking frankly about domestic violence* (survey). Personnel journal.

National Women's Study. (1992). *Risk factors for substance abuse: a longitudinal study* (D. G. Kilpatrick, principal investigator, Grant # RO1-DA05220). Washington, DC: National Institute on Drug Abuse.

National Workplace Resource Center on Domestic Violence. (1995). A project of the Family Violence Prevention Fund, San Francisco, CA.

New York State Office for the Prevention of Domestic Violence. (1996). *Domestic violence: Finding safety and support.* Rensselaer, NY: Author.

Pennsylvania Coalition Against Domestic Violence. (1997). Fact sheets. Harrisburg, PA: Author.

Pennsylvania Coalition Against Rape. (2000). *The trainer's toolbox: A resource guide for sexual assault counselor training.* Harrisburg, PA: Author.

Pennsylvania State Child and Adolescent Service System Program Advisory Committee. (1995). *Core principles: Pennsylvania child and adolescent system program.* Harrisburg, PA: Office of Mental Health and Substance Abuse Services.

Rosen, L. E., & Amador, X. F. (1996). *When someone you love is depressed: How to help your loved one without losing yourself.* New York: Free Press.

Shalala, D. (2000, April). *HHS reports new child abuse and neglect statistics.* Washington, DC: U.S. Department of Health and Human Services.

Shore, D. (Ed.). (1986). *Schizophrenia: Questions and answers* (DHHS Publication No. [ADM] 86–1457). Washington, DC: U.S. Department of Health and Human Services, Schizophrenia Research Branch.

Stroul, B. A., & Friedman, R. M. (1986). *A system of care for children and youth with severe emotional disturbances* (Rev. ed.). Washington, DC: Georgetown University Child Development Center, CASSP Technical Assistance Center.

Stroul, B. A., & Friedman, R. M. (1996). *Children's mental health: Creating systems of care in a changing society.* Baltimore, MD: Paul H. Brookes.

Summers, N. (2001). *Fundamentals of case management practice.* Pacific Grove, CA: Brooks/Cole.

Teyber, E. (1992). *Helping children cope with divorce.* New York: Lexington Books.

Tjaden, P., & Thoennes, N. (1999, November). *Prevalence against women: Findings from the National Violence Against Women Survey.* Washington, DC: National Institute of Justice, Office of the Justice Programs, U.S. Department of Justice.

U.S. Center for Substance Abuse Treatment. (1995). Treatment Improvement Protocol (TIP) Series #7. Rockville, MD: Department of Health and Human Services.

U.S. Department of Health and Human Services. (1999). *Mental health: A report of the Surgeon General—Executive summary.* Rockville, MD: U.S. Department of Health and Human Services Administration, Center for Mental Health Services, National Institutes of Health.

U.S. Department of Justice, Office of Justice Programs. (1994, November). *Domestic violence: Violence between intimates* Washington, DC: Bureau of Justice Statistics.

Worcester, N. (1993, July/August). A more hidden crime: Adolescent battered women. *Network News.* Madison, WI: National Women's Health Network.

Index